THE U.S. OPEN®

THE U.S. OPEN
Golf's Ultimate Challenge

Robert Sommers

New York ATHENEUM *1987*

Library of Congress Cataloging-in-Publication Data

Sommers, Robert (Robert T.)
The U.S. Open.

Bibliography: p.
Includes index.
1. United States Open Golf Championship Tournament—
History.   2. Golfers—Biography.   I. Title.
GV970.S65   1987   796.352′7   85–48137
ISBN 0–689–11525–3

To Dad,
who bought me my first book,
and Helen,
who saw me through this one.

ACKNOWLEDGMENTS

Everyone, I suppose, has his heroes. I've had mine. Some were athletes, some were warriors, some were neither. My most lasting hero was among the last group. As a young man in the early years of a career in writing about sports, I looked forward each morning of the golf season to the reports by Al Laney, in the *New York Herald Tribune*. Later, when I began attending such happenings as the United States Open, the Masters, or the National Amateur, I maneuvered to the typewriter next to his, and I walked with him in the galleries of the great men we wrote of. Back inside once again, I marveled at how quickly he created his graceful, fluid, and literate work while I struggled, unsure of myself, to write a simple declarative sentence. I'd become morose and discouraged, but Al would reassure and advise me. Without that encouragement from him and from so many others I've met and mingled with over the years, this book would not have been born.

Certainly it could not have been done without the guidance and companionship of so many friends both here and abroad who made watching the great occasions so much pleasure: Ken Bowden, without whom it never would have happened; George Eberl, who offered wise counsel indeed; Jerry Tarde, Nick Seitz, Ross Goodner, Dick Taylor, Peter Ryde, Michael Williams, Michael McDonnell, John Hopkins, Dick Miller, Mark Wilson, and Peter Dobereiner; Merrell Whittlesey, from earlier days; Janet Seagle, the USGA's librarian and museum curator, who is always ready to blaze a trail through the maze of written works; and

ACKNOWLEDGMENTS

Herbert Warren Wind, whose tutorials, delivered on the run as we roamed here and abroad, were both beguiling and inspiring.

Many others were of immense help: Ralph Guldahl, who went to great trouble, Johnny Farrell, Red Hoffman from Robert Trent Jones's office, Trent Jones himself, George Fazio, Dave Marr, Lew Worsham, Joe Dey, Isaac B. Grainger, Eddie Miller, an old USGA hand, Jack Fleck, Cary Middlecoff, Claude Harmon, and many others. They made it fun.

Bridgewater, New Jersey
March 1987

CONTENTS

Prologue   3

PART ONE
Wellspring

1 The Early Heroes   11
2 Johnny McDermott Leads the Homebreds   27
3 Francis Ouimet Awakens America   33

PART TWO
Between Wars

4   Vardon and Ray in Reprise   53
5   Bobby Jones at Inwood   58
6   Jones Against the Field   69
7   The Revival of Gene Sarazen   89
8   Dog Days of the Thirties   99
9   The Frustrations of Sam Snead   110
10 Byron Nelson's Poor Timing   125

PART THREE
Hogan, Palmer, and the New Era

11 Snead's Final Agony   133
12 The Emergence of Ben Hogan   140

CONTENTS

13 Top of the World   157
14 Hail and Farewell   169
15 A Legend Is Born   178
16 Heavy Hangs the Head   199
17 One Brief Shining Moment   206
18 So Near, So Far   214

PART FOUR

Nicklaus and Beyond

19 Baltusrol and the Record   223
20 Another Rival   230
21 One More to Go   248
22 The Best Round Ever?   256
23 The Journeymen   264
24 Jack Is Back   279
25 Waiting for Watson   286
26 From Nelson to North   295

    Epilogue   308
    Appendices   319
    Selected Bibliography   331
    Index   335

ILLUSTRATIONS

The great Willie Anderson sits with his friend and arch rival, Alex Smith, at an early Open.   *United States Golf Association*

The classic, graceful form of Harry Vardon   *United States Golf Association*

John J. McDermott, the first American-born champion   *United States Golf Association*

Francis Ouimet during the playoff of the 1913 Open   *United States Golf Association*

Ouimet, Harry Vardon, and Ted Ray on the 18th green of the playoff   *United States Golf Association*

Walter Hagen   *United States Golf Association*

Harry Vardon driving at Inverness, 1920   *United States Golf Association*

Harry Vardon and Bob Jones before the qualifying round at Inverness in 1920   *United States Golf Association*

Bobby Jones saving a tie in the 1929 championship at Winged Foot   *The Bettmann Archive*

The smooth style of Jones as he begins the 1930 Open   *United States Golf Association*

1932: Gene Sarazen cradles the U.S. Open trophy in his right arm and the British Open trophy in his left.   *United States Golf Association*

Sam Parks holing the final putt in the 1935 Open   *United States Golf Association*

The powerful swing of Ralph Guldahl   *United States Golf Association*

With Johnny Goodman watching, Sam Snead plays the first shot of his Open career.   *Associated Press/Wide World Photos*

ILLUSTRATIONS

The fluid power of Sam Snead at the height of his career   *United States Golf Association*

One of the game's great innovators, Byron Nelson   *United States Golf Association*

Ben Hogan at the peak of his career   *United States Golf Association*

Julius Boros   *Pongracz*

Ed Furgol after winning the 1954 Open   *United States Golf Association*

Jack Fleck defeats Ben Hogan in the 1955 playoff   *United States Golf Association*

Cary Middlecoff   *United States Golf Association*

Arnold Palmer holing his final putt in the 1960 Open   *United States Golf Association*

No one attracted galleries better than Palmer.   *Washington Star/Elwood Baker*

Ken Venturi in the 1964 championship   *Washington Star*

Gary Player   *United States Golf Association*

Jack Nicklaus at Baltusrol in 1967   *United States Golf Association*

The Golden Bear winning his third Open, in 1972   *United States Golf Association*

In 1980 Nicklaus wins a record-tying fourth Open.   *John Kelly*

Lee Trevino, the Open champion of 1968 and 1971   *Don Brooks*

Tom Watson's dramatic pitch from the rough wins the 1982 championship.   *Lawrence Levy*

Andy North   *United States Golf Association*

The United States Open Championship trophy   *United States Golf Association*

THE U.S. OPEN®

PROLOGUE

At 630 yards, the 17th hole at Baltusrol is the longest in championship golf, a true three-shot hole, one of the few remaining that asks the modern professional to play a wooden club for his second shot and place his ball in a precise location for the approach to the green. To reach the fairway, the drive must carry 200 yards of heavy rough and settle on a narrow tract no more than thirty-five yards wide tilting to the right. The second shot must then clear a nest of bunkers crossing the fairway and land on a level spot on the right, because the ground rises sharply on the left; a ball that stops on the hillside leaves a more difficult shot to the green, perched on a plateau well above eye level and beyond a rising grade covered with matty rough and pitted with bunkers.

Late in the afternoon of June 15, 1980, Jack Nicklaus stood on the tee of this mammoth hole emotionally drained from a day-long struggle with Isao Aoki, the Japanese golfer, battling him for the United States Open championship. Even though he was playing some of the best golf of his career, Nicklaus had not been able to shake off Aoki. He was two strokes ahead with two holes to play, but a golfer with the putting stroke of Aoki could make up those strokes in quick order, particularly since both of the last two holes at Baltusrol are par 5s.

Drawing back his driver in that familiar long and upright swing, Nicklaus lashed into the ball and hit a high, soaring shot that drifted slightly to the right, and finished 275 yards from the tee. From a good lie he then ripped into an iron that streaked over the cross bunkers and onto the level ground near the base of the incline, the ideal spot on the fairway. From there he pitched his ball onto the green, twenty-two feet to the right of the hole. When he climbed the slope and saw Aoki's ball lying five feet from the hole, also in three strokes, Nicklaus felt sure Aoki would hole his putt. If he wanted to avoid a playoff, if not the outright loss of the Open, he would have to birdie either this hole or the 18th.

Nicklaus was forty years old, and he had won the Open three times before, but he wanted a fourth badly; winning four Opens would raise him to a higher level. While he had already won seventeen tournaments of national—indeed, international—consequence, four U.S. Opens would do what nothing else could. At his age he would not have many more opportunities.

His face was drawn as he stood over the putt, reflecting the strain of the last four days. He drew the putter blade back smoothly and stroked the ball. As it rolled toward the hole, Nicklaus stared anxiously, as if willing it to fall. The ball ran dead on course, took a slight right-to-left break in the last two feet, and tumbled into the cup.

As the ball fell, the huge gallery clustered around the green broke into wild cheering, and Nicklaus screwed up his face into a grin that was uncharacteristic of the man. Normally stoic, he had been stirred upon occasion to show a pleased, tight-lipped smile, but only once before, when he won the 1970 British Open at St. Andrews, had he reacted like this. This was an expression of pure joy, of total fulfillment, of immense satisfaction, for, barring a miracle by Aoki on the seventy-second hole, the Open was his. Aoki performed no such miracle, and Nicklaus won his fourth Open.

The United States Open Championship is the ultimate goal in golf, because it is as close as the game comes to deciding the best golfer in the world. The British Open has the more cosmopolitan field, drawing players from many more countries, but the U.S. Open has the strongest, if only because the United States has more first-class golfers than any other country. Winning the U.S. Open, therefore, assures a man a place in golf history. In a moment of reflection after winning in 1975, Lou Graham said quietly: "Now my name will be on that trophy just like Ben Hogan and Bobby Jones."

The U.S. Open also stands apart because of tradition. Conducted by the United States Golf Association®, the governing body of golf in the United States, the Open is the oldest tournament in North America. It has been won by the greatest golfers of all: by Harry Vardon in its early years, and since then by Bobby Jones, Walter Hagen, Gene Sarazen,

4

PROLOGUE

Ben Hogan, Byron Nelson, Arnold Palmer, Jack Nicklaus, Lee Trevino, and Tom Watson. Of the great golfers of the twentieth century, only Sam Snead failed to win the U.S. Open, but, oh, how he tried.

The U.S. Open is by far the largest of all golf tournaments worldwide. Each year more than 5,000 golfers enter, both professional and amateur, even though they know only 150 or so places are available. All but about fifty of that final field must survive one or two qualifying rounds, and those fifty are exempt strictly because of outstanding recent playing records. The odds against an unknown's even reaching the Open site are staggering. For a player to go through both qualifying rounds is difficult enough; for him to win is nearly impossible. Since 1959, when the two-stage qualifying system was adopted, only Ken Venturi in 1964 and Orville Moody in 1969 survived both and won. Each year it becomes more difficult.

The Open is difficult to win for other reasons. Traditionally it is played over the nation's best courses: Merion in Philadelphia; the Olympic Club in San Francisco; Oakmont in Pittsburgh; Oakland Hills in Detroit; Medinah in Chicago; and Baltusrol and Winged Foot in the suburbs of New York City. With one exception, clubs like these might be the occasional site of the PGA Championship, but not of regular PGA Tour events, so the Tour players rarely see them. The one exception is Pebble Beach, that majestic course on the Monterey Peninsula of California that was for so long the annual site of the Bing Crosby Pro-Am. Pebble Beach has been the venue of two Opens (1972 and 1982), and one PGA Championship (1977), and the exception is justified: Pebble Beach is the best golf course in the world.

Not only does the USGA take the Open to the best courses, it sets them up to be much more testing than the players are accustomed to. In the philosophy of the USGA, a champion golfer should be able to hit his driver both long and straight, so fairway widths are narrowed to between thirty and thirty-five yards, depending on the length and general configuration of each hole, and bordered by rough up to five inches deep. The Open champion is expected not only to hit the greens, but also to place his ball where he'll have a chance for a birdie. To test that ability fully, the greens are kept firm and very fast. At Merion in 1950, Julius Boros hit a shot onto the 16th green close to the front, where the ground rises to a level plateau. Although his ball didn't quite reach the crest of the slope, it stopped just at the edge and seemed safe. As he picked his way through an old stone quarry filled with wild and scraggly undergrowth, a gentle puff of wind ghosted across the green. That was all the ball needed; it glided off the green. On the first hole at Winged Foot twenty-four years later, Jack Nicklaus faced a twenty-five-foot downhill

5

putt with a left-to-right break. Tapped a little too firmly, the ball rolled down the grade, took the break, and was still picking up speed as it passed the hole, leaving Jack another twenty-five-footer coming back. He had played his approach onto the wrong part of the green, leaving himself a downhill rather than an uphill putt. Late that night a vandal drove his car across that green, but the ground was so firm he caused little damage. It remained playable.

A day or two before the first round of the 1977 Open, a man stood at the rear of the 18th green at Southern Hills in Tulsa and dropped a ball from shoulder height. When it hit the ground, it popped up once and then began to roll. On and on it rolled, very slowly but very steadily. It crept by the hole, curling slightly to the right, and as it moved toward the front of the green, it caught a downgrade and gathered speed. It was moving increasingly faster as it rolled off the green, over the collar, and onto the fairway. The man looked at his watch; the ball had rolled for twenty-four seconds. P. J. Boatwright, whom the USGA relies on to see that Open conditions are met, thought the Southern Hills greens were just fine.

A phrase has become attached to another part of U.S. Open course preparation and, indeed, has become part of the language of golf. The term is "Open rough." Open rough means deep, dense, unyielding grass that seems a foot deep and feels like steel wool. Its underlying objective is to extract a penalty of about half a stroke a hole for an inaccurate shot. That is, a player who hits his ball into the rough on two holes should par only one of them.

Sometimes the plan doesn't work out, and the penalty is too severe. Ben Hogan drove into the rough on the 18th hole at the Olympic Club in 1955 and needed four more strokes to reach the green. In the 1983 Open at Oakmont, Jack Nicklaus didn't even consider going for the green when he missed the 11th fairway; instead, he chopped out sideways, over to the adjacent 10th fairway. Influenced by that and similar incidents, the USGA relented and doubled the width of the secondary rough immediately bordering the fairway—grass held to about two inches high—from six feet to twelve feet along a few holes. At the same time, a mobile machine shop that follows the PGA Tour did a brisk business sharpening the leading edges of players' iron clubs so they could slice through the grass more easily.

Rough like this keeps the players off balance. The modern tournament golfer becomes accustomed to blithely whaling away at his tee shot, because the penalty for missing fairways is hardly ever severe in the weekly Tour events. In the Open he hesitates and often drives with an iron or a fairway wood, because he lacks confidence in his ability to hit

6

the driver straight enough. And then, of course, he accuses the USGA of "taking the driver out of golf." At Oakmont in 1983, Severiano Ballesteros, a very long but sometimes erratic driver, used his 1-iron on all the par four holes except the second (he used a 5-iron there), and the driver only on two par 5s.

Rough creates other problems unique to the Open. With his ball lying only three or four yards off the green, a player can often do no more than try to bulldoze it onto the green—*anywhere* on the green—with a technique similar to playing a ball buried in sand. At the 1983 Open, Johnny Miller's approach to Oakmont's 10th hole rolled off the left side of the green, through the collar, and into the heavy grass. Miller was surely not more than a foot or two into the rough, within two yards of the green and less than twenty feet from the hole, and yet he had to draw his wedge back to shoulder height to cut through the grass.

Forced to struggle for pars from a few feet off the green, the players grumble further that the Open has also eliminated the chip shot. They're right, to a degree, but then how important is the chip shot anyway? Shouldn't the player who hits greens have the advantage over the player who only comes close? Jack Nicklaus hits greens. At Baltusrol in 1980, for example, Nicklaus hit fifty-nine greens and Aoki hit fifty-one. Who was the better golfer? If we judge by who plays the better full shots, then Nicklaus clearly was the better man that week, and by more than the two strokes he eventually won by. That is what the Open tries to establish.

Golf can be intractable, however. The winner is the man who gets the ball into the hole in the fewest number of strokes, no matter how, and the Open is usually won by someone other than the man who hits the most fairways and greens. In 1982, when Tom Watson finally won an Open, he hit only forty-six greens at Pebble Beach, while Nicklaus hit fifty-three. Nonetheless, Watson shot 282 and Nicklaus 284. In 1984 at Winged Foot, Greg Norman hit fifty-three greens, the most of anyone in the field, but lost a playoff to Fuzzy Zoeller, who hit fifty-one.

Conditions in an Open are the most severe the players face each year, and because of those conditions, which are further compounded by the emotion of the occasion, to win is the most difficult accomplishment in golf.

As its name suggests, the Open is open to anyone, either professional or amateur. Unlike the Masters, it is not an invitational tournament; unlike the PGA, it is not for members of a certain organization (the PGA of America plus a few guests); and unlike the regular weekly tournaments, it is not only for members of the PGA Tour. Anybody can play in the Open, provided only that he is good enough.

PROLOGUE

What makes so many golfers want to play in the Open? Certainly not the prize money; although it isn't bad, it has never been the highest of the year. When Jack Nicklaus won the Open in 1980, total prize money was $356,000, but three other tournaments in the United States offered more. That, however, is better than it had been in earlier times. In 1953, when Ben Hogan won his fourth Open, the prize money was $20,000; eight other tournaments offered more. Hogan won $5,000 in that Open. During the same year, Earl Stewart won $6,900 in the Ardmore Open, a relatively undistinguished affair played in central Oklahoma, and Al Besselink collected $10,000 for winning the Tournament of Champions in Las Vegas. Hogan said he never made a dime from the Open, but by winning he was in demand for exhibitions, and he made his money from them.

Clearly, it isn't the money.

It is fame, certainly, for the names of the Open champions are seldom forgotten, and the designation of Open champion stays with a man throughout his lifetime.

To the golfer who strives for it, winning the Open offers the ultimate satisfaction and the pride of knowing that for one week when it mattered most, he was the best player of them all.

This wasn't always the case, however. The United States Open began not as the most important competition in the game but as hardly more than an appendage to the Amateur championship, a sideshow that gave wealthy men the opportunity to gamble on what they considered the lower orders. While everyone acknowledged that the professionals were the best players, and the United States Golf Association was organized partly to conduct an Open championship, it was of secondary interest; the Amateur was the important event. Years went by before the Open surpassed the Amateur in the minds of the USGA and of the public at large.

But, then, the Open goes back even further than the birth of the United States Golf Association.

PART ONE
Wellspring

ONE

The Early Heroes

Willie Dunn, Jr., was a small, neat man, about five-foot-six inches tall and weighing 125 to 130 pounds. He wore a trim mustache that curled up at the ends, in the fashion of the late nineteenth century, had bright, clear eyes, a fresh, eager face, and, when the occasion called for it, sported a winged collar with a four-in-hand tie, stirrup trousers (so that too much shoe didn't show), a coat of just the right length, and a fedora set squarely atop his head.

Willie Dunn cut a handsome and elegant figure; and why not? In the early 1900s, while living the good life in France, he was said to have taught golf to more earls, lords, and duchesses than any other professional golfer. In the custom of the day, he had overseen the condition of the golf course at Biarritz, the ultraexclusive resort on the Bay of Biscay just north of the Spanish border, while giving lessons to aristocrats, noblemen, and other men and women of enormous wealth who wintered there. Among others, he taught Queen Natalie of Serbia and impressed her so much she hired him to lay out a golf course on her Biarritz estate.

Dunn also became acquainted with W. K. Vanderbilt, the American socialite, who was a frequent visitor to Biarritz. When Vanderbilt showed an interest in golf, Willie demonstrated the techniques by playing a few shots across a deep depression and stopping each ball within a few feet of the hole. Vanderbilt was so impressed he invited Dunn to teach the game in the United States. Dunn accepted, arrived in New York in 1893, and was taken to the Shinnecock Hills Golf Club, in Southampton, on Long Island, a summer encampment for the moneyed class.

Dunn came from a family of fine golfers. In a famous challenge match in the old country, his father, Old Willie Dunn, and his father's twin, Jamie, teamed against Old Tom Morris and Allan Robertson, the first man to break 80 over the Old Course of St. Andrews. The match was played over three courses, one round at St. Andrews, one at North Berwick, the other at Musselburgh, the home of the Dunns. While Robertson and Morris won (they are said never to have lost a match without giving strokes), the Dunns had the immense satisfaction of beating them 12 and 11 at Musselburgh.

This is how big-time golf was played in the days before championships were born. The first tournament of national scope was an amateur competition at St. Andrews in 1858. Two years later, in 1860, the British Open was born at Prestwick, on the other side of Scotland, but for many years the money match remained the game's most important test.

Willie Dunn, Jr., was one of an army of Scottish professionals who migrated to the United States to teach the game to Americans and to build their golf courses. Willie Campbell came over from Musselburgh and settled at The Country Club in Brookline, Massachusetts, and Willie Davis, who had first come to Montreal, moved on to Newport, Rhode Island. With so many professionals in the country, debates naturally developed over who was the best player. Not many of the immigrants had been at the top of the class back home—most of the best players remained in Britain—but of those who moved to the United States, it was generally believed that Willie Dunn was the best. To test that hypothesis a series of matches was arranged for early 1894 between Dunn and Willie Campbell. Campbell won at Newport, but Dunn was to have his revenge later in the year under much more impressive circumstances.

Golf had come to the United States permanently in the late 1880s when Robert Lockhart, an immigrant Scot who had become a linen merchant in Yonkers, New York, returned from a visit to his homeland with a supply of golf clubs and balls (later in the year he was arrested for hitting some of them around the sheep meadow in Central Park in Manhattan). Hearing about Lockhart's equipment, John Reid, another resident of Yonkers with Scottish roots, invited him and some other friends to his house on February 22, 1888, George Washington's Birthday—which, by the way, was a balmy, pleasant midwinter day—for a game of golf. Reid laid out three rough holes in his pasture, and he and his guests, sharing Lockhart's clubs, knocked the ball around through much of the afternoon.

12

At a dinner at his house shortly after that pleasant day, Reid and his friends founded the St. Andrew's Golf Club (they used the apostrophe). Other golf clubs sprang up simultaneously and independently in Boston, Newport, and Southampton, and at the same time Charles B. Macdonald was organizing the Chicago Golf Club. Although all of them followed the rules of the Royal and Ancient Golf Club of St. Andrews, Scotland, each club conducted its tournaments and other affairs independently, without the guidance of a central authority. In an atmosphere like that, conflicts were bound to spring up and, inevitably, two clubs became rivals.

In 1894 both the Newport and St. Andrew's clubs held national amateur tournaments. The first was at stroke play at Newport on a windy September morning. The skill of American golfers of the time was so low that of the twenty starters, only eight finished and just two scored under 200 for thirty-six holes. W. G. Lawrence of Newport shot 188 and beat Macdonald by one stroke. A month later, St. Andrew's held its version of the National Amateur at match play. Twenty-eight men entered; in the final match, L. B. Stoddard, a St. Andrew's man, defeated Macdonald in nineteen holes.

Unlike Newport, St. Andrew's also invited professionals to participate in a simultaneous Open championship. Four accepted—Willie Dunn, Willie Davis, Willie Campbell, and Samuel Tucker, recently appointed the professional at St. Andrew's. Like the Amateur, the Open was conducted at match play. No one knows why; the British Open had been decided by strokes since it began, but the big money matches, both in the United States and in Britain, were still at match play.

If that wasn't the determining factor, then conducting the Open at match play could have been a reaction to the criticism of Newport's first Amateur. Some of those more sensitive to transatlantic golf tradition dismissed the Newport event by claiming champions could only be determined by match play.

Whatever the reason, on a bright, clear morning in October, Willie Dunn defeated Willie Davis, 3 and 2, in the first match, and Willie Campbell eliminated Sam Tucker, 2 and 1, in the second. Now Dunn had his opportunity to get back at Campbell for beating him earlier in the year. He did, winning by 2 up and becoming the first Open champion of the United States. To commemorate his victory, Dunn was given $100 and a gold medal. He wore the medal with pride for the rest of his life.

When Macdonald, piqued by missing the Amateur title for a second time, claimed that no single club could arbitrarily conduct a tournament to decide a national championship, the charge also tarnished Dunn's

Open title. Willie, however, remained forever adamant that he was the first Open champion of the United States, and he had a logical response to anyone who questioned his claim: When Gentleman Jim Corbett won the heavyweight boxing championship from John L. Sullivan, no national organization was behind the fight.

Precedent was also on his side. The British Open began as a promotion of the Prestwick Golf Club and was played at first as part of the club's autumn meeting, toward the end of a long week of amateur matches. Indeed, not until 1920 did the Royal and Ancient Golf Club take over and give the British Open the backing of an organization of national scope. Yet no one denies that Willie Park, Sr., who won over seven players at Prestwick in 1860, was the first champion.

The rivalry between Newport and St. Andrew's, along with the controversy over the two amateur championships, caused so much turmoil that something clearly had to be done. Golf needed a central body authorized by the clubs themselves to govern the game in the United States.

Shortly after the St. Andrew's tournament, Henry O. Tallmadge, secretary of St. Andrew's, Theodore Havemeyer of Newport, and Laurence Curtis of The Country Club, near Boston, invited representatives of those three clubs, plus delegates from Shinnecock Hills and the Chicago Golf Club, to a dinner in New York City. They met on December 22, 1894, and formed what is now the United States Golf Association, with the mission, as laid down in its constitution, of determining the sites for the Amateur and Open championships.

As they had been at St. Andrew's, the 1895 Amateur and Open were scheduled by the new USGA for the same week in October, at the Newport Golf Club in socially chic Newport, Rhode Island. The Amateur, at match play, would be decided first, followed by the Open, at stroke play over thirty-six holes, or four times around Newport's nine-hole course, all in one day.

Had he been in America at the time, Willie Park would have been heavily favored to win the Open, for early that summer he had been almost invincible in a series of money matches in the Eastern states, defeating Willie Campbell, Willie Norton, and Joe Lloyd, and winning two of a series of three matches with Willie Dunn, at $200 a match. For some forgotten reason, however, Park returned to Scotland in July, shortly after his last match with Dunn. As he sailed for home on the *Etruria*, he was handed a message from Dunn, wishing him a pleasant voyage. One imagines it was more pleasant for Dunn than for Park, because with Park gone, Dunn had a much better chance of winning at Newport.

14

Of the nine other professionals and one amateur lined up against Dunn that windy autumn morning, Willie Campbell seemed to have the best chance to dislodge him as Open Champion. While all the professionals had emigrated from Britain, only Campbell had ever finished high in the British Open, placing second, third, fourth twice, fifth, seventh, and ninth in the seven championships from 1883 through 1889. It was not an impressive field by the standards of British golf, but nevertheless, those ten men represented the best in America.

The golf course they faced was not the same as it had been a year earlier. Willie Davis had revised and rerouted the holes and made the course a more reasonable and interesting test, turning it into a 2,755-yard, par-35 layout with six par-4 holes, the longest at 385 yards, two par 3s, and a 485-yard par 5. A large part of the course ran through low, swampy ground, rising at times to higher ledges covered with rough boulders. A stone wall cut diagonally across the 5th, a 340-yard par 4.

Newport's most distinctive feature was a rock that rose about thirty feet high a few yards ahead of the 7th tee. Since blind holes were common in those times, Davis routed the hole so the drive had to clear the rock. Adding to that problem, the green was protected by a semicircular bunker across the front and along both sides. Fortunately, the hole measured only 300 yards. Among Newport's other features: The first shot had to carry a series of three earth bunkers, or mounds, that rose six to seven feet above ground, swampy ground to the left of the 2nd hole and an open ditch six feet wide about 280 yards from the tee, and a stone quarry directly in front of the 6th tee. Judged by later standards, the Newport Golf Club of 1895 was a dinosaur, but it was a fine course for its time.

October 4, 1895, was bright and clear, but a strong wind blustered in from the northeast. Golf shots would be difficult to control, and it was not at all certain the best man would win. The Amateur had concluded the day before, with Macdonald finally winning, and many of the amateurs had remained for the Open, to watch, to serve as markers, to referee, or to bet heavily. The New England money was on Campbell, the Chicago money on Jim Foulis, and the New York money on Dunn.

When he began with birdies on the 1st and 2nd holes, Campbell looked as if he might run away from the field, but he dropped strokes on the next two, both par 3s, made 7 on the 5th, where he ran into all kinds of trouble, and went around in 41. He was two strokes ahead of Dunn and four ahead of three others, but with the chilly wind still ripping in off the Atlantic Ocean, Campbell played badly on his next circuit and shot 48. Even with 89, though, he held onto a share of the lead, along with Dunn, who had made only one 6 on his first nine, and Foulis, a long-hitting Chicagoan who had survived an 8 on the 6th, a hole that took a terrible toll throughout the championship.

After lunch, while those three were watching one another, Horace Rawlins moved into contention.

A twenty-one-year-old Englishman whom Willie Davis had brought over in January to be his assistant, Rawlins had shot 45-46—91 for the first eighteen. With a good birdie on the 1st hole and the only birdie made throughout the championship on the 8th, he sped around the third nine in 41, taking over second place, with 132, only a stroke behind Campbell and upsetting the smart money. The amateurs, who were betting even more heavily now, were further upset when Campbell fizzled on the last nine, allowing Rawlins to take command. After 5s on the first two holes, Campbell flew his tee shot into Price's Neck Road, behind the green of the 3rd, a 165-yard one-shotter, losing the ball. Upset by this lapse of tempo, he teed up another ball and pushed the shot to the base of the stone wall that followed the curve of the road, took a penalty of one stroke to move clear of the obstruction, and ended up with 9. Out of the race now, he completed the nine in 48 and finished the championship with 179.

Rawlins, meantime, strung together another 41, shooting 82 for the eighteen and 173 for the thirty-six holes. No one could catch him. Willie Davis shot a pair of 42s for a fine 84, but it had no effect, since he had had 94 in the morning. Dunn and A. W. Smith, the Canadian amateur, both shot 86s, and Foulis had 87. With 175, Dunn finished second to Rawlins, followed by Foulis and Smith at 176. For his victory, Rawlins won $150 and a gold medal.

Horace Rawlins had learned to play golf as a caddie on the Isle of Wight off the southern coast of England, where, ironically, he had attracted the attention of Willie Dunn's brother Tom, who was impressed with the rough youngster and helped him refine his game. Rawlins had played in only one tournament in England before coming to the United States, and while he had beaten Dunn in a match, he had finished well off the lead in a tournament at Shinnecock Hills two months before the Open.

The result of that first Open conducted by the United States Golf Association was a bitter disappointment for both Dunn and Campbell. Dunn never won again—he and Foulis tied for third at the Chicago Golf Club, in 1897—but he continued to wear his medal proudly until he died, in 1952. Campbell was thirty-three in 1895. He played in a few more Opens, but he died five years later, at thirty-eight, without winning the Open.

16

While Rawlins continued to play very well, he could never win again. He finished second the following year at Shinnecock Hills, where Foulis won with 78-74—152. By then six holes had been added to Shinnecock, turning it into an eighteen-hole course, and Foulis' 74 stood as a record until the rubber-cored ball came into wide use. It was matched by Laurie Auchterlonie in 1902 and then beaten in 1903 by Willie Anderson's 73.

Rawlins last appears in the record book in the 1909 Open, when he finished in sixtieth place, but his place in history was assured as the first United States Open Champion under the banner of the USGA.

In 1897 Foulis was succeeded as champion by Joe Lloyd, an Englishman who divided his time between the Essex County Country Club in Manchester, Massachusetts, and the spa town of Pau in the French Pyrenees. He would be the last winner over thirty-six holes, for now the USGA decided to separate the Open from the Amateur and lengthen it to seventy-two holes, playing thirty-six on each of two days, as the British Open had been conducted since 1892. Making the change just then was awkward, because the 1898 championship was scheduled for the Myopia Hunt Club, a nine-hole course in a suburb of Boston; to get in seventy-two holes, every one of the forty-nine entrants would have to play eight times around. Even then Myopia was a demanding course, for even though he broke 84 only once, Fred Herd won with a score of 328, an average of 82 for each eighteen-hole round. The next year the championship moved back to an eighteen-hole course, the Baltimore Country Club, laid out by Willie Dunn. Carnoustie-born Willie Smith won there by eleven strokes, a margin that is unlikely to be broken.

Through its first five years, the Open had been won by British-born players who had settled in the United States for at least part of the year. It hadn't grown important enough to draw the best of the British golfers across the Atlantic just to play in the championship, but in 1900 its prestige rose substantially when Harry Vardon and J. H. Taylor decided to enter. By then, they had established themselves as the greatest players in the game, but neither was drawn by the importance of the championship; they came for reasons of commerce.

Because Vardon had won three of the last four British Opens, the A. G. Spalding Company took advantage of his popularity and introduced a new ball called the Vardon Flyer. To help promote it, the company arranged a series of exhibition matches for 1900 that would last the entire year, except for a quick trip home for the British Open, and cover some 20,000 miles, taking Vardon from Canada to Florida. The tour was a roaring personal success for Vardon and an absolute revelation to American golfers. Even though he usually played against the better ball of two opponents, Vardon won over fifty matches, halved two, and lost thirteen. Only two of the losses were against a single opponent. Bernard Nicholls beat him at Ormond Beach, Florida, over a course without a single blade of grass, and again at the Brae Burn Country Club near Boston. Some of Vardon's victories were monumental. Twice he beat Willie Dunn by absurd margins—16 and 15 at Point Comfort, Virginia, and 15 and 14 at Scarsdale, New York.

American golfers had never seen the likes of Vardon's easy grace. Jerry Travers, who would become one of the greatest American amateurs, said Vardon was easy to identify. "If you run across one man who is making the game so easy a child could play it, whose form is the last word in poetry, and who from one hundred and eighty to two hundred and twenty yards is putting a full shot closer to the hole than most others can put a mashie, your quest for Vardon will be over."

While J. H. Taylor couldn't match Vardon as a stylist, he had won the British Open twice before Vardon won his first, and some years earlier had joined with George Cann, a boyhood friend, to form a club-making firm. Convinced golf had a fine future in the United States, Cann and Taylor opened a branch in Pittsburgh. Cann settled there permanently and left Taylor to run the business in Britain. After Taylor won the British Open in 1900 (his third), he and Cann agreed J.H. might help business by touring America, as Vardon was doing. Taylor was also hired by Harper & Bros., the American publishing house, to write articles for the magazine *Golf*, the first golf magazine published in the United States. For this he was paid £2,000, a large amount for the times.

The Open was scheduled for early October at the Chicago Golf Club once again. With both Vardon and Taylor on hand, no one else was given a chance, even though a very good field had entered, led by Willie and Alex Smith, brothers from the famous Carnoustie family, who had come over to live in America, Jim Foulis and his brother Richard, Laurie Auchterlonie, Alex Campbell, Horace Rawlins, Tom Hutchison, and Dave Bell.

Vardon and Taylor were an interesting contrast in styles. Vardon played high, soaring, slightly faded shots that were occasionally tossed about by the wind. Taylor hit low, running, right-to-left shots, which weren't as effective in America as on his native links because the entrances to so many American greens were protected by cop bunkers (those with a high bank on the greenward face). Except for the strong southerly wind that would blow for most of the championship, Vardon's style seemed the more suited for the golf course.

Because agronomy had not yet reached the stage where strains of fine-bladed grasses were available, American putting greens tended to be coarse and bumpy. In attempting to eliminate grain, the Chicago Golf

Club used a machine to brush the grass. Taylor said the result was like a boy's hair brushed the wrong way, and he could hole nothing. Nevertheless, he jumped to a three-stroke lead over Vardon in the first round, with 76 to 79. Vardon didn't putt very well either, but he played some marvelous recoveries after a number of his shots were blown off line by the strong wind.

Vardon added a 78 in the afternoon, and when Taylor struggled to 82, the morning positions were reversed, with Vardon ahead by one stroke. He should have led by two, but after missing a putt for par on the last green, he rather carelessly tried to tap the ball into the hole, snagged the blade of his putter against the wiry grass, and whiffed.

With 76 in the third round against 79 by Taylor, Vardon extended his lead to four strokes, and with eighteen holes to go, he was obviously playing with great confidence. On the 7th hole of the final round he turned what looked like a stroke of bad luck into a birdie. With the wind at his back, he drove 270 yards, an amazingly long shot with the old gutta-percha ball, but his ball bounded into a cross-bunker.

Five strokes ahead by then, Vardon played a wonderful niblick close to the cup and holed the putt for a 3. When Taylor made 4, Vardon had increased his lead to six strokes.

Taylor nibbled away throughout the last nine, cutting Vardon's lead to two strokes by the 17th, but it was all over when Vardon played a full brassie to the back of the 18th green and got down in three for his 5. Vardon shot 80 to Taylor's 78 and won by two strokes, 313 to 315. Taylor did have some bad luck—over the last thirty-six holes at least four of his putts rimmed the cup—but Vardon had played the shots he had to play when he had to play them.

Vardon and Taylor were well clear of the field at the end. Dave Bell, playing out of Midlothian, another Chicago club, was third at 322, nine strokes behind Vardon, and Laurie Auchterlonie, from Glenview, Illinois, was fourth at 327. Willie Smith, the defender, finished fifth at 328.

The 1900 championship showed decisively that British golfers were still the best. Even so, American fans were beginning to create their own heroes. The first of these was even then ready to assert himself, and, indeed, had nearly won three years before Vardon made his visit. Only Joe Lloyd's superb 3 on the last hole had prevented Willie Anderson from winning the 1897 Open when he was just seventeen. Scottish-born Willie was already in with 163 when Lloyd came to the 465-yard 18th needing a 4 to tie. He ripped a big drive, then scorched a brassie eight feet from the cup and holed the putt. A slight, self-contained golfer, Anderson needed a few more years to break through, but when he did, he dominated the game in the United States as no one had before. From 1901 through 1905, he was nearly unbeatable, winning the Open four times, the Western Open twice, and losing a playoff to Alex Smith, his great rival, for the first Metropolitan (New York) Open Championship, in 1905. From 1897 through 1910 he played in fourteen Opens. In addition to winning four, he finished lower than fifth only three times, second once, third once, fourth twice, fifth three times, eleventh twice, and fifteenth once. He was the only man to win the U.S. Open with both the gutta-percha and the rubber ball (Vardon, Taylor, and James Braid—the Great Triumvirate—won the British Open with both). Willie Anderson was the first encompassing hero of American golf.

Sadly, Anderson's career was as brief as it was brilliant. He died at the age of thirty, it was said from arteriosclerosis, normally a disease of the elderly, but probably from causes related to alcohol, for, like many golf professionals of that era, he drank heavily.

How good was Willie Anderson? Those who played against him and watched the great players of later years said he was as good as anyone who ever played. He was the complete golfer, skilled in every phase of the game. He had a full, flowing, although somewhat flat swing—at least compared to Vardon's upright style—and he moved into the ball with an unhurried ease that disguised his power. He putted with a smooth, rhythmic stroke, but he was probably at his best with the mashie, the equivalent of the modern 5-iron. It was his favorite club.

His accuracy was legendary. Some years after Anderson's death, Gene Sarazen was practicing from a bunker, obviously pleased with himself as he laid shot after shot within easy holing distance. Spotting Bill Robinson, an old professional and golf course architect standing nearby, Sarazen called, "Hey, Bill. Could Willie Anderson get out of traps like that?" Robinson sneered, then turned his head and spat. "Get out of them?" he snarled. "He was never in them."

While Anderson often seemed dour and phlegmatic—which might be the ideal temperament for a champion golfer—he had his moments.

Club members of those days felt justified in barring professionals from their clubhouses because they were generally a rough, crude band, short on social graces, and long on alcohol intake (they drank a raw, brutal liquor that scalded the throat and ravaged the insides—it wasn't Chivas Regal). The USGA required Fred Herd to put up security for the Open trophy after he won in 1898, fearing he'd pawn it for drinking money.

Nor was their language out of Yale or Harvard. Most of them had very little schooling. They swore, often heavily, and the immigrant Scots and English spoke a dialect that was difficult to understand, laced with strange back-alley expressions.

Club members might find these characters suitable subjects for heavy betting—like Dan Patch—but they had no wish to mingle with them socially; they were of a different stratum of society and were to be kept in their place. The professionals couldn't do anything about this, but they found some snubs hard to accept. Where they would eat lunch at championships was always a problem.

On the morning of the first round of the Open at Myopia, the year after Vardon's victory, a club member told the professionals they were to take their lunch in the kitchen. Anderson was standing on the fringe of the group, idly swinging his mashie. As the substance of the message became clear, the pace of Willie's swing picked up speed, and for a moment he lapsed into the dialect of his youth. "Na, na," he snapped. "We're na goin t' eat in the kitchen." Furious, he slashed at the ground with all his power and gouged a huge divot from the velvety lawn. Astonished, the member retreated inside. Sometime later the professionals were told they could have their lunch in a tent that would be raised for them.

That incident seemed out of character, because Anderson was essentially a modest man who got along extremely well with the other players. Even though he beat them regularly, they admired him, respected him, and liked him. The public, however, seemed indifferent to him, and Willie was upset by the indifference.

Tom Mercer had come over from Edinburgh and was working at the Sound Beach Golf Club in Old Greenwich, Connecticut, when Willie was at the Apawamis Club close by in Rye, New York. Although Mercer was older than Anderson, they had become close friends, and in moments of gloomy introspection Willie would mutter to him, "They don't know me. They don't know me."

Anderson was born in 1880 in North Berwick, where his father, Tom Anderson, Sr., was greenkeeper at that famous old course that skirts the headlands above the Firth of Forth. While he never caddied, Willie had the run of the course and often played in caddie tournaments. By the mid-1890s, with so many opportunities opening up in golf in the United States, he was persuaded to emigrate by Frank Legh Slazenger, of the sporting goods family, who had left his brothers in charge of their London establishment and opened a business in New York. Willie was only fourteen, but Slazenger found him a position at the Misquamicut Golf Club in Watch Hill, Rhode Island.

Anderson spent the summer at his new club, but, becoming homesick, he returned to Scotland for the winter. Back in the United States the following spring, Willie spent the year teaching members and working on his own game, and by the following season he felt he was ready to test himself in serious competition. His narrow defeat by Lloyd convinced him that, despite his age, he could play with anybody, but like many other great players still to come, he needed a few more years to develop fully. He finished third to Fred Herd in 1898, fifth to Willie Smith in 1899, and eleventh when Vardon and Taylor came over in 1900.

The 1901 Open was the second at Myopia, but by now the course had been lengthened to eighteen holes, measuring 6,130 yards and made so difficult that the players complained. The ground was hard, the turf thin, and the greens abnormally fast. One man putted boldly from above the cup on the 8th hole and watched his ball roll off the green and disappear into some shrubs. Anderson missed one very short putt on the 13th and two at the 17th. Laurie Auchterlonie missed one on the 8th during the last round so short it seemed ridiculous, and Willie Smith missed three just like it during the third round.

In the difficult conditions, the competition was tense, and the lead changed hands by the round. Auchterlonie opened with 81, Alex Smith shot two 82s and went ahead after thirty-six holes, then Stewart Gardner moved to the front with 249 after fifty-four holes. Anderson lay second, with 250, Smith stood another stroke behind, and Auchterlonie, David Brown, Bernard Nicholls, and Willie Smith tied at 252—seven men within three strokes of one another, the tightest struggle yet for the Open championship.

When Anderson closed with 81, for a total of 331, he looked safe, for Gardner had collapsed, along with Nicholls, Brown, and Willie Smith. Only Alex Smith was left, and he needed three 4s to tie Willie. A long putt fell for a 3 on the 16th, but he dropped a stroke to par at the 17th. Now he must have that 4 on the last hole.

The 18th measured only 335 yards, but under the circumstances, a par was no cinch. Smith drove well, then hit a glorious iron only ten feet from the hole. The gallery of about 500 crowded close around the green as Smith studied his line. He stroked the putt nicely, right at the center of the cup, but he misjudged the speed, and his ball stopped just short. It was a tie, and the Open would be decided by a playoff three days later—the golf course was reserved for members over the weekend.

Anderson shot 85 to Smith's 86. One era was drawing to a close, and another had begun.

The gutta-percha ball had been the standard golf ball since the 1840s, when it replaced the centuries-old featherie, a leather pouch stuffed with boiled goose feathers. The gutty had a number of advantages over the featherie. It was less expensive, and it was easier to make. A feather ball had to be cut, stuffed, and sewn by hand; gutta-percha is a rubbery substance that can be heated and molded into a sphere easily and quickly. When it was wet or mishit with an iron club, a feather ball often flew apart, but a gutta-percha ball that was nicked, knocked out of shape, or even split apart could be heated and remolded. Above all, though, the gutta-percha ball flew yards farther than the featherie. Compared to the featherie, the gutty seemed the ideal ball for golf.

Still, man is a restless and inventive species, and the gutty was never allowed to rest easily. New ideas were tried regularly; some of them were better than others.

A ball called the Eclipse was introduced during the 1880s. A mixture of cork and rubber, it was the original Bounding Billy, the liveliest ball ever seen to that time, bounding along the ground, leaping over bunkers, and flying out of control on pitches to greens. Strangely, it seemed to fly farther off the face of an iron club than from a wood. It had the further benefit of wearing very well and not breaking apart as the gutty sometimes did. But its major feature was also its major weakness—it was much too lively and couldn't be controlled. It had a short life and soon disappeared.

Someone else developed a ball called the Putty. Softer than either the gutty or the Eclipse, it too was lively and uncontrollable and it too failed. An American manufacturer developed still another ball called the Maponite that combined the wearing qualities of the Eclipse with the click of the gutty. The company behind it failed, however, and this ball also disappeared.

All these and most of the many other experiments were based on molding a solid mass into a sphere. But in 1898 Coburn Haskell, an indifferent golfer from Cleveland, Ohio, conceived the idea of winding thin strips of rubber thread around a solid core and holding it all together with a thin cover of gutta-percha. With this invention, Haskell created a new form of golf. His ball flew farther than the old gutty, ran farther, and was more forgiving of a mis-hit shot. Above all, it could be controlled. It made the game altogether more enjoyable for the less skilled player.

In spite of all its wonderful qualities, however, the Haskell ball was not an immediate success; the great players were reluctant to switch from the gutty. Haskell sent a supply of the new balls to J. H. Taylor, asking him to use them in the 1900 Open, but after playing a few shots with them in practice, Taylor was afraid he might lose his touch with the gutty and put them aside.

Nevertheless, he was eager to give the Haskell a thorough test. A week or so later he teed one up on the 1st hole of the Rockaway Hunting Club on Long Island as a group of players stood on the green about 240 yards away. Since he was not a long hitter—his normal drive covered about 175 yards—Taylor assumed they were well out of range, but his ball shot off like a rocket and rolled to the feet of a man who was holing out. Taylor had never hit a ball that far, but as he rushed up and apologized, he realized the gutta-percha ball was doomed. The Haskell simply went too far for the gutty to survive.

Walter Travis won his second consecutive U.S. Amateur Championship in 1901 using the new ball, but still it wasn't catching on with professionals; the conservatives felt the game might be hurt by the added distance of the Haskell and that the game would no longer be golf. When word got around that a group of British professionals were considering a trial of the ball, traditionalists flooded golf magazines with indignant letters. Then, on the eve of the 1902 British Open, John Ball, the great British amateur, gave a Haskell ball to Sandy Herd, the brother of Fred, who had won the U.S. Open four years earlier. When Sandy used it and won the championship, the rush was on to buy the Haskell ball. The gutty was gone forever.

Back in the United States, scores in the U.S. Open quickly reflected the change. In winning the 1902 championship with 78-78-74-77—307, Laurie Auchterlonie finished six strokes ahead of Travis and Stewart Gardner, and became the first man to shoot under 80 in each round. His scoring was so steady he had only two nines in the 40s.

Over his fourteen-year career, Willie Anderson held jobs at ten clubs. He had been at Baltusrol in Springfield, New Jersey, twenty miles west of New York City, shortly before the turn of the century, and since the 1903 Open was coming there, it was like a homecoming. Making the most of his knowledge of the course, he led by six strokes with one round to go, but the expected runaway didn't develop. David Brown, an ex-plasterer from Musselburgh, who had won the 1886 British Open, picked up the six strokes with a 76 against Anderson's 82, and at the end of the day both men had 307.

Willie's form had been slipping round by round, and he was no better in the playoff, but Brown had lost his touch, too. Anderson shot 82, Brown 84, and Anderson became the first man to win the Open twice.

By now there was no question that Willie Anderson was the best golfer in America. Not only had he won the Open twice and matched the record seventy-two-hole score of 307, he had also won the Western Open of 1902, the nation's second most important professional tournament, shooting the remarkable score of 299 at the Euclid Club in Cleveland. A year later he won them both again.

The Western Golf Association had been organized in 1899 as a rival to the United States Golf Association, chiefly because golfers in the West felt their interests didn't coincide with those of the Eastern clubs. Perhaps to assure Westerners they were not being ignored, the USGA took the 1904 Open to the Glen View Club in suburban Chicago, after three years of playing close to either Boston or New York.

In cold and drizzly weather, Anderson shot 75 in the first round to tie Stewart Gardner, but when the clouds drifted away after lunch, Willie's game floated off with them. He struggled around in 78 that afternoon, then added another 78 the next morning. By then, Fred McKenzie, yet another Scottish import, was two strokes ahead, but Anderson would not be beaten. Going for everything, he began the last round with four 4s and a 3 and turned in 37. Coming home he was flawless. After a 5 on the 10th, he played the last eight holes in two under 4s, sensational golf for those times. With 35 on the second nine, he shot 72 and a total of 303, setting both the eighteen- and seventy-two-hole scoring records and winning by five strokes over Gil Nicholls.

In two years then Willie had won two National Opens and two Westerns, but he wasn't through yet. In 1905 the Open went to Myopia for the third time in eight years. While Anderson opened poorly with rounds of 80 and 81, leaving him five strokes behind Stewart Gardner and his old nemesis, Alex Smith, Willie was one of those rare men who play their best on the great occasions. Full of confidence, he began the third round par-birdie-par, and then, when a long putt dropped on the 4th, he told the crowd, "That's the championship." He finished the nine in 35 and shot 41 coming back. His card showed five 3s, another remarkable exhibition of scoring, and his 76 brought him within a stroke of Smith.

Sensing that the battle was between Smith and Anderson, two proved winners, the gallery divided into two parts, the larger group following Anderson. Willie gave them a fine show. Out in 37, he started home with a par and a bogey and caught Smith, who was playing ahead of him and on his way to a third consecutive 80. After two more bogeys, Anderson birdied the 14th, a tightly bunkered 350-yard par 4, then added pars on the 15th and 16th.

Four strokes ahead with two holes to play, the little Scotsman gave his backers a scare by making a 6 on the 17th, but they need not have worried. At the 18th Willie hit a long straight drive, pitched safely onto the green, and took two putts for a par 4 and a round of 77. While his 314 was the highest winning total since the rubber-cored ball had become widely used, it was two strokes better than Smith's 316.

Only twenty-five then, Anderson seemed certain to dominate the game for years, but curiously he never won another Open. A year later he and Alex Smith fought a tight duel at Onwentsia, where Willie had become the professional. Two strokes behind Smith after thirty-six holes, Anderson lost another stroke in the third round, even though he turned in a strong 74, but he wasn't the same man after lunch. He staggered home in 84 and finished fifth. Smith shot 75, joining his brother Willie as an Open champion and with 295 became the first man to break 300 in the Open.

This was Anderson's last serious threat. While he appeared to be robust, his health was failing. He was under a doctor's care in the 1907 Open, when he shot 316 and finished fourteen strokes behind Alex Ross. Forever on the move, in 1910 he took a job at the Philadelphia Cricket Club, which was to be the site of the Open that year. This was to be his last Open. He could still play well enough, and the competitive fires still burned fiercely, but he wasn't up to the challenge. While he broke 80 in every round—78 was his highest score—the overall level of scoring had become much better. Alex Smith won with 298, and Anderson's 303 left him in eleventh place. Even Willie's younger brother, Tom, beat him by a stroke.

By then a good player could earn decent money in exhibition matches, and in the fall Willie set off on a series of thirty-six-hole matches around Pittsburgh. On October 19 at the Fox Hill Club, he teamed with Isaac Mackie of the home club against Alex Smith and George Low. Mackie and Smith both shot 147, Low 153, and Anderson 156. On October 21, Anderson and Gil Nicholls lost to Jock Hutchison and Peter Robertson. Two days later Anderson played his last match.

Teamed with Nicholls again, Willie played thirty-six holes at the Allegheny Country Club against William C. Fownes, the current National Amateur champion, and Eben Byers, the 1906 champion. The match was a classic. Playing terrific golf, the amateurs shot a better ball score of 69 in the morning against a par of 72 and stood 2 up at noon. After lunch, Anderson and Nicholls went to work and, playing at the same level as the amateurs had in the morning, pulled even by the thirty-fifth hole. Then, from just off the edge of the 18th green, Byers holed a chip for a 3 to win the hole and the match.

Anderson had tired noticeably over the last few holes. After dragging himself into the clubhouse and sprawling in a chair, he groaned that he wouldn't play another round of golf that year. Two days later, on October 25, he died at his home in Philadelphia.

TWO

Johnny McDermott Leads the Homebreds

By 1910, Macdonald Smith had left Carnoustie, a grim, gray little town on Scotland's east coast, to join his brothers Willie and Alex in the United States. With his graceful, flowing swing, Mac Smith seemed certain to become successful in America. He wasted no time, shooting 71 in the last round of the 1910 Open and tying his brother Alex for first place at 298. That round took place on Saturday, June 18, three months exactly after Mac's twentieth birthday, and since competitive golf wasn't played on Sunday, the playoff was held over until Monday. Mac had cooled off by then, shooting a 77 to his brother's 71, and Alex became the champion.

A third man was in that playoff. John McDermott, the eighteen-year-old son of a Philadelphia mailman, shot 75, losing by four strokes to Alex but beating Mac by two. While Alex never won another Open (he was thirty-eight at the time), and Mac would never win the Open at all, McDermott developed into one of the great players of the age.

In 1909, George Sargent, yet another expatriate Briton, had lowered the seventy-two-hole Open record to 290 by shooting 75-72-72-71 at the Englewood Golf Club in New Jersey. Playing in his first Open, Johnny McDermott had scored 322 and placed forty-ninth in the field of sixty. He was a more polished player a year later, winning the Philadelphia Open, then tying the Smiths in the national championship, beaten in the playoff by a man who was twenty years older and vastly more experienced.

PART ONE

McDermott was a quiet, mannerly young man; he didn't drink or smoke, and he rarely missed Sunday mass. He had been a good student at West Philadelphia High School, but he dropped out to become a professional golfer, taking a job at the Merchantville Field Club in southern New Jersey, then switching to the Atlantic City Country Club. Johnny drove himself. He began the day's practice at dawn, often five o'clock in the summer, and continued until eight o'clock, when he opened the shop. After closing late in the afternoon, he played until dark, then practiced putting by lamplight.

McDermott's mashie became the stuff of legend. He practiced by hitting shots at a large tarpaulin spread on the ground about 150 yards away, reducing the target gradually to spread-out newspapers. The more he practiced, the better and more confident he became. Early in 1911 he challenged Philadelphia professionals to eighteen-hole matches for $1,000 each. After he won three straight, the competition dried up.

By then, McDermott was definitely ready for bigger things.

The Open that year was returning to the Chicago Golf Club, where Vardon had won in 1900, and while the layout was much the same, the greens were smoother and putted balls ran much truer than they had eleven years earlier. Nevertheless, Chicago turned out to be difficult and demanding, and the June weather was scorching, with just an occasional drifting cloud giving momentary relief from the blazing sun. Only Alex Ross scored under 75 in the first round. One of two brothers who had come to the United States from Dornoch in the north of Scotland—Donald became one of our great golf course designers—Ross shot 74 and led by a stroke over H. K. Barker. Still two months short of his twentieth birthday, McDermott had opened with a disappointing 81, but his game sharpened considerably in the afternoon, and he shot a fine 72.

As the leaders collapsed the next day, McDermott had a great opportunity to run off with the championship, but he struggled around in 75 and 79 to match Mike Brady and George Simpson at 307 and stumbled into another three-man playoff.

Johnny normally played a Rawlings Black Circle ball, but when a manufacturer offered a $300 bonus if the playoff winner used a brand called Colonel, he switched, then hit two of them out of bounds from the 1st tee. He escaped with a 6, but he had lost two strokes to Brady and one to Simpson, who was playing despite pain from inflamed muscles. Neither Brady nor Simpson was a match for McDermott this day, though. One hole later all three were tied, and by the end of nine, Johnny had the playoff in hand. With a 39 out, he led Brady by four strokes and Simpson by five, and went on to beat Brady by two and Simpson by six.

At nineteen, McDermott was not only the youngest player to have won the Open, but the first American-born champion as well. He had ended the domination by immigrant British golfers, and he was leading a wave of young homebreds, like Mike Brady and Tom McNamara, who were to revolutionize the way the game was played.

McDermott's victory had not only shown that American-born golfers could outplay the best of the imports, it also quickened interest in the Open. On the first day of August 1912, a field of 125 golfers turned out at the Country Club of Buffalo, the first time the Open entry topped 100. The Amateur still drew a larger field (217 in 1910 and 186 in 1911), but the Open was gaining.

Scoring was improving, too. In the decade since the birth of the wound-rubber ball, subpar rounds had become common. David Hunter had shot 68 and Tom McNamara 69 in the 1909 Open, the lowest until then, but no one expected scores like those at Buffalo. The course measured 6,326 yards, the longest ever for the Open. Par, however, was a forgiving 74.

McDermott scored 149 for the first thirty-six holes and went into the third round trailing Mike Brady and Alex Smith by two strokes. Momentarily losing control, he drove two balls out of bounds and made 6 on the 1st hole. Another pulled tee shot on the 2nd was his last mistake. Johnny played the remaining sixteen holes in one-under-4s, but his 74 dropped him another stroke behind Brady. Mike now led with 220, but at 223, McDermott was well within range.

Brady had a wretched start in the afternoon, and McDermott continued to attack. Playing the first nine in 35, with eight 4s and a 3, he had caught Mike at the 2nd, passed him at the 3rd, and led him by three as he turned for home. Brady was through, but Tom McNamara was still in the hunt. McNamara had already won the North and South and the Metropolitan Opens, and he had been third in both the Massachusetts and Wykagyl Opens. Now, playing three or four holes ahead of McDermott, the Boston Irishman was doing wonderful things. Four strokes behind Johnny when the round began, he was out in 35 and had begun the home nine with three birdies in four holes. He was five under par by then, the hottest burst of scoring ever seen in the Open, and he was closing in. If he could play the last five holes in even par, he'd have 69, and then they'd wait to see what McDermott was made of. Four quick pars and McNamara was at the 18th, a short, 333-yard par 4. He could make a birdie here, and a birdie would give him 68 and put more pressure on McDermott. He didn't get it, but with a par he was back in 34 and had a superb 69, which made him the first man to break 70 twice in the Open.

PART ONE

McDermott was finishing the 15th when McNamara, smiling broadly, walked off the 18th green with his 296, even par for seventy-two holes. At that point Johnny was one under par on the second nine and still had two strokes in hand. McNamara's dazzling stretch run had cut only two strokes from McDermott's lead. At the 155-yard 16th, McDermott hit a tee shot that covered the flagstick all the way and came down only a few yards from the hole. Using the style of putting that had developed in the United States—heels together, erect stance, pendulum stroke—McDermott rolled the ball dead into the heart of the hole for a birdie 2. Now he had three strokes in hand with two holes to play, and the Open was his. A lost stroke on the 17th meant nothing; with 36 for the second nine, he had 71 for the round and 294 for the championship.

Never had American golfers seen such sensational scoring. With 73 and 69, McNamara had played the last thirty-six holes in 142, the lowest finish yet, and McDermott had been only three strokes behind, with 74-71—145. While their seventy-two-hole scores were four strokes higher than George Sargent's 290 at Englewood, they had played a more demanding golf course.

Although McNamara had shown that he was capable of wonderful bursts of scoring, McDermott was clearly the better golfer. He had now won the Open twice before he had reached the age of twenty-one, and he was being compared to Willie Anderson. There seemed to be no limit to what he might accomplish. He was doing well financially: Clubs were marketed under his name, he endorsed balls, played exhibition matches, gave lessons, and invested his money. The world was a lovely place.

As 1913 dawned, McDermott, Brady, and McNamara planned a trip to the British Open, at Hoylake in northwestern England. McDermott had two purposes in mind. Fiercely American, he wanted to show the British that he and his comrades were the better golfers, and he also wanted to erase the memory of what had happened to him at Muirfield a year earlier. He had gone over as the American champion in 1912, announcing he had come to win, an American attitude that still irritates Europeans. He had looked especially sharp in practice, playing several rounds in the low 70s, but his game deserted him in qualifying. He shot a humiliating 96 and was on his way home before the championship began.

Some of McDermott's problems had been caused by his method of striking the ball. Americans by then had developed their own type of golf swing, a long, loose, flowing motion somewhat like the old St. Andrews swing of the feather ball period, but with more body turn. Because it emphasized a flattish motion, it often caused a hook, which Johnny couldn't control at Muirfield. The British swing, on the other hand, was

30

shorter, with a restricted follow-through that made more use of the arms and wrists.

Johnny's swing was well under control at Hoylake. Despite an 83 in the wind and the sheeting rain of the last day, he shot 315 and finished fifth, the best an American had ever done. While his score was nowhere near the leaders—J. H. Taylor ran away from the field, with 304—McDermott sailed for home pleased with his game and with his performance. He realized that except for two nasty breaks when his ball failed to clear bunkers by inches, he would have finished higher, but he knew that he had played some of his best golf in the worst conditions, and his driving had been straight and long.

Just as life was looking ever brighter, though, Johnny McDermott's good times were ending. When he arrived home, he was shaken to learn he had lost heavily in some stock transactions. He kept the news from his family—he was a bachelor and lived with his sisters and their parents—but he brooded so much they knew something was wrong. Other problems deepened his depression.

Harry Vardon was on another tour of the United States then, accompanied by Ted Ray, a fellow Englishman. They entered a tournament at Shawnee-on-Delaware, Pennsylvania, a mountain resort on the upper Delaware River, that attracted about the same field as the one that was to play in the Open a few weeks later. Putting beautifully, McDermott shot 293, eight strokes better than Alex Smith, the runner-up and thirteen better than Vardon. Ray was another stroke behind.

McDermott was boosted onto a chair at the presentation ceremony and the crowd called for a speech. Cocky to the point of arrogance, McDermott said, "We hope our foreign visitors had a good time, but we don't think they did, and we are sure they won't win the National Open."

The crowd was stunned. The Englishmen's faces flushed, but they said nothing. Trying to smooth things over, their friends only added to the embarrassment. American players seemed more indignant than the foreign-born pros; they felt the remarks were particularly ungracious coming from McDermott, since the British had received him so cordially on his two visits. One of the home pros remarked that the news reports would be full of the matter within hours and that "American professionals can be sure of a cool reception abroad for years to come."

McDermott wasn't aware he had said anything wrong, but when he was told he had insulted the Englishmen, he found them and apologized. The older men were understanding. Realizing that Johnny was young and flushed with victory, they accepted the apology.

Others were not so forgiving. McDermott was criticized in one newspaper account for his "unsportsmanlike remarks," which led to more criticism. He received a letter from an official of the USGA, who stated that because of Johnny's "extreme discourtesy," his entry for the 1913 Open might be rejected. Crushed, McDermott brooded even more. Even though his entry was accepted, he was depressed when he went to Boston for the championship, which was out of character for him, but he was such a great player he missed tying for first place by only four strokes.

After returning to Atlantic City, McDermott kept to himself even more for a time, but then he seemed to recover his confidence in Florida over the winter and entered the British Open once again.

He didn't even tee off. On the first day of qualifying he missed a ferry that would have connected with a train to Prestwick, where the championship was being played. The round was already underway when he finally arrived, but when he explained what had happened, understanding officials offered to let him play even though he was late. Johnny refused, saying it wouldn't be fair to the other players. Downcast, he booked passage home on the *Kaiser Wilhelm II*, the speed queen of the North Atlantic.

Thick fog that had covered Europe for days was especially heavy when McDermott sailed. With its foghorn blaring, the liner was making way slowly through the English Channel when suddenly, out of the mist, the grain carrier *Incemore* loomed dead ahead. Both ships maneuvered violently, but they rammed. The *Kaiser Wilhelm's* hull was ripped open beneath the waterline. It was doomed.

McDermott was in the barber shop when he was rocked by the collision. A steward led him to a lifeboat, and he was picked up a few hours later and returned to England. While he seemed unharmed, the experience affected him more than anyone realized.

The series of events over the last year—his stock losses, the incident at Shawnee, then the shipwreck—preyed on his mind. He entered the 1914 Open, but by then his spirit was shattered, and he was never in position to win. Later that season he blacked out as he entered the professional's shop at Atlantic City. Only twenty-three, his career was finished. He was taken to his parents' home in Philadelphia and spent the rest of his life in and out of rest homes taking an endless series of treatments. He never played in another golf tournament, although he watched a few. He saw his last Open in 1971 at the Merion Golf Club, close to his home in the suburbs of Philadelphia. Not long afterward he died, quietly and in his sleep. He would have been eighty within a month. He could have been the greatest of them all.

THREE

Francis Ouimet Awakens America

With their growing success at home, and especially after Johnny McDermott's high finish in the British Open at Hoylake, American golfers moved onto a higher level. As they had improved they had developed their own style, and their confidence was climbing. By 1913 some of them felt they were as good as anybody. They'd have their chance to show it, later in the year, because Harry Vardon was planning another American tour, which would include another try at the Open, scheduled for September at The Country Club near Boston.

Vardon's tour was backed by Lord Northcliffe, the owner of *The Times*, London's leading newspaper, who was more interested in having him win the U.S. Open than he was in the rest of the tour. As his traveling partner, Vardon chose Ted Ray, a big, burly man, six feet tall and weighing over 200 pounds, who wore a bush mustache and usually smoked a pipe. The winner of the 1912 British Open, Ray was the ideal partner for Vardon; while Harry was the game's consummate stylist, Ted was its long-distance king.

They arrived in New York in the midst of a heat wave, and they were both surprised and annoyed to find they were due in Philadelphia the next day for a match against Ben and Gil Nicholls. With no preparation, the Englishmen shot a better-ball score of 68 and won by 3 and 2. Maybe the Americans weren't quite as ready to handle the cream of British golf as they thought.

The suspicion grew as Vardon and Ray won match after match. They played forty-one altogether and lost only to Alex and Macdonald Smith, but that was after the Open.

With each loss, the confidence of the Americans sank; only a few felt they were a match for the two Englishmen. Predictably, McDermott was one of them. He believed he was as good as anybody, and when he won the tournament at Shawnee-on-Delaware, he not only convinced himself he was the best player in the game, but helped restore the fading confidence of the other Americans as well.

As the Open drew near, interest grew intense. Entries soared to 165 players, by far the largest ever, causing qualifying to cover two days rather than one. Many players entered as a response to what they perceived as a foreign challenge. Walter Hagen came in from Rochester, introduced himself to McDermott, and told him, "I'm here to help you boys take care of Vardon and Ray."

There were other foreign challengers. Wilfred Reid had come over from England and Louis Tellier from France. This was the most important and the most cosmopolitan U.S. Open played so far.

Although American confidence had grown with McDermott's victory at Shawnee, it sagged after the qualifying rounds. In different halves of the field, Vardon led the first day's play with 151, and Ray led the next day's with 148. Still, it was only qualifying; the real test would come over the next two days.

McDermott had played in three Opens by then, and no one had beaten his seventy-two-hole scores. He began at Brookline as if he would keep that record intact, playing iron shots so precisely he had little work to do on the greens. He began 4-3-4-4-3-4-3, but he lost three strokes over the next two holes, went out in 36 and shot 74 for the round, leaving him three strokes behind Alex Ross and Macdonald Smith, both with 71s. Tom McNamara and Walter Hagen had 73s, Wilfred Reid 74, Vardon 75, and Ray a disappointing 79.

Recovering from his dismal start, Ray shot a superb 70 in the afternoon, and when the day ended, he was two strokes behind Vardon, who had played a steady 72, and Wilfred Reid, the coleaders, at 147.

With the British players as much on edge as the Americans, the tensions that had simmered below the surface broke into the open the evening after the first day's play. When an argument over the British system of taxation developed into an exchange of insults directed at each other's places of origin, Ted Ray reached across the dinner table and pummeled Wilfred Reid's nose with two powerful blows, driving him to the floor of the Copley Square Hotel's dining room. His nose bloodied, Reid leaped to his feet and went after Ray, but the headwaiter sprang between the two men, and the others in the party pulled them apart.

While nerves were on edge, the weather turned miserable. Rain that had begun falling shortly after midnight continued throughout the next day. The golf course became sodden, and the ball often plugged in the soft ground. Putting became particularly difficult. Whether he was affected by the weather or his scuffle with Ray, Reid's game collapsed. Playing erratic irons and putting badly, he shot 85 and 86. Ray, however, scored 76 and climbed into a tie for the lead with Vardon and Francis Ouimet, the twenty-year-old Massachusetts Amateur champion. All three had 225.

As Francis was beginning his fourth round, Ray was finishing with 79. He had 304 for the seventy-two holes, but his score looked vulnerable. Vardon was playing a few holes behind Ray, and by the time Francis had played five holes, Harry had finished, too, also with 79 and 304. Those were the best scores in, but Francis didn't think they were very good. He didn't waste much time thinking about it, though.

Without public scoreboards, no one could be sure what was going on, and rumors flew about the golf course. First, Jim Barnes has the Open locked up. Then, bad luck, he's blown sky high.

Tellier will win in a walk. No, he'll finish behind Vardon and Ray.

Walter Hagen is making a run for the lead. Could he keep it up?

At 227, Hagen had been only two strokes behind the three leaders as the last round began, but he was off to a horrible 6-5-7 start in the afternoon. He seemed finished, but Walter could never be counted out of a golf tournament until he had actually lost. After a good drive on the 4th, he holed a full mashie for a 2, then followed up with a pair of 3s. Out in 40, he had picked up the two strokes he needed to catch Vardon and Ray. Perhaps an American would win.

Fighting the rising tension, Hagen got through the 10th and 11th with pars, but he missed a twelve-footer on the 13th that would have given him the birdie he needed to inch ahead. With the holes running out, his best chance would be the 14th, a par 5. His drive was so good he felt he could reach the green with a solid brassie. Hagen lashed into the ball with all he had, but the force of his swing upset his timing. He topped the shot, and the ball rolled along the wet grass throwing spray in its wake like a whirling waterwheel. He hooked his next badly, finally holed out in 7, and shot 80. His 307 left him three strokes behind Vardon and Ray.

Ouimet was the only American within range now, but his prospects looked grim. Needing 78 to win or 79 to tie, he had gone out in 43, then thrown away two more strokes on the little 140-yard 10th, jerking his head up as he swung, scuffing his ball barely twenty feet, and three-putting from eight feet. Now he'd have to play the last eight holes in one under par to shoot 79 and match the Englishmen. It wouldn't be easy.

PART ONE

Walking through a narrow lane of spectators on his way to the 11th tee, Francis heard a man say, "It's too bad he's blown up." It was just what he needed, for Francis was a fighter, and that remark put him in the proper frame of mind to battle on.

A par on the 11th steadied him, but a hard 5 on the 12th was no help, because the hole measured only 415 yards, and he had counted on a 4 there.

Standing on the 13th tee, Francis assessed his chances. He would have to play the last six holes in two under par to tie, and he figured he had two holes left where he might save strokes—the 13th, a drive-and-pitch where he had made 3s regularly, and the 16th, a one-shotter. He got a boost when he played a good drive from the 13th tee, but with a simple pitch left, he mis-hit the ball, barely missing a greenside bunker. The ball skipped off the green and stopped about thirty feet from the hole. Instead of a reasonably short putt for a birdie, he faced a difficult chip to get the ball close enough to save par. Then he chipped right into the hole.

Francis followed this stroke of luck with a routine 5 at the 14th, then saved his par on the 15th after another mis-hit approach. Now for the 16th, where he had a hunch he could make a 2. Once again he played a loose shot and instead of a birdie, he had to hole a testing nine-footer to save still another par. To catch up now, he would have to birdie one of the last two holes.

The 17th at The Country Club is a 360-yard par 4 whose fairway bends left around a cluster of bunkers. Francis drove wide of the sand, then, using a jigger, a shallow-faced iron with the loft of a 4-iron, he hit a crisp shot that sat down on the soggy green fifteen feet beyond the hole. At last a chance for the birdie he needed so badly. Telling himself to be sure to give the ball a chance, he struck the putt as firmly as any he'd ever played. As the ball rolled toward the hole, it seemed as if he might have hit it too hard, but it smacked into the back of the cup and dropped in. He had caught the Englishmen; now all he needed was the par on the 18th.

The fairway runs through an old polo field encircled by a racetrack. The ground rises beyond the track, and the green sits on the higher ground. It is a substantial hole that measures 410 yards from tee to green, and it was playing longer in the rain. Francis hit his drive far enough to have a long iron to the green. He struck it well, and when the ball cleared the track, he thought he saw it kick onto the green. His excitement rising, he said to little Eddie Lowery, his ten-year-old caddie, "I've got a putt to win."

As he climbed the bank leading up to the green, Ouimet saw it wasn't over yet. His ball had not kicked onto the green as he thought but had stopped short, where it had hit the ground. His chip left him a four-foot putt for the par, and he rolled it in. There would be an eighteen-hole play-off the next day, with a twenty-year-old amateur against two accomplished professionals who had been among the game's great champions longer than Ouimet had been playing. Indeed, had his father not bought a house near The Country Club, it is possible that Francis would not have played the game at all.

Francis Ouimet was born in Brookline in 1893. After the family moved to the house across Clyde Street from The Country Club, Francis found he could save time on his way to and from school by cutting through the club's grounds. Occasionally he'd stumble across a lost ball, and by the time he was seven, he had an impressive collection of Silvertowns, Ocobos, and Henleys—and lately a few of the new Vardon Flyers—all gutta-percha balls, but they weren't much use without a club. About two years after Francis had begun his golf ball collection, someone gave a club to his older brother, Wilfred, who had become a caddie, and when Wilfred was away, Francis would knock balls around the yard. He often paused on his way home from school to watch the golfers. If one of them played a particularly good shot, Francis would rush home and try to copy it.

By then he had a crude course to play on, laid out by Wilfred in a pasture behind the house. The first hole was roughly 150 yards long with a brook 100 yards from the tee, the second was fifty yards long, and the third was a combination of the first two, leading back to the house. The course was fraught with hazards—a gravel pit, swamps, brooks, and high grass. Such as they were, the fairways followed the higher ground, but a ball hit off line was lost.

Francis became immersed in the game and thought of little else. He read anything he could find about golf in newspapers or magazines. When he was eleven, he began to caddie, and he saw such good players as Walter Travis, Chandler Egan, Jerry Travers, Fred Herreshoff, Willie Anderson, Alex Smith, Tom McNamara, and, of course, Alex Campbell, the professional at The Country Club. He had a brassie and a mashie of his own by then, and he spent hours playing the rude course behind the house. His game improved steadily. At first he couldn't carry the brook that crossed the first fairway, but after a year of steady practice, he could do it regularly.

As he improved, he outgrew the little course out back and played most of his real golf at Franklin Park, a public course in Brookline; occasionally he'd slip across the street at 4:30 or 5 in the morning and play The Country Club, until a greenkeeper chased him away. He had his first taste of competition in a high school championship in 1908, qualifying with 85 and losing in the second round.

At sixteen, Francis won the Boston Interscholastic Championship, and immediately began thinking grand thoughts about the 1910 National Amateur, scheduled for The Country Club. He entered, played badly, and missed qualifying for match play by one stroke. He failed again in 1911 and 1912, but as the 1913 season swung into full bloom, he was doing better. Playing in the Massachusetts Amateur, Francis was 2 down to John G. Anderson after twelve holes of the semifinal, then played the next five holes in 2-3-3-3-3 and closed out the match, 3 and 1. The next day he wiped out Fred Hoyt, 10 and 9.

The National Amateur was at the Garden City Golf Club, a marvelous old course on Long Island near New York City. Encouraged by winning the state championship, Ouimet entered and shot 151 in the qualifying rounds. Chick Evans had to shoot 32 on the last nine to beat him out as medalist.

Francis won his first match handily and then faced Jerry Travers in the second. Travers had won the Amateur three times already, including 1912, leaving little question that he and Evans were the country's top amateurs. Evans was a superb striker of the ball, immeasurably better than Travers, but Travers was a deadly putter. Francis was up against the best.

Neither man could open any kind of a lead through the morning, and the match was even coming to the 18th hole, a par 3. Both balls were on the green, Ouimet thirty feet from the hole, Travers twenty feet away. Ouimet's putt rolled to the edge of the cup but didn't fall. Travers holed. One up with eighteen to play.

The biggest crowd Francis had ever played before waited for them to begin the afternoon round. Travers won the first and increased his lead to two holes, but Francis kept chipping away, hole by tortuous hole, and inched ahead after the 7th. The match reached its climax on the 8th, the twenty-sixth of the day. A poor wooden-club player, Travers often drove with a driving iron, and here he played a powerful shot that carried beyond Ouimet's ball. From 180 yards, Ouimet then played a terrific shot eight feet from the hole. It was a winning stroke, and Francis was proud of it. Travers topped him, hitting a glorious iron that flew straight at the hole and stopped ten inches away. Francis was finished. He had lost a hole he seemed likely to win, and he couldn't recover. Travers won the match, 3 and 2, and later defeated John Anderson, 5 and 4, in the final match.

Believing he was through with competitive golf for the year, Francis went back to his job with Wright and Ditson, the sporting goods manufacturer. He had entered the Open, coming up later in September, because Robert Watson, the president of the USGA, wanted to assure a good group of amateurs, but he had taken vacation time for the Amateur, and he wouldn't ask for more. When the qualifying round pairings were published in the Boston newspapers, however, John Merrill, Ouimet's supervisor, saw his name and said, "I see you're now going to play in the Open Championship."

Embarrassed, Francis explained that Watson had asked him to enter, but he did not intend to play. He would be gratified, though, if he could see Vardon and Ray. "Well," Merrill said with a gleam in his eye, "as long as you're entered, you'd better plan to play."

Elated, Francis arranged a game with some friends at the Wellesley Country Club the weekend before the Open. With the championship only two days away, he shot 88 over a short and easy course. His friends believed they may have ruined his game, but Francis told them to forget it, that he had probably got a lot of bad golf out of his system. Possibly he was right, because now he was playing for the Open championship.

Awaking early the morning of the playoff, Ouimet looked out his window and saw the fine rain still falling. He dressed and walked across the street to The Country Club, where he noticed pools of water collecting in the low spots, particularly inside the racetrack that encircled the 1st and 18th fairways. He changed into his golf shoes, and after half an hour warming up, he was told Vardon and Ray were ready to play. As Francis walked toward the 1st tee, Johnny McDermott took his arm and told him, "You're hitting the ball well; now go out and play your own game. Pay no attention to Vardon and Ray."

As Francis teed up his ball and saw the large gallery crowding around him, he felt his first tinge of excitement. It was as if at last he had realized both what he might accomplish and what he was up against. Vardon and Ray weren't concerned about him; they were confident the championship would be settled between them, and at first they paid him little attention.

All three men drove remarkably well at the 1st hole, a 430-yard par 4, but because of the length of the hole and the soggy turf, only Ray could reach the green with his second. Drawing out his brassie, he pushed the shot and missed the green. All three made 5s. Francis had to hole a four-footer, but he didn't hesitate at all over the putt, and from the instant the ball dropped, the tension and his awe of the other men fell away. He remembered McDermott's advice, and little Eddie Lowery reminded him on every shot to keep his eye on the ball and to take his time.

As the holes flew by, the crowd grew to enormous proportions. Some estimated that 10,000 spectators crowded around the three golfers as marshals armed with megaphones shouted them into order. The misty rain soaked the players and their clubs, and Ray's pongee coat hung limp from his body like an old sack.

PART ONE

Through the soaking rain Ouimet matched Vardon and Ray stroke for stroke. He was driving as long and as accurately as either of them, and it was clear after only a few holes that he was the best putter. More important, however, he seemed to have no nerves. When he misplayed a shot, he shrugged it off and made up for it with the next. He hit his only truly bad shot on the 5th, a 420-yard par 4, where the drive is played from an elevated tee. Ouimet outdrove the others and stood by while they both missed the green with their second shots. Sensing a chance to pick up a stroke, Francis played a brassie, but his hands slipped on the club as he moved into his downswing, and the ball flew off at an acute angle to the right and fell out of bounds.

Ouimet was lucky; if the ball had remained in play among the trees and underbrush, he might have made any score, but under the rules of the time, that terrible shot cost him only one stroke. Still calm, he dropped another ball, played a wonderful shot onto the edge of the green, and made his 5, matching Vardon and Ray. Francis not only avoided losing a stroke, but he realized right then he could keep up with the Englishmen. This would be a long and trying day.

The golf had been fairly ordinary through the first five holes, but now the pace picked up. Vardon dropped a lovely little pitch close to the cup to birdie the 6th, Ray birdied the 7th and then holed a forty-footer on the 8th, where Ouimet had set off a roar by playing a blind mashie shot over the brow of a hill within twelve inches of the cup. After nine holes all three were even with 38. The break came on the 10th. The ground by now was a bog, and when Vardon and Ray played short of the pin, their balls hit the mushy turf and drew back toward the front of the green, leaving deep pitch marks on their lines to the hole. Ouimet's ball carried beyond the hole; it was covered with mud, but he had a clear run to the cup. Both Vardon and Ray took three putts, and when Francis coaxed his ball down the slight grade and into the cup in two, the gallery whooped and cheered. Ouimet had pulled clear of the Englishmen and led for the first time.

Vardon was stunned. He realized he had been wrong to believe this boy had no chance. He was even more shocked when Ouimet increased his lead to two shots with a par on the 12th. In the hardly bearable tension, Vardon took a stroke back on the 13th, and then Ray felt he might cut a stroke from Ouimet's lead if he could get home in two on the 14th, the par 5. Off the tee last, he hurled himself into the shot, straining for the extra distance he needed, and then threw every bit of his power into the second. The strain was beginning to tell on him, though; the ball shot off to the right into a growth of trees. Luckily for him, he had an opening through the branches and saved his par, but he had lost his best chance to close ground. When he made 6 on the 15th, he dropped four strokes behind and was out of it.

The strain was telling on Vardon, too. Usually a left-to-right player, he had hooked both his drive and approach on the 14th, and on the 15th he lighted a cigarette, something he rarely did on the golf course. Only Ouimet seemed calm and sure of himself. He hadn't made a mistake since he had played a weak chip on the 7th, and he was one under par since then.

Both Ouimet and Vardon made their pars on the 16th, but Ray, no longer interested, took three putts. Now for the 17th, where Ouimet had birdied in the fourth round to force the tie.

Vardon desperately needed a birdie, because Francis was leaving no openings. Still holding the honor, Harry felt he could save a few yards by shading his drive close to the bunker at the bend of the fairway. The gamble didn't work. Once again he pulled the shot, and his ball flew into the bunker, so close to the front bank he had no chance to reach the green with his second. A shot lost rather than gained.

Francis, meanwhile, had driven down the middle and dropped another jigger fifteen feet from the hole. When his putt fell for a birdie once again, he had three strokes in hand with only one hole to play. Nothing could stop him now. Splitting the final fairway with his drive, he had to wait agonizing minutes while marshals, their megaphones blaring, cleared a path through the throng that milled about cheering him on. Then, with order restored, he took one practice swing and drilled his iron directly at the flag. It was a winner all the way, and he made his 4 easily. Francis shot 72, Vardon 77, and Ray 78.

The crowd had barely been held in check through those final moments, and now, as Francis, his knees trembling, holed that final putt, it broke loose and swarmed around him, a few men lifted him onto their shoulders and paraded him around the grounds. As he accepted the trophy from John Reid, Jr., the secretary of the USGA, Ouimet said he was as surprised and pleased as anyone there.

"Naturally it was always my hope to win out. I simply tried my best to keep this cup from going to our friends across the water. I am very glad to have been the agency for keeping the cup in America."

Francis Ouimet became a national hero. To the public he was the all-American boy, the young man from a family of modest means who had entered a field dominated by professionals and amateurs of wealth and social position and had shown he could play the game better than any of them. He was an unassuming hero, partly because of his solid upbringing. As he was riding about on the shoulders of the gallery, the parade was stopped for a moment by a small woman. He leaned forward on the shoulders of his captors as she spoke to him quietly, then he said, "Thank you, Mother. I'll be home soon."

America was a young country when Ouimet won the Open. The continent had been linked by rail only forty-five years, the last of the Indian wars had petered out only thirteen years earlier, and vast stretches of prairie remained unsettled. Still largely agricultural, the country was beginning to realize its industrial might. Manifest destiny had claimed the continent, and now the United States was becoming a colonial power. Commodore Perry had opened Japan to commerce sixty-five years earlier, and by the end of the nineteenth century, America had kicked Spain out of the Western Hemisphere, annexed the Philippine Islands, and quelled the insurrection. The Great White Fleet had circled the globe, showing off America's naval might, an American doctor had conquered yellow fever, and the Panama Canal was to open within a year.

While Americans played different games from Europeans, its sons had startled the world by dominating track and field events in the 1896 Olympic revival, and in the 1912 Games, Jim Thorpe, an American Indian, had won both the decathlon and pentathlon and been declared the world's greatest athlete.

Baseball had been played since the Civil War, but the American League was only thirteen years old then. Within weeks of the Open, Ty Cobb would win his seventh consecutive batting championship, although his .390 average was his lowest in three years (he hit .420 in 1911 and .410 in 1912), but Babe Ruth hadn't made it to the major leagues yet.

Football was back in fashion after having been banned during the Teddy Roosevelt administration because of its rough character, and within a month of the Open, it would be changed for all time. With Gus Dorais passing to his broken-nosed roommate, Knute Rockne, little Notre Dame, an unheard-of college in South Bend, Indiana, would slaughter Army, 35–13, in the first meeting between the two schools.

The country was growing. Arizona had been admitted to the Union a year earlier, the last of the forty-eight contiguous states, and with immigrants flooding in, the population had reached 90 million by 1910. The United States was strong, and it was vibrant. Americans were confident they could do anything better than anyone else and could be anything they wanted to be.

It is impossible to judge if Ouimet's victory affected the spread of golf in the United States, but the game grew rapidly. In September 1913, about 350,000 Americans played golf. Ten years later 2 million played, and by then they played better than anyone else, in part because of the intervention of the First World War, which kept a generation of Britons from playing the game, and in part because of the American's natural competitiveness.

While the 1913 Open might have been stimulating to the game's expansion, it was devastating to Walter Hagen, the twenty-year-old professional from Rochester who had come so close but had been ruined by one shot. Discouraged by his finish, he was convinced golf was not his game, and instead dreamed of a baseball career. He seemed about to realize that dream the following winter. With the Country Club of Rochester closed, Hagen went to Florida, where he became friendly with Pat Moran, the manager of the Philadelphia Nationals, who went through spring training at Tarpon Springs. Moran allowed Hagen to pitch in a few practice games, and when the Nationals broke camp and headed north, Walter had the distinct impression he would be given a thorough trial the next year.

Hagen floated back to Rochester on a cloud, prepared to work at his club and pitch semipro baseball. He had decided not to enter the 1914 Open, but Ernest Willard, the editor of the *Democrat and Chronicle* newspaper, thought Walter had done surprisingly well in his first attempt and offered to pay his expenses to the Midlothian Country Club near Chicago. Walter accepted the offer.

Always concerned with his image, Hagen took as much care with his clothes as he did with his game. At Brookline he had worn white flannels, with the cuff turned up just once, a loud striped silk shirt, a red bandanna knotted around his neck, and white buckskin shoes with red rubber soles. The outfit cost him plenty—$10 for the shoes alone. He packed the same outfit for Midlothian, with one exception. His feet had slipped on the wet turf at Brookline, so he left his white bucks behind and substituted shoes with hobnails, a short nail with a rounded head protruding from the sole that gripped the ground like the later spiked shoes.

Walter took the day coach from Rochester to Chicago in time to play some practice rounds, but at first the trip seemed wasted. Even though he was barely old enough to vote, he liked the taste of first class, and since someone else was paying the bill, he could afford it. On the evening before the first round he went to the best restaurant he could find and ordered his first lobster dinner. He awoke in the middle of the night with stomach pains, and by dawn he could hardly stand. The hotel's physician gave him some pills, recommended he eat only milk toast, and told him to take two aspirins before he played—if he felt well enough to start. He would try.

Riding the South Shore Railroad to Midlothian on a sweltering August

43

day with the steam engine belching soot and cinders through the open windows, Hagen was miserable, but he was determined to play, even though every swing caused him pain.

Walter was never known for his accurate driving or his classic form. His swing began with a decided sway, and he gave the illusion of hurling himself at the ball as he brought the clubhead through. Consequently, although fairways were not virgin territory, neither were they always familiar ground. Now, with every movement painful, his driving was worse than ever. The first hole was designed for the drive to carry over a pond, but Hagen pushed his ball so badly it didn't go near the water. Undismayed, he recovered neatly with an iron onto the green and saved his par.

He played like that all day, one loose shot followed by a remarkable recovery. With nine holes behind him, Walter was a stroke under par with 35, and then he spurted home with birdies on four of the last five holes and shot 68, setting the course record. Elated because he had taken a potentially ruinous round and turned it into a triumph, he rushed to the scoreboard expecting to find himself miles clear of the field, but his shoulders sagged when he saw that Francis Ouimet was only a stroke behind him with 69.

Walter was disappointed, but in spite of the continuing pain, he went around in 74 in the afternoon, then waited while one player after another made a run at his 142.

Tom McNamara nearly caught him with 143, and when Ouimet shot 76 in the afternoon, he was only three strokes behind, at 145.

Relieved that he had not only survived the day at all but was actually leading the field, Hagen stuck to steak and potatoes that night, played two steady rounds of 75 and 73 the next day, and finished with 290, matching the record set by George Sargent in 1909. Neither Ouimet nor McNamara could keep up. Francis shot 298, and McNamara, closing with a ragged 83, finished with 302. Those two were gone, but a new menace had surfaced in the morning.

Although he was an amateur, Chick Evans was the finest striker of the ball in American golf. He hit every iron squarely and crisply, and he was a marvel with his brassie and spoon. Jerry Travers recalled seeing Evans hit drive after drive straight down the middle of the practice ground, then play twenty-five consecutive iron shots within six feet of where his caddie stood. Few men have had it all, though, and Chick had his flaw. A marvel at every other shot, he was a terrible putter. He usually played with only seven clubs—the brassie and spoon, a mid-iron (approximately a 2-iron in a modern set), a jigger, a pitching club with the loft of a 7- or 8-iron, a niblick (like a 9-iron or wedge), and a putter—but he was so bad on the greens that occasionally he carried more than one putter, switching back

44

and forth, hoping one of them would work. If he had had the touch of Jerry Travers, he would have been unbeatable, but while he had won the Western Amateur three times and the Western Open once, he had not won a tournament of national scope. Now, after years of failure, he was closing in.

With 150 for the first two rounds, Evans had stood eight strokes behind Hagen, but after a routine 37 on the first nine of the third round, he thrust himself into the battle with a stunning burst of four birdies on the next six holes, came back in 34, shot 71 for the round, and moved to within four strokes of the lead.

As the last round began, Hagen was playing three holes ahead of Evans before only a handful of spectators while Chick, a Chicago boy, had a gallery of over 1,000 openly pulling for him. Hagen could listen for the cheering and tell how Evans was doing, and he was doing well. When Walter dropped three strokes to par on the 8th and 9th, Chick pulled to within one stroke of him with nine holes to play. He should have been tied, but after a wonderful iron to the 9th, he missed a three-foot putt.

It is never safe to say that one missed putt cost a championship, but it must have hurt Chick's composure, because he had dreadful luck on the home nine. He missed from inside ten feet on the 11th, took three putts on the 12th, and his fifteen-footer on the 16th grazed the cup as it slipped by. He was two strokes behind Hagen by then, but when he coaxed home a twenty-five-footer on the 17th, he stood even par for seventy-one holes. Now he would need an eagle 2 on the 18th to catch Walter, and an eagle on the 18th was not impossible. While it was a par 4, it was only 277 yards long; a big drive might reach the green. Hearing that Evans had a chance to catch him, Hagen rushed out to watch, joining the crowd that ringed the green four and five deep, cheering for Evans. Chick tore into his shot and drove his ball to the edge of the green, about fifty feet short of the cup, setting up the chance to chip in for his 2. The crowd was so hushed as Chick crouched over they could hear the *click* as he hit the ball. He had judged the pace perfectly, but he had pulled the ball slightly, and it settled about a foot left of the hole. Chick finished with 291, one stroke too many.

Hagen forgot about baseball. He went back to Rochester and almost immediately realized he could make a lot of money playing golf. Offers for exhibitions poured in, and he accepted as many as he could. A natural showman, he played to the fans, and except for the few times he was in the same field as Bob Jones, throughout the 1920s he attracted the largest galleries.

Hagen had a further distinction: From 1913 through 1916, he was the only professional to win the U.S. Open. Ouimet had won in 1913, Hagen in 1914, then Jerry Travers took the 1915 championship, and Evans finally would have his day in 1916.

Travers was the best amateur golfer of his time. Both Evans and Ouimet hit the ball better, but Travers dominated the National Amateur Championship. By 1915 he had won it four times; only Bob Jones, who came along later and won five, has ever won as many. Because he was so erratic with his full shots, Travers was more dangerous in match play than in medal, but, nevertheless he was capable of sustained stretches of low medal scores, which is what is needed to win an Open. Furthermore, with the 1915 Open set for Baltusrol, close to his home, Jerry would have the support of the gallery.

He qualified easily, shot 78 in the first round, added 72 in the afternoon, and crept into good position, just two strokes behind Jim Barnes, an Englishman then living in Philadelphia, and Louis Tellier, a tidy little Frenchman based a few miles west of Baltusrol in Summit, New Jersey.

When he shot 73 the next morning, Travers found himself a stroke ahead of Tellier, Mike Brady, and Robert McDonald, but with the Open championship in sight, the last round unfolded as a growing disaster. Using his driver, Travers hooked his tee shot and lost one stroke on the 1st, three-putted the 4th, then dropped two more strokes on the 7th. He was out in 39, sliced out of bounds on the 10th, topped his drive on the 11th, and overshot the 12th green. He might reasonably be out of the race after such shoddy work, but he was such a wonderful putter he had lost only one stroke to par over those last three holes. Even so, he figured he would have to play the last six holes in even par to tie, and that was a long shot.

He made it through the next two holes all right, but on the 15th, a 462-yard par 5, it looked as if he would fail when his mid-iron second nipped the lip of a fairway bunker. Luckily, the ball bounded forward and stopped ten yards short of the green. A neat little pitch left him an easy putt for the birdie 4, and now he needed three pars to win.

Taking no more chances with his unreliable woods, Jerry switched to his black driving iron and made the pars he needed for his 75. With 297 he finished one stroke ahead of Tom McNamara.

That was the peak of Travers' career. He concentrated on his business as a cotton broker on Wall Street and never played in another national championship, although he appeared in a few exhibition matches for the American Red Cross during the First World War. When the stock market crashed, Travers was ruined. He became a professional and played some exhibitions that drew very little money. After one match, he left his jigger behind to be auctioned for whatever he could get. It was sold for $6. He arranged to manufacture a Schenectady-type putter bearing his name, but only his friends bought it. He also tried selling the Spalding Red Dot, a golf ball he had helped make famous, and had even worse luck. His former caddie bought a dozen and gave them back, saying Jerry needed them more than he did. Travers died in 1951. Three years later his medals from the Amateur and the 1915 Open turned up in the safety deposit box of a friend along with a note, which read in part, "in appreciation for your many favors."

With the 1916 Open scheduled for the Minikahda Country Club in Minneapolis, the entry dropped off markedly. Where 130 had come to Baltusrol, only eighty-one showed up at Minikahda. Travers had withdrawn from competitive golf, and Ouimet had decided not to play, but Evans was back, and so was Hagen.

Evans was twenty-six in 1916, a perpetual and inconsolable flop in national competitions. Although he had great success in Western Golf Association affairs, he had never played his best golf in USGA events. He had been a semifinalist in four National Amateurs, but he'd reached the final match only in 1912, and then he was thrashed 7 and 6 by Travers.

Although Evans had made his move too late at Midlothian, he was in the fight from the start at Minikahda. With the course softened by heavy overnight rains, Chick flew around the first nine in 32, but instead of opening a wide gap, as he might have expected, he was only a stroke ahead of Wilfred Reid. Both men cooled off coming in and finished with 70s. Reid went out in 34 in the afternoon, but again he couldn't keep it up and posted 72. Evans' 69 was all he needed to hold the thirty-six-hole lead at 139.

The gray clouds were gone the next morning, and the weather turned hot. So did Reid. Once again he blistered the first nine, streaking around in 32 and moving ahead, but then he made three consecutive 7s coming home, shot 43, and no longer was a factor. Evans, meanwhile, shot a steady 74, but even with Reid falling apart, he wasn't clear of danger. Jock Hutchison moved into contention with 72 in the morning, and when he shot a wonderful 68 in the afternoon, he completed the seventy-two holes in 288, two strokes under the record 290 that had stood since 1909.

Evans was waiting to play the 13th when he learned how Hutchison had finished and that Jim Barnes was only a stroke back at 289. Assessing his situation, Chick felt he needed a birdie here, but the 13th was the longest hole at Minikahda. It measured 525 yards, but it played even longer because of a creek that cut across the fairway about 100 yards short of the green. Most players laid up short rather than try to clear it with their second shots.

Standing in the fairway after a powerful drive, Chick turned to a friend and said, "I think I can afford to take a chance." Lashing into the shot with his brassie, he watched the ball soar well past the creek, hit the ground, and run onto the green. Two putts, and he had his birdie.

Chick finished the round in 73 and beat Hutchison by two strokes, shooting 286, a stunning score for the time. It became one of the game's enduring records, lasting twenty years. Its life, however, must be measured by more than time.

Done with seven wooden-shafted clubs, it lasted through an era when golfers routinely carried twenty-two or more. Whereas Evans and his contemporaries had to manufacture shots to fit the occasion, golfers of the 1920s and 1930s carried clubs for all purposes. Furthermore, the wooden-shafted clubs were both imperfectly made and difficult to control, because the shaft tended to twist when the head made contact with the ball. Steel-shafted clubs were approved by the USGA in 1924, but even though they eliminated much of the torque and performed more consistently, the record endured. It was set in a period when golf balls were of no standard size or weight, and it survived until four years into the period of the third standard ball (the ball that measures 1.68 inches in diameter and weighs 1.62 ounces was adopted in 1932). No other scoring record survived such radical changes in equipment.

With Europe at war, the British Open hadn't been played since 1914. When the United States joined with the Allies in April 1917, the USGA suspended the U.S. Open for the duration, substituting in its place an Open Patriotic Tournament at the Whitemarsh Valley Country Club, near Philadelphia, in June. Jock Hutchison shot 292 and won by seven strokes over Tom McNamara. It was played only in 1917.

While some golf was being played—the PGA Championship was suspended, but the Western Open was held in 1917—most of it was for war relief. Before he went into the Army, Francis Ouimet teamed with Jesse Guilford, a big, strong man from New Hampshire, in exhibitions, many of them against Mike Brady and Louis Tellier. Every weekend as he waited to enter the air service, Evans played for the American Red Cross and other charities. Since he had married in January of 1917, Walter Hagen had been exempted from military service, and like the rest, he played exhibitions for war relief. When the war ended, in November of 1918, he was the best golfer in America. Except for the war years, he had never been without a title since 1913. He had learned to control his sway, but while he had no equal from 100 yards in, he had remained an unpredictable driver. He could be driving beautifully, splitting the fairways with shot after shot, when suddenly his timing would fail, and the ball would soar off out of control. Not to worry; Walter could forget that shot and work on the next, which he'd often drop close enough to the hole to set up a birdie. Without that peculiar knack, he probably wouldn't have won the 1919 Open, at Brae Burn Country Club near Boston.

With 221 for fifty-four holes, Mike Brady led Hagen by five strokes and seemed to have the Open locked up, but he was one of those tragic figures who are never quite good enough. He shot 80 in the fourth round, finished with 301, then slumped into the clubhouse to wait.

Hagen had reached the 10th tee when he heard of Brady's collapse. He had not been a model of sound golf himself, and he would have to play the second nine in par to match Brady's score. All seemed lost when he hooked out of bounds on the 11th, dropping one precious stroke, but that was only a temporary setback; two holes later he picked up a birdie. One more and he'd win.

His chance came at the 18th, a demanding par 4 with an out-of-bounds wall close behind a two-level green. Hagen hit a useful drive, but he had a long iron left, and the pin was set on the back upper level of the green close to the wall. Never one to back off, Hagen hit a solid shot that stopped hole-high about eight feet to the right of the cup.

As he strode toward the green, Hagen sent word ahead for Brady to come out and watch him finish. With Mike standing by, Hagen stroked his putt straight for the hole. The ball caught the lip and spun out. They were tied at 301.

In the playoff the next day, Hagen jumped to an early two-stroke lead, and he was still two ahead with two holes to play. The 17th called for a drawn tee shot, but Hagen pushed a high soaring drive into a patch of muck. After a short search, Brady found Hagen's ball sunk about four inches down into the soft turf. Walter's cause seemed hopeless, but he was a man of many resources.

Seeing his ball so deeply embedded, Hagen claimed a spectator must have stepped on it and that he was entitled to a free lift. Since no official had seen anyone near the spot where the ball was found, Hagen's claim was denied. Then Walter demanded the right to identify his ball. The officials had to allow that.

Hagen plucked the ball from its burrow, wiped off the mud, agreed that it was indeed his ball, then replaced it very gingerly. It did not sink below ground, and now he could play a shot. Even though he made 5 to Brady's 4, he had saved the day.

Both men made par on the last hole, and Hagen won the playoff, 77–78.

Walter Hagen was twenty-seven years old in 1919, and he went on to dominate professional golf through the 1920s. He won the PGA Championship five times—four years in succession—the British Open four times, and he continued to be a factor in the U.S. Open. He finished fourth by two strokes in 1928 and third by three in 1935, when he was forty-three. When his career ended, he had placed among the leading five in eleven Opens and among the leading ten in five others. His was one of the remarkable Open records. But he never won again.

PART TWO
Between Wars

FOUR

Vardon and Ray in Reprise

In July of 1914, Harry Vardon won the British Open for the sixth time. In August, Europe erupted into war, and the championship was suspended for six years. When it resumed, in 1920, Vardon was fifty, well beyond the age when a man might dream of winning another important golf competition. Vardon, however, was no ordinary man. No longer loose and limber but still playing with style and grace, he finished thirteenth, not bad for a man who had won it twenty-four years earlier and had been confined to sanitariums at various times, battling tuberculosis.

Within a month after the championship ended, Vardon and Ted Ray were in the United States on another tour that would take them through the East and Middle West to play a hundred or so matches. So long as they were in the country, they decided to enter the Open, played at Inverness Club in Toledo, a course superbly designed by Donald Ross.

They had begun their tour on July 18. By August 10, the day of the Open's first qualifying rounds, they had played twenty-two matches. Ray had also played in the Shawnee Invitational, finishing second to Jim Barnes, but Vardon hadn't entered because he had injured his thumb. In their last match before the Open, they defeated D. K. (Deke) White and Charley Lorms, both of Toledo, 2 and 1, at Inverness, and they went into the qualifying rounds as confident as they had been in 1913.

Jock Hutchison played beautifully in the qualifying—72 in the first round, 69 in the second—then opened the championship proper with another 69. With 76 in the afternoon, he held the halfway lead, with 145, a stroke better than Leo Diegel, a twenty-one-year-old fledgling professional, and Barnes, winner of the first two PGA Championships, in 1916 and 1919. Vardon and Ray had been off form in qualifying, but they had recovered once the championship began and lurked at 147, tied with Walter Hagen, just two strokes off the lead.

Hagen's defense of his 1919 championship ended when he went out in 41 the next morning. He never recovered. Vardon seemed to be dropping from contention, too, when he butchered the 1st hole, hooking both his first and second shots, then three-putting from ten feet (he missed his second putt from eighteen inches). A start like that might have ruined a player of less character, but Vardon tore around the next seventeen holes in sixty-five strokes. With 218, he stood one stroke ahead of Diegel and Hutchison and two ahead of Ray.

Although he was dog-tired, Vardon kept up his remarkable golf through the early afternoon, gaining another stroke on par through the first five holes. He lost that stroke with a bunkered tee shot on the 8th, and it looked as if he might lose another when his drive kicked behind a tree on the 9th, a par-5 hole. Blocked from a direct shot at the green, Vardon aimed at a bunker to the left and put so much cut on his brassie the ball curled right, headed directly toward the pin and stopped a few yards short of the green. He pitched to two feet, and then, with a relatively easy chance for a birdie, he missed the putt.

Vardon was out in 36; another nine holes like that, and he would be an easy winner. Par on the 10th, then a birdie on the 11th and he had four strokes in hand with seven holes to play. The crowds were flocking to him now, thrilling in his easy grace as he played one flawless shot after another, and awed by his stamina. Over the last three days he had played ninety-nine holes—thirty-six in qualifying and sixty-three in the championship proper—in just eleven over par. He was a marvel, but his stamina was about to face a severe test.

The 12th at Inverness was a par 5 of 522 yards. The fairway ran level for the first 200 yards, then fell away down a gentle slope, to more level ground before rising to an elevated green. As Vardon stood on the tee, a gentle breeze turned into a gale. By the time he had played his drive, the wind was whipping in from Lake Erie, wrenching the leaves from the trees and churning sand from the bunkers. It was blowing directly into the 12th at such strength Vardon couldn't reach the green with three solid shots. One stroke gone. Then his putting touch left him.

Vardon had been a good putter as a young man, but as he aged he developed a nervous condition in his right hand and forearm. Often as he stood over short putts, a muscle in his right forearm jumped so badly it could be seen by the gallery. As he stood over a two-foot putt he needed to par the 13th, the muscle began to dance out of control, and he played an awkward jabbing stroke. The ball shot off the face of the putter, slammed into the back of the hole, and sat on the lip. He was lucky; if the ball hadn't hit the cup, it would have rolled six or eight feet past. His composure shattered, Vardon took three putts on each of the next three holes, and now he needed two 4s to win where he should have been miles ahead of the field.

His round reached its frustrating climax on the 17th, a 430-yard par 4 that under the best of conditions called for two very long shots to clear a brook that purled across the fairway only a yard short of the green. Playing directly into the full force of the storm, Vardon hit a short drive. Trying to reach the green with his second now was a gamble, but he had to try because his putting was so bad it was unrealistic to believe he could lay up short of the creek and still save his par. To hit the ball that far he would have to use his brassie and throw his body into the swing, something he never liked to do. As soon as he moved down into the shot, Vardon realized his timing was off, and as the ball flew from the clubhead and climbed into the wind, he felt the championship slipping away. He hadn't hit the ball quite well enough; it cleared the front bank of the brook, but it slammed against the far side of the ditch and toppled back into the water.

Vardon seemed to age as he walked toward the green, lost in the large gallery that milled around him. He stumbled on and finished the 17th with a 6; he had lost seven strokes over that agonizing stretch beginning at the 12th, far too many. With a par 4 on the 18th, he had played the last nine holes in 42, and shot 78. His 296 was too high. He had come so close, but in the end age and the storm, combined with his own abominable putting, had cost him one last victory.

As Vardon plodded toward the clubhouse, weary with fatigue, the crowd raced back to pick up Ray, Diegel, and Hutchison, now suddenly back in the hunt. Ray was next. Off well in the afternoon, he stood a stroke under par after six holes with excellent prospects of gaining another stroke at the 7th, where he had already made three birdies. Although the 7th measured 320 yards, it doglegged sharply left in the drive zone at an angle of almost 90 degrees, which made it play much shorter. Ray had driven the green in the three previous rounds, sending high, soaring drives across the wide, scrub-infested ravine that knifed across the front of the tee and ran along the left side, following the bend in the fairway. Once again he went for the green and once again he birdied.

Two under par for the round now, Ray squandered strokes at the 8th, where he bogeyed, and at the 9th, where he missed a putt from less than two feet, but he was out in 35 and closing in. After dropping another stroke at the 11th, where Vardon had birdied, Ray was three strokes behind Vardon's pace with seven holes to play.

A 6 on the 12th was no help, but he picked up one valuable stroke on Vardon at the 13th and one more at the 14th. Another par 4 on the 16th, and Ray was six over par for seventy holes, exactly how Vardon had stood earlier. With his enormous power, Ray overshot the 17th green, but he made his 5, a stroke less than Vardon, and he had finally moved ahead with one hole left. He made his par on the short but devilish 18th, and with 75 he was in with 295, waiting for Hutchison and Diegel to finish.

Leo was closing in. He was four strokes over par for 67 holes and stood three strokes ahead of the Englishman; par golf over the last five holes and he'd be an easy winner. The crowd was pulling for him, and when he had made the turn for home in 37 and had climbed to within two strokes of Vardon and one behind Ray, Chick Evans had rushed out and taken his bag, replacing Diegel's caddie. A topped drive on the 14th didn't seem too costly, but Diegel was on edge. As he prepared to play his second shot, a friend rushed up and told him Ray had bogeyed the 17th. He slammed his club to the ground and snapped, "I don't care what Ray took. I'm playing my own game."

Upset, he hooked his second into a bunker, barely got out with his third, and made 6. Two strokes gone there and two more on the 15th and 16th. Back in 40, he tied Vardon at 296. Hutchison was next.

He had been three over par on the first nine, but with Vardon falling apart, he needed only a break or two to catch up. Instead, he lost a stroke at the 14th, a three-footer rimmed the cup on the 15th, and his chip on the 17th stopped an inch short of falling. Another gallant putt slipped past the hole on the 18th, and Jock also finished one stroke behind Ray.

At forty-three, Ray became the oldest man ever to win the Open. He had played in 1913 and in 1920, and no one had beaten his seventy-two-hole score in either championship. He had won once and had lost in a playoff. He returned in 1927, when he was fifty, but he was never a threat.

Vardon did not return. He had played three times, won in 1900, tied in 1913, and finished one agonizing stroke out of first place in 1920. He played in a few more British Opens, but retired from competition a few years later and lived out his life quietly down the road from South Herts, his old club near London. He died in 1937.

Their golf in 1920 was an uncomfortable reminder of the quality of the best British golfers. The British, however, were not to see their like again, and we were about to enter a new age.

As a footnote, from the beginning, professional golfers had been treated traditionally as a lower caste, not acceptable in the clubhouses or the locker rooms; they changed their shoes in their cars or under a convenient tree, and they took their lunch somewhere other than in the clubs' dining rooms.

In 1920 the members of Inverness broke that old tradition and invited them into their clubhouse, where they were free to use all the facilities.

Not long after the championship ended, a delegation of professionals led by Walter Hagen, a man of instinctive grace, presented the club a cathedral chime clock well over six feet tall. Its dark wood cabinet bears the rich patina of age, and its polished brass works gleam behind a beveled glass front. It has stood in the club's foyer since 1920. A brass plate fastened to the front is inscribed:

> God measures men by what they are,
> Not what in wealth possess.
> This vibrant message chimes afar,
> The voice of Inverness.

FIVE

Bobby Jones at Inwood

In his two qualifying rounds at Inverness, Vardon had been paired with Robert Tyre Jones, Jr., an eighteen-year-old amateur from Atlanta who was studying for a degree in mechanical engineering at the Georgia School of Technology. They were the oldest and the youngest in the field.

They were also the greatest pairing of golfing talent the world had ever seen. It would not see another to match it until forty years later, when Ben Hogan and Jack Nicklaus would play together at Cherry Hills in Denver in the last two rounds of the 1960 Open.

Although he was barely old enough to shave, Jones had been a well-known prodigy since he was fourteen and had lost a tough battle to Bob Gardner, the defending champion, in the 1916 National Amateur. Although he had played in two Amateur championships by 1920, this was his first Open, and he was understandably nervous because he was paired with Vardon.

Even at this stage of his career, Jones could play astonishing shots. From a hanging lie in the rough, he played a brassie hole high to the right of the 5th green. Vardon said later it was one of the longest recoveries he'd ever seen. But even though he could play wonderful shots, Jones knew precious little about playing golf. Despite a wobbly 78 in the first round of the Open proper, he had climbed to fifth place after fifty-four holes and stood only four strokes behind Vardon with eighteen holes to play. In the full flush of youth as he wound up his lunch with pie and ice cream, Bobby told himself he could win the Open with 70. Indeed he could have, but he started badly, tried foolish and desperate shots, went around in 77, and finished fifth. A 72 would have won; he would learn later that even the great players lose strokes in tense situations.

Jones was back the following year at the Columbia Country Club in suburban Washington, still only a teenager but a player of unlimited potential. With a rocky 78 in the first round, he was nine strokes behind Jim Barnes, but even though he shot 71 in the afternoon and climbed into third place, he was never really in position to win. With 77s in the last two rounds, Jones shot 303 and tied for fifth place. Jim Barnes shot 69-75-73-72—289, led every round, and won by nine strokes over Walter Hagen.

With the impatience of youth, Jones went into the 1922 Open wondering if he would ever become a national champion. He'd won tournaments, of course—the Georgia Amateur at fourteen, the Southern Amateur at eighteen and again at twenty, and he had been runner-up in the Southern Open twice—but never a national championship.

He began 1922 by having surgery on his left leg to correct swollen blood vessels. Entering the Southern Amateur less than two months after leaving the hospital, Bobby played eighteen holes of qualifying and five subsequent matches in ten under par, his best sustained series of low scores. Arriving in Glencoe, Illinois, for the Open, he felt his game was just about right and that Skokie Country Club was an easy course. When he played the first three rounds in 74, 72, and 70, he was tied for the lead with Wild Bill Mehlhorn, a blunt man with a forty-four-inch chest and a twenty-nine-inch waist who was one of the game's great ball strikers and at the same time one of its most uncertain putters.

Bursting with confidence, Jones felt sure he could shoot 68 in the fourth round, which should be good enough to win. No one paid much attention to Gene Sarazen, another twenty-year-old.

Playing steady, controlled golf, Sarazen had breezed around in 72 and 73 the first day, and under the mounting strain had birdied three of the last five holes to save a 75 the next morning. Now he was only four strokes behind Jones and Mehlhorn, the coleaders at 216.

The first of the leaders to start, Mehlhorn was out in 38 and losing ground. Behind him Sarazen dropped a stroke on the 2nd, but he made two quick birdies at the 3rd and 4th. Gaining confidence, he began striking the ball harder, and the more he put into each shot, the straighter it flew. Just as Mehlhorn finished with 74, a loud cheer rose from the 9th green; Sarazen was out in 33, a stroke under par and closing in.

A bogey on the 10th; not good, but another quick birdie on the 12th, then five straight pars, and Sarazen was still one under par. A par 5 on the 18th would give him 69 and 289. Would that be good enough? He checked to be sure of Mehlhorn's score: 290—a par would do it.

PART TWO

Sarazen split the fairway with a long drive and found his ball sitting up nicely. At 485 yards, the hole was usually reachable in two shots, but the wind was blowing directly into Gene's face. A brassie wouldn't make it, but with such a good lie he could hit a driver, and that might do it. Sarazen lashed into the ball and sent it screaming low into the wind. Just as it was losing momentum, it hit the edge of the green and rolled fifteen feet from the cup. Two putts, and Gene had birdied. His 68 was the lowest finishing round ever shot in the Open, and his 288 gave him a two-stroke lead over Mehlhorn. Now let them come to him.

By then Jones had gone out in 36 and had given up on his own 68, but he could still tie Sarazen if he could shoot another 36 coming in. A missed putt cost him a stroke on the 10th, and he lost another when he pitched over the 12th green. Now he had to pick up two strokes to tie. A thirty-footer fell on the 14th; one stroke back. Now to hold on through the next three holes and go for the birdie on the 18th. Steady pars on the 15th and 16th, then a bad break on the 17th. He tried to cut the corner of the dog-leg, but his towering drive took a bad kick and stopped on a roadway under a billowing tree. Even though he had only a short distance to the green, his ball was in such a bad lie he had no chance. He bogeyed, and his opportunity was gone. A birdie on the 18th saved him only a tie for second place.

When Jones entered Harvard in the fall, his clubs went into the closet while he studied English literature, but he rushed home to Atlanta when the term ended and began preparations for the Open.

Significant developments had been taking place abroad for the last two years. Hardly any Americans had gone to Deal for the 1920 British Open, but Jock Hutchison, an American citizen by then, had won in 1921 and Walter Hagen in 1922. The results of those two championships showed clearly that the Americans of the postwar era played the game better than the British. Some suspected that Jones was the best of the Americans, but by the time he arrived at Inwood Country Club on Long Island, New York, in June of 1923, he was beginning to doubt himself. His constant failures were getting on his nerves, and his practice rounds had been depressing. Because Inwood was a narrow course that punishes the wild player, Jones was constantly in trouble. He was spraying his shots so badly he had trouble breaking 80.

Sometimes, though, poor practice rounds mean nothing. As soon as the championship began, the shots flew from his clubs with all their old assurance, and he streaked around Inwood in 71 and 73. Only Hutchison with 142, Jones at 144, and Bobby Cruickshank with 145 were under 150.

Hutchison was one of those men jinxed by the U.S. Open. While he could win the British Open, the PGA, the Western Open, and the North

60

and South, he wasn't up to the U.S. Open. He shot 82 in the morning and dropped like a rock. Jones, meantime, shot 76, and Cruickshank followed him in with 78.

Running ahead now, Bobby figured another 73 would win. Maybe even 74. Probably 75.

From early disappointments, Bobby had learned to ignore the other man and play against par, but now he set himself to play against Cruickshank, the only man in position to catch him. He paid the price. Starting badly, Bobby was out in 39, but a 35 would give him 74, and he had not been over 35 on the second nine yet. Starting back smartly, he holed from eighteen feet to birdie the 10th and from ten feet to save par on the 11th. Pars on the 12th and 13th, then his pitch to the 14th rolled about a yard from the hole. Another birdie. Two under now, his tee shot on the 15th veered left into a greenside bunker, but again he nursed the ball a yard from the cup for his par. Still two under with three holes to play. Par was 4-4-4, but Bobby had needed all twelve strokes only once before, and twice he closed 4-4-3. If he parred them all, he'd have 33 on the second nine and 72 for the round. No one would catch him.

Believing he had the Open won, Jones eased up. After a good drive on the 16th, he pushed his approach out of bounds, and only luck saved a bogey 5. Dropping a second ball, he pulled it, but it caromed off a mound and rolled seven feet from the cup. He holed the putt. Two hooked shots cost him another stroke at the 17th, and now he needed a par 4 on the 18th to shoot the 74 he wanted.

Could Bobby do it? Maybe not. He had just thrown away two precious strokes, and he was facing Inwood's strongest hole. It was 425 yards long with the fairway running level for the first 200 yards, then easing down a gentle grade and ending at a wide pond Inwood members called a lagoon. The green was set against the far bank.

Losing those two strokes seemed to take some of the fight out of Bobby. He hit a short drive, then hooked his spoon. The ball cleared the pond but curled left and rolled under a chain stretched around the 12th tee.

While officials removed the chain, Jones brooded over his loose play, reviving the old doubts. Was he really good enough to win?

To make his 4, he would have to clear a deep bunker blocking the direct line to the flag and stop his ball quickly. With the crowd hushed, Bobby tried to play a soft lob, but he caught a little too much turf. The ball dropped into the bunker, and he made 6. He had lost four strokes the last three holes, shot 76 instead of the 74 he wanted, and his 296 opened the way for Cruickshank.

By the time Jones had stumbled into the clubhouse, stunned by his miserable finish, Cruickshank had played five holes at the cost of one lost stroke. He could win, but he would have to play the next thirteen in one under par. The odds were against it, but odds never worried Cruickshank; he had survived a much tougher fight. As a British soldier, he had seen his brother blown apart by a German shell. Captured later, he had escaped from a prisoner-of-war camp and had worked his way through enemy lines to rejoin the fighting. A spirit like that would not be intimidated by a game of golf.

Knowing what he had to do, Cruickshank played the next seven holes in 2-3-3-4-3-4-3, one stroke over level 3s and three under par. If he could play the last six holes in even par, he would beat Jones by three strokes.

With the Open in his hands, Cruickshank played the 13th through 15th holes in 5-5-4 against par of 4-5-3, and his cushion was gone; now he'd have to finish 4-4-4 over three punishing holes.

He broke on the 16th. After a good drive, he missed the green, played a timid pitch, and took three putts for a wretched 6. He couldn't win now; he'd have to birdie one of the last two holes to save a tie. On the 17th green in two, he almost holed his fifty-footer, but he made 4. Only the 18th left.

He drilled his drive straight down the middle, then ripped into a mid-iron that covered the flag all the way, cleared the pond, and stopped six feet from the cup. It was a majestic shot, one of the greatest ever played in championship golf, and when he holed the putt, Cruickshank had earned a place in a playoff.

His birdie had had further significance. It had given Bobby Jones a chance to redeem himself. When Jones made that terrible 6 on the home hole, O. B. Keeler, a reporter from the *Atlanta Journal*, told him he thought he probably would be the champion because it seemed unlikely that Cruickshank would catch him.

"Well," Jones answered, "I didn't finish like a champion."

Back in his room in the clubhouse waiting for Cruickshank to finish, Jones continued to brood. Everybody said he was a great golfer, but was he? If he was, why couldn't he win anything? He could hit the shots—he knew that—but was he a golfer or simply a great shot-maker who couldn't put enough of those shots together to win anything? He had been trying for seven years, ever since he was fourteen. Others may have considered his showing in the 1916 National Amateur a triumph; to Bobby it was the first failure. It was a disappointment, of course, but it shouldn't have been. He was lucky to be alive.

Bobby Jones was born in Atlanta on March 17, 1902, to Clara Merrick Thomas Jones and Robert Purmedas Jones. He was their second child; their first, William Bailey Jones, died at three months. Through his first five years, six doctors had predicted little Bobby wouldn't survive, either. He was a frail, sickly infant with a thin and spindly body and an oversized head. Unable to digest solid foods, he lived mostly on Farina, pablum, and egg whites. When Bobby was five, his father moved the family to the country for the summer, where they boarded in a big house close to the 2nd fairway of the East Lake golf course. There was no history of golf in the Jones family, but Bobby's father had played baseball well enough at Mercer College and the University of Georgia to be offered a contract by the Brooklyn club of the National League. His father, Robert Tyre Jones, a huge (six-foot-five), humorless textile merchant for whom little Bobby was named, refused to let him sign.

Living so close to a golf course now, Bobby's parents took up the game. When one of the other boarders gave Bobby a sawed-off cleek—an iron club with very little loft—he and Frank Meader, the son of the landlady, laid out a rough course along the dirt road running past the house and batted the ball around by the hour. When the occasional wild shot bounded into a briar patch, little Bobby would jump up and down in a rage; even at five he couldn't accept less than his best.

He had other diversions, too—a creek that ran through a field that Bobby insisted swarmed with fish he never caught, and a mule Bobby was never able to coax more than a few steps from its stable. For its stubbornness, Bobby named it Clara, an honor his mother failed to recognize.

Summer over, the Joneses returned to Atlanta, but they were back again the next year and moved into a house on the club grounds. In a fortunate accident of timing, Stewart Maiden became the club professional that summer. He was a man who seldom spoke, but he swung with a flowing rhythmic motion. Even though he was only a child, Bobby recognized the grace of Maiden's swing and followed him whenever he played. After a few holes, Bobby would run home and try to copy Maiden's shots. Like most children with an athletic inclination, Bobby was a natural mimic. He spent hours pitching a capful of balls onto the 13th green, close by the house, all the while imitating Maiden's style and, at the same time, developing his sense of feel and touch.

He was still thin, with skinny arms and legs, but the days in the sunshine, the golf, the fishing, and the tennis he dabbled in gradually had their effect. Now that he was able to digest anything in sight, his appetite grew, and soon his body filled out. As his health improved, so did his golf. He had a natural gift. Although at nine he was the youngest boy in the field, he won the club's junior championship, defeating Howard Thorne, a boy of sixteen, by 5 and 4. Bigger, stronger, and seven years older, Thorne hit the ball farther than Jones, but Bobby destroyed him around the greens.

PART TWO

At ten he was shooting around 90; at eleven, fighting to control his trembling hands and shaking knees, he holed a four-foot putt on the home green and for the first time shot 80. Bobby played that day with Perry Adair, who was three years older and a little bit better. In 1914, Perry went to the final of the Southern Amateur and became the first boy wonder of golf. The following year, when the Southern came to East Lake, Bobby placed third in qualifying and lost in the second round.

Although he had played invitation tournaments in Mobile and Birmingham, Alabama, the Southern Amateur was his first sectional competition. The next year, when he was fourteen, he won the Georgia Amateur, the first one ever played, defeating Simpson Dean in the semifinal round, but for the second time experiencing a strange phenomenon that would follow him throughout his career: He brought out the best in his opponents. In the Montgomery, Alabama, Invitational earlier in the summer, he had played the first nine in 33 and had had Perry Adair 3 down, but Perry had come back in 33 and won, 1 up. Then, in the Georgia Amateur, Bobby was 5 up with five holes to play, but Dean won the next three, and facing a five-foot putt for another win on the 17th, he left it only an inch short.

While Bobby brought out the best in others, he could play pretty good golf under stress. After defeating Dean, he faced Adair in the final. Bobby had been growing steadily, and by now, at five-foot-four and a chunky 165 pounds, he was bigger and stronger than Perry. Three holes down after the first eighteen, Bobby began the afternoon with a wild drive, but from then on he played unbeatable golf, finishing the round with a medal score of 70 and winning 2 up. With that match, Bobby had replaced Perry as the boy wonder.

Back home in Atlanta, Perry's father persuaded Bobby's father to allow him to go to Philadelphia for the National Amateur. His career in national competition had begun.

With national championships suspended during the war, J. A. Scott, of Wright and Ditson, arranged a series of matches for the Red Cross. Bobby and Perry joined Alexa Stirling, an Atlanta girl, and Elaine Rosenthal, a promising young golfer from Chicago, and toured through Massachusetts, Maine, New Hampshire, and Connecticut, and later Bobby and Perry teamed against other prominent amateurs—Chick Evans, Bob Gardner, Warren K. Wood, Jim Standish, and Kenneth Edwards. Bobby was also invited to play against professionals for war relief. In one memorable match he lost the first three holes to Cyril Walker, played the next six in 4-3-4-4-4-2, and won, 1 up.

The Red Cross and War Relief funds realized more than $150,000 from matches Bobby played, and he became famous. More important to his career perhaps, he also gained experience playing against older and better golfers.

With the war over, the 1919 National Amateur was set for the Oakmont Country Club, a severe and brutal golf course a few miles up the Allegheny River from Pittsburgh with as many bunkers as shell holes at Verdun and greens as slick as waxed marble. Bobby had grown up playing on slow greens of Bermudagrass, a coarse-bladed strain common throughout the South. He hadn't seen the faster and finer-bladed bentgrass greens until he had played at Merion three years earlier. They had shocked him. He hit one putt much too hard; as the color of his cheeks rose, his ball, picking up speed, rolled off the green, raced down a slope, and tumbled into a stream. By now, though, he had learned to cope with the speedy greens of the North through his experience in wartime exhibitions, but Oakmont's were the fastest he had ever seen.

Since he had lost to Jim Barnes by one stroke in the Southern Open and had finished second to Doug Edgar in the Canadian Open earlier in the season, it was hardly surprising that he breezed through four matches, but he was no match for Davey Herron in the final. A twenty-year-old Oakmont member familiar with those glassy greens, Herron played thirty-two holes in four under level 4s and polished off Jones, 5 and 4.

Encouraged by his showing against the professionals and in going to the final of another Amateur, Bobby entered the 1920 Open. He played remarkably well at Inverness, and a month later lost to Francis Ouimet in the semifinals of the Amateur. Recognized as a player of remarkable talent, he was picked to join a group of Americans making the first organized assault on the British Amateur Championship in 1921. Bobby lost in the fourth round, then stayed on for the British Open at St. Andrews. He humiliated himself in the third round, and for the rest of his life he didn't forgive himself.

After two reasonably good rounds, he shot 46 on the first nine of the third round, made 6 on the 10th, a par 4, and then, seething because he had left a putt short and was about to make another 6 on the 11th, he picked up his ball. Although he continued to play—he didn't leave his partner to play alone, and, indeed, went out in the afternoon and shot an unofficial 72—he had quit.

Bobby had had earlier bursts of temper, but his galleries were so captivated by his bold and dashing game, they overlooked his appalling behavior. Back home again after the British Open, he gave his fans another example of his gambling, all-or-nothing style. With only eighteen holes to go in the U.S. Open, he had been nine strokes behind Jim Barnes and hopelessly out of the running, but he had played the first four holes in birdie, birdie, par, par. The 5th hole was a 560-yard straightaway par 5 with a massive bunker slicing across the fairway well beyond the drive zone and with a fence running close along the left. The bunker was no problem to golfers of this caliber, but they had to be careful of the fence.

Bobby pounded his drive so far he had only 275 yards left, and he felt he could reach the green with his brassie and cut another stroke from Barnes's lead—possibly two. He tore into the shot, but he came over the top and pulled the ball over the fence and out of bounds. Never one to flinch from a challenge, he dropped another ball and once again pulled it over the fence. He completed the hole eventually in nine strokes and shot 77, not nearly good enough to catch Barnes, but good enough for a fifth-place finish.

Playing in the National Amateur two months later, Bobby tried to cut the corner of a dogleg and drive the green, but his ball hit the tallest shoot of the tallest tree and fell straight down into a stony depression covered by underbrush. He had been 2 up on Willie Hunter, the British Amateur champion, but he lost, 2 and 1.

Told later that bold shot had cost him the match, Bobby answered:

"I can play this game only one way: I must play every shot for all there is in it. I can't play safe."

Daring like this worked as often as it failed and made him a favorite of the galleries. But he hadn't won.

He had felt he had a good chance in the 1922 Open, but Sarazen had come in with 68, and then, in the semifinal round of the 1922 Amateur at The Country Club, Bobby had played first-class golf, but he was wiped out 8 and 7 by Jess Sweetser, a big strong Yale man.

Was Jones indeed a great golfer who didn't have what it takes to win? Back in 1916 someone asked Walter Travis if Jones would improve much.

"He can never improve his shots if that's what you mean," Travis replied, "but he will learn a great deal more about playing them."

Five years later, Walter Hagen told O. B. Keeler, "He's got everything he needs to win any championship except experience and maybe philosophy. He's still impetuous. But I'll tip you off to something. Bobby will win an Open before he wins an Amateur."

Now, in July 1923, Bobby had the opportunity to do just that and at the same time redeem himself for the horrible 6 he took on the seventy-second hole the previous day.

Sunday morning of the playoff was gray and overcast with just the hint of a storm to come later in the day. Assuming the role of chaperon, Francis Ouimet, Bobby's idol as a boy, had seen that Jones had a good night's sleep, brought him to the golf course the next morning, and then, with Keeler, Francis Powers, another newspaperman, and Sol Metzger, he wandered out to the 3rd green, where all four sat on a bank and talked and sang, trying to relieve their tension. Keeler could recite verse endlessly, and now he was haunted by a line from Kipling:

"I'm dreading what I've got to watch, the color sergeant said."

Then it was time to go.

A huge crowd of about 8,000 fans had swarmed through the gate by the time Jones and Cruickshank strode to the tee for the two o'clock start. Bobby's face was drawn and pinched, and his eyes were sunken. He did not project confidence.

First off the tee, Cruickshank sliced his drive into the rough, had to lay up short of the green, and lost a stroke to Bobby's routine par 4. Cruickshank turned right around and birdied three of the next four holes, parred the other two, and jumped two strokes ahead after six holes. But Jones wasn't whipped; he fought back and birdied two of the next six, and picked up four strokes.

Back and forth they went, first one man gaining a stroke, then the other. Neither could take command. Over the first fifteen holes, only three holes were halved, and the two men were even. Jones was frustrated. Cruickshank's drives were yards shorter than Bobby's, and he had continually missed the greens, but he had made up for his mistakes with his short game. From the 10th through the 15th, Cruickshank had hit only two greens in standard figures, and he had been in the rough on two of the five driving holes, but still he clung to Jones, fighting for every stroke and playing miraculous recoveries when hope seemed lost.

Now the strain began to tell even more. Cruickshank's approach fell into a bunker by the 16th green, dropping him a stroke behind with two holes to play. Once again he drove poorly on the 17th, hooking his ball over the trees and into the 16th fairway, but he scraped out a par 4, and when Jones made 5, they were even again with only the demanding 18th left to play.

For Jones, all the years and all the disappointments came down to that one hole. A failure here could mean the end of a career before it had ever begun.

With the equipment of the day, reaching the green of a hole as long as the 18th called for two solid shots. With each hole the tension had grown more unbearable for both men, but it seemed to have affected Cruickshank more. He hadn't hit a green since the 14th, and he had hooked his last two drives. Still, he had birdied the 18th on Saturday, and now, with two more good shots like those, he could win. First he needed a good drive. He set himself firmly, but he lunged feebly at the ball, half topped it and sent it veering off to the left behind a clump of trees barely 150 yards away.

PART TWO

Jones next. With all the grace and rhythm of his legato swing, he drove his ball at least 100 yards farther than Cruickshank's, but it settled on a patch of bare ground in the right rough. Neither man seemed to have an advantage; both would probably have to lay up short of the pond. Cruickshank played first and hit a high pitch that nicked the leaves of a tree as it began its rise and settled in mid-fairway, past Jones's ball. Now it was up to Bobby.

With his ball resting on bare dirt, Bobby had a clean lie, but he was 190 yards from the green, and if he didn't hit the ball perfectly, it would probably drop into the water and finish him. Hesitating barely an instant, Bobby sized up the shot, drew out his mid-iron, set himself quickly, then tore into the ball. It started off on a low line, and the crowd sucked in its breath as it rose in the heavy, humid air. When it came down safely on the far side of the pond, stopping six feet from the cup, the gallery burst into a thundering roar. There was no doubt now that Jones would win, for Cruickshank was fumbling to a 6.

Bobby coaxed his first putt close to the hole and tapped in for his par, winning the playoff with 76 to Cruickshank's 78. Jones was a champion at last, and great things lay ahead.

SIX

Jones Against the Field

With the 1923 season over, Bobby returned to Harvard, then dashed home again the following spring to prepare for the 1924 Open, scheduled for the Oakland Hills Country Club in suburban Detroit. Its undulating greens were tightly bunkered, and at 6,880 yards it was brutally long. Seven of its eleven two-shot holes stretched beyond 400 yards, and the 9th, one of its four one-shotters, measured 242 yards. Over a course like that, it seemed logical that the championship would go to one of the longer hitters. Jones was one of the longest; so were Walter Hagen, Gene Sarazen, Bill Mehlhorn, Mac Smith, and Bobby Cruickshank.

Cyril Walker hardly looked like the man to beat. A spare man, he weighed a strapping 118 pounds, had a thin face capped by brownish hair that came to a point above a high and broad forehead, ears that stood out from his head, and uneven teeth that showed through his happy smile. Thirty years old by then, he had done little else except finish second to Hagen in two North and South Opens and defeat Gene Sarazen in an early round of the 1921 PGA.

An Englishman, Walker had learned to play golf on the Lancashire coast, in the west of England, where the wind whips in from the Irish Sea. It was good training, for the wind was up at Oakland Hills, and midway through the first round it was clear that anything close to par would be a very good score indeed. Playing his shots so low the wind would have a minimum effect, Walker shot two steady rounds of 74, two strokes over

par, and when the day ended, he stood one stroke behind Jones and Mehlhorn, who shared the lead at 147.

Another 74 in the third round, and Walker had caught Jones at 222.
Growing more confident with every shot, he started the fourth round with
38 on the first nine, made his par 4 on the 10th, and then learned that
Bobby, playing well behind him, had begun 6-4-5-4. When Jones made 6
on the 10th, Walker's confidence soared. He had picked up two strokes on
Bobby, and the others were dropping out of the hunt. Mehlhorn had
been playing the steadiest kind of golf until the 12th, where he had taken
6 on a par-5 that could be reached with two good shots, Hagen had hung
on until the 16th, where he heeled his mashie into a pond in front of the
green, Cruickshank had made 6 on the 18th, and the 10th had ruined
Jones. (A par 4 of 440 yards, the 10th cost Bobby 6s in the first, third, and
fourth rounds and a 5 in the second—twenty-three strokes in four rounds.)

Walker faced his last serious test at the 16th. After a solid drive, he still
had a long iron across a menacing body of water into a strong headwind.
His caddie wanted him to play his driving iron—clear the water at any
cost, even if it meant reaching a deep bunker behind the green—but
Walker chose the shorter mid-iron. As soon as he hit the shot he knew
he'd won the Open. The ball cleared the water easily, thumped onto the
green, and stopped eight feet from the hole. Taking no chances, Walker
eased his first putt close and made his 4.

Against a rising flood of emotions, Walker had played the last nine
holes of this unforgiving course in even par 37 and had 75 for the round.
His total of 297 had beaten Jones by three strokes.

Golf was growing rapidly in the postwar years. The handful of clubs at
the beginning of the twentieth century had grown to nearly 4,000 by the
middle 1920s. They were springing up in every part of the country, some
of them the result of enlightened marketing both by sporting goods com-
panies and by real estate promoters. The A. G. Spalding Company hired
Tom Bendelow, a Scottish immigrant, to tour the country laying out golf
courses, which, in turn, created golfers to buy Spalding's clubs and balls.
An able golfer and religious zealot, Bendelow laid out 650 courses, often
taking no more than one morning. He established the routing and length
of the holes and left the actual construction to others. There was nothing
unusual in this; it was how the job was done in the game's early years.

Other architects had been busy, too—A. W. Tillinghast, Donald Ross,
Devereaux Emmet, Bill Flynn, Max Behr, and Alister MacKenzie, a
former physician. They were all professional architects. A number of
talented and dedicated amateurs dabbled in the field and gave us some
of our best courses. Hugh Wilson had created Merion, Jack Neville had

designed Pebble Beach, and George Crump, a Philadelphia hotelier, had dedicated the last years of his life to the creation of Pine Valley. Those three are the best golf courses in the United States and among the ten best in the world.

While Merion was built before the First World War, Pine Valley and Pebble Beach were done after the Armistice, beginning a period of remarkable growth in both number and quality of American courses. Tillinghast had come out of Philadelphia and created the two new courses at Winged Foot and two more at Baltusrol, both in the suburbs of New York City; Donald Ross had done Oakland Hills and continued to work on Pinehurst No. 2; Willie Park had designed one of the four courses at Olympia Fields near Chicago, and Bendelow another; Bill Flynn had done Cherry Hills in Denver and created an entirely new design at Shinnecock Hills, where the second Open had been played; Sam Whiting had laid out the Olympic Club in San Francisco, a club whose membership included Bob Fitzsimmons, the heavyweight boxing champion of an earlier era; and MacKenzie had stopped on his way from England to Australia long enough to design Cypress Point.

These were all wonderful and enduring golf courses, whose style and integrity would stand up through periods of changing and improving technique and equipment. While it is true that some of the bunkering of those masterworks had to be adjusted and some of the greens reshaped as the ball became progressively longer, their basic designs remained valid.

As more and more Americans took up the game, more and more good players were created, and the size of the Open fields grew. From the eleven men who had played at Newport in 1895, the entry had grown to 165 in 1913 and to 265 in 1920. When the 1923 Open attracted 360 players, the traditional thirty-six holes of qualifying at the site had to be extended over four days rather than two, as it had been for years. It was obvious a new qualifying format had to be found. In 1924 the USGA played eliminations at Worcester, Massachusetts, and Oak Park, Illinois. Forty players from each region qualified for the championship proper; there would be no qualifying at the site.

A year later, in 1925, the entry reached 445, causing the USGA to set up three qualifying sites, one near Chicago, another in San Francisco, and a third at the Lido Country Club on Long Island. Jones was among those who had to qualify at Lido, an unusual course designed by Charles Blair Macdonald, the irascible 1895 National Amateur champion, and financed by real estate promoters.

Overbearing, domineering, and bull-headed, Macdonald had a gift for golf course design. His National Golf Links of America, which he had begun on eastern Long Island in 1908, was among the first modern golf courses in North America. He also designed the early Chicago Golf Club, the Mid Ocean Club in Bermuda, the Yale Golf Club, and the Piping Rock Golf Club. All are first class. Lido, however, was special.

For a site, the promoters had chosen 115 acres bordering the Atlantic Ocean on the south shore of Long Island. The tract was mostly marshland and swamp, with a big lake in the middle. Seeing the ground for the first time, Macdonald had walked away, saying the job couldn't be done. He was finally persuaded by the promise that he could do anything he liked—create hills, dig hollows, form mounds and lakes, shape the very ground.

The more he thought about it, the more he had become fascinated by the challenge. It was like a dream, and the prospect had made him feel like a creator. He accepted and then set about building a wonder course.

With the help of Bernard Darwin, a Dickensian scholar and golf correspondent of *The Times* of London (and, incidentally, the grandson of the evolutionist Charles Darwin), Macdonald sought a fresh design for a classic two-shot hole between 360 and 400 yards long. Since Darwin also wrote for the British weekly magazine *Country Life,* he had arranged for a contest among its readers. A design by Dr. Alister MacKenzie had been judged to be the best of the eighty-one entries and had won the prize of 15 guineas (a little more than £15 sterling). With some revisions to fit the terrain, Macdonald had adopted MacKenzie's plan as the 18th hole.

Begun in 1914, Lido was a marvel of engineering. To fill the marsh, two million cubic yards of sand were sucked up from the ocean floor, piped overland, and then spewed out to create hills and valleys, to make the fairways roll, and to contour the greens. On top of the sand, Macdonald laid blocks of meadow bog five inches thick in slabs measuring fifteen by thirty inches, and on that poured muck from an adjacent meadow. He built a lagoon to create an island fairway on one hole, with sluice gates to control the flow of water in and out of the channel.

The cost reached $800,000, enormously high for the time, but it was an imaginative and inventive period, and the course was a wonderful test of the game. But it didn't last. The real estate venture failed during the Great Depression, maintenance was neglected, and part of it was sold off.

Lido was at its peak when Jones qualified for the 1925 Open with what he called some of his greatest golf. With eight 3s on his scorecard, Bobby shot 72 in the morning under sunny skies and a light breeze. The wind picked up after lunch, rain pelted down, and he needed all his skill to get around in 71 and win a place among the ninety-two who would start at the Worcester Country Club, in Worcester, Massachusetts.

Bobby began the Open badly. Calling a penalty on himself for causing his ball to move in the rough near the 11th green, which cost him one stroke, he opened with 77, but he rallied, shot 70, 70, and 74, and finished with 291, tying Willie Macfarlane, whose third round 67 broke a record that had stood since 1909.

At least ten men could have won in the last eighteen holes, but they all failed. Leo Diegel was three under 4s with seven holes to play, made 6 on the 12th and 8 on the 18th, shot 78 and 296. Francis Ouimet, Walter Hagen, and Johnny Farrell could have tied with birdies on the 18th, but they all missed. Even Jones might have won, but needing a 4-4-4 finish to post 67 in the third round, he shot 5-5-5 and 70.

Macfarlane also had had a chance to win outright. He had been three strokes ahead of Jones with only seven holes to play, and had lost them all.

Although it had been scheduled for eighteen holes, the playoff had to go thirty-six, the longest so far. Twice Macfarlane looked as if he would win in eighteen holes, but Jones birdied the 14th by holing a full pitch, and then Willie missed a six-footer on the 18th. Both men shot 75; they would have to play again in the afternoon.

Jones went ahead quickly, and when Willie missed a putt from inside a yard on the 9th, Bobby led by four strokes. Out in 39 against 35 by Jones, Macfarlane's cause seemed hopeless, but he rushed home in 33 and shot 72 while Jones shot a ragged 38 coming back and finished with 73.

Macfarlane was a slender man, just under six feet tall, with dark, wavy hair and a prominent nose, and he wore steel-rimmed glasses. He seemed to have no driving ambition; he hadn't played in an Open since 1920 and had played only thirteen rounds since the previous October when he had gone to Lido to qualify, but he had a graceful, flowing swing that needed little tuning up. He was so unusually well coordinated that, after hurting his wrist playing from hard ground at the Baltimore Country Club early in his career, he found he could shoot from 77 to 83 playing one-handed.

He was a streaky player. In a series of rounds around New York, Macfarlane had shot 64 at Quaker Ridge, 64 at Hudson River, 66 and 67 in one day at Dunwoodie, and 64 at Oak Ridge in Tuckahoe, his home club. He had also shot 61 at Oak Ridge, but it couldn't stand as the course record because of an interruption. Willie had 30 on the first nine, but on his way to the 10th tee, he had been overcome by the aroma of broiling steaks wafting from the clubhouse and stopped for lunch, then shot 31 on the second nine.

By the middle 1920s it was evident that the postwar American was a better golfer than the postwar Briton. While no Briton had won the U.S. Open since Ted Ray in 1920, Americans had won three of the four British Opens since 1921, and the American amateurs had won all three Walker Cup Matches through 1925, twice by wide margins. Any lingering doubt that the United States was now the world's leading golf power evaporated in 1926. Jess Sweetser, suffering from a heavy cold, became the first native American to win the British Amateur, the United States won the Walker Cup match, and Americans dominated the British Open, taking the first four places and seven of the first ten. Bobby won, Al Watrous was second, George Von Elm third, and Walter Hagen fourth.

Jones played some of his greatest golf in winning the British Open. In the qualifying rounds at Sunningdale near London, he shot 66 and 68, two of the finest rounds ever played in championship golf. His 66 was a marvel—he was out in 33 and back in 33, had 33 putts and 33 other shots, and his holes were all 3s and 4s—not a 2 and not a 5.

He was not nearly so sharp at Royal Lytham and St. Annes in the championship itself, but lying two strokes behind Watrous after sixty-seven holes, he played the last five tough holes in 4-3-4-4-4, shot 74 and 291, and beat him by two strokes.

Since the United States Open was scheduled for early July, at the Scioto Country Club in Columbus, Ohio, Jones had no time to waste. He sailed on the *Aquitania*, stayed in New York long enough for a parade up Broadway, then took the sleeper to Columbus.

The Open had always been played over two days, but because of the continuing growth both in the number of entries and the size of its galleries, the USGA adopted a three-day format for 1926: 147 men would play eighteen holes on each of the first two days, and then the low fifty scorers would play thirty-six holes on the third day. Not only would more players start, but admission fees from the additional day of play would help cover the escalating prize money. From the $335 paid to professionals in 1895, the prize fund had grown to $1,200 in 1916, and to $1,745 in 1919. By 1926 it had climbed to $2,145, to be shared by twenty players.

Bobby opened with 70, but after 79 in the second round—the worst he had ever scored in an Open—his prospects seemed hopeless. He was tired and emotionally drained, and once again he had taken a penalty stroke for causing his ball to move.

Six strokes behind Mehlhorn with thirty-six holes to play, Bobby recovered his poise the next morning and went around in 71 to Mehlhorn's 75, but now Joe Turnesa was in front, leading Bobby by three strokes, with Mehlhorn second.

Turnesa was one of seven sons of a Westchester County, New York, greenkeeper, who thought their preoccupation with the game was a waste. When word reached the Pelham Country Club in midafternoon on July 10 that Joe was leading the Open, a member rushed out to tell his father.

"He should be," he grumbled. "All he ever does is play golf."

A hot wind was blowing across Scioto, increasing in strength by the hour. It was blowing very strong as the last round began, and rain fell occasionally. Mehlhorn dropped out early, leaving the battle to Jones and Turnesa. Playing two pairs ahead of Bobby, Joe added another stroke to his lead on the first nine with a 37 to Bobby's 38, and when both men made their 4s on the 10th and 11th, Jones had only seven holes left to make up four strokes. To win now he would have to play inspired golf, and Turnesa would have to slip.

The break came on the 12th hole. From a downhill lie, Turnesa's low-flying approach caught a corner of the rough, costing him one stroke. Moments later Bobby birdied, holing an eight-foot putt, and now he was only two behind with six to play. Turnesa began to struggle; his swing became choppy, and the strokes began flying away. He lost another at the 13th, where he was bunkered, and still another on the 16th, where his approach rolled over the green. His lead was gone now, for Jones was picking up one par after another, and with a bogey on the 17th, Turnesa fell a stroke behind and lost all hope of winning outright. Still, he might force a playoff if he could birdie the 18th, a 480-yard par 5.

After a good drive that left him within range of the green, Turnesa pushed his second to the right, then played a nerveless pitch to seven feet and holed the putt. He was in with 77 and 294.

Back on the 17th green, Bobby had holed a four-foot putt to save par and then climbed to the 18th tee, knowing he needed a birdie to win. With about 10,000 spectators lining the fairway and crowding around the green, Jones unleashed a long and straight drive that left him about 200 yards from the green. An unnatural silence settled over the gallery as Jones ripped into his iron, but they began cheering as the ball flew straight at the flag, hit the front edge of the green, barely slipped past the cup and stopped ten feet away. He took two putts for the birdie. Jones had played the last nine holes in 35, picking up five strokes on Turnesa, shot 73, and won with 293. Jones had become the first man to hold both the U.S. and British Open championships in the same year.

Two months later he reached the final of the Amateur, losing to George Von Elm by 2 and 1. In one season of superb golf, he had gone to the sixth round of the British Amateur, had won both the British and U.S. Opens, and had lost in the final of the U.S. Amateur. An idea was born. Would it be possible to win all four in one year? The next opportunity would come in 1930, when the British Amateur and Open would be scheduled close enough together for Walker Cuppers to play in all three events on the same trip.

Jones was twenty-four in 1926 and held degrees in mechanical engineering and English literature. In the fall he entered Emory University in Atlanta to study law. In the spring he won the Southern Open and then headed for Pittsburgh to defend his Open championship at Oakmont. With its length (more than 6,900 yards) and swift putting surfaces, it was as challenging as Oakland Hills. Bobby wasn't up to it; he had the worst Open of his career and was never a contender after the 4th hole the first day. A misplayed long iron dropped into a bunker, he took four strokes to get out, and he spent the rest of the week steering his shots. He didn't have a score as low as 75, finished with 309, and placed eleventh.

The championship was won by Tommy Armour, a thirty-two-year-old Scottish immigrant who had lost the sight of an eye in the war. Over as tough a finish as there is in championship golf, Armour played the last six holes in two under par to tie Harry Cooper at 301, then shot 76 in the playoff and beat him by three strokes. Cooper was a luckless young man from England. Like Macdonald Smith, he was one of the great players who never won a national championship, although he was perpetually close. His 79 in the playoff was his worst round of the tournament, while Armour's 71 in the second round was his only score under 76.

Jones recovered quickly from this spell of indifferent golf, sailed abroad and played St. Andrews in 68-72-73-72—285, led every round of the British Open, broke the record by six strokes (he had set it the previous year), and won by six strokes from Aubrey Boomer and Fred Robson. Returning home, he played in the National Amateur at Minikahda in Minneapolis, won the qualifying medal with 142, tying the record, then defeated, in order, Maurice McCarthy, Gene Homans, Jimmy Johnston, Francis Ouimet, and Chick Evans. He beat Johnston 10 and 9, Ouimet 11 and 10, and Evans 8 and 7, all in thirty-six-hole matches.

Golf over for the year, Bobby returned to Emory, but he withdrew before the term ended, passed the Georgia bar examination, and entered practice in the spring of 1928. With his new responsibilities, he cut down on his golf schedule and played in only the Open, the Warren K. Wood Memorial, and the Amateur. Even though he had won the last two, he passed up the British Open.

Johnny Farrell had also declined to join the large group of Americans who had gone to the British Open at Sandwich, England; he was tired from a heavy winter schedule. At twenty-seven, he was a year older than Jones and had been a consistent winner for the last few years. He had won five tournaments in 1926 and eight in 1927, and he was doing nicely in 1928, winning the Miami Open, teaming with Gene Sarazen to win the Miami Four-Ball, and in March winning the LaGorce Open, whose $5,000 first prize was the richest in golf. Since he had never been worse than seventh in the last five Opens, had missed tying Jones and Macfarlane by one stroke in 1925, he figured to be a strong contender at Olympia Fields, a mammoth complex near Chicago.

Because its Fourth Course had been the site of several tournaments, including the Western Open, the club had records of the hole-by-hole scoring averages that exposed some weaknesses. In preparing for the Open championship, club officials strengthened some of the more vulnerable holes, principally by extending the yardage. The result was a course of 6,741 yards—not as long as Oakmont, but about 250 yards longer than the original design. Par was established at 35-36—71.

With 73 and 71 the first two days, Jones led George Von Elm and Bill Leach, a Philadelphia professional, by two strokes, but Bobby's unruly gallery had upset Farrell so badly he shot 77-74—151 and was back in fifteenth place.

Most of the leaders played sloppy golf the last day. Jones struggled around in 73 and 77, Leach shot 73 and 80, Von Elm 76 and 74, and Walter Hagen finished 73-76. Among the early starters, Farrell shot 71 in the morning, picking up two strokes on Jones, then 72 in the afternoon, gaining five more. They completed the 72 holes tied at 294, the best scores in.

None of this seemed to matter, though, because Roland Hancock, a burly, twenty-one-year-old professional from Wilmington, North Carolina, needed only 5s on the last two holes to win.

Deep in despair from another close but futile finish in the Open, Farrell strolled out to watch Hancock finish. He picked him up as he crossed the narrow footbridge leading from the 16th green to the 17th tee, passing over a small brook reeking with the overflow from bootleggers' stills upstream. As he approached the bridge, a spectator, perhaps dizzied by the fumes, cried, "Make way for the new champion."

No one will ever know if the remark made Hancock overconfident, but he butchered the last two holes. He pushed his drive on the 17th onto a patch of bare ground in the right rough, then became flustered. Without asking for a ruling, he assumed the bare patch was a hazard, held his club-head well above ground to avoid a penalty for grounding his club, and hit a perfectly terrible shot. The ball was never airborne; it rolled along the ground and expired in thick, unyielding rough no more than ten or fifteen feet ahead. He needed two more shots to reach the green, and made 6. Unsettled, he made another 6 on the last hole and finished one stroke behind Jones and Farrell. Bobby would be in his third playoff in six years.

Convinced that eighteen holes was not a fair or thorough test, the USGA set the playoff for thirty-six holes. A light drizzle began falling as Jones and Farrell walked to the 1st tee, and Johnny pulled on a bright green sweater. Bobby grinned; the Irishman had his lucky colors.

Perhaps the sweater really was a charm; after they struggled through the first fourteen holes with neither man giving ground, Johnny stunned

Jones by making four consecutive birdies and going to lunch three strokes ahead.

Bobby won those strokes back quickly after lunch when Farrell three-putted each of the first two holes, and once again they played stroke-for-stroke through the 15th. Then Jones bogeyed the 16th to fall one stroke behind, and Farrell pitched to two feet for a sure birdie on the 17th. Jones seemed to be finished. His ball lay thirty feet from the cup, hardly birdie range, and unless he holed it he would be two strokes down with only one hole to play. But Bobby was dangerous when he was cornered. He holed his thirty-footer, and Farrell had to struggle to make his two-footer and save his one-stroke lead. Now the Open hinged on the 18th hole, a mild enough par 5 of 490 yards.

Farrell was in trouble from the start. Two loose shots left him in the rough fifty yards short of the green, but Jones was on with his second and had two putts for the birdie that would probably force another playoff. Fighting off the tension, Johnny pitched to eight feet, and after Jones rolled his first putt close enough for a certain 4, Farrell holed his birdie. He had beaten Jones by one stroke.

Later in 1928, Jones won the Amateur for the fourth time, again ravaging his opponents and winning his last three matches by 14 and 13, 13 and 12, and 10 and 9.

Even though he had lost the Open to Farrell, it had been obvious for years that Jones was a better golfer than any of the professionals. Since 1922 he had been beaten over seventy-two holes in the Open only in 1924 and 1927, and he had won the Amateur four times and the British Open twice. Walter Hagen had won five PGA Championships from 1921 through 1927, four of them in succession, but as an amateur, Jones wasn't eligible for the PGA, and he had played in none of the three British Opens that Hagen had won. On the other hand, Jones had beaten Hagen in only the 1926 British Open.

The public adored Bobby. He was young—only twenty-seven in 1929—he was good looking, he had a natural open charm, and he succeeded at what he tried. Americans might love the underdog, but they worship the winner.

If the era when he ruled golf wasn't the greatest age of sport, it was the greatest age of sports heroes. Babe Ruth and Lou Gehrig were at the height of their powers, although the Yankees were about to give way to the Philadelphia Athletics of Jimmy Foxx and Mickey Cochrane, the Four Horsemen had come and gone, but Knute Rockne was consistently turning out great Notre Dame football teams. Jack Dempsey and Gene Tunney reigned over boxing, Bill Tilden was the lord of tennis, Earl Sande was our leading jockey, and Tommy Hitchcock was romping around the polo fields.

Lindbergh had flown the Atlantic alone, Jimmy Walker was mayor of New York, the Teapot Dome scandal had come and gone, but the Broadway Limited came every day. Rudolph Valentino stalked sultry maidens through the desert, air mail was coming in, flappers were going out. It was the era of Florenz Ziegfeld and George White, of Paul Whiteman and George Gershwin. Mussolini governed Italy, but hardly anyone outside Germany had heard of Adolf Hitler and fewer of Francisco Franco. But fortunes were being made on Wall Street and everybody knew about J. Pierpont Morgan.

Only a genuine hero could stand out in those times, and Jones stood out. Whenever he played, it was Jones against the field—even money.

Once again Bobby went back to business after the Amateur and played only weekend golf until late June of 1929, when he came to Winged Foot, a fairly new and tough course in the suburbs of New York City. When A. W. Tillinghast was hired as the designer, he was told, "Give us a man-sized course." It was man-sized, indeed—6,786 yards, par 72, tightly bunkered, and cut through forests of oak, maple, linden, ash, birch, beech, and pines, and set on rolling green meadowland salted with outcroppings of grayish rock scraped bare by the great glaciers of the Ice Age. It was a stiff test that would probably put the field on the defensive. It seemed to be having that effect on Jones when he opened the first round with 6-4-5 against a par of 4-4-3. But suddenly he began firing his shots at the pins and played the next fifteen holes in six under par, finishing with 69, the best score of the day. Winged Foot struck back the next day, and Bobby shot 75, but he came back with a 71 Saturday morning and went into the last round leading Gene Sarazen by four strokes and Al Espinosa by five.

Sarazen was always dangerous, but he could get nothing going and gradually fell out of the chase. Now only Espinosa seemed a threat. A veteran of the First World War and a member of one of the old Spanish families that settled California, Espinosa had gone out in 38, but then he began striking the ball with precision and played the last six holes in twenty-two strokes, two under par, finishing at 294. It was the best seventy-two-hole score yet, but would it be good enough?

Jones had been picking up one par after another through the first seven holes, giving no one an opening, when without warning he began playing like a fifteen-handicapper on a bad day, pitching back and forth from bunker to bunker across the 8th green and taking a 7, losing three strokes to par. The attack of jitters seemed only momentary, though, for Bobby settled down and once again began grinding out his figures. Then he floundered again. Needing only pars on the last four holes to beat Espinosa by four strokes, he overclubbed his approach to the 15th, misjudged a soft lob, and failed to clear a knoll, and before he knew it he had another 7. Now instead of having strokes in hand, he needed three tough pars to shoot 293 and edge Espinosa by a stroke. When he took three putts from twenty feet on the 16th, all his strokes were gone, and to tie now he would have to make 4s on two holes that measured 450 and 419 yards.

He made his 4 on the 17th with no trouble, but he pulled his approach to the 18th into rough grass on the bank of a bunker. Now he had to get down in two to tie. From an awkward stance with his feet above the ball, Bobby popped the ball out of the grass with his niblick and stared after it as it ran true toward the hole. It stopped twelve feet short. To make the 4 he needed he would have to hole a difficult side-hill putt that would break about a foot and a half from left to right on a slippery green.

The huge gallery hushed as Bobby studied the putt. Finally satisfying himself with the line, he stood up to the ball in his familiar stance—heels close together, his body bent only slightly from the waist—soled his putter behind the ball, then tapped it smartly. The ball ran straight for a few feet, took the break, and tumbled into the cup.

The crowd had held its breath as the ball rolled along the slick green, but now it erupted into a crashing roar. Bobby had come through once more.

Again he would be in a thirty-six-hole playoff, but unlike those that went before, Bobby was never in trouble. He shot 72-69—141 while Espinosa, well off his game, stumbled around in 84-80—164. Bobby had his third Open.

For four years now Jones had been looking forward to 1930 and the chance to win all four national championships, but with a goal of this magnitude in mind, he would have to play in more tournaments than usual to keep his game sharp. He hadn't played four tournaments in one year since 1927, and he'd been in only five altogether through 1928 and 1929, but he determined to play in four others before the British Amateur, the first of the Grand Slam events. He would play in the Savannah and Southeastern Opens before sailing for Britain, and, once there, in the *Golf Illustrated* Gold Vase and the Walker Cup.

The Savannah Open was a classic. Horton Smith, himself not quite twenty-two but the winner of eight tournaments in 1929, shot 278 and beat Jones by one stroke. A little later, Smith and Jones faced each other in the Southeastern Open, played at the Augusta (Georgia) Country Club. Jones shot 284 and won by thirteen strokes (many years later he told a friend this was the best he ever played). Those two over, Bobby sailed to Britain, shot 143 for thirty-six holes at Sunningdale, winning the Gold Vase, then won both his foursomes and singles matches in the Walker Cup.

The British Amateur was played at St. Andrews, which he had come to love. Even though he played magnificent golf—143 holes in six under even 4s—and had the best card of anybody in the field in every one of his eight rounds, it was not an easy victory. Cyril Tolley, a brawny British Walker Cupper who was one of the longest hitters of his day, missed a twelve-foot putt on the 18th hole that would have beaten Bobby in the third round, and then Jones laid him a stymie (his ball blocked Tolley's line to the hole) and won on the 19th. George Voigt, a Walker Cup teammate of Bobby's, had him 2 down with five to play, but he drove out of bounds on the 14th and into a bunker on the 16th, and Jones won the match when Voigt missed from six feet on the 18th green.

Bobby had become such a great favorite with the Scots, especially the St. Andreans, that on the day of the final match, hardly a citizen was left in town; they were all at the golf course watching Jones play against Roger Wethered, an Englishman and close friend. The gallery was estimated at 15,000, and with most of them rooting for him, Bobby won, 7 and 6. The match ended on the 12th hole, almost as far from the dull gray stone clubhouse of the Royal and Ancient as one can be, and Bobby needed help from the Scottish police to fight his way through the worshiping crowd that swarmed over him as soon as his last putt fell.

Alone with O. B. Keeler later in the afternoon, Bobby said he had wanted to win this tournament more than any other, and that no matter what happened now, he was happy. But then he had said the same thing when he had won the 1923 Open.

With the British Open two weeks off, Bobby and his wife, Mary, celebrated in Paris, but the British Open was on top of him before he was ready for it, and he hurried back to Hoylake.

While the holes near the clubhouse of the Royal Liverpool Golf Club are laid out over flat and featureless ground, those that border the sea weave among rolling dunes that create all manner of lies. Hoylake begins easily enough, but its finish is brutal. Its last five holes—two par 5s and three par 4s—cover 2,318 yards, one third the length of the entire course.

Opening with stunning golf, Jones matched the course record of 70 in the first round and added 72 the next day. As well as he had played, he held a bare one-stroke lead over Fred Robson, an Englishman, and a three-stroke edge on Horton Smith, with Archie Compston five behind, and five strokes could evaporate quickly over this course.

A big, strong Englishman, Compston had beaten Walter Hagen by 18 and 17 in a seventy-two-hole match in 1928, and he looked as if he might bury Jones too as he began the third round 4-3-4-2 an hour after Bobby had started 4-5-6-3. Compston had wiped out Jones's lead in four holes, and when Bobby played the last five holes in four 5s and a 4 and shot 74, Compston followed him in with 68 and moved a stroke ahead.

As quickly as he climbed into the lead, Archie dropped out, shooting 82 in the afternoon. Jones, meanwhile, was out in 38, but now Leo Diegel and Mac Smith were closing in. Bobby felt he needed a birdie on the 16th, a par 5 of 553 yards, to have a chance. A long drive put him in position to go for the green with his brassie, but to get there his ball would have to cross a portion of the practice field, which was out of bounds. Mis-hit the ball and it would be all over. Swinging smoothly, Bobby cracked his ball cleanly over the range, but it carried a trifle too far and settled in an awkward position in a greenside bunker. He would have to play a delicate shot from a downhill lie in sand.

After studying his shot, Bobby reached into his bag and pulled out a strange instrument, a heavy iron club with a thick hickory shaft, a broad sole that rode through the sand rather than dug in, and a concave face that cradled the ball and flung it rather than hit it. This was the first of the sand wedges; it had been given to him by Horton Smith.

Jones took his stance, his right foot almost atop the back bank of the bunker and his body bent low, drew the club back slowly, then brought it down in a smart descending blow. The ball popped up cleanly, cleared the front lip of the bunker, carried onto the green, and rolled a bare two inches from the hole. He had his birdie. He finished with 75 and a 291 total. It was a tough score to match, but Diegel and Mac Smith might do it. Now Bobby could only wait.

He went into the clubhouse and ordered a whiskey and soda, but the strain was telling, and his hands, so steady in the heat of competition, trembled so badly he couldn't hold the glass. Gripping it in two hands, he drank quickly, then ordered another, waiting and watching through the clubhouse windows. First Diegel faded, and then Mac Smith reached the last hole needing an eagle 2 to tie. As Mac's ball rolled past the cup, Bobby took his left hand from the glass.

With the drive for the Grand Slam halfway over, Jones dropped the first clue that 1930 might be his last year of competitive golf.

"This is my last shot at the British Open," he told the Associated Press. "It's quite too thick for me. I feel I'm not strong enough to play in another one."

It was June, and with the U.S. Open coming up in a month, Bobby headed home. Cyril Tolley, who had won the British Amateur twice by then, had entered the U.S. Open and was traveling with the Jones party.

On the train from London to Southampton, he asked Bobby how long he had been in Britain.

"Six weeks," Jones answered.

"Have you ever played so badly for so long?"

"No," Bobby said.

He had indeed been off his game and hadn't begun to hit the ball as he liked until he shot 66 in an exhibition match with Harry Vardon, James Braid, and Ted Ray a few days before he sailed. As a fatalist, however, he believed his winning the British Amateur and Open was preordained.

Sailing on the steamship *Europa*, Jones arrived in New York on July 2 to another parade up Broadway under a shower of ticker tape streaming from the windows of brokerage houses. Those who labored in those buildings had very little else to do. Wall Street had collapsed eight months earlier, setting off the Great Depression. Only 1.3 million shares of stock had been traded that day, the slowest day in two years.

In the evening, Jones and 400 friends gathered for a dinner in his honor, and the next morning he boarded the Twentieth Century Limited for the trip west. He had seven days to hone his game and study the ground of the Interlachen Country Club, a heavily wooded course on gently rolling land eight miles west of Minneapolis.

Bobby's game responded to practice, and he began playing noticeably better than he had in Britain. It was obvious from the start he had peaked. Off at 9:45, he shaved two strokes from par over the first nine, going out in 34, and even though he dropped a stroke in the steamy afternoon, coming home in 37 and shooting 71, he was playing heady, confident golf. As the day wore on, both Mac Smith, a constant menace, and Tommy Armour shot 33s on the home nine and came in with 70s, and Wiffy Cox, a gravel-voiced ex-sailor from Brooklyn, matched Bobby's 71. Close behind lurked Walter Hagen, Harry Cooper, Horton Smith, and Joe Turnesa, all desperately eager to stop Jones.

A heat wave had gripped the Middle West since early in July, sending temperatures climbing over 100 degrees on the golf course. Bobby had played the last nine in the heat of the day, dressed in light gray slacks, a white shirt, white cap, and red foulard tie. With the humidity almost as high as the temperature, he had perspired so heavily the red dye from his tie had stained his shirt, and the knot had drawn so tight it had to be cut off. Someone grabbed it for a souvenir.

In more comfortable weather the next day, with the temperature down to the low 90s and the air noticeably lighter, Bobby began with a nervous bogey on the 1st hole, but quickly picked up ground with birdies on the 4th and 5th and needed a par 5 on the 9th for 35. At 484 yards, the 9th could be shortened by hitting the second shot across a clear blue lake with water lilies floating on the surface. Bobby had birdied the hole consistently in practice, but now he pushed his drive slightly, and the ball settled in a tight lie near the bank of the lake. Regardless of his lie, Bobby had decided to go for the green, but as he reached the top of his backswing, two little girls darted out of the crowd up ahead. Seeing them from the corner of his eye, Jones flinched and half topped his shot. The ball streaked off in so low a trajectory it could not clear the lake; he was probably headed for a 6.

Luck and the laws of physics saved him. The ball hit the water on such a low plane it skipped like a flat stone—once, then again—hopped over the bank, climbed up the hill, and stopped thirty yards short of the green. Some spectators thought the ball hit a lily pad, but it had hit only the water. Buoyed by his good luck, Bobby pitched dead to the hole, made his birdie 4, and turned for home in 34, two under par for the day. Running into trouble coming back, he shot 39 and finished at 144, tied with Cooper and Charlie Lacy, two strokes behind Horton Smith. Ten players were bunched within five strokes.

Jones broke away in the third round. Off early, he played the first nine in 33, picked up three more birdies coming home, and with two holes to play he was headed for 66, the best score ever shot in a U.S. Open. The strain was too much. He lost a stroke on each of the last two holes and finished with 68. Still, he began the last round leading Cooper by five strokes.

If 10,000 people were at the 1st tee in the morning, 15,000 crowded around it in the afternoon, all of them straining to see if Bobby could keep his string alive. Marshals carried ropes to hold the crowd in check while the players hit their shots, but as soon as the ball was in flight, fans bunched around them again. Jones and Joe Turnesa had to fight their way through the gallery. The day grew even hotter, and in the crush the temperature had to be well above 100 degrees.

Never comfortable in the lead, Bobby began the last round 4-5-5, losing three strokes to par, but even more frightening, losing four to Mac Smith. Playing an hour behind Jones, Smith had been seven strokes behind after fifty-four holes, but when he began the final round 4-4-2, he cut the lead to three strokes, then picked up two more with a par 3 at the 13th, where Bobby had made a 5. This was Jones's second double-bogey on a par 3 hole; he was in trouble, but as usual, he fought back.

At the 14th, a 444-yard par 4, Bobby ripped a 3-iron to ten feet, taking back one stroke, then pitched to a yard on the 16th, making his third straight birdie there. He was back to two over par and led by three strokes once again, but he faced a grueling finish.

At 262 yards, the 17th was a monstrous par 3. Throwing every ounce of his power into his swing, Bobby pushed his tee shot badly; the ball cleared a bunker on the right side of the green, hit a tree, and was never seen again. It might have fallen into a dried-up water hole covered by tall brown reeds and swamp grass, but no one saw it.

Turning to Prescott Bush, the referee, Jones said, "What shall I do?"

"The ball went into the parallel water hazard," Bush answered. "You are permitted to drop a ball in the fairway opposite the point where the ball crossed the margin of the hazard."

Bobby took a penalty shot and dropped another ball, pitched onto the green, and made 5.

The decision was the most controversial of Bobby's career. First, the status of that area as a hazard hadn't been clarified. Furthermore, since no one actually saw the ball fall into the hazard, many people felt the ball should have been declared lost, and Jones should have played another ball from the tee. He should not have been told to drop another ball near the marsh, leaving himself an easy pitch rather than another tee shot. In a newspaper column under his name, Gene Sarazen said the ruling tainted Bobby's victory, but an editorial in *The American Golfer* supported Bush's decision that the ball had gone into the swamp, entitling Jones to the drop. The decision stood, of course, but even so, Jones was four over par and once again only one stroke ahead of Smith.

Feeling he needed a birdie on the 18th, Bobby followed a good drive with a 3-iron onto the front of the green forty feet short of the cup. To reach the hole, his ball would have to run a short distance up a gentle slope, then climb a steeper grade. Over the years he had learned not to putt while he was breathing hard, and his breath was coming fast now. He studied the putt for a long time while he calmed himself, then struck it perfectly. The ball ran up both slopes, took a right-to-left break, and fell into the hole. A birdie 3 and a round of 75. His 287 was one stroke off the record Chick Evans had set in 1916, and once more he led Mac Smith by two strokes.

An hour later Smith came to the 18th still two strokes behind, needing an eagle 2 to tie, just as he had in the British Open. Because of the delay caused by the Jones ruling on the 17th, about six groups were waiting on the 18th tee, but they all stood aside and allowed Smith to go through. There would be no eagle; Mac made his par and finished at 289. Jones had won his fourth Open and the third trick of the Grand Slam.

Four thousand miles to the east, Bernard Darwin rose early to read the reports from Minneapolis, because, like most Britons, he was pulling for Jones. Seeing that Bobby had won, he went for a walk, and along the way he met J. H. Taylor.

PART TWO

"So Bobby has done it again," Darwin said.

"Wonderful, sir, wonderful," Taylor said. "I can't understand how Mr. Jones can keep it up."

Nor could Bobby. The demands of golf at this level were too much to bear. Whenever he played, he was expected to win, and the constant strain had worn on his nerves. He had had enough. In the stillness of a small room on an upper floor of the Interlachen clubhouse, Bobby decided that no matter what happened in the Amateur at the Merion Golf Club, he would end his career there, where it had begun, and play no more competitive golf.

Seeming to play stronger golf each day, Jones won the Amateur, racing through his first two matches by 5 and 4, his third by 6 and 5, then avenging an earlier 8 and 7 loss by defeating Jess Sweetser by 9 and 8 in the semifinals. After defeating Gene Homans, 8 and 7, in the final, Jones announced his retirement on November 17, 1930. He was twenty-eight. He left behind a staggering record. During the last eight years he had played in twenty-one national championships and had won thirteen. In the last eleven years, beginning in 1920 when he played in his first U.S. Open, through 1930, he had played in fifteen U.S. and British Opens and had won seven.

While he would no longer play competitively, Jones did not retire from golf. To maintain his own standards of amateurism, he had turned down a number of offers within the rules that would have earned him a lot of money, but now he was free to accept them. He signed a contract with Warner Brothers to write and star in a series of films called "How to Play Golf," showing him giving lessons to prominent movie stars like W. C. Fields, Joe E. Brown, Guy Kibbee, Douglas Fairbanks, Jr., James Cagney, Loretta Young, Edward G. Robinson, and Warner Oland (an early Charlie Chan).

He became a director of A. G. Spalding and designed a set of clubs that bore his name (they remained in production through 1973), and he wrote extensively on the game in newspapers, magazines, and books. Even though he no longer played in the Open, he came and watched. In 1932 at Fresh Meadow, not far from Inwood where Bobby had won his first Open, he was seen in the back row of Gene Sarazen's gallery wearing a dark blue suit, vest, tie, and straw boater, straining to see above the crowd.

He began building the Augusta National Golf Club, his dream course, and originated the Masters Tournament. He attempted a modest comeback in the first Masters in 1934, but he had been away too long, and instead settled easily into the role of host, playing the last round with the leader.

86

When the Second World War began, he entered the Army Air Forces as a captain and left in 1944 as a lieutenant colonel.

The Masters had been suspended from 1943 through 1945, but it resumed in 1946 with Jones again playing and acting as host. In 1947 he withdrew after two rounds because of what he described as a crick in his neck. It was nothing to worry about; he'd had them occasionally since 1926. He was forty-five; he never played in the Masters again.

He developed double vision for a period of six weeks in the spring of 1948. In May he had trouble using his right hand. At the same time he began stubbing his right foot as he walked, and his right side burned whenever he swung a club. On August 15, a small group of spectators followed as he played the Wahconah Country Club in western Massachusetts. He played poorly. He never played again. By 1950 he had to use leg braces and canes to walk.

In May of 1950 he was admitted to the Lahey Clinic in Boston for surgery to relieve a damaged spinal disk, believed to be pressing on a nerve. The following January at the annual meeting of the USGA in New York, Al Laney, a graceful and literate writer for the *New York Herald Tribune*, approached him as he sat on a low chair near the speakers' dais. As Bobby took Al's hands in both of his and pulled him close, Laney thought he looked the same as ever, but as they embraced, he looked down and saw the cold steel of a leg brace shining beneath the cuffs of Bobby's trousers. Laney was shocked; after a sudden indrawn breath, he moved away as quickly as he could, hoping Jones wouldn't see his distress.

The following April Jones saw Laney at the Masters and invited him to sit in his golf cart.

Placing a hand on Laney's knee, Jones said, "You ran away from me at the meeting."

Embarrassed, Laney muttered that he hadn't wanted to bother him, but Jones answered that he wanted his old friends to bother him. Laney asked about his condition.

"I've known you longer than anyone in golf," Jones said. "I can tell you there is no help. I can only get worse. But you are not to keep thinking of it. You know that in golf we play the ball as it lies. Now, we will not speak of this again, ever." And he smiled.

Jones had syringomyelia, a rare disease that attacks the spinal column, withers the muscles, dulls the sense of feel, causes persistent pain, and eventually kills.

Outwardly Jones maintained a sense of dignity and cheer. Inside he fought it. At first he refused to use a wheelchair, and he'd be damned if he'd acknowledge sympathy.

PART TWO

One morning, in the strange semiconscious state of first awakening, he tried to step out of bed and dropped to the floor. At first he lay there, not understanding, but in the next moment he realized he could not stand, could not walk, and never would again. The anger, the bitterness, and the hopelessness welled within him until at last the rage broke. With balled fists he pounded the floor and pounded and pounded and swore and cursed the chance that had changed him from a vibrant and vital man into an invalid.

The disease usually takes from ten to twelve years to kill. Jones fought it for twenty-three years. At the end he was bedridden, his body so emaciated he weighed only ninety pounds. He died on December 18, 1971, at sixty-nine.

Years before he died, Jones had talked about his condition and himself.

"When it first happened to me, I was pretty bitter, and there were times I didn't want to go on living. But I did go on living, so I had to face the problem of *how* I was to live. I decided I'd just do the very best I could."

Told of Jones's death, Ben Hogan said:

"The man was sick so long and fought it so successfully, I think we've finally discovered the secret of his success. It was the strength of his mind."

SEVEN
The Revival of Gene Sarazen

In the two decades following Coburn Haskell's invention of the rubber-cored ball, the integrity of the old established golf courses had been under constant attack. With no restriction on the size or weight, manufacturers had made balls that flew farther and farther, and as a result, the courses were playing shorter and shorter. Something had to be done. In 1921, the USGA and the Royal and Ancient tried to control distance by limiting the weight of the ball to no more than 1.62 ounces and the diameter to no less than 1.62 inches, smaller than the balls in common use until then. It worked, to a degree, but the change had other effects as well.

The old gutta-percha balls had been lighter (some had weighed only 1.3 ounces), and some had been bigger. Harry Vardon had played with a ball 1.7 inches in diameter. Some early Haskell balls had been 1.71 inches in diameter and some had weighed 1.72 ounces. Because the ball's girth had caused it to sit high up on the grass, early heroes like Vardon, Taylor, Anderson, and McDermott had played a sweeping stroke, picking the ball cleanly. Vardon was said to have played irons without nicking a single blade of grass.

The new standard ball caused a change in technique. Because it was smaller, it snuggled down in the grass, making it more difficult to hit. For solid contact, it had to be struck a descending blow, a difficult method that increased the possibility of hitting the ground behind the ball. On the other hand, when the ball was struck properly, it spun like a buzz saw and stopped quickly on the greens, an action that was ideal for American golf. While the low, running shot was proper for British seaside courses with their fine-bladed, close-cropped grass, firm soil, and consistent high winds that tossed a high-flying ball about, the more lofted shot was better for American courses, which were principally wooded inland layouts not subject to the sea winds.

This was the beginning of target golf. With the new technique, the ball could be carried to the green, flying over hazards and stopping within a few feet of the hole.

Uniformity was to last only ten years. Since the small ball still flew too far for American courses, in 1924 the USGA began experimenting with a ball that was lighter and larger. The new ball measured 1.68 inches in diameter and weighed 1.55 ounces. It flew higher than the smaller, heavier ball, but it required more precise striking, because with more surface acting against the air, a mis-hit shot veered off line more easily. Furthermore, it wouldn't fly as far or roll as much; golf courses, therefore, would play longer.

It was a failure.

Put into play in 1931, it lasted one year. It was so light the wind tossed it about too easily, and when it was putted, it quickly lost momentum and wouldn't hold its line. New specifications adopted for 1932 returned the maximum weight to 1.62 ounces but maintained the minimum diameter at 1.68 inches. The new ball was successful (it was in effect only in the United States; the rest of the world clung to the R&A's standard).

The game was advancing in other areas. The USGA had approved the steel shaft in 1924 (the R&A held off until 1931) and toward the end of the decade, steel had almost completely replaced hickory shafts. Jones had used hickory throughout his career, but toward the end of the 1920s, other players had learned that shots were easier to control with steel because the shaft twisted less at impact than hickory.

More important, however, the steel shaft led to the phenomenal growth that lay ahead. Because they were mass-produced in large factories, they could be manufactured quickly and in quantity. Expansion, however, was years away; by 1931 the world was entering the Depression.

With Jones gone, the game had no king, and attention at Inverness over the July 4 weekend focused on who might succeed him as Open champion. Walter Hagen was still around, but he was thirty-nine years old, and he had lived rather well. Mac Smith was still swinging smoothly and still finishing second, but Harry Cooper might still become a champion, and there were Horton Smith, Tommy Armour, Johnny Farrell, Leo Diegel, Bill Mehlhorn, and Gene Sarazen. Not one of them, though, had the star quality of Jones, and even if they had, it wouldn't have mattered.

The championship involved none of them; it was settled between a former amateur standout and a little-known club professional.

With eighteen holes to play, George Von Elm had 217 and led Billy Burke by two strokes, with Guy Paulsen, a young professional from Fort Wayne, Indiana, another stroke back at 220, followed by Hagen, Mac Smith, and Mortie Dutra at 221. A truly gifted player, Von Elm had been one of the country's leading amateurs through the 1920s, but at the end of the 1930 season he had announced he had become a businessman golfer, a classification unfamiliar to most of the public but perfectly clear to Von Elm. He had explained that while he didn't feel qualified to call himself a professional, if money prizes were available, he'd treat them as he would any other business income. Von Elm lived in California, where life is different.

He was thirty years old at the time, had a thin face, slicked back blond hair, walked with a swagger, and moved into the ball with a violent pivot. He was also a formidable competitor. When he played the first nine holes of the last round in 36, he seemed to have the Open won, because Burke had shot 36, too, and had failed to pick up any ground. No one else was close.

A moon-faced twenty-eight-year-old professional at the exclusive Round Hill Club in Greenwich, Connecticut, an expensive suburb of New York, Burke plodded steadily through the second nine, not making a move but not giving away strokes, either. Playing ahead of Von Elm, he shot 37 coming in, a stroke over par, finishing the seventy-two holes with 292.

Von Elm, meanwhile, was running into trouble, dropping one stroke at the 12th, and three more from the 14th through the 16th—four strokes gone at a critical stage. Now he was behind, needing a birdie on the short, 330-yard 18th to tie. After a drive into the fairway and a gorgeous pitch to twelve feet, Von Elm studied the line with unusual care, because he had missed a very short putt on the 16th. Satisfied, he rapped the ball firmly with his heavy putter and holed it, forcing a thirty-six-hole playoff.

Burke shot 73 the next morning against Von Elm's 75, but when he slipped to 40 on the first nine in the afternoon, Von Elm led by two with nine holes to play. Once more Von Elm let strokes slip away and again had to birdie the last hole to tie, 149–149. There would be a second thirty-six-hole playoff. Burke won the next day with 77-71—148 to Von Elm's 76-73—149. It had taken 144 holes to settle the championship. It was far too much. There would be no more thirty-six-hole playoffs; hereafter they would be over eighteen holes.

The Open had grown steadily through the 1920s. The fields had become larger and qualifying more complex. Only 360 players had entered in 1923,

91

when Jones had won his first championship, but 1,177 had entered in 1930, when he had won his last, and 1,011 in 1932. Sectional qualifying, which had begun with two sites in 1924 and three in 1925, had expanded to twenty by 1932. Prize money had grown from $1,745 in 1919, the first postwar Open, to $5,000 by 1929, with $1,000 going to the winner. While it had climbed no higher by 1932, it was a substantial amount of money for those grim times.

To help finance the growing prize fund, the USGA had begun charging admission fees in 1922, the year Gene Sarazen won at Skokie. Sarazen had been a cocky twenty-year-old then, but now he was a veteran of ten years of tournament golf and had been around so long he seemed much older than thirty.

Born to Italian immigrant parents and christened Eugenio Saraceni, Sarazen had grown up in Harrison, New York. His father, Federico Saraceni, was a bitter and solitary man who had studied for the priesthood in Italy but had given up his dream when his parents died. Disillusioned, he became a carpenter and later a contractor. He expected Gene to follow him.

A poor businessman to begin with, Federico also had wretched luck. He contracted to build twenty-five houses just before the United States entered the First World War, and when the cost of building materials shot up beyond what he could pay, his business failed. To help support the family, Gene left school and took a job as a carpenter. Later he worked in a munitions factory making artillery shells for Russia before it dropped out of the war, but he caught pneumonia and almost died. He was made a happy boy when his doctor told him not to return to the factory but to find a job outdoors.

A caddie as a young boy, Gene turned to golf, hoping to become another Francis Ouimet. He played at Beardsley Park, a nine-hole course in Bridgeport, Connecticut, where the family had moved a few years earlier, and found he had a flair for the game. Needing a job after he recovered fully, he became the shop boy at the Brooklawn Country Club, the plushest club in the city, and played well in some local tournaments. A professional now, he went to Florida for the winter tournaments late in 1919, played good but not spectacular golf and, most important, met Ramsey Hunter, the professional at the Fort Wayne, Indiana, Country Club. Ramsey was the youngest brother of Willie Hunter, the Englishman who had won the 1921 British Amateur and defeated Bobby Jones in the third round of the U.S. Amateur later that year. After playing a few rounds with Sarazen (Gene had changed his name before going to Brooklawn; Saraceni didn't sound crisp enough), Ramsey offered him a job as his assistant. Gene accepted.

He loved the informality of Indiana, and the club members liked him. Impressed with the low scores he had been turning in, they sent him to Inverness for the 1920 Open and were even more impressed when he finished third in qualifying. Gene, however, was disappointed when he placed thirtieth in the Open itself; he believed he was as good as anybody in the field.

A chunky five-foot-four inches, he was a very long hitter for his size, able to reach many par 5 holes in two strokes. He was cocky and sometimes abrasive, and like Jones, he fought a hot temper. When he and Jones were paired together in the 1921 Open in Washington, they made a deal: Every time one of them threw a club, he'd pay the other $5. No money changed hands; both of them could face down a challenge.

Born in February 1902, a month before Jones, Sarazen reached his peak first and, in fact, overshadowed Bobby for a time. After his first look at Skokie, weeks before the 1922 Open, Gene had written to a friend, "Bet on me."

The Open ended on July 15. In August he won the PGA at Oakmont, defeating, among others, Jock Hutchison and Bobby Cruickshank. Since Walter Hagen had won the British Open, promoters arranged a seventy-two-hole match between them for the "world championship," thirty-six holes at Oakmont and thirty-six holes at the Westchester Biltmore near New York. Sarazen won, 3 and 2.

After a weak defense of his Open championship the following year—he opened with 79, finished with 80, and placed sixteenth—Gene met Hagen in the final match of the 1923 PGA and beat him again on the second extra hole. No doubt about it; the cocky kid could play, and he wouldn't be intimidated by anyone.

He made exhibition tours, one of them around the world, and he became a celebrity. While he continued to play reasonably good golf, he began thinking life might offer something more. Under the spell of some agents who had lured him to Hollywood to film a series of slapstick one-reelers, he began to see himself as another Rudolph Valentino. It was all very flattering and alluring, and his ego, never restrained for very long, went out of control.

His idyll ended quickly, for Sarazen was also a man of good sense. In a moment of clarity after waking up one morning, he saw he had no future in movies—he was a golfer. He sprang out of bed, packed his bags, and went back to doing what he did best.

Sarazen played very well through the rest of the 1920s, winning the Miami Open three times, the Metropolitan New York Open, the Met PGA, the Long Island Open, and the Western Open, finishing second twice in the Canadian Open, and in 1928 placing second in the British

Open. He was usually a threat in the U.S. Open—fifth by two strokes in 1925, third by four in 1926, third by one in 1927, sixth by five in 1928, and third by two in 1929—but he couldn't win. After winning the 1923 PGA, he lost before the semifinal round of the next six. Yes, he was playing well, but not well enough. He thought of himself as a champion, and champions came in first.

Something was wrong. But what? It had to be his driving. Once a long, straight driver, he had become erratic. He could win in Florida, but the courses down there were more forgiving than those where the big championships were played. Sarazen's natural shot was a right-to-left draw, but too often he hooked wildly. Looking frantically for a cure, he changed from the interlocking grip he had grown up with to the overlapping Vardon grip. No help; back to the original. He tore down his swing and rebuilt it. That wasn't it, either.

Studying the swings of the more consistent players—like Jones, for example—he noticed they kept their grips firm throughout the swing. In contrast, he realized he relaxed his hands at the top of his backswing, and the club changed position on the way down, causing his loose shots. Perhaps he could maintain a better grip if his hands were stronger. Ty Cobb once told him he wore lead in his shoes as he warmed up to make his feet feel light when he took it out. Adapting this principle, Sarazen built a thirty-ounce driver, more than twice the weight of a normal club, and swung it an hour a day to strengthen his hands.

He did one more thing. He had never been good from sand, but although the USGA had banned the concave-faced sand iron after the 1930 season because of its cradling effect, he had seen what the flanged sole of that and other early sand wedges could do. Applying layers of solder to his niblick to create the flange and adding a few degrees of loft, he developed his own version of the sand iron, much lighter than the heavy original, which sometimes weighed twenty-three ounces. Sarazen's wedge transformed him from an indifferent sand player into one of the best—even money to get down in two from any bunker.

Gene's game slowly responded to his new training methods, but he lost the final match of the 1930 PGA to Tommy Armour because he smothered his drive on the last hole, a recurrence of his chronic ailment, and he was never a contender in the 1930 Open, placing twenty-eighth, beaten nineteen strokes by Jones. Still, he was encouraged by his fourth-place finish in 1931, and he felt 1932 might be a good year. His sand iron was working well, and he had taken steps to avoid a jinx. Gene had spent six years at the Fresh Meadow Country Club, a 6,815-yard par 70 course in New York, about a half-hour subway ride from Times Square, but he had left when the club was assigned the 1932 Open, because according to superstition, nobody wins at his home course. Hadn't he lost the PGA to Armour at Fresh Meadow? Furthermore, he had decided to change his tactics.

Sarazen had always been daring, ready to play a forcing shot if it might help him to win. It was one of the qualities that made him so attractive, but sometimes those bold shots had cost him dearly. He had made 7 on a par 5 hole in the 1928 British Open by trying to play an impossible shot and finished second. But even then he had lost heroically.

As 1932 began, Sarazen determined to be more conservative and not so impetuous. It seemed to be working; in fact, everything was coming together—his swing, always very simple and economical, slipped back into its old groove, the shots ranged far and true, and his sand play improved enormously. After a good winter, he went off on his annual campaign to win the British Open, played that year at Prince's, in southeastern England. Starting off with 70-69-70, Gene left the rest of the field reeling, closed with 74, and won by five strokes over Mac Smith. His 283 was thirteen under par (a high 36-38—74) and broke the record 285 set by Jones at St. Andrews in 1927. He didn't have a 6 on his card.

Gene hadn't much time to glory in his British Open championship. When he arrived back in New York, he had only about a week to prepare for the U.S. Open, which didn't seem like nearly enough time. It was only natural for his game to slack off after it had been so good in Britain, but his troubles went deeper. He was tired, and he didn't like the strain of being the favorite. Wanting to win is one thing; being expected to win is quite another.

As the championship began, Sarazen stuck to his conservative tactics, avoiding the deep bunkers that pinch the narrow openings to Fresh Meadow's greens and not firing his shots at the flags in his normal style, but he had to putt like a demon on the flattish greens to shoot 74 and 76. Those insignificant scores left him five strokes behind Phil Perkins, the former British Amateur champion, but he wasn't out of it yet. Five strokes wasn't too much to make up over thirty-six holes, particularly for a man who could finish like Sarazen.

Continuing to play cautiously the next day, Gene lost four strokes to par over the first eight holes, dropping seven strokes behind with twenty-eight holes to play, and that might be too much to make up. Gene had never been interested in second place; if he couldn't win, he had often simply gone through the motions, and now he seemed listless as he walked onto the 9th tee needing a par for 39 (par was 35-35—70).

The 9th was a little par 3 of only 143 yards with a menacing bunker across the front and others encircling the green. The green itself was narrow in front and broad to the back. With the pin set in the right rear corner, Sarazen drilled a 7-iron directly at the flag, but as the ball rose into the pale sky, it looked like it might be too long. It carried directly over the flag, hit the back of the green, and rolled onto the apron. After lining up the putt carefully, Gene rapped the ball right into the hole for a birdie 2.

Jones was watching from the veranda when Sarazen's putt fell. Turning to Reg Norton, a friend, he said, "This might set Gene off. Let's go see what happens."

Perked up by the birdie, Gene began spanking his shots with more authority and once again found that the harder he swung, the straighter the ball flew. His approaches were soaring straight at the flags, constantly leaving him within birdie range. After four routine pars, he holed a putt for a 2 on the 14th, another for a 3 on the 15th, and still another for a 4 on the 16th, a monstrous 587-yard par 5—three birdies in a row. Routine pars on the 17th and 18th, and Sarazen had played the last nine holes in 32, salvaged a 70, and picked up four strokes on Perkins. He was in the thick of the fight now, only one stroke behind with eighteen holes to play.

After having lunch with Jones and Norton, Gene rested, then went back to work. The last of the contenders to go out, he felt he needed 68 to win. The course wasn't playing easy, and nobody was tearing it apart, but three men had shot 69 in the morning, including Bobby Cruickshank, and two others had had 70s. Yes, he'd have to beat par to win.

A routine par 4 on the 1st—good start—but a pushed tee shot and a short approach into a bunker cost him a stroke on the 2nd.

Gambling on the 3rd, Gene cut the corner of the dogleg with a long, towering drive and had only a short pitch left. He made his birdie there, then another on the 4th. One under with a par 5 coming up, a chance for a third straight birdie. Two woods and a pitch to fifteen feet set it up, but the putt slipped past. No birdie there, but he made one on the 6th with a drive over a pond 220 yards out and a low, boring 2-iron to four feet. Two under now. A safe par on the dangerous 7th, a 412-yard par 4, and on to the 8th, 435 yards with a slight dogleg to the right and a light following wind blowing straight down the fairway. After a solid drive, Gene dropped his pitch on the front of the green and played two safe putts for another par.

Now for the 9th, the hole that had sparked his revival in the morning. Of all the holes at Fresh Meadow, Sarazen knew this one best. Since it lay close to the shop, he had often used the green to practice his putting; it didn't have a break he didn't know. Gene hit another lovely 7-iron shot fifteen feet away, then rammed the putt home. Another birdie 2, and he was out in 32. A 36 coming back would give him the 68 he wanted, but he had to guard against overconfidence.

A drive that cut the corner of the dogleg on the 10th, and a 7-iron left him fifteen feet from another birdie, but again a putt failed to drop. A drive and 6-iron to the 11th, and an eighteen-footer glided a few inches beyond the hole. One more par.

The 12th was another par 3, 155 yards to a long and narrow green tightly guarded by a cross bunker about 100 yards from the tee, with rough behind it and another bunker across the narrow opening. Another long peanut-shaped trap ran parallel to the left, and three more ringed the back left, back right, and the right.

Sarazen played a mashie, but his timing was off, and he hit behind the ball. He was lucky; it cleared the first cross bunker and fell into the rough forty or fifty feet from the hole. With the cup close to the near edge of the green, Gene faced a delicate shot. He felt he couldn't afford to give away a stroke by playing safe; he had to take a chance. He played his sand iron, hoping to drop the ball just a yard or so beyond the far bank of the bunker and give it a chance to roll close to the hole. Digging his feet into the ground, he came into the ball cleanly. It popped up, cleared the bunker, dropped softly onto the green, and trickled two feet from the cup. A soothing par; what a relief.

Meanwhile, Perkins and Cruickshank had been playing almost as well as Sarazen, and they had already passed the 13th, 14th, 15th, and 16th, four very tough holes. Gene couldn't let up now. He covered the 448 yards of the 13th with a drive and a 4-iron and made one par, then played a spoon to the 14th, a 219-yard par 3, and made another—five straight pars coming in.

As he walked to the 15th tee, word raced back that Perkins had finished with 70 and Cruickshank with 68, tying them at 289. To beat them, Gene would need that 68. He was three under par; four more pars would give him 67.

The 15th was a dangerous hole. It measured 424 yards—well within range of an iron club second—but out-of-bounds bordered the left, and since Gene drew his shots, even a slight mis-hit could cost him dearly. Steering away from the trouble, Gene drove into perfect position, but he underclubbed his approach and his 7-iron dropped short. Just then he had a lucky break. His ball came down on a patch of hard, bare ground, bounded onto the green, then stopped ten feet from the cup. He holed the putt for a birdie 3. Four under now; with three more pars he'd shoot 66. Two woods and a sand iron to the 16th and two putts for his par 5, another driver and another sand iron to the 17th, but a ten-footer hung on the lip. Three strokes ahead now and only one hole left. A solid drive split the 18th fairway, but with only a 7-iron left, Gene somehow pushed his approach into the right greenside bunker.

As the ball dropped into the sand, spectators swarmed around the green, forcing Sarazen to wait until marshals cleared an opening wide enough for him to play his shot. Putting his faith in his sand iron, Gene swung through the shot smartly. The ball jumped out of the sand and rolled eight feet from the cup.

Once again the gallery surged forward and formed a tight circle. He could take three putts from there and still win, but he tapped the ball right into the hole for his par 4.

Sarazen had shot 66, played the last twenty-eight holes in 100 strokes, and scored 286 for the seventy-two holes. He had won the Open by three strokes, matched the seventy-two-hole record Chick Evans had set back in 1916, and by playing the last thirty-six holes in 136 strokes, had set another record that would last fifty years.

Once again he had clawed his way to the top and revived what had seemed to be a moribund career. He would remain a familiar figure long after he could compete.

EIGHT
Dog Days of the Thirties

When Gene Sarazen blistered Fresh Meadow with his closing 66, Bobby Cruickshank, Abe Espinosa (brother of Al), and Johnny Goodman had each shot 68. Cruickshank and Espinosa were experienced professionals, but Goodman was a twenty-four-year-old amateur from Omaha who was already known as a first class player. He had beaten Jones in the first round of the 1929 Amateur, and a year later had shown it was no fluke by tying for eleventh place in the Open. In 1933, he was threatening again at the North Shore Country Club near Chicago.

The fifth of ten children who had been orphaned when they were quite young, Goodman had left school to help support the family, but he had enough resolve to complete high school at night. Times were hard then, and his finances were in such a sorry state in 1929 that to play in the Amateur he had traveled to Pebble Beach, California, on a railroad pass given to him by a friend. It was for a cattle car.

Insolvent he might have been, but Goodman was an outstanding golfer. Not a particularly long hitter, he was consistently straight despite a quick, three-quarter backswing and hand action that closed the clubface at the top. His irons were crisp and true, but his strength was in his short game.

After beating Jones, Goodman had lost in the next round to nineteen-year-old Lawson Little. He missed playing in the 1930 Amateur and lost his first-round match in 1931, but in 1932 he reached the final, eliminating a series of great players—forty-eight-year-old Chandler Egan, who had won the 1904 and 1905 Amateurs, Charlie Seaver, a Walker Cup player whose son Tom was to become a great pitcher, Maurice McCarthy, and Francis Ouimet, the defending champion. Goodman had lost in the final to Ross Somerville, a Canadian.

A short man with thick blond hair combed straight back, Goodman opened the 1933 Open with a dull 75 that left him seven strokes behind Tommy Armour, but then he began stringing together some great shots the next day, went out in 32 with four birdies and came back in 34 with one birdie, one bogey, and an eagle 3. While his 66 was a sensational score, it had its rugged elements. Goodman had hit only twelve greens, but chipping and pitching like a dream, he had saved par on each of the six he missed. His driving was superb. He hit every fairway, reached one par 5 hole in two shots, one-putted ten greens, took three putts from fifteen feet on the 11th, and of the twelve greens he hit, he was inside ten feet on four and never more than twenty feet from the cup. He had chipped in for his eagle on the 15th.

When Johnny followed with 70 the next morning, he jumped six strokes ahead of Ralph Guldahl, a twenty-one-year-old Texan, with 211 to 217, and when he began par-eagle-birdie in the afternoon, he figured he was eight or nine strokes ahead of the field. Then, believing he had the Open won, he began playing defensive golf. With the change in tactics, the shots that had been so crisp and decisive grew timid and tentative, and he lost six strokes in the next six holes. The harder he tried, the more frustrating it became as one by one the strokes slipped away. Mac Smith, Johnny's playing partner, finally settled him down, and he played the last nine in 37, for 76, but even though he had played well enough to post 287 and had come within one stroke of the seventy-two-hole record, he was in trouble.

Playing an hour behind him, Guldahl sprinted to the turn in 35 and started home with three pars and a birdie. In the eleven holes from the 4th through the 14th, he picked up nine strokes and caught Johnny. Not able to make up any more ground because of shoddy putting, Guldahl needed a par 4 on the 18th to tie and a birdie to win, but he hit only a fair drive, and his 3-iron approach slid off to the right and into a bunker. He blasted within five feet of the cup, but he missed his putt. Goodman won by a single stroke. When he holed out in 5, Guldahl snatched his ball from the cup and slammed it to the ground. Then he smiled sheepishly.

Throughout the early years of golf in the United States, a few gifted amateurs like Ouimet, Travers, and Evans had competed on fairly even terms with professionals, not only because of their natural talent, but also because they played in nearly as many tournaments and developed as sharp a competitive edge (Jones was the exception; somehow he kept himself competitive even though he played in only a few tournaments each year), but as the 1920s gave way to the 1930s, amateurs could no longer keep up with professionals. Goodman was the fifth amateur to win the Open, and he will probably be the last. An amateur hasn't won since, nor is one likely to. Times were changing.

Through the growing number of tournaments, professionals as a group were becoming tougher competitors. There was no Tour yet, but the seeds had been planted, and the professional was playing the game more and spending less time in his shop. The great players like Sarazen and Hagen could tour the country and the world playing exhibitions, but those with less talent and appeal looked to tournaments. Some of those tournaments had been around a long time, and some were relatively new. The Western Open began in 1899, and the North and South Open followed in 1903. New events grew, sponsored principally by regional or state associations. In 1905 the Canadian Golf Association conducted the Canadian Open, and the Metropolitan Golf Association inaugurated the Metropolitan Open.

As press coverage increased, resort managers staged their own events, aimed at grabbing newspaper space and luring tourists. By the middle of the 1920s, tournaments were played throughout Florida. The idea spread. The Texas Open began in 1922, the Los Angeles Open in 1926.

These were held during the winter, when many northern clubs were closed and the club professional was free to play. The living was often crude. When Sarazen first played in Florida, he bought a third-class steamship ticket from New York to Jacksonville for $23.50 and lived in an attic room of a boarding house for $5 a week. Bill Mehlhorn went to Florida in stages, stopping from town to town to give lessons and sell subscriptions to the magazine *Golf Illustrated*, and when he got there, he stayed in a tiny room furnished with an iron bed, a few scatter rugs to cover a bare wooden floor, and one window. The rate was $3.

Even though the players learned to live cheaply, it took determination to survive, because only a few tournaments paid prize money to more than fifteen or twenty places. Nevertheless, with more events to play in, the professionals became stronger tournament players, better able to control their emotions in tense competitive situations.

Fans loved to watch the pros play, and soon tournaments expanded into the spring and summer. The Florida swing began with the Miami Open in early January, then crossed the Intracoastal Waterway for the Miami Beach Open. The Pensacola Open followed next, then the pros went to Savannah, Georgia, back to Miami for the rich LaGorce, offering the staggering purse of $15,000, and to Pinehurst for the North and South Open the last week in March, which usually ended the tournament season. By 1930, though, tournaments had crept into the schedule later in the year. The St. Paul Open set its dates for August, and the St. Louis Open was played in September. Both offered prize money of $10,000, double the U.S. Open purse. The season ended with the Capital City Open in Washington, D.C., and the Mid-South Open in Pinehurst, both in the fall.

Western pros had their own circuit, beginning in December with the San Francisco Match Play Championship, then swinging through Pasadena, Glendale, and Long Beach. The Los Angeles Open offered $10,000 in prize money. The Southwestern tour began in El Paso in late January and moved through San Antonio to the Texas Open, to Waco, then to Hot Springs, Arkansas, for the South Central Open.

Players skipped from region to region, going wherever prize money was to be won. With the Depression deepening, tournament winnings became a means of survival.

Curiously, golf prospered during the Depression's early years. While factories closed and unemployment grew, play on Seattle's municipal courses rose from 190,000 rounds in 1929 to 280,000 in 1930. With the addition of a new public course in Atlanta, play increased by 73,668 rounds and climbed even further when its new course, named for Bobby Jones, opened toward the end of 1930.

Construction fed the increase. Seven new courses were opened around San Francisco in 1930 and three more were planned for 1931. Total cost, including improvements to existing courses, was less than $1 million.

Other cities and regions showed the same pattern of growth. Cincinnati had its best season ever, and so did Wilmington, Delaware, Philadelphia, and Albany, New York.

The euphoria couldn't last; within a few years the cycle reversed, and clubs were being abandoned faster than they were being built. In 1930, a year after the Wall Street collapse, the USGA had 1,134 member clubs, and in 1931 membership increased to 1,154. Then the slide began. Membership fell to 1,138 in 1932, not a significant drop, but the losses mounted as the Depression wore on, fed by the drought that struck the Great Plains. The USGA lost 283 clubs in 1934, the worst single year it ever had, reducing its rolls to 855, and it lost another eighty-eight in 1935. Membership stood at 767 clubs that year; it would never be that low again.

The loss of clubs also meant the loss of jobs for professionals; winning money in tournaments became essential. Bobby Cruickshank's club had closed only a month or two before the 1932 Open, which probably inspired him to his 69-68 finish. The declining number of club jobs made tournaments even more attractive.

At the same time, travel became too expensive for sizable numbers of Americans to play in the British Open. Beginning with Walter Hagen in

1922, Americans had won every British Open except for 1923, but with the world suffering hard times, Denny Shute, a twenty-eight-year-old Ohioan who won at St. Andrews in 1933, became the last American champion until Sam Snead in 1946, after the Second World War. Some Americans continued to play in the British—Gene Sarazen made it an annual rite, and Snead, Byron Nelson, Ed Dudley, Horton Smith, and Ralph Guldahl played at Carnoustie in 1937—but it was too expensive for most American professionals, and the small prize money wasn't worth the risk.

When Americans stopped coming in significant numbers, the British Open's stature diminished. Whether they could have won against the Englishman Henry Cotton in 1934 is moot; it was their absence that mattered.

Back home, Jones had retired, and Hagen had grown old, and none of those who looked so promising in the 1920s had developed into big winners. Mac Smith was forty when Jones retired, past the time when he could win, and good as he was, Harry Cooper didn't have a national championship in him. The game needed a hero, but no one stood above the crowd. From 1934 through 1936, the Open was won by Olin Dutra, Sam Parks, and Tony Manero, each of whom climbed briefly to the top, then dropped from sight.

Like Al Espinosa, Dutra was a descendant of one of the original Spanish landholders in California. Smitten with golf as a boy, he rose at four o'clock every morning and practiced before going to work. He did this for eight years, from the time he was fourteen until he was twenty-two and could play a very sound game. Then he gave up his job in the hardware business and became a professional. When he took the job as club professional at the Brentwood Country Club in Los Angeles, he taught relentlessly. For one four-week period he gave lessons from 8:30 in the morning until 5:30 at night, with half an hour off for lunch, six days a week.

A big, burly man standing six-foot-three and weighing 230 pounds, Dutra turned to tournament golf and won the PGA Championship in 1932. With that championship on his record, he was one of the better-known players in the 1934 Open at Merion, but he was off to a ragged start, with 76-74—150, leaving himself eight strokes behind the leader and trailing seventeen other men. The prospects of his winning were remote at best. They became worse than that when he was stricken overnight with an attack of dysentery, but he struggled around in 71 and 72 the next day and squeezed past Sarazen by one stroke, 293 to 294.

While it wasn't expected, particularly after his first two rounds, Dutra's winning couldn't be considered a shock, but by taking the 1935 Open,

PART TWO

Sam Parks became a folk hero, the man against whom all unexpected winners are compared. The only man to break 300 at brutally hard Oakmont, Parks shot 299 and beat Jimmy Thomson by two strokes, shooting 76 in the fourth round against Thomson's 78. Not one of the leaders broke 75 in the last round. This was the only tournament Parks ever won. A graduate of the University of Pittsburgh, he eventually left professional golf, became a salesman for U.S. Steel, and later joined Oakmont as a member.

Tony Manero was another who won only the Open, but he did it in style, closing with 67 in 1936 and breaking the seventy-two-hole record by four strokes. The record had stood at 286 since Chick Evans set it in 1916, but Manero played the Upper Course at Baltusrol in 282.

Those three Opens were played over remarkable sites that were landmarks in golf course design. Merion was laid out in 1912, Oakmont in 1903, and Baltusrol in 1921.

Created as a cricket club—somehow baseball never caught on—Merion crammed a golf course onto 100 acres of its property on the outskirts of Philadelphia in the middle 1890s, but the rubber-cored ball quickly made it obsolete. Golf had a firm hold by then, so the club reached farther into the country and bought 127 acres of worn-out farm land with a rock foundation covered by a thin surface of clay. Part of it had been used as a stone quarry, but even that was worn out by 1910.

Club officials assigned the job of designing the new course to a group of young members—H. Gates Lloyd, Rodman E. Griscom, Dr. Henry Toulmin, Richard S. Francis (an engineer who could read a transit), and the most fortunate choice of all, Hugh Wilson, an insurance salesman and first-rate golfer. Wilson spent seven months in England and Scotland learning the elements that make outstanding golf holes, and when he returned loaded with drawings of famous holes, he had a perception that few in the business of golf course design ever grasp.

Merion's new course was opened in 1912, but Wilson continued to refine it until he died in 1925. He relocated tees and greens to avoid a road that cuts through the property, put in new bunkers here and there, and remodeled some greens. Joe Valentine, the course superintendent, helped Wilson place the greenside bunkers. After Wilson chose the sites, Valentine spread white bedsheets while Wilson retreated down the fairways and called for adjustments until the effects were just what he wanted. In its final form, Merion had 128 bunkers, each created individually and faced with white sand. In his wish to give Merion the feel of British golf, Wilson planted Scotch broom hard against some of the bunkers and pampas grass in others. Scotch broom is a spiky bush that resembles the gorse that abounds through Scotland; a ball in the broom is probably unplayable.

104

Pampas grass is a tall clump that grows two or three feet high, then arches gracefully downward toward the sand.

While its bunkers give Merion its special look, its greens are what make the course great. They come in a variety of shapes and sizes, big when they must receive a long shot, small for the pitch; some shelved into a shoulder of a hill, some plateaued, some set at a sharp angle to the line of play, some sloping away at the back. Each is protected by some feature—a bunker, a creek, or impenetrable thatchy rough.

Merion has about all that can be asked for in a golf course. It is not excessively long—at its longest it measures only 6,500 yards—but it has long par 4s and short par 4s, one par 5 of 600 yards, another of 535, and its four par-3 holes range from 224 yards to 129. Some fairways bend left, others bend right; it has no blind approach shots and only three holes where the drive zone is hidden. Its last three holes are classics, perhaps the strongest finish of any American course that has had an Open: a 430-yard par 4 with an approach that must carry across the old quarry to a plateaued green, followed by a 224-yard par 3 played from an elevated tee back across the quarry to a low-lying green framed by bunkers and with a deep depression on the front, and ending with a 458-yard par 4 calling for a blind drive back across the quarry one final time, then a medium-to-long-iron approach played from a downhill lie to a bunker-guarded green that falls away at the back. To play those holes well in the heat of competition is to play first-class golf.

In completing the Grand Slam, Bobby Jones closed out Gene Homans on the 11th, one of the greatest holes in golf. At 370 yards it is just a drive and a pitch, but it is a masterpiece of design that proves the principle that great holes don't have to be long and brutal; they must, however, demand careful planning and precise execution. The ground runs level for about 180 yards, then begins a gentle drop of some eighteen feet to a lower level, bending slightly left. A narrow brook flows in front of the green, curls around the right and back, framing the green before it disappears into wooded land behind. Protected on the left by a bunker, the green is narrow in front and broad to the back, curving behind the bunker, and the surface is very firm. It is a teasing hole that invites birdies but collects a stiff price from those who take the chance and fail.

Sarazen was leading the 1934 Open when he reached the 11th. Playing cautiously, he drove with a 2-iron but hooked into the brook. He dropped another ball, played his third short of the green, pitched over with his fourth, hit a poor fifth onto the green yards from the hole, then took two putts. Three shots were gone, and he lost to Dutra by one.

The 11th has seen its lighter moments, too. In the same Open, Bobby Cruickshank was leading when he reached the 11th in the third round.

His mis-hit second dropped into the creek, but the ball hit a rock and bounced onto the green. Cruickshank flung his club heavenward, tipped his white linen cap, and cried, "Thank you, Lord." Suddenly his ears rang as the club whistled down and cracked him on the skull. Wiffy Cox, who was paired with him, fell to the ground laughing.

Merion is among the three best golf courses in the United States, ranking with Pine Valley, in the sandy wasteland of southern New Jersey, and with Pebble Beach. It is a model of strategic design, rewarding the well-executed shot, one of the two basic architectural principles. Oakmont, on the other hand, is an example of the other; it is perhaps the most severely penal course in North America, featuring hard and slick greens, bunkers everywhere you look, narrow fairways bordered by thick unyielding rough, and more than adequate length. Even under normal conditions it gives up low scores grudgingly, and under tournament conditions it can be impossible.

It is difficult to believe Oakmont was built in 1903, only five years after the invention of the rubber-cored ball. Courses built years later have become obsolete through advancements in the performance of the golf ball, but not Oakmont. With the exception of the Old Course at St. Andrews, it is the oldest course in the world where national championships were still being played in the 1980s.

It is equally difficult to realize that this masterpiece was designed by an amateur architect who had taken up the game shortly after his fortieth birthday, only a few years earlier. Henry C. Fownes, an iron and steel tycoon from Pittsburgh, not only laid it out, he also organized the club and served as president for twenty years. Obviously he knew how to get things done, because Oakmont was built in only a few months. Construction began on the morning of September 15, 1903, using hand labor. Twelve holes were finished six weeks later, when work was suspended for the winter, and the other six were done the following spring. It was ready for play by the fall of 1904, and it has remained basically the same ever since.

It is a point of pride among Oakmont members that every green except one has remained where Henry Fownes put it. The 8th was moved ten feet in 1951 to make room for the Pennsylvania Turnpike, which was built beside an old railway roadbed that separates the property into two tracts.

Anyone who plays Oakmont comes away muttering about its greens and its bunkers. Built on a base of only six inches of topsoil over a foundation of clay, Oakmont's greens are the hardest and fastest in championship golf. A ball dropped from shoulder height will roll off some of the more tilted greens and run into the rough.

It is the bunkers, though, that dominate the course. In the club's early years, Henry's son William, who won the 1910 Amateur, would wander about watching how the course was being played. If he saw someone taking a short cut or perhaps going unpunished for playing what he considered a bad shot, a bunker appeared practically overnight, because the Fowneses believed "a shot poorly played should be a shot irrevocably lost." One year after Oakmont opened it was pitted with 350 bunkers, an average of almost twenty a hole.

Nearly half of them disappeared over the next fifty years, filled in after William Fownes relented under pressure from members, but 180 remained, some of them golf landmarks. A serried series of ridges rising from sandy waste to the left of the 3rd and 4th fairways, creating eight bunkers from one, is called the Church Pews. A smaller copy borders the left side of the 15th. At 244 yards, the 8th hole is long enough as par 3s go, but in addition to its great length, it is protected by the Sahara, a huge expanse of sand that covers a quarter of an acre. The Sahara is 130 yards long and thirty yards wide; to keep it raked in the era before the powered raking machine, it took one man an hour a day three days a week.

In the beginning Oakmont's bunkers had a further distinguishing feature. Instead of being raked smooth, they were ribbed with deep, wide furrows that gave the old brown sand the look of a freshly plowed potato field. The grooves were dug the diameter of a golf ball and ran perpendicular to the line of play; a ball that settled between furrows was as good as buried.

Seeing Oakmont for the first time in the 1927 Open, Ted Ray spoke to O. B. Keeler:

Ray. Now those bunkers with the ribbed sand, I'll give you an illustration. What sort of game do you shoot?

Keeler. A feeble sort of 90.

Ray. Yes, and I'm a fairish sort of professional and a big chap to boot. And when we both get into one of those plowed bunkers, all I can do is knock more sand out of it than you can, because I'm bigger and stronger. We both have to play the same shot, whether we shoot 90, 100, or 75. There is no option. Two hundred yards from the pin or twenty yards, you pick out the niblick and blast. Now I think that is not as it should be. The recovery shot from sand—wind blown sand, not plowed sand—is a distinct golf shot; it calls for great skill and execution. The green may be a couple of hundred yards away, but in the furrow you or I or any man has nothing to do but explode. We are all on a level.

The furrows were modified and then eliminated after Fownes died, but aside from the altered position of the 8th green and the loss of half its bunkers, Oakmont has remained basically the same. Some greens are smaller than they were, and new tees have been built, stretching its length from its original 6,400 yards to more than 6,900 yards for championships—one, on the 17th, reduced the possibility of driving the green—but through the 1980s it remained a monument to the foresight of Henry and William Fownes.

Both Merion and Oakmont were designed by amateurs, but Baltusrol was done by A. W. Tillinghast, an eccentric genius who gave the country some of its finest courses—both the Upper and Lower Courses at Baltusrol, the East and the West Courses at Winged Foot, the San Francisco Golf Club, and Five Farms in Baltimore. National championships have been played on nineteen of his designs.

Tillinghast was an outrageous character with a remarkably diversified interest in and influence over golf. He was a decent player on the national level, an early syndicated columnist who annually ranked the country's leading amateur, professional, and women players (in 1916 he ranked Bobby Jones twelfth and predicted a great future for him), a contributor to and later editor of the magazine *Golf Illustrated*, a photographer of golf subjects, one of the founders of the PGA of America, an early collector of golf art and other memorabilia, and a promoter and organizer of golf tournaments. He put together the Shawnee Open that Johnny McDermott won in 1913.

Tillinghast was also a heavy drinker. Sometimes he would disappear for a month at a time, and when he drank at home, he'd frighten his family by reeling around the house waving a loaded pistol.

At other times he was a charmer. He was a flashy dresser, played the piano by ear, had a talent for sketching, talked like a dream, and he knew an amazing assortment of people. Walls of his house were covered with photographs of Lillian Russell, Jack Dempsey, and some alleged Czarist nobility. He knew everybody. He was invited to Mexico by the president of the country, and once he went to lunch with a man who called him by his first name and spoke at length of events in Russia. After lunch, Tillie's wife asked who the man was.

"Didn't I introduce you?" he asked. "He's some wild Russian—Trotsky."

While his behavior might have been outlandish, Tillinghast created wonderful courses that featured wide and generous fairways but small, tightly bunkered greens that demanded precise iron play. Tillinghast created the Baltusrol courses in the early 1920s when the club acquired enough additional property to expand to thirty-six holes and enough money to hire a professional architect. The club had been organized and the original eighteen holes laid out by Louis Keller, a squeaky-voiced gentleman farmer who also founded the New York Social Register. He named the club for Baltus Roll, a wealthy farmer who had owned the property and had been the victim in the area's most famous crime of the nineteenth century. On Washington's Birthday of 1831 he was dragged from his house and beaten to death by two thieves who believed he had money hidden away. Roll's land eventually came to Keller.

The Baltusrol property lies at the base of one of the Watchung Mountain ranges, a series of high ridges that run in a westerly direction through central New Jersey. The Upper Course, where Manero set the Open record, is the less heroic of the two, but it is a fine test of shots, nonetheless. It is rather tight and not overly long, clinging to the lower slopes of the mountain. The Lower Course is more Herculean, laid out on bottomland, where the ground levels off after its plunge down the slopes of the Watchung. The mountain is a critical element on the Upper Course, since a putted ball tends to fall away from it, but its effect is not so pronounced on the Lower, where tactics are influenced more by water hazards, which can be in play on six holes, and by its 126 bunkers.

The greens on both are generous, although they tend to be slightly larger on the Upper. Tillinghast was unique among the golf course architects who developed their technique in the United States—men like Charles Macdonald and his spiritual heirs Seth Raynor and Charles Banks, Donald Ross, Devereaux Emmet, and those who came later, like Robert Trent Jones and his sons Bob, Jr., and Rees, Pete Dye, and George and Tom Fazio. Not only was he a good player, which helped him design good tactical holes, but he was also an aesthete—he dabbled in art—which helped him create scenically beautiful holes. The 10th at Five Farms, for example, is lovely; its green is set behind a pond fed by a shallow brook, and a small arched footbridge leads through a line of weeping willows to the 11th tee.

Americans had become the best players in the world, and now, because of the imagination and understanding of the game by men like Tillinghast, Ross, the Fowneses, and Hugh Wilson, it had most of the greatest courses as well. More were coming.

NINE
The Frustrations of Sam Snead

At the time Manero won at Baltusrol, Tillinghast courses had been sites of the 1928 PGA, the 1929 Open, and the 1935 Ryder Cup Match. He had risen to the top in architecture, but another of his ventures was about to collapse.

Golf Illustrated was the lesser of the two major American golf publications. Its rival, *The American Golfer,* was the best golf magazine ever published. It began in 1909, filling a void left after a magazine called simply *Golf* folded. Walter Travis founded *The American Golfer* and served as its first editor. Other publications followed. Chick Evans edited *Golfers Magazine,* and when *Golf Illustrated* began publishing in 1914, we had three golf magazines of national scope.

Those early publications reflected the relative importance of the Open and the Amateur championships in the eyes of the editors and presumably the public. In 1909, for example, *The American Golfer* devoted seventeen pages to the National Amateur and only nine pages to the Open. In 1914, when Walter Hagen won his first Open, it rated six pages in *Golfers Magazine,* but Francis Ouimet's victory in the Amateur was given ten pages. While it was the same immediately after the First World War—the 1919 Amateur rated twenty-four pages in *The American Golfer* against eighteen for the Open—the difference narrowed in the 1920s, when Jones and Hagen were at their peaks. In 1926 Jones was given seven pages in *The American Golfer* for his U.S. Open championship, two less than for his loss to George Von Elm in the Amateur. By the middle 1930s, the ratio was eight for the Open and nine for the Amateur.

Golf magazines were flourishing. From its beginning the game attracted the more literate of the sports fans, and its literature is the best of any game's. To a large segment of British literati, Bernard Darwin was known as one of the world's ablest authorities on the works of Charles Dickens; to those who followed golf, he was known as the chap who wrote those perceptive unsigned pieces in *The Times* and the signed articles in *Country Life*. He also wrote regularly for *The American Golfer*. Others from unexpected backgrounds dabbled in golf writing. Arthur Balfour, the British prime minister from 1902 to 1905 and foreign secretary in the wartime cabinet, wrote extensively on the game. Chick Evans wrote; Max Behr was primarily a golf course architect, but he became *Golf Illustrated*'s editor, and Tillinghast was a terrible but enthusiastic writer. Jones was exceptionally good; his *Down the Fairway* and *Golf Is My Game* belong in any serious golf library.

Well known authors worked the game into their plots. Agatha Christie used golf in several novels (*Murder on the Links* and *Why Didn't They Ask Evans?*), Rex Stout wrote a mystery that ran in serial form in *Golfers Magazine*, and of course, P. G. Wodehouse composed roaringly funny stories on golf.

It was all great fun, and everybody was making money. Then it ended. In the desperate economic climate of the middle 1930s, advertising dried up, and the magazines collapsed. *The American Golfer* tried to keep afloat by combining with another publication called *Sports Illustrated*, but it lost its identity, and eventually *Sports Illustrated* died in 1937 (Time, Inc., bought the title and created a new magazine in 1954). For the first time since the early 1900s, America was without a purely golf publication with national distribution. The times were grim, indeed.

Against this backdrop of despair, a remarkable group of young golfers was struggling through the early years of their careers, driven by a fierce determination to succeed. Ralph Guldahl was born in 1911, Byron Nelson, Ben Hogan, George Fazio, and Sam Snead in 1912, and Lloyd Mangrum, Jimmy Demaret, Vic Ghezzi, Dutch Harrison, and Toney Penna were all about the same age. The money they could win sounded good, but tournament golf quickly ate up the profits, and it was not an easy life. They drove from city to city in broken-down cars barely able to move, lived in the cheapest hotels, washed their own socks and underwear in their rooms, and lived on chicken salad sandwiches when they could afford them. Sometimes two of them pooled their expenses and winnings so they could survive. They practiced long and hard and survived on determination alone. Despite the advances in equipment, course maintenance, and playing techniques of the next forty years, they would have dominated the pro Tour of the 1980s by force of will alone.

While he was the last of that group to take up tournament golf, Snead was the most colorful of them all. He was a genuine prodigy. He came out of the hills of western Virginia with a motley collection of clubs, some of them with hickory shafts, some with steel, and outplayed the most celebrated golfers of the day. He had his first success in September 1935, shortly after becoming a professional. Trying his luck in the Cascades Open in Hot Springs, Virginia, he finished third behind Billy Burke and Johnny Revolta and won $275, which seemed like a fortune. His performance, along with his long, loose, fluid swing, so impressed Fred Martin, the manager of the Greenbrier Hotel across the border in White Sulphur Springs, West Virginia, that he offered Snead a job as one of the Greenbrier's professionals for $45 a month, room and board, and any money Sam could earn teaching hotel guests at the resort's golf courses. Martin promised the teaching fees would not be penny ante. Sam's future was assured.

At the Greenbrier he practiced, played with guests, gave lessons (Alva Bradley, president of the Cleveland Indians, hired Sam as his personal instructor), and played in exhibitions. In one memorable match he teamed with Johnny Goodman, who was still an amateur, and beat Lawson Little and Billy Burke, 3 and 2. Burke was long, and Little was longer, but they couldn't match Snead's power. In winning the closed pro championship of West Virginia later in the year, Sam shot 61 over the Greenbrier's Old White course. He was ready for bigger things.

He made his debut as a full-time tournament player in September of 1936, at the Hershey Open in Pennsylvania. He finished fifth and won $285. He also made an impression on Craig Wood, his playing partner in the first round. Recognizing Snead's potential, Craig signed him to a contract to represent the Dunlop company, which meant $500 cash, two dozen balls a month, and a new set of clubs. Since he owned only eight clubs at the time, they were welcome.

Snead's power attracted the crowds, but it wasn't his major strength. He was superb with the pitching clubs—put him within 100 yards of the pin, and he'd get down in two strokes—an excellent putter, a terrific long-iron player, and he could recover from the sand with anybody. His driving caused him the most problems. He had an unpredictable and uncontrollable hook; when it was bad, the ball never rose more than a few feet off the ground and swerved sharply left. It became so bad he was ready to go home early in January 1937, but just before the Los Angeles Open, Henry Picard handed him a George Izett driver that weighed 14.5

ounces and had a swing weight of E-5—heavier than his old club—8 degrees of loft, and a stiffer shaft. (The normal driver bought from the shelf weighs about 13.5 ounces and has 11 degrees of loft.)

His driving straightened out right away. The harder he swung, the straighter the ball flew, and his confidence flooded back. A week later, Picard was leading the Oakland (California) Open after three rounds, but Snead closed with 67 and won by two strokes. First prize was $1,200; he was solvent again. Three weeks later he shot 68 at Rancho Santa Fe in San Diego and won the first Bing Crosby pro-amateur tournament, a one-day affair that paid $500 to the winner.

Snead decided to keep the driver and gave Picard $5.50 for the club, which was all Henry asked. Sam never parted with it. The insert was replaced many times and he had copies made, but no club ever felt as good. With it, Snead developed into the longest straight driver in the game. The galleries loved to watch his powerful shots that roared off right of center, then curled back with a slight right-to-left draw and ran forever once they hit the hard ground. Jimmy Thomson hit enormously long shots, but he wasn't as accurate. When they were paired together, their days turned into driving contests. It didn't help their scores, but it drew crowds.

Coming out of the hill country added to Snead's appeal. He was raw and unrefined, and he said funny things. After he won at Oakland, he saw his picture in a New York newspaper and wondered how it got there.

"I never been to New York in my life," he drawled.

He was a sensation, the biggest attraction since Jones, and he brought new life to professional golf. By early June he was listed as the favorite in the National Open, scheduled for Oakland Hills once again. Denny Shute had won the PGA and Byron Nelson had won the Masters, but they weren't given as good a chance as Snead, who had won nothing more than a run-of-the-mill tournament and a one-day pro-am.

Given a preferred starting time, Snead was off at 1:25 the first day, paired with Goodman, and in spite of a wobbly start, he made the prophets look good. He struggled through the first four holes, playing six terrible shots and twice taking four strokes to reach greens, but he picked up two birdies and fought back to even par after eight holes. He needed a par 3 on the 9th to make the turn in 36, but the 9th was a terror that day, 213 yards played through a left-to-right crosswind. Where earlier starters had used wooden clubs, Snead played a 2-iron and drilled a low, boring shot that found an opening no more than fifteen yards wide and died twenty-five feet from the cup. He holed the putt for a birdie 2. Out in 35, he played the home nine in 34 and tied the course record at 69, three under par. While it was a stunning start, Sam wasn't alone. Denny Shute tied

him, and five others were only a stroke behind. Even though Oakland
Hills had been extended to 7,037 yards, 157 yards longer than it had
played in 1924, it was not the terror of thirteen years earlier, when Al
Espinosa's 71 was the lowest score of the week and only Cyril Walker
had broken 300.

A 73 in the second round left Snead in fifth place, but with 70 and 71
on the last day he had 283, five under par and just one stroke over the
record. Sam's finish was spectacular. The 18th then was a par 5 of 537
yards that bent right at the drive zone. Snead covered the distance in two
strokes—a stinging drive and a 3-wood from a close lie that carried to the
green, bit into the turf, and braked eight feet from the cup. He coaxed
the putt home for an eagle 3.

It was common then for an announcer stationed at the 18th green to
call out the scores as each man finished. Some of them had loud voices
that carried long distances. Ralph Guldahl was on his way to the 10th tee
when he heard the announcer bellow, "Sammy Snead, 283." Guldahl
had seemed out of the race two holes earlier, but now he was the only
man left who had a chance to beat Snead. He had begun the last round
tied with Sam at 212, four under par and a stroke behind Ed Dudley, but
after playing the first five holes in two under par, he had dropped strokes
on both the 6th and 7th, two short par-4 holes. Even par for the round
then, he would have to play the last eleven holes under par to have a
chance, and that wasn't likely the way he was going. He might pick up a
stroke on the 8th though. Originally a strong par 4 of 450 yards, it had
been lengthened to 491 yards for the Open and made into a short par 5
that the longer hitters could reach with their second shots. It was definitely within reach of Guldahl, a big, strong man who stood six-foot-three
and weighed 210 pounds.

Knowing he had to make his move here, he cracked a long and straight
drive, then lashed a 2-iron that carried onto the green and checked
thirty-five feet from the hole. Two putts here would give him one of the
birdies he needed.

Normally a slow-moving deliberate man, Guldahl took hardly any time
with his putt. He looked it over quickly and gave it a firm rap. The ball
rolled on and on, took a slight break to the right, and dived into the cup.
Never mind the birdie, he had an eagle 3. Then, after a stinging 1-iron
to ten feet, another putt fell on the 9th, and Guldahl was out in 33. With
Snead in at 283, Ralph knew a 37 would beat Sam by a stroke, and a 38
would tie; if he couldn't shoot 38, he thought, he didn't deserve to be
Open champion.

Suddenly he was in trouble; as quickly as he had picked up those three
strokes, he lost two of them with bogeys on the 10th and 11th. Now he'd

have to play the next seven in even par for his 38, and that was no sure thing. At 555 yards, the 12th was the longest hole on the course, but if he were to pick up any more strokes, this hole and the short 13th offered the best opportunities.

After two big shots, Guldahl's ball lay on the edge of the fairway about thirty yards from the 12th green, leaving him a narrow opening between two bunkers. The ground leading to the green rose to a bold contour, then sloped downward to the hole, cut about twelve feet from the crest of the grade and another twelve feet from the troublesome rough along the green's edge.

Guldahl played an exquisite knock-down pitch that bit twice, trickled down the slope, and expired a yard past the hole. One stroke taken back. Now for the 13th, a treacherous little 142-yard par 3. A glorious 6-iron only a foot-and-a-half from the cup and another birdie. Three under par once again, and now, with pars the rest of the way, he'd have the Open. A chip-and-putt 4 at the 14th, then a mis-hit approach to the 15th looked costly. His ball sailed off to the right, heading for the 16th tee, but as a spectator jumped out of the crowd, the ball hit the heel of his shoe, bounced into a bunker, and settled next to a cigar butt. Guldahl blasted cigar and ball onto the green and saved his par.

Confident now, he made his figures on the last three holes, shot 69, and with 281 he beat Snead by two strokes, lowering the seventy-two-hole record once again.

While the 1937 Open was a triumph for Guldahl, it was the first of a series of disappointments for Snead. As the favorite, he had played under immense pressure he should not have been asked to endure and had done remarkably well. The tension had shown in practice, and it had shown in the first few holes of the tournament itself. He was a marvel to have pulled himself together and come so close to winning in his first attempt. With a swing like his, with all his power and finesse, he would surely win the Open soon—probably more than once. In the popular wisdom, his time was coming, but it wasn't there just yet. The popular wisdom was wrong.

Meantime, Guldahl gloried in his victory, which established him as the best player in the game only two years after he had given up in disgust. He had come close to winning the 1933 Open, but when he had needed a birdie to nip Johnny Goodman by a stroke, he had made a bogey. He was only twenty-one, though, and he had lots of time. He came back the next year and finished eighth, but when he dropped to fortieth place in 1935 and didn't do well in other tournaments, he went home to Dallas and announced he was giving up golf; his putting touch, always unreliable, had left him entirely. He tried selling cars with no luck at all, but other jobs were hard to find. Then someone asked him to lay out a nine-hole course in Kilgore, Texas, and he was back in the game. He began working hard on the practice ground, and when the feel of the clubs gradually returned, he tried the winter tour once again.

Because his young son, Buddy, had developed a lingering cold, Guldahl took his family to the California desert, where he worked at a few odd jobs and played in a few tournaments, winning practically no money. Then he ran across Robert Woolsey, who was in the movie business, and Rex Bell, an actor. After a few rounds together, Guldahl impressed Bell and Woolsey so much they staked him to $100 and sent him to the True Temper Open in Detroit in the spring of 1936. He won $240. Suddenly he was hot. He finished eighth in the Open at Baltusrol, won $360 in another tournament, then won the Western Open. At the end of 1936 he had won the Radix Trophy with a strokes-per-round average of 71.65, the lowest on the Tour. He had another great year in 1937. In addition to the Open, he won the Western, finished second in seven tournaments, including the Masters, and third in another. He was still going strong as 1938 began.

Through the first forty-one years, only Willie Anderson, Johnny McDermott, and Bobby Jones had won the Open in consecutive years. Guldahl became the fourth, winning easily at Denver's Cherry Hills Country Club, shooting 74-70-71-69—284, matching par, and beating Dick Metz by six strokes.

Guldahl had been comfortably in fifth place, four strokes behind Henry Picard after thirty-six holes, but their superb golf was overshadowed that day by a stranger event. As the sun settled behind Pikes Peak that cool spring evening, reporters swarmed around Ray Ainsley, an obscure professional from Ojai, California, insisting that he tell again how many fish he had killed slashing at his ball as it tumbled through the brook that purls beside the 16th fairway, and what exactly did he scream after every one of his nineteen strokes. Nineteen strokes on one hole was an Open record, superseding the eighteen taken by Willie Chisholm in a rocky ravine at Brae Burn in 1919. (Told how many strokes he'd taken, Chisholm insisted that Jim Barnes, who was ticking them off on his fingers, must have been mistaken. "Oh, Jim," he cried, "that cannot be so; you must have been counting the echoes.")

Guldahl had climbed to a level very few have reached. Beginning in 1936, when he had returned to tournament golf, he had won three consecutive Western Opens, the 1937 and 1938 U.S. Opens, placed second in the Masters Tournaments of 1937 and 1938, and won it in 1939. He was not at his best at match play, though, and never did well in the PGA until he reached the semifinals in 1940.

He had his best year in 1939, winning three tournaments in addition to the Masters, placing seventh in the Open and finishing the year as third leading money winner. He finished fifth in the 1940 Open and then teamed with Snead to win the Inverness Four-Ball. That was the last tournament he was to win. He played only occasionally through the war years, and then his game left him once again, and he quit.

While he was at his peak, Guldahl was the most dangerous big-tournament player in the game, but while he could play inspired golf, he didn't excite the galleries. When he and Snead won the Miami Four-Ball in 1939 and the Inverness Four-Ball in 1940, he played the better golf of the two, but Sam drew the crowds. Snead had that glorious, flowing, rhythmic swing, his hands set well above his head at the top of the back-swing, his feet planted firmly as he moved toward the ball, and then his hands whipping through the hitting zone in a burst of power, and his lithe, athletic body carrying into the finish, hands high again; Guldahl, on the other hand, squirmed himself into position, took a full shoulder turn, keeping his feet firmly anchored and moving his lower body very little, drew the club back with explosive speed, and struck the ball with what looked like an uppercut delivered with the force of a sledgehammer. It looked awkward, but it worked. While Snead's personality sparkled, Guldahl's was drab. With a more athletic build, Snead's clothes fit as if they were tailored specifically for him; Guldahl's hung like wash on a clothesline. Snead stood erect and walked with a long, loping stride and a spring in his step; Guldahl slouched and plodded along with bent shoulders. Snead's face showed emotion when he hit either a good or a bad shot, and occasionally he amused the gallery with a funny remark delivered in a funny accent; Guldahl was quietly impassive.

Snead had the personal magnetism Guldahl lacked.

Sam came along at just the right time. Professional golf—indeed, all golf—needed a star, and he looked like the answer. Seeing Snead's swing, Jones said he couldn't understand how he ever shot above 70. Nor could others, and they followed him faithfully, glowing as he played one flaw-less shot after another. He might not have saved the professional Tour, because plenty of great golfers were around—Byron Nelson, Gene Sarazen, Henry Picard, Denny Shute, Harry Cooper, Dick Metz, Paul Runyan, and Guldahl—but he created newspaper copy when golf needed a bright personality.

Because of his personal appeal, Snead drew a devout following that never wavered in its belief he was the greatest player ever, but the more objective fans wondered if he might be just a passing phenomenon when he shot 77-76-76-80—309 at Cherry Hills and tied for thirty-eighth place, twenty-five strokes behind Guldahl. A year later, at the Spring Mill Course

117

of the Philadelphia Country Club, Sam created a spark of doubt in even his most passionate fans.

Like Cherry Hills, Spring Mill was designed by Bill Flynn, who had worked on the construction crew that had laid out Merion. When the job was finished, Flynn and Hugh Wilson, Merion's designer, had planned a partnership, but Wilson withdrew because of his failing health and Flynn joined instead with Howard Toomey, a prominent Philadelphia engineer, in the firm of Toomey and Flynn (the name had a nice bouncy rhythm). Flynn handled the designs and Toomey the construction and finances. While they did a number of outstanding courses other than Cherry Hills—a completely new course at Shinnecock Hills replacing the old Willie Dunn layout, Indian Creek in Miami Beach, Kittansett near Boston (site of a Walker Cup Match), the Cascades Course of The Homestead at Hot Springs, Virginia, and the James River Course of the Country Club of Virginia near Richmond—Spring Mill was not one of their better works.

Trying to identify what sets one golf course apart from another is a futile exercise. Some courses simply play better than others, make better use of the land, or perhaps have better land to begin with. Spring Mill simply didn't play as well as the four previous Open courses. As it was set up for the championship, it had a par of 34-35—69, the lowest par ever, and even though it measured a reasonable 6,786 yards, it didn't have the heroic finish of Merion, which was shorter, or of Oakland Hills, Cherry Hills, or Baltusrol. Spring Mill finished with two mild par 4s of 328 and 368 yards, then an uphill par 5 of 555 yards. Although the members played two other holes as three shotters, the 18th was Spring Mill's only par 5 for the Open. The 8th, at 479 yards, and the 12th, at 480, seemed long enough to be three-shot holes, but because of the great distances tournament players were hitting the ball and the hard ground in the days before full-scale irrigation systems, both were within range of second shots and were designated par 4s.

In his third full year on the circuit, Snead had played superb golf since the beginning of 1939. He had won three tournaments by June, tied for third in another, and finished second in the Masters, beaten a stroke by Guldahl. This time he looked like a sure winner.

Opening with 68, 71, and 73, Snead had gone into the final eighteen holes a stroke behind Johnny Bulla and tied with Craig Wood, Denny Shute, and Clayton Heafner, a gruff redhead from North Carolina who had blistered Spring Mill with 66. Both Bulla and Heafner fell apart in the afternoon, but Sam returned to his form of the first two rounds, lost two strokes on the first nine, birdied the 11th, then began picking up one par after another. Byron Nelson, meantime, had been in top form, winning the North and South and Phoenix Opens, but rounds of 72, 73, and 71 had left him five strokes behind Bulla. With faint hope, Nelson began the fourth round with a birdie on the 1st, a strong 450-yard par 4, but he dropped a stroke at the 3rd, a tricky downhill par 4 with a tightly bunkered green, and then played thirteen consecutive holes in par. A putt finally fell on the 17th, dropping him to one under par, and he played the 18th in a steady par 5 for a 68.

In with 284, all he could do was wait and hope, and he had very little to hope for, because Snead, playing behind him, was on the 17th tee needing two pars for 70 and 282.

The fairway of the 17th swings right in the drive zone, and the ground climbs to a higher level at the small, bunker-guarded green. Sam drove into just the right spot, but in making sure to clear the trouble in front, he overshot the green, chipped five feet short of the hole, and then inexplicably left his putt short. A bogey 5. No harm done; a par 5 on the 18th would give him 283, still good enough to beat Nelson, and with two good shots he might even reach the green and make an easy birdie. Still, Sam looked rattled.

While Nelson had already finished, Wood and Shute were playing behind him, and Sam didn't know how they were doing, but he could hear an occasional cheer, leading him to believe he needed a birdie.

Tearing into his drive a touch too vigorously, Snead hooked the ball into a tight lie in the rough 275 yards from the green. In spite of his bad lie, Sam believed he might get there with a good brassie, and even if he didn't catch the ball flush, he'd have only an easy pitch left. The birdie was within reach.

His decision was a disaster. Sam topped the shot; the ball bounced and rolled up the slope and dived into a steep-faced bunker probing into the fairway from the left about 110 yards short of the green. Now he had a serious problem. The bunker face was about five feet high, low enough to clear with a wedge, but trying to reach the green, Sam played an 8-iron. The club didn't have enough loft. The ball slammed into the face of the bunker and wedged between the cracks of some freshly laid sod. Three strokes gone. From an awkward stance, he chopped at the ball through sand and sod, tore it loose, and sent it hopping into another bunker forty yards short of the green. With his feet on the grass outside the bunker, Sam played his fifth shot onto the green, but the ball rolled forty feet beyond the hole. He putted three feet past, then left his next putt short. An 8.

An awful hush settled over the crowd as Sam staggered off the green and lurched toward the clubhouse. Women's eyes watered, and men patted him softly on the back. Other players turned away to save him embarrassment.

Sam shot 74 and finished with 286. Now Nelson, not Snead, was the man to beat.

Wood followed Snead to the 18th needing a birdie to tie. After two decent woods, his approach stopped on the front edge of the green, and he holed the putt for 72 and the tie. Like Snead, Shute needed only to par the last two holes to win, but he bogeyed the 17th, hitting his approach behind a tree, and joined Nelson and Wood at 284.

While Shute was never a threat in the playoff, Nelson and Wood struggled throughout the long afternoon, never more than a stroke apart. Both men were out in 33, and when Nelson three-putted the 17th and Wood birdied, Craig went ahead for the first time. He had the Open in his hands with only one hole to play, but he pulled his second shot into the gallery lining the 18th fairway, hitting a spectator (a relative of Alfred M. Landon, the losing candidate in the 1936 presidential election). The mistake didn't look too costly when he struck a superb pitch four feet from the cup, but Nelson meanwhile had played his second shot close to the green and pitched eight feet away. Nelson made his birdie, but Wood's putt veered off and slipped past the cup. Both men had 68; they would have to play again the next day.

Nelson effectively ended the second playoff in the early holes. From a downhill lie on the 3rd, he pitched next to the hole for a birdie, and on the 4th, a long, sweeping dogleg to the right, he drove past the nest of bunkers at the bend and ripped a low 1-iron directly at the pin. The ball hit the front of the green, rolled past the hole, then curled back, following the contour of the ground, and wedged between the flagstick and the edge of the cup. An eagle 2. He had played consecutive par 4s in five strokes and had left Wood far behind, finally shooting 70 against Wood's 73. His accuracy over the thirty-six holes of the playoff had been phenomenal. Six times his approach shots had hit the pin, each time with a different club—a wedge, a 9-iron, 6-iron, 4-iron, 1-iron, and a driver.

Nelson finally had his Open, but Snead's problems continued. A year later he opened with 67 and was only one stroke off the lead going into the last round at the Canterbury Golf Club in Cleveland, but he closed with 81, his worst Open score ever, and dropped to sixteenth place. Lawson Little, the man who had won the U.S. and British Amateur championships in 1934 and 1935, tied with Gene Sarazen at 287 and won the playoff.

One other man shot 287, but he was disqualified for playing out of turn. Ed (Porky) Oliver, an overweight, good-natured man was among six players who dashed to the 1st tee when they saw a storm making up. Joe Dey, the USGA's executive secretary, had been starting the field, but he was in the clubhouse having lunch, and only a marshal, the unofficial lady scorer, and a few reporters were standing by the tee when the over-eager players arrived. The marshal told Oliver he wasn't to start, but Porky insisted. Merrell Whittlesey of the *Washington Post* and Maury Fitzgerald of the *Washington Times Herald* pleaded with him, telling him of another player who had been disqualified for playing out of turn in a qualifying round, but Porky ignored them. Five others played out of turn also, and they were all disqualified.

Hearing what had happened to Oliver, the other players objected, and Little and Sarazen insisted on including Porky in their playoff. It was no use; the disqualification stood.

Oliver was heartbroken. He sat at his locker for a long time with his head bowed and an occasional tear running down his cheek.

"It's not just the honor of having a chance to win the Open," he said. "I need the money, and I need it badly."

The disqualification of Oliver, followed by the emotional scene in the locker room, had a further unfortunate effect. They clouded a round of golf that should not be forgotten.

Little was in the clubhouse with 287 when Sarazen holed out on the 9th green. As he walked toward the 10th tee, Gene was told he needed 34 to tie. Most of the other leaders were blowing up. Frank Walsh, whose 213 had led at fifty-four holes, was on his way to 79, Snead was shooting 81, Picard 76, Nelson and Mangrum 74, and Ben Hogan, the new sensation, 73.

Sarazen was thirty-eight years old. He had won the Open eighteen years earlier, and he had just shot 38 on the first nine, two strokes over par. To shoot the 72 he needed, he had to better his first nine by four strokes over a trying course that finished with a 615-yard par 5, a 230-yard par 3, and a 441-yard par 4. He knew in his soul that this would be his last chance at another Open—those opportunities didn't come often to men of his age—and while he was among the strongest finishers the game had ever known, he wasn't overconfident.

"I'll try to get it," he said.

He picked up one birdie on the 11th and another on the 13th, a short par 5, but ahead lay some of the toughest holes in golf. He got past the 14th and 15th with routine pars, but he had to hole a breaking eight-footer to par the 16th. Now for the 17th and 18th, two holes that had cost him bogeys in the first two rounds.

When he missed the 17th green and left his pitch thirty feet short of the hole, Gene's cause seemed hopeless, but never in his life had Sarazen given up. He rammed that thirty-footer home, then played two powerful shots onto the home green. He had a fifty-footer for a birdie 3 that would have won, and he almost pulled it off; the ball stopped eight inches from the cup. He tapped it in, grinned, waved to the crowd amid thundering applause, and strode to the clubhouse. He had his 34 and had caught Little. Maybe he had one more Open in him.

Sarazen was no match for Little the next day, shooting 73 against Little's 70.

Little had been the greatest amateur since Jones. Through 1934 and 1935 he had won thirty-two consecutive matches in two U.S. and British Amateur championships and the 1934 Walker Cup. The public had expected great things of him when he became a professional in 1937, and he looked as if he would live up to those predictions by winning the 1940 Open, but he never threatened to win again. He developed into a reliable player who could win the weekly events, but not the major championships.

He was succeeded as Open champion by Craig Wood. Born a year before Sarazen, Wood was a member of three Ryder Cup teams, but he seemed jinxed. The 1935 Masters had been in his hands when Sarazen holed a 4-wood for a double eagle 2 on Augusta's 15th hole, and he had missed a four-foot putt on the 18th at Spring Mill in the first playoff round against Nelson. By 1941 he had a problem with his back and had to play with a heavy leather and steel corset strapped around him. It restricted his movement, but he couldn't play without it.

The 1941 Open was played at the Colonial Country Club in Fort Worth, Texas, the first time it had been south of the Potomac River. When Wood took seven strokes on the first hole, a long par 5, he was about to walk in, but he was talked out of it, and he finished the round in 73. He added 71 the next day, and in a driving rainstorm posted two rounds of 70 on Saturday. His 284 beat Denny Shute by three strokes.

After the presentation ceremony, Wood piled into a car with Fred Corcoran, tournament director of the PGA, and Bill Cunningham, sports columnist for the *Boston Post*, to drive to his hotel. As they approached a driving range, Corcoran suggested that Wood might want to hit a few balls, just to keep his swing grooved.

"You're right," Wood laughed. "It comes and goes. It's the kind of thing you can't turn loose once you've got it going or it might never come back."

They stopped, and in front of a dazzled group of weekend golfers and the astonished range owner, the new National Open champion hit a bucket of balls.

That was on June 7. Six months later, Pearl Harbor was bombed, and America entered the war. The Open was suspended for the duration.

Several developments had taken place in the previous few years. Prize money for the Open, which had risen to $5,000 in 1929, reached $6,000 in 1938. It was climbing, but other tournaments offered more. The Los Angeles and the Miami Opens paid $10,000, the Tam O'Shanter $11,000, and the St. Paul Open, played over a municipal course, offered $7,500, less than it had in 1930, but still more than the national championship. But money was never the main attraction of the Open; this one was played for glory.

Meanwhile, two matters involving equipment were troubling the USGA.

Through most of his career, Harry Vardon had carried six clubs—a couple of wooden clubs, a putter, a cleek, mashie, and a pitching club. Chick Evans had used only seven when he set a scoring record that lasted twenty years. This was common; the players relied on their skill in creating shots with the clubs they had—the runup, the high pitch, the half shot. While most men played a niblick from the sand, Fred McLeod had used his mashie. He rarely failed to recover.

As golf swung into its first great expansion, following the First World War, the number of clubs in a set grew. Jones carried fifteen clubs, but as we moved into the 1930s, players carried more and more. At the peak of his amateur career, Lawson Little carried thirty-one clubs. A public links player named Arthur Anderson carried thirty-two, because, he said, he couldn't afford for someone else to have an advantage.

Most tournament players carried from twenty-one to twenty-five clubs. It was common to carry two or three putters—one for fast, one for slow, one for medium-speed greens—maybe two drivers, some trouble clubs like a baffy or wooden cleek (a shallow-faced wood with a short shaft used to play from the rough), and perhaps a putting cleek. More lofted than the normal putter, the putting cleek was used for long putts over bumpy greens, a common condition in a time when many professional tournaments were played over heavily used municipal courses.

In this atmosphere, the game's governing bodies grew increasingly alarmed and afraid the game was being changed by the specialty clubs. Some believed the USGA should have acted years earlier and banned the sand wedge, and they certainly didn't approve of chippers.

After a few years of debate, spurred by those who believed a tournament should be won by the man with the best swing, not by the man with enough clubs to fit every situation, in 1938 the USGA and the R&A imposed a limit of fourteen clubs. Caddies applauded.

PART TWO

The ball had been causing at least as much concern as the clubs. As technology improved, manufacturers had added more zip and made it go farther. No golfer ever lived who didn't yearn for more distance, but the leading professionals and the top amateurs—the showcase of the game— were turning some of the grand old courses into obsolete antiques, too short to test the best players. Of the fifteen courses where the Open had been played from its beginnings through the First World War, none had been used since then. Gone from the rota were Myopia, the site of four Opens in eleven years, and the Chicago Golf Club, the host to three. Baltusrol, The Country Club, and Shinnecock Hills returned, but their courses were entirely new. The game had changed, and it didn't fit those grand old courses.

Recognizing that even those courses built in the 1920s and 1930s might become obsolete, the USGA established a limit on the golf ball's performance. Size and weight had been regulated since 1921, but in 1941 its distance was limited, too. At one time the USGA had planned to standardize construction of the ball, but the regulation didn't pass a vote of the executive committee, and a velocity test was adopted instead.

Experiments had been conducted for years. A golf ball testing machine was built in 1926 by Harold A. Thomas, a professor at Carnegie Tech in Pittsburgh. The machine incorporated a series of pulleys that served some mysterious purpose and fired the ball by compressed air. Never used by the USGA, the project was dropped in 1930, but the Armour Research Foundation of Chicago developed a more reliable machine. Balls were struck by a metal hammer and driven through a tube 10.6 feet long and timed by a photo-electric device. Occasionally a ball escaped the tube and ricocheted around the room while the startled engineers dived for cover, but it worked. It became the official testing machine, and the rule limiting a ball's initial velocity went into effect in 1941.

One other minor development changed the appearance of the game. From the beginning, golf was considered a game for the fall, when there's a nip in the air. Players wore coats. As its popularity grew and the game moved into summer, the golfer shed his coat, but he continued to play in a long-sleeved shirt and tie. The more vain wore their shirts with French cuffs and flashy cufflinks.

Old conventions were breaking down. When he beat Craig Wood at Spring Mill, Byron Nelson became the first Open champion to win wearing the kind of short-sleeved, open-necked shirt we've all come to associate with golf.

TEN

Byron Nelson's Poor Timing

Ever since Sam Snead made his 8 on the seventy-second hole at Spring Mill, the 1939 Open has been remembered as the one Snead kicked away. While that is indeed what happened, it is regrettable it is so little remembered as the Open Byron Nelson won, for Nelson was just as much a victim of a cruel fate as Snead.

No man can be more than the best of his time, and Nelson was that. His time, however, coincided with the Second World War, when the Open was suspended for four years, and golf was confined mainly to less memorable Tour events. Were it not for the war, who could tell how many more Opens—or PGAs or Masters—Nelson might have won. As it was, when the Open resumed, in 1946, Nelson was burned out, ready to give up the life of a touring professional golfer. During those few years, though, he was one of the six best golfers to have come along since the First World War, ranking with Bobby Jones, Ben Hogan, Jack Nicklaus, Arnold Palmer, and Sam Snead. Some will say Nelson was the best of them all.

As the years flew by, the memories of his accomplishments dimmed. This is unfortunate, for Nelson was more than a great player. He not only raised scoring standards to levels never seen before (he shot a monotony of 66s), he developed a new method of striking the ball that eliminated his chronic hook, became the most reliable driver the game has known, and probably was the best long-iron player ever. No man has it all, however. Nelson was not an escape artist; if he missed a green, he lost a stroke. Nor was he a first-class putter. He had a wristy stroke and lacked the finely tuned touch of the great putters like Jones and Walter Hagen.

But Nelson was a leader, an innovator, and because of him, golf, unlike other games, improved during the war years. From 1942 through 1945, Nelson won twenty-eight tournaments. In 1945 alone he won eighteen Tour tournaments, eleven of them in succession—a record that is to golf what Joe DiMaggio's fifty-six-game hitting streak is to baseball. He averaged 68.33 strokes per round, an incredibly low figure.

It is generally assumed that Nelson had no competition when he won those eighteen tournaments, that all the other great players were in the armed services (Nelson was classified 4-F because his blood needed an unusually long time to clot). That isn't true. Nelson played in thirty-one tournaments in 1945, but Snead, who was still in the Navy, played in twenty-seven and won six. Ben Hogan spent most of the year in the Army Air Forces, but he had finished second to Nelson in the Tam O'Shanter Open in July, and after being released from the service in August, he joined the Tour full time a week after Nelson's streak of eleven consecutive victories ended. Hogan played in nineteen tournaments that year and won five. Other well-known players competed, too: Craig Wood, Jimmy Demaret, Claude Harmon, Henry Picard, Denny Shute, and Harold (Jug) McSpaden, who finished second to Nelson seven times. (Like Nelson, McSpaden was exempt from military service.)

Nelson was setting his records against the best players in the game, not against weak fields. In one six-week period beginning with the Knoxville Open, Hogan's first tournament after his discharge, the winners were, in order, Nelson, Hogan, Snead, Snead, Nelson, Hogan. Jimmy Hines intruded then, but Nelson and Hogan won the next two.

While Hogan and Snead lived to play golf, to Nelson it was a means to an end. His heart was in a cattle ranch near Fort Worth, Texas, where he had grown up, and whenever he won money, he'd think of it in terms of how much livestock he could buy. He won lots of money; he was, in fact, the most consistent money winner the game has known.

In most tournaments in those times, only the low twenty to forty players won prize money, and some paid fewer. The Henry Hurst Invitational of 1941, for example, paid twelve places, the 1941 Open paid only twenty-eight, the Western Open twenty-five, and the 1942 Masters only twelve. From 1940 through 1944, Nelson was *in the money* in 113 consecutive tournaments.

He was capable of dazzling streaks of scoring. He shot 66 in the opening round of the 1937 Masters without holing a sizable putt, and then, trailing Ralph Guldahl by four strokes going into the last round, played the 12th and 13th holes in five strokes— a birdie 2 followed by an eagle 3. On those same holes, Guldahl scored 5 and 6, a six-stroke swing. Now leading by four (he had picked up two strokes in the early going), he went on to win.

Five years later, in 1942, Hogan and Nelson tied at 280 in the Masters. In the playoff, Hogan covered the eleven holes from the 6th through the 16th in one under par and lost five strokes. Nelson was devastating: He birdied the 6th, a par 3, made an eagle 3 on the 8th, and at the dreaded Amen Corner, birdied the 11th, 12th, and 13th. Nelson shot 69, Hogan 70.

Even though Nelson dominated golf for the next three years, winning tournaments at a rate never seen before and raising scoring and playing standards to higher levels, he considered 1939 his best year, because, in addition to winning the Open, he also won the North and South and the Western Opens and reached the final of the PGA Championship, where he lost to Henry Picard in thirty-seven holes. Those were four of the game's most important tournaments, and he had nearly won them all.

Nelson was twenty-seven then, and no one could guess how long he could go on. But the war years wore him down. During 1943, Nelson and McSpaden played 110 exhibition matches at military hospitals, War Bond sales drives, and fund-raising functions for the Red Cross and USO. At one stretch Nelson played for nineteen straight days on a tour with Bing Crosby, Bob Hope, and Johnny Weissmuller. It wasn't as bad as being shot at, but it dulled his interest in tournament golf. Still, his golf had been profitable. In 1944 and 1945 Nelson won $101,303.45 in War Bonds. (This was their mature value; if he had cashed them right away they would have been worth $75,977.51.) The cattle ranch was coming closer.

When the fighting ended with the promise of a postwar paradise and the Open was revived, along with the full pro Tour, Nelson decided the 1946 season would be his last. He was no longer willing to pay the cost demanded by championship golf. The tension tore at him inside and made him physically sick. He had been so violently ill the morning of his 1942 Masters playoff with Hogan that Ben had gone to his room at the Bon Air Hotel and offered to postpone the round. Nelson declined.

The 1946 Open was played at Canterbury once again, and Nelson was in the thick of it, two strokes behind Hogan and Vic Ghezzi after thirty-six holes. An estimated 12,000 spectators swarmed unchecked over the hills of Canterbury the last day, restrained only by ropes carried by marshals. Players and caddies had to push and shove through the crowds, and the players hit their shots through narrow funnels of fans. The unruly crowd might have cost Nelson the championship. After he played his second shot on the 13th hole, a par 5, the gallery rushed ahead and crowded close behind his ball. The marshals strung their ropes, hoping to hold back the fans, but they were so close to Nelson's ball that when Eddie Martin, his caddie, ducked under the rope carrying the heavy golf bag, he lost his balance and stumbled into Byron's ball. The accident cost Nelson a penalty stroke. Even with it, he shot 69, three under par, and held the fifty-four-hole lead with 211. Ghezzi and Lloyd Mangrum, a former soldier who had been wounded in combat in Europe, were next at 212, followed by Hogan at 213.

The first of the leaders to go off in the afternoon, Ghezzi shot 72, but his 284 didn't look good enough. Nelson and Mangrum next. Nelson was a stroke ahead of Mangrum, and he could beat Ghezzi's score by two strokes if he could par the last three holes. He made his figures on the 16th, but his birdie putt on the 17th grazed the edge of the cup, and he missed again from three feet. One shot gone, but a par on the 18th would do it. He never had a chance. He hooked his drive, hooked his second, leaving it thirty yards short of the green, and made 5. He was tied with Ghezzi. Mangrum played the last three holes in par, picked up two strokes on Nelson, and also climbed into the tie.

Meanwhile, Hogan and Herman Barron had been closing in. Ben had made a miserable 7 on a par 4 hole early in the round, but he had fought back and needed only to par the last three holes to inch ahead. He made his 5 on the 16th and his 3 on the 17th, and with only the 18th to play, he could win with a birdie or tie with a par. After a good enough drive, he fired his approach directly at the flag and watched the ball come down eighteen feet above the cup, leaving him a downhill putt on a slick green. Hogan never flinched. Going boldly for the cup, he putted two feet past, then missed coming back. He finished a stroke out of the tie. Barron faltered, too, and tied Hogan. The first postwar Open would be decided by a playoff.

Nelson, Ghezzi, and Mangrum all shot 72 the next morning, forcing another round for the afternoon. Nelson and Ghezzi raced ahead over the early holes, but then they began playing wobbly golf. Some putts fell for Mangrum, and after seventeen holes he led Ghezzi by one stroke and Nelson by two.

The strain was telling on Byron. Already annoyed by the incident with his caddie and with his shaky finish in the fourth round, his nerves were on edge. When he played a miserable chip on the 17th, he slammed his club back into his bag, wrenched out his putter, and then rammed it back in when he bogeyed. His last chance had gone; he was two strokes behind with only one hole to play. Ghezzi, though, could still catch Mangrum.

It was late in the day as the three men moved to the 18th tee. Rain poured down, and the sky was luminescent with flashes of lightning streaking from the black storm clouds above. First up, Mangrum hooked his drive into the left rough, but the others hit the fairway. To reach the green, Lloyd would have to hook his second around a tree jutting into his line of play. The shot didn't come off, and Mangrum's ball landed on the face of a bunker. Ghezzi's approach ran over the green, and Nelson's was short. (Byron eventually made his par, but it didn't matter.)

Mangrum was away. Taking too much sand, he left his ball well short of the hole. Ghezzi next. From rough grass at the edge of a bunker, he chipped his ball true to the hole but with enough pace to roll four feet past. Mangrum's putt for the 4 missed, and now Ghezzi could force another tie by holing his putt. The 4,000 spectators who hadn't fled the storm crowded around the green as he crouched over his ball. His stroke was a little too light, and the ball stopped inches short of the cup. Mangrum holed out for 72, while Nelson and Ghezzi shot 73. Mangrum became the first postwar Open champion.

Nelson never entered another Open. Two months later he lost to Porky Oliver in the quarterfinals of the PGA and retired. Burned out from the years of competition, he went home to his wife, Louise, and his 230 acres in Roanoke, Texas. He was thirty-four.

PART THREE
Hogan, Palmer, and the New Era

ELEVEN
Snead's Final Agony

The war had ended in 1945, and by 1947 everyone who had seen combat was out of the military service if he wanted to be. Released veterans flocked to colleges, and many of them took up golf. Courses that had been out of action during the war were revived. Part of the Congressional Country Club in the Maryland suburbs of Washington had been a training ground for the OSS, but it was turned back to the club. Wykagyl in suburban New York had plowed up its 1st and 2nd holes for a victory garden. Augusta National had become a turkey farm, and beef cattle had grazed the fairways of Baltusrol. By now they were all back in shape, and the game was poised for enormous expansion. We had had 5,691 golf courses operating in 1931, but only 4,870 in 1947. We had lots of ground to make up.

Open prize money, which had climbed to $6,000 in 1938, jumped to $8,000 in 1946 and to $10,000 in 1947, with a first prize of $2,000. No tournament offered less, and several of no lasting merit offered more. Prize money for the Reno, Denver, and *Philadelphia Inquirer* Opens, along with the Colonial Invitational, reached $15,000; the Western Open offered $12,500, and the carnivalesque All American Open outspent them all. Played at the Tam O'Shanter Country Club in Chicago and run by George S. May, a Barnum-like former Bible salesman, the All American put up $30,000 in prize money. Judged by money alone, the Open stood shoulder to shoulder with the Richmond (California), San Antonio, and Esmeralda Opens.

PART THREE

Still, the Open had other rewards, like the promise of high-paying exhibition matches, bonuses from equipment manufacturers, and lasting fame. Mangrum had won only $1,500 in prize money at Canterbury, but he was swamped by offers the next day. First he received $10,000 to represent Tam O'Shanter on the Tour, another showbiz coup by May; Wilson Sporting Goods gave him $5,000 for using its equipment; he was given $2,000 in appearance money at another tournament (the PGA killed that type of arrangement within a few years); and he received $3,000 for other endorsements. As Open champion, Mangrum could also command the same money for exhibitions as Nelson and Hogan, the highest paid players—$300 for weekdays, $500 for weekends.

Fame is fleeting, though, and you had to cash in quickly. Five years after Nelson retired to his ranch, he and a MacGregor salesman tried to set up an exhibition tour, but they had trouble lining up dates; Nelson had been away too long. He wanted the exhibition tour, though, so when he received an invitation to the Crosby, he practiced for a month, won the tournament, and the exhibition dates were filled.

Nelson's ordeal was over, but Snead's was in full flower. By now it was generally agreed he was jinxed in the Open. He had been only one stroke off the lead after fifty-four holes in 1940 but stumbled home in 81; shot 76 and 77 in 1941 and never figured, and after an opening 69 in 1946, had followed with indifferent scores of 75-74-74. Nonetheless, it was inconceivable that Snead would not win the Open.

Since the beginning of 1945, when he had rejoined the Tour full time, Sam had won eleven tournaments—five in 1945 and six in 1946—but 1947 was shaping up as an off year. While he had finished in a tie for third place in the fifty-four-hole Crosby, he hadn't threatened to win anything else. He had finished twenty-fourth at Los Angeles, twentieth in the Masters, and out of the money in most of the others. Then, a week before the Open, Sam shot 273 and finished in a tie for fourth place in the National Capital Open near Washington. His game was coming together at just the right time.

The Open was set for the St. Louis Country Club, not a particularly difficult test. While Colonial had measured 7,005 yards in 1941 and Canterbury 6,926 in 1946, St. Louis could stretch out to only 6,532 yards. Among the great courses, only Merion at 6,544, was as short, but St. Louis wasn't nearly as strong as Merion. The players quickly took advantage of its leniency; thirteen men broke its par of 71 in the first round, and Harry Todd, Henry Ransom, and Chick Harbert shared first place with 67s. When Bobby Locke, a puffy-jowled South African, shot 68, the Open had a serious foreign threat for the first time since 1920.

To call Locke unorthodox was to understate. He dressed in knickers and usually wore a long-sleeved white shirt with four-in-hand tie and a white linen cap. Every ball he hit headed to some distant target off to the right, then made a sweeping turn like a boomerang and landed in the geometric center of every fairway. He even hooked his putts. Using a wristy stroke with a hickory-shafted blade putter old enough to grow moss, he swept the face open on the backstroke, then flapped it closed coming through the ball. He holed everything he ever looked at.

Along with a number of others, Locke was lucky to be in the Open, because some of the qualifying rounds were chaotic. In St. Louis the whole round was canceled and played again because some players had been permitted to improve their lies and others hadn't. Locke qualified in the Metropolitan (New York) section, but he should have been disqualified because he cleaned his ball on the greens, which was permitted in PGA tournaments but not in USGA events. It violated the Rules of Golf. Since some 70 percent of the field did the same thing, however, everyone was excused.

They were not excused from another violation. The PGA also permitted players to carry sixteen clubs; some who forgot the USGA's fourteen-club limit were thrown out.

Controversies over the rules continued into the championship itself. Club manufacturers had agreed seven years earlier to limit the depth and width of the grooves that line the faces of iron clubs. The control became effective in 1942, but five years later some manufacturers still made clubs with wider and deeper grooves than the rules allowed. Players had to buff them down at the site of the Open.

In this atmosphere, Snead came as close as he ever would to winning the Open, but he had to play some of the best clutch golf of his career to get there. With nine holes to play, Lew Worsham, a twenty-nine-year-old Virginian who had played most of his golf around Washington, D. C., seemed to have the championship in hand. He had opened with two 70s, shot 71 in the morning round of the last day, then rushed around the first nine of the afternoon round in 33. A 36 on the second nine—level par—would bring him in at 280, a record score. His prospects looked good after a birdie 3 on the 10th dropped him to five under par for sixty-four holes, but he lost three strokes over the last eight holes, shot 38, and finished with 71 and 282. Now Snead had a chance.

Playing about half an hour behind Worsham, Snead had rallied after a shaky start, and with a birdie on the 15th, he had pulled even with Lew. If he could pick up one more stroke, he'd have 281, all he needed to win. He made his par 3 on the 16th, and his fans scrambled ahead to watch him play the 17th, a short par 4 of only 365 yards. They groaned when he bogeyed. The best he could hope for now was to tie, and to do that he'd

135

have to birdie the 18th, a much harder hole than the 17th. Snead tore into his drive, hitting it about 300 yards right into the middle of the fairway, then strung a lovely iron eighteen feet right of the hole. As his adoring gallery fidgeted, Sam had to wait for Dick Metz and Bud Ward to hole out; then, while Worsham watched, he rolled his ball right into the bottom of the cup.

The crowd roared, Sam smiled, and Worsham walked over and shook his hand. It was as courageous a putt as any man ever holed, and it forced the fourth playoff in the last five Opens.

Playoffs are often anticlimactic, but in this one both men played superb golf, and the finish is among the best remembered in the game's lore.

Snead was in command throughout the early holes, leading by one stroke after a first nine of 34. Worsham pulled even with a birdie on the 12th, but Sam moved two strokes ahead with birdies on the 12th and 15th. With three holes to play, Snead looked unbeatable, but Worsham hadn't given up. His tee shot to the 16th, across a valley to a plateau green, ran to the back edge, perhaps twenty feet past the hole, and he rolled it in for a birdie. One behind now, with two to play.

Both men played sloppy tee shots on the 17th. With the best approach from the left side, the drive should be played into the bend, where the fairway takes a gentle turn to the right, but Worsham hit a big soaring hook that carried over the gallery, past the rough, over the trees, and into the 18th fairway, which runs parallel to the 17th. Snead tried to cut his shot around the corner, but instead hit the ball into the right rough. From where the two balls lay, Worsham had the better angle to the green, even though he was much farther away. Lew's approach dropped onto the green and held, but Sam's pitch came out of the tall grass with very little backspin, hit the front edge of the green, and rolled all the way across, six or seven feet into the rough. He chipped six feet from the cup, then missed the putt. When Worsham got down in two, they were even, and it was down to the home hole.

The fairway of the 18th climbs over two levels, leaving a blind approach to a heavily guarded green. A bank rises behind and to the right of it, rough lurks to the left, and a bunker reaches across the front. Outdriven throughout the day, Snead was away and hit a gorgeous approach about twenty feet from the hole. Worsham's ball skidded across and off the back edge, stopping just short of heavy grass crowding the borders of the green. He would have to chip.

Taking very little time, Lew played a firm shot that rolled to the hole with a bit too much pace, grabbed a corner of the cup, then dribbled two-and-a-half feet past.

Now, with the Open there to be won, Snead played a perfectly terrible shot. Putting downhill on a somewhat racy green, he left his ball well short. No quick killing, but if he holed this delicate little downhiller, he'd have no worse than a tie, and if Worsham missed, well, Sam would have his championship. He walked immediately to his ball and began to set up, but with the easier putt, Worsham wanted to put more pressure on Snead by holing out first. Who putted first depended on whose ball lay farther from the hole.

"Wait a minute," Lew called to Sam. "Are you sure you're away?"

Snead stopped. Not sure of the proper procedure, they called to Ike Grainger, the chairman of the USGA's rules committee, who was standing at the edge of the green. When Grainger reached them, Sam insisted he had the right to continue putting.

"Sam," Grainger said, "not unless you're away."

Grainger called for a steel tape measure. Stretching the tape from the cup first to Snead's ball, then to Worsham's, Grainger found that Sam lay thirty and one-half inches from the hole and Lew twenty-nine and one-half inches. Snead would putt first. But the damage had been done.

About 5,000 spectators ringed the green, but only the steady drone of a passing plane broke the deathlike stillness as Snead settled over his ball. He did not have an easy putt; it was downhill with a left-to-right break. Sam tapped the ball a touch too lightly for it to hold its line; the crowd moaned as the ball turned away from the cup and stopped two inches outside the hole. Worsham rolled his putt in for 69 to Snead's 70. Worsham was the Open champion, and Snead was frustrated once again.

Sam had two other close finishes in later years, but neither was as tragic as those failures in 1939 and 1947. Two years after his loss to Worsham, carelessness or bad judgment cost him a chance to tie Cary Middlecoff at Medinah near Chicago.

Opening with 75, Middlecoff played the next thirty-six holes in 67 and 69 and went into the last round at 211, three strokes ahead of Clayton Heafner, who had 214, and six ahead of Snead with 217. Strung tight from the tension, Middlecoff stumbled around the last eighteen holes in 75 and finished with 286, two over par. Now both Heafner and Snead were within range.

Heafner pulled even by the end of fourteen holes, but then he bogeyed the 16th and missed a birdie opportunity on the 18th: 73 and 287.

Sam still had nine holes to play when Middlecoff finished. Out in 36, he'd have to play the rugged second nine in 33 to catch up, and he hadn't shot under 71 so far. Suddenly the putts began to fall, and he birdied two of the next five holes, picking up the strokes he needed. If he could match par the rest of the way, he'd have the tie. Par on the 15th, and another on the 16th; two more to go. Before Medinah was revised in the early 1980s, the 17th was a dangerous par 3 of 230 yards with a massive carry across a wide body of water. A deep bunker guarded the front, and the rear of the green rose sharply. The tee shot was all carry, with no room for error. Snead hit a good-looking shot dead at the pin, but a slight wind blowing into his face held the ball back a trifle. It hit well to the front of the green, drew back down the incline, and rolled three feet off the putting surface.

He seemed to be in no danger; he could either putt the ball or chip it. He chose to putt, planning to hit down on the ball and let it skim across the apron, which should brake it. It was a common shot, one used all the time, but Sam didn't notice that his ball was sitting in a small depression. When he stroked the ball, it popped up quickly, jumped across the fringe, and rolled eight feet past the hole. He missed his par putt, and now he needed a birdie on the 18th, a par 4 of a little over 400 yards with a gentle left-to-right swing. His approach skipped over the green, and his chip stopped three feet short. He shot 34 instead of 33, and finished with 70 and 287, one stroke too many. Again.

The agony went on, but that was Sam's last close approach to winning, although he was second once again, at Oakmont in 1953. He went into the last round a stroke behind Hogan, but Ben outplayed him and won by six strokes.

Snead never lost his sense of humor over his failures (perhaps they were offset by his enormous success in everything else). Talking to a friend about Oakmont, Sam was asked about that last round.

"Were you tight, Sam?" the friend asked.

"I was so tight you couldn' a' drove flax seed down my throat with a knot maul."

He continued to play, nevertheless, and when he wrapped up his career, he had appeared in thirty-one Open championships. As late as 1968, when he was fifty-six, he placed ninth. He played his last Open in 1977, when the USGA extended him a special exemption from qualifying to honor the fortieth anniversary of his first appearance. He missed the thirty-six-hole cut. He had made the cut in twenty-seven Opens, the last time in 1973 when he was sixty-one, and shot 295, placing twenty-ninth. A year later, at sixty-two, he felt he had a chance to win at Winged Foot after some wonderful practice rounds, but he had to withdraw before the tournament began because of severe chest pains. He thought he might be having a heart attack, but X rays showed he had broken two ribs when his tractor had overturned on him on his Virginia farm.

Hardly anyone has meant so much to the Open as Snead, and certainly no one else captured—and broke—so many hearts. He was the focal point so many years, and so often he seemed ready to win, but he always failed.

He added continuity, someone the fans could rely on, giving them hope one moment, despair the next.

Through his forty-year Open career, Sam finished second four times, third once, fifth twice, and placed among the low ten in five others. While he was struggling with the Open, he won three Masters Tournaments, three PGA Championships, one British Open, and seventy-eight other Tour events. In 115 Open rounds, from 1937, when he was twenty-five, through 1977, when he was sixty-five, Sam averaged 73.37 strokes per round; for every seventy-two holes he averaged 293. But he never won.

TWELVE
The Emergence of Ben Hogan

In the spring of 1949, a secretary ripped open a special delivery letter in an office building on East 57th Street, a fashionable shopping district in New York littered with art and antique dealers, expensive department stores like Bergdorf-Goodman, high quality tailors, and the jewelry emporium of Van Cleef & Arpels. The secretary sat in none of those monuments of commerce; she toiled in the office of the United States Golf Association. She frowned as she took an entry form from the envelope and saw the signature. It was from Ben Hogan, which of itself shouldn't have been surprising, because entry forms from Hogan had been arriving since 1931, but she knew that Hogan had been injured gravely when his car had collided with a Greyhound bus on a misty morning in February near the small west Texas town of Van Horn. Ben and Valerie Hogan had been on their way home to Fort Worth from Arizona, where Ben had lost a playoff to Jimmy Demaret in the Phoenix Open.

Hogan had won the National Open in 1948, shooting 276 at the Riviera Country Club in Los Angeles. He would be the defending champion at Medinah, if he played. A note addressed to Joe Dey, the USGA's executive secretary, arrived with the entry form. It read:

> I am getting along great just now, up all day and walking as much as possible. The doctor tells me walking is the only cure for my legs, so that's my daily thought and effort.
>
> Enclosed is my entry for the Open, with the hope that I will be able

to play. Up to now I haven't taken a swing, but miracles may happen. Would you please do me a favor and not release my entry? If I can play I should like it to be a surprise. I hope and pray that I may see you in June.

Hogan did not play; he withdrew before the qualifying rounds.

The accident, a head-on collision, took place on February 2. Seeing the headlights of the bus and realizing he couldn't avoid the collision, Hogan flung himself across Valerie to protect her. The reaction probably saved his life; he would have been killed if he hadn't moved, because the shaft of the steering wheel rammed through the car seat. Although the shaft missed him, the rim of the wheel caught his left shoulder, breaking his collarbone, and the motor was driven backward, pinning his left leg and slamming into his stomach. Valerie was trapped under Ben and couldn't move. It took an hour to free them.

Hogan was laid on the back seat of a car, becoming grayer by the moment and slipping in and out of consciousness. After what seemed like an age, he was taken to a hospital in Van Horn for X rays, then rushed to a larger facility in El Paso, about 120 miles away. When the damage was assessed, Hogan had a broken collarbone, a broken pelvis, a broken ankle, a broken rib, and damage to his bladder. The injury to his left leg would have the most lasting effect on his career, and in the weeks ahead it would become serious.

Hogan was lucky to be alive, but he was a tough man with a strong mind and a lean and hard body. His recovery was going so well he was to be released from the hospital on February 16, only two weeks after the accident. He wasn't. A blood clot moved from his bruised leg through his heart, into the pulmonary artery, then into his right lung. His condition became critical. Another larger clot could kill him. The vena cava, a vein leading from the leg to the heart, travels through the stomach. It would have to be tied off in the abdomen. A specialist was flown in from New Orleans, by a B-29 bomber on a training mission, to perform the two-hour operation. Hogan was encased in a cast from his armpits to his hips, and he was given six blood transfusions over the next few days. But he was alive.

Before he submitted to the operation, Hogan asked the surgeon if he would be able to walk and play golf again. He was assured he would, and so, still in his cast and lying in his hospital bed, he began squeezing rubber balls to strengthen his hands. The long, slow, painful trek back had begun.

He was released on April 1 and went home to Fort Worth on a train. His legs were still swollen, and doctors told him the swelling would last another five months. They advised him the only way to strengthen his legs was by walking. Home again, he'd walk around the living room every morning, adding five laps each day.

As his strength grew, he walked outdoors. Occasionally he'd be gone a long time, and Valerie would comb the neighborhood in the car, often finding him waiting for her.

By late summer he was strong enough to chip and putt. In September he went to England as nonplaying captain of the American Ryder Cup Team. The match was played at Ganton Golf Club in Scarborough, where Harry Vardon and Ted Ray had been the professionals.

While he had been confined in the hospital, Hogan had been deeply moved by the public's concern, and talk had circulated about a newer, mellower Hogan. When the Americans lost three of the four foursomes matches, the players learned he was as tough and as competitive as ever. Under the sting of Hogan's displeasure, the Americans overwhelmed the British and Irish the next day, winning six of the eight singles. Dutch Harrison won by 8 and 7, Jimmy Demaret by 7 and 6, Sam Snead by 6 and 5, Lloyd Mangrum and Chick Harbert by 4 and 3, and Clayton Heafner by 3 and 2. Only Johnny Palmer and Bob Hamilton lost. The United States won, 7–5.

Back home again, Hogan continued his recovery. In November he was at the Colonial Country Club hitting balls. On December 10 he played his first full round. He played again the next day. In January of 1950 he entered the Los Angeles Open.

Throughout his confinement, while others had wondered if he would walk again, Hogan had dreamed of returning to the Tour. In his two rounds at Colonial he found he had the shots—he was close to par on both days over a severe course—but he had ridden a cart both days. He would have to walk in tournament golf, and Hogan's legs had not fully recovered. They never would. To control the swelling and cramps, he wore heavy elastic athletic bandages. Even then his legs hurt. Only by playing could he know if he could make it.

The Los Angeles Open began on January 6. Hogan arrived in late December and played four practice rounds. When the tournament began, he shot an erratic 73 in the first round, but followed up with 69 the next day. Rain caused the third round to be postponed, giving Ben's legs a day of rest, and then he shot two more 69s. He finished with 280, which looked good enough to win, but Snead birdied the last two holes to catch him. Sam won the playoff, which was delayed a week for the Crosby, but Hogan had found he could play tournament golf once again. Not only play, but play well enough to win. Now he looked toward the 1950 Open.

Because of interruptions for two wars, this would be the fiftieth, the

Golden Anniversary United States Open. It was set for Merion, one of the USGA's favorite clubs. Hogan practiced endlessly through the first few months of 1950, but he played sparingly, saving his legs. He had played in the Crosby but placed nineteenth, and he had shot a poor 76 against Snead's 72 in the Los Angeles Open playoff. Phoenix renamed its tournament the Ben Hogan Open, and he played there, too, but not well. In April he was in position to win the Masters, two strokes out of first place with eighteen holes to play, but he scored 76 in the last round. Jimmy Demaret shot 69 and beat him by five strokes. Snead passed him, too, with 72. After that Hogan won the Greenbrier Pro-Am at Snead's home course and placed third at the Colonial National Invitational. Now it was time to get ready for the Open.

No one prepared for an Open the way Hogan did or could analyze a course as he could. He usually arrived at least a week early and played some practice rounds, mostly alone. Trying to develop a feel for the course, he would hit two balls on every hole, each to a different spot, then find a secluded spot and practice the shots he felt the course demanded. His approach was based on his belief he had to be inside twenty feet to make birdies.

His planning was meticulous; he seemed to know every flat spot on a course and how a ball would bounce wherever it landed. In preparing for the 1953 British Open, he sent Cecil Timms, his caddie, ahead to the 6th green. Hogan was going to play three shots to the green with his 2-iron, one to the left front, one to the center, one to the right front. Timms was to tell him how each ball bounced.

After a few rounds on a strange course, Hogan knew precisely how it should be played. On his way to England for the 1956 Canada Cup, he asked Snead about the Wentworth Golf Club, where they were to compete as partners for the United States. Snead had played Wentworth before, but he offered a vague description. After one round, Hogan gave Snead a detailed plan of how the course should be played. He advised Sam to use a 3-wood rather than a driver on one long par 4. When Snead did and complained he needed a 5-iron to reach the green where he had used a 7-iron before, Hogan reminded him he had played his 7-iron from a hanging lie.

More than any other player, Hogan had the control to follow his plan. If he wanted to approach from a level place on the left side of the fairway, that's where he drove the ball. Hogan gave the impression that if he hit the ball into a bunker, that's how the hole should be played.

When he finished his preparations, he knew what shots he would have to play and what clubs he would need to play them with. While the rules set a limit of fourteen clubs, every tournament golfer has more to choose from for any round. After days of meticulous study, Hogan decided there were no 7-iron shots at Merion; he left it out of his bag.

Ben also had the knack of figuring what score would win, then setting his plans to make it. Even though Merion was short, its fairways were narrow, its rough high, and its greens rock-hard and slick. Nothing new there. Hogan decided scores would be high, just as he liked. His only question was whether his legs could hold up to the punishment of the double round on Saturday.

Hogan shot 72 in the first round, two over the par of 70, which should have been close, but when the day ended, he was eight strokes off the lead. Lee Mackey, an obscure young professional from Birmingham, Alabama, scored 64, an eighteen-hole Open record. Ironically, Mackey almost hadn't qualified. He had tied for the last spot in Birmingham and won his place on the 3rd hole of a playoff.

Mackey began as if he'd be lucky to finish. He drove into a fairway bunker on the 1st hole and hit a 5-iron into another bunker by the green, but then he blasted six inches from the cup. After that he played superb golf. Par at Merion is an unbalanced 36-34. Mackey was out in 33, then birdied three of the next six holes. After losing a stroke at the 17th, a monstrous par 3 of 230 yards, he struck a good drive on the 18th, then a 3-wood that hit short of the green, hopped up the incline, and rolled eight feet from the cup. He holed it for a birdie 3 and an inward nine of 31. He had only one question when he finished; he asked Joe Dey, "What do you think will make the cut?"

The question was appropriate, for Mackey shot 81 the next day, then finished with 75 and 77, his final score of 297 tying for twenty-sixth place. When he learned his 64 was a record, he gave the ball to his caddie as a souvenir. Midway through the second round, when things weren't going so well, the caddie fished the ball from his pocket and handed it back, saying, "Better try this one again."

While Mackey was breezing around the first nine, Hogan was having trouble. He made five 5s, only two of them for pars, and shot 39. The greens were so unusually fast he didn't ground his club when he had a downhill putt so that he wouldn't be penalized if the ball moved. The precaution was wise. As he took his stance on one green, the ball suddenly trickled four feet closer to the cup. Startled, Hogan looked up quickly, and a USGA official standing nearby confirmed he had not addressed the ball. (Technically, you have not addressed the ball unless you have both taken your stance and grounded your club.)

Ben shaved one stroke off par on the second nine and came back in 33 for his 72. The next day he shot 69 and climbed into fifth place at 141, behind Dutch Harrison, Johnny Bulla, Jim Ferrier, and Julius Boros, who was beginning a distinguished career in the Open. (Boros shot 68 in the first round with eight 3s; Mackey had seven 3s and a 2.)

Hogan's legs ached; each night he unwrapped the bandages that reached from his ankles to his crotch and soaked in a tub of hot water. It had helped, but now he faced that torturous double round.

Saturday was a lovely, warm spring day in Philadelphia. The sun was bright, a few puffy clouds hung milk white in the pale blue sky, and the branches of the maples and oaks swayed in the moderate breeze coming out of the southwest. Hogan shot another 72 in the morning for a fifty-four-hole score of 213, three over par, tying Cary Middlecoff, who was paired with him the final day, and Johnny Palmer. They were two strokes behind Lloyd Mangrum, the leader at 211, and one behind Dutch Harrison. One more round to go.

After a light lunch, Hogan started out with a 4 on the first hole and a 5 on the second, both pars. The third had given him trouble in the first round, and it did again now. A par 3 of 195 yards across a valley to a two-level green protected by bunkers on the left and a billowy sycamore on the right, it cost him a stroke, and he finished the first nine in 37, one over par.

While his first nine wasn't inspiring, it was considerably better than either Mangrum's, Harrison's, Palmer's, or Middlecoff's. Middlecoff had slipped to 39, and the others had floundered around in 41. Now, even though he was four strokes over par for sixty-three holes, Hogan was in front. Middlecoff and Mangrum were six over, and Harrison was seven over par.

Meanwhile, up ahead, George Fazio had finished with 287, seven over par. The first man off the tee in the morning, Fazio was one of the game's finest ball strikers, but although he played a lot of tournaments, he was not a regular on the pro circuit. A Philadelphian, Fazio liked to stay close to home and dabble in business; at different times he owned a Cadillac dealership in Cambridge, Maryland, and dealt in scrap metal. In 1950 he was listed from the Woodmont Country Club in Washington, but he wasn't there very often.

Fazio had begun the last round at 217, six strokes behind Mangrum. Out in 37, he seemed headed nowhere, but then he had begun playing wonderful shots, starting back with three solid pars, then dropping a birdie putt on the 13th, a little par 3 of 133 yards. He lost that stroke on the next hole, but he birdied the 15th, played the next three in par, and finished with 70.

While his score wasn't particularly promising at first, it looked better and better as the day wore on and one after another of the leaders began

145

to collapse. Playing an hour ahead of Hogan, Mangrum was all over the place on the first nine, but he settled himself and came home in 35, matching Fazio at 287. Half an hour later Harrison struggled home in 35 too, but that was a stroke too many: 288.

By the time Harrison finished, Hogan was ahead—Middlecoff had taken two strokes to recover from the huge bunker by the 10th green and then steadily lost ground—but Ben was also struggling. His legs throbbed with pain, his caddie had to pick his ball from the cup, and Middlecoff marked his ball for him when it was necessary. Hogan wasn't sure he could finish. He was three strokes ahead as he stood on the 12th tee, but his round nearly ended there.

As Ben lashed into his drive, his legs locked, and he almost fell. He struggled to hold his balance, then staggered toward Harry Radix, a friend standing at the edge of the tee. His legs felt like stone.

"Let me hang on to you, Harry," he gasped. "My God, I don't think I can finish."

Like an infestation of locusts, 13,000 fans swarmed over Merion that day, and by now almost all of them had clustered around Hogan. They stood hushed when he hit his shots, but then they darted ahead, caring nothing for the other men struggling with this trying and baffling course, ignoring them, shouting as they tried to play their shots, and running ahead to find a place near a green where another player was putting. Marshals had no control, and progress was painfully slow. Very few of the fans saw Hogan flinch after his drive; all but a few had raced ahead to the 12th green, where Harold Williams and Loddie Kempa were holing out. They seemed to have no effect on Williams—he made his par 4—but Kempa fought to make 8.

Ben hung on Radix's shoulder while the pain gradually eased. Slowly he moved his foot, then he took a tentative step. He could walk, but could he play? His iron hit the 12th green, bit, and stopped, but he took three putts. One stroke gone, but he still had two in hand. Pars on the next two holes, but it was agony. The 15th is a marvelously conceived short par 4 of 395 yards with an elevated tee, a plateau green, and a fairway that bends right around a grouping of bunkers. The drive must either clear the bunkers or come close to them; if it doesn't, it could run out of bounds into a road bordering the left. The green, guarded by deep, steep-faced bunkers, has two levels. Hogan played the hole perfectly—a lovely drive into the narrow fairway, followed by a soft pitch that braked itself eight feet below the hole. Then he took three putts again. One stroke ahead now with three hard holes to play, back and forth across the old stone quarry.

Two stout shots got him on the 16th for his par, but he bunkered his

Players and caddies of an early Open. The great Willie Anderson, whose record of three consecutive championships has never been matched, sits with his arm across the shoulders of his friend and arch rival, Alex Smith. Not allowed inside the clubhouses early in the century, the players changed their shoes under a convenient tree.

The classic, graceful form of
Harry Vardon, who ushered in the
era of the modern swing.

John J. McDermott, the first
American-born champion, and the
youngest. His iron play was
legendary.

Francis Ouimet's victory over Harry Vardon and Ted Ray in the playoff of the 1913 Open remains the most significant in the development of golf in the United States. Eddie Lowery, Ouimet's ten-year-old caddie, was offered ten dollars to step aside and allow someone more mature to carry the bag in the playoff, but he refused.

Ouimet lining up his putt on the 18th green of the playoff, while Harry Vardon (left) and Ted Ray stand by helplessly.

Walter Hagen remained a force in the Open long after he won his two championships in 1914 and 1919.

Coats were still being worn as late as 1920. Harry Vardon driving at Inverness, while eventual winner Ted Ray watches.

One of the greatest pairings
of golf talent: Harry Vardon,
who was then fifty, and Bob Jones,
who was eighteen, before
the qualifying round at
Inverness in 1920.

Bobby Jones holing the breaking twelve-footer on the seventy-second green at Winged Foot, saving a tie in the 1929 championship. The next day he defeated Al Espinosa in the playoff.

The smooth style of Jones as he begins the 1930 Open, the third championship of the Grand Slam. This was the last Open he would enter. Jock Hutchison is at the left.

At the end of 1932, his greatest year, Gene Sarazen cradles the U.S. Open trophy in his right arm and the British Open trophy in his left. He is one of four men who have won both in the same year. The others are Bobby Jones, in 1926 and 1930; Ben Hogan, in 1953; and Lee Trevino, in 1971.

Sam Parks holing the final putt in the 1935 Open, one of the greatest upsets the championship has ever seen. The only man in the field to break 300 (he shot 299), Parks never won another tournament.

The powerful swing of Ralph Guldahl. From 1937 through 1939, he was the best player in the game, winning the Open in 1937 and 1938 and the Masters in 1939.

With Johnny Goodman watching, Sam Snead plays the first shot of his Open career, driving from the first tee at Oakland Hills in the 1937 championship. Forty years later, he played in his last.

The fluid power of Sam Snead at the height of his career, when he could win anything except the Open.

tee shot on the 17th and his last stroke was gone. Now came the long hard 18th, 448 yards with a blind drive that must carry 210 yards over the crest of a hill to clear the quarry and reach the fairway. Hogan hit a fine straight drive to a level spot well over the brow of the hill. Now he faced a long shot into a difficult green. The hole was cut on the right rear; a bunker reached around the right front, and the green ran uphill for a distance, then fell away. Too strong a shot would run off the back and into the crowd.

Hogan pondered what to do. If he needed a birdie to tie, he'd hit a 4-wood and try to cut the ball around the bunker and stop it close to the hole. It was a dangerous shot, but what good was second place? If he could get away with a par 4, he'd play a safer shot, use his 1-iron and aim for the left front corner.

He looked around and saw Jimmy Hines, who had missed the cut, and Fred Corcoran.

"What's low?" he asked Hines.

"Two eighty-six. Bill Nary, I think."

Corcoran interrupted. "No," he said, "two eighty-seven is low."

Hogan glared and froze Corcoran with that icy wide-eyed stare. Corcoran, as Irish as Hogan, glared back.

"Two eighty-seven is low," he repeated in a slow, measured, emphatic tone.

Hogan thought for a moment, then drew out his 1-iron. He'd play the safe shot.

An unbroken line of fans encircled the hole, from behind Hogan, along both sides of the fairway, and around behind the green, standing quiet as death as he set himself for the shot. He went into his usual routine: feet set, a look at the hole, a waggle or two, then the quick backswing, powerful downthrust, the long exaggerated extension through the ball, and the high, full finish, perfectly balanced. The ball could do nothing but what he willed. It streaked toward the green and stopped on the left front corner, forty feet from the hole.

The crowd roared, then thundered toward the green. Nothing else mattered but a chance to see the finish by this gallant fighter who by now was eating his last reserves of strength. They ignored everyone else still on the course. P. J. Boatwright, locked in a battle with Frank Stranahan for low amateur, was ready to drive from the 14th tee, which is close by the 18th green, when the gallery broke. Ignoring him, the crowd ran across the tee and knocked his ball from its peg.

Hogan was a pathetic figure as he limped up the rise before the green. He had been on the course for six hours in this one round, and the last nine holes had been agony. He had thrown away a three-stroke lead over the last six holes, and right now he was as close to not caring as this tough, hard, determined man would ever be.

He sized up the forty-footer and rapped it toward the hole, expecting it to break to the right and hoping it would fall. It broke left and rolled four feet past. The crowd groaned. Discouraged at throwing away a three-stroke lead and taking as little time as he ever took over an important putt, Ben rolled the ball into the cup for his par. He had come back in 37, and his 74 had tied Fazio and Mangrum. They would play eighteen more holes the next day for the championship.

It was as gallant a finish as any man ever made. Hogan had fought the wracking pain of his legs and the questions in his own mind: Could he hold up to thirty-six holes in one day? He could, and he had shown he could still play with anybody. Could he win, though? Remember, he had lost a playoff in Los Angeles. Tomorrow would answer the final question.

In his hotel room that night, Ben peeled away the bandages and soaked for hours in a hot tub to relieve the dull ache in his legs. Already punished beyond what an ordinary man would ask of them, they would have to carry him through eighteen more holes. There was doubt that they could.

The next morning he rewrapped his legs and drove to Merion. No matter what happened, Hogan had already accomplished a miracle. Barely a year earlier he had survived a risky operation, and through the strength of his will had struggled to walk again. Now he was playing for the most important championship in golf.

Both Hogan and Mangrum had 36 at the end of nine holes. Fazio, meanwhile, was hitting the ball better than either of them but getting less out of it. Perhaps overexcited, he had overshot three greens and had driven out of bounds on the 7th. Despite those mistakes he shot 37. He was still strong with his irons coming back, and with five holes to play he was even with Mangrum, one stroke behind Hogan. Then he overshot four of the last five holes and gradually yielded, coming home in 38 for 75.

Mangrum had fallen two strokes behind with bogeys on the 12th and 14th, but when he birdied the 15th, he was within one stroke of Hogan with three holes to play. If he could par in, he might catch Ben, because those were tough holes where the slightest mistake could cost a stroke, and Hogan's legs ached, and he was very tired. Instead, Lloyd made the mistake. He missed the 16th green with his approach and chipped weakly, leaving himself a tough eight-footer for his par 4.

Lloyd studied his line and then stood up to the putt, but as he took his stance, he saw an insect crawling over his ball. Without thinking, he placed the head of his putter next to the ball to mark its position, lifted the ball, blew the bug away, replaced the ball, holed the putt, and walked toward the 17th tee thinking he was still one stroke behind with two holes to play.

He wasn't. Cleaning a ball on the green violated the rules. As Mangrum slipped through the gallery ropes and onto the 17th tee, the USGA's Ike Grainger caught up and told him he was penalized two strokes.

"You mean I had a 6 instead of a 4?" Mangrum asked.

"Yes," Grainger replied.

Mangrum glared—a hard, piercing glare. Then he softened.

"Well," he said, "I guess we'll all eat tomorrow."

Realistically, the playoff was over; Hogan was now three strokes ahead with two holes to play. The pressure off, he holed a fifty-footer for a birdie 2 on the 17th and won by four strokes, with 69 to Mangrum's 73.

Since Byron Nelson had retired, Hogan had been the best player in the game, but his accident had caused everyone to wonder if he could still play at his old level. In those four days in June 1950, he had proved he was still the best. Over the next three years he would become even more than that.

Hogan's climb to the pinnacle of golf was no more remarkable than his having ever become a professional golfer.

The will to win must never be mistaken for the wish to win. The 1950 Open was a victory of Hogan's will, a fierce, unyielding will, partly born in him, partly shaped in his childhood. After the death of his father when Ben was nine, he sold newspapers on trains passing through Fort Worth, occasionally sleeping in the waiting room of the station if he had not sold out, and later became a caddie at the Glen Garden Country Club. Other young boys have done the same things, but something within Hogan drove him harder.

Born with high intelligence to complement his determination, Ben Hogan probably could have become anything he wanted to be. He chose to be a golfer; then he became the best of his time. The best ever? If anyone has been, it was Hogan.

None of the great players took as long to develop or worked so hard. Hogan grew up in Fort Worth, caddied with Byron Nelson, who was seven months older, and as a boy played against Nelson, Ralph Guldahl, and Gus Moreland. He showed the least promise of them all.

He became fascinated by the game, but because he worked to help support the family, he seldom had enough money to buy clubs. When he did, he would buy an old used club from a barrel at a W. T. Grant store, sometimes spending an hour picking out one he liked. He was never easy to please. Later, when he and Nelson became affiliated with the Mac-Gregor Sporting Goods Company, Hogan would spend two or three days assembling a set of clubs, looking over the shoulder of machinists as they ground the clubs to his satisfaction, creating just the right look to the top edge and shaping the sole just the way he liked it. Nelson, on the other hand, could assemble a set in half an hour from clubs already manufactured.

Hogan's first full set was a gift from his mother. She had objected to his spending all his time playing golf and caddying and felt he should be more like his older brother, Royal, who had become sales manager of a local office supply business before he had graduated from knickers into long pants, but when she finally understood that Ben had a dream, she surrendered. She gave Royal $40 and told him to buy Ben a set of clubs. They would be a Christmas present.

Ben practiced and played, and his game responded. When he was fifteen, he and Nelson tied for first place in the Glen Garden caddie championship. Nelson holed an eighteen-foot putt for a par to win the nine-hole playoff. Still no one believed Hogan had much potential. But Ben persisted. He spent so much time away from school he didn't graduate. At nineteen he became a professional after an undistinguished amateur career. He played his last amateur tournament in Shreveport, Louisiana, and didn't win anything. He sold his watch to pay his caddie, then hitched a ride home to Fort Worth in an open touring car. It rained all the way. Nothing came easy.

Ben entered his first Open in 1931, the year he became a professional. The qualifying field in Dallas included him, Nelson, Jack Burke, and Jack Grout, who later taught Jack Nicklaus. A thirty-six-hole score of 151 qualified. Burke shot 151 and lost in a playoff, Grout shot 161, Hogan 165, and Nelson withdrew after shooting 80 in the first round.

Bad scores had no effect on Hogan. He was determined to succeed. In January of 1932 he took $75 and headed for California and the winter Tour. He won $8.50 for placing thirty-eighth in the Los Angeles Open and $200 in the Agua Caliente Open despite a 74 in the last round. In mid-February, after shooting 78-81-80-76—315 at New Orleans and finishing twenty-five strokes behind Gene Sarazen, the winner, he went home again broke. He was terrible. He tried again the next year, but once again he had to quit when money ran out. He was getting nowhere, but he simply would not give up the dream of becoming a professional golfer.

Hogan qualified for the Open for the first time in 1934, but shot 79-79—158 at Merion and missed the cut. Back again two years later, he led the qualifying at Dallas, but in the championship proper at Baltusrol, he missed the cut once more. With each failure he drove himself harder. He practiced for hours, until his hands blistered and bled. In 1935 he had married Valerie Fox; if no one else had faith in him, she did, but it was tough going. Ben was an erratic player with a wild uncontrollable hook that kept him constantly in trouble. In January of 1938, they reached a point of utter despair. They had been living on little else but oranges for a month when the Tour reached Oakland. Hogan stayed in contention through the first three rounds, but when Sam Snead and some others arrived at the Claremont Country Club the morning of the last day, they found him beating his fists against a brick wall.

"What's the matter?" someone asked.

Hogan stopped.

"I can't go another inch," he said, then hissed, "some son-of-a-bitch stole the wheels off my car."

That day, playing harder than he ever had, Hogan shot 69, finished second to Harry Cooper, and won $380. It was the turning point of his career. He was never close to giving up again. His game began to come around, and he developed into a consistent money winner. He finished the year with $4,150, ranking fifteenth on the money-winning list. Snead led with a remarkable $19,534; Johnny Revolta, who was second, won only $9,555. A year later Hogan finished seventh in money winnings. He was making progress.

He finally made it through seventy-two holes of the Open in 1939, but he had a dismal finish. He shot 78-80 the last day, finished with 308, beat just one other golfer, and finished twenty-four strokes behind Byron Nelson, his old caddie mate. He had to feel a certain bitterness. Nelson by then had won the Open and the Masters, and Guldahl had won two Opens, three Westerns, and a Masters, but after three years on the Tour, Ben had won nothing on his own (he had teamed with Vic Ghezzi to win the Hershey Four-Ball, but he didn't count that). Within a year that would change.

The North and South Open signaled the end of the Winter Tour. Prize money was only $5,000, but the players were put up free at the old Carolina Hotel, a place of great charm, where diners often dressed in black tie, and coats were required for breakfast. The tournament was played over the Number 2 Course, the masterpiece Donald Ross spent a career refining. Hogan opened the 1940 tournament with birdies on three of the first four holes and shot 66 in the first round; finished 3-3-3 (eagle-par-birdie) for 67 in the second; played cautiously in the third, constantly underclubbing, and shot 74; then closed with a 70, for 277. He beat par by eleven strokes, the previous record by two, and Sam Snead by three.

His first victory finally tucked away, within a week and a half Ben won the Greensboro and the Asheville Land of the Sky Opens. He finished the year as the leading money winner and won the Vardon Trophy, which in those times was awarded to the professional with "the finest tournament record in competitive play." Ben Hogan had finally arrived.

PART THREE

Byron Nelson wondered what had taken him so long. For some years Nelson had been convinced Hogan would become outstanding. In 1938, when Ben was invited to the Masters for the first time, Nelson bought him for $100 in the Calcutta pool. It was a waste of money; Hogan shot 75-76-78-72—301, sixteen strokes behind Henry Picard. Hogan and Nelson were close friends then. Away from golf they went duck hunting together, sometimes with Guldahl, and Nelson once bought two drivers and gave one to Hogan.

When two men as fiercely competitive as Hogan and Nelson are thrust against each other day after day, each one passionately committed to beating the other, friendships can't remain close. The flame that drove them and would allow neither man to concede to the other burned away a close relationship. Later they became hostile.

By the end of 1940, Hogan and Nelson stood at the top of the game, but that wasn't enough for Ben. While he had won four tournaments (he added the Goodall Round Robin later in the year), he had won neither the Open nor the PGA, the really big ones. He had made it into the 1940 Open as an alternate and had missed tying Lawson Little and Gene Sarazen by three strokes by shooting 72-73 the last day, and Guldahl had beaten him, 3 and 2, in the quarterfinals of the PGA. For a man who had been hanging on by his fingernails in 1938, Hogan had come an immeasurable distance in three years, but he lusted for more.

Hogan had a remarkable year in 1941. In twenty-six stroke-play tournaments, he was never lower than sixth. He won five, including two four-ball affairs, one with Sarazen and one with Jimmy Demaret. Once again he was leading money winner and Vardon Trophy leader, but once again he failed in the Open and PGA. A bad start of 74-77 cost him any chance in the Open, and Nelson put him out, 2 and 1, in the quarterfinals of the PGA.

Only two men broke 70 in the Open—Denny Shute, with 69 in the first round, and Ben, with 68 in the third. Hogan added 70 in the pouring rain during the last round, and in spite of his poor start, placed third, with 289, five strokes behind Craig Wood.

The golf schedule was cut back in 1942 because of the war, but Hogan still won six tournaments, including the North and South once again, and lost the Masters to Nelson in a playoff. With the Open canceled, the USGA joined with the PGA and the Chicago District Golf Association in sponsoring the Hale America National Open, with proceeds going to the Navy Relief Society and the USO. Although the draft was claiming players and the country's transportation system was overtaxed, a remarkably good field turned out at the Ridgemoor Country Club, a good but not great course in Chicago. Even Bobby Jones entered, although he was never a factor.

Hogan ran away with it. He opened with an indifferent 72, but he was always capable of blistering bursts of scoring, and suddenly began knocking the flagsticks out of the holes with glorious irons and shot 62 in the second round. When he followed with 69 and 68, he beat Mike Turnesa and Jimmy Demaret by three strokes, Nelson by seven, Little by nine, and Wood finished twelve strokes adrift. He had beaten the last three Open champions soundly.

Could this count as an Open? Hogan thought it should, but not many agreed.

The season ended with Hogan both the leading money winner and Vardon Trophy leader for the third consecutive year.

Mobilization for war was in full swing by then, and Ben spent the next two years in the Army Air Forces. With Hogan out of action and the rivalry put aside, Nelson became the biggest name in golf. When Ben was released late in 1945, Byron was in the midst of his sensational season. Ben was eager to challenge him.

The two men were not at all alike, either physically or emotionally. At six-foot-one, Nelson was taller. He had a soft, pleasant voice and pale blue eyes. Hogan stood five-foot-eight-and-a-half, and in his prime weighed a sylphlike 135 pounds, all bone and muscle. He had a square face with the prominent bone structure photographers dream about, a strong, square jaw, a wide row of white, even teeth, dark, slightly wavy hair, a deep, commanding voice with only the trace of a Southwestern accent, and the coldest slate-gray eyes God ever made. At a glare from Hogan, a grown man could lose his voice. He glared often; he couldn't stand stupid questions or inane remarks.

Through thorough analysis and endless practice, Hogan had learned to control his wild hook. By shortening his wildly overlong backswing, weakening his grip with his left hand, and rolling his wrists to open the clubface on the way back, then keeping a fractionally open position coming through the ball, he hit shots that drifted slightly right after they reached apogee, instead of buzzing off to the left while they were still climbing. As Hogan stood on the practice tee at Pinehurst before the 1951 Ryder Cup Match, Max Faulkner, the current British Open champion, thought he spotted a flaw in Hogan's method as shot after shot shaded off to the right. Finally he spoke.

"Ben," he said, "I think I can help you get rid of that fade."

Hogan glared.

"You don't see the caddie moving, do you?" he snapped.

He could say more in fewer words than any man alive.

Nelson was gentler, and their methods were different, too. Nelson had an abbreviated upright swing; at the top, the shaft of his club barely went past the vertical. Taking the club back, he slid his hips to the right, then slid them to the left as he came into the ball. The effect was to keep the face of the club moving along the target line for a longer distance through the ball than in the idealized swings of the time.

Hogan developed the same effect in a different manner. He had a flat motion with a long sweeping backswing (at least he did in his youth) that took the club well past horizontal. Coming through the ball, he uncoiled his body with all the strength he could put into it, and as his hands began to cross his body coming through, his wrists still seemed fully cocked; he had carried the theory of the late hit as far as it could go. His left arm was straight as a rod going back, his right arm just as straight going through; he developed a longer extension through the ball than any great player ever.

In comparing Nelson and Hogan, Nelson was probably a little better with the driver and the longest irons, Hogan was probably better with the medium through short irons. Hogan had a decided edge in short putts; he was deadly from inside ten feet.

Hogan was also a magician in getting out of trouble. In his match against Charles Ward in the 1951 Ryder Cup, he was 1 down after the first nine, then drove badly on the long, 600-yard 10th. He was deep in the woods with no hope of escape, and Ward seemed certain to win another hole. With only the narrowest opening, Hogan threaded his ball through the pines with a pitching club, and from a good lie in the fairway ripped a driver toward the green. The ball hit short, bounced a few times, and rolled thirty feet from the cup. Hogan holed the putt for a birdie 4. Expecting to be 2 up, Ward was suddenly even. Hogan won the match, 3 and 2.

While Nelson's and Hogan's methods and temperaments were as different as Springsteen and Sinatra, the results—in both cases—were the same. They were the best. Nelson won eighteen tournaments in 1945, Hogan won five. The following year, Hogan's first full season of tournament combat since his release from the military, Ben won thirteen tournaments, Nelson six. In two years they had won forty-two tournaments between them. Nelson seldom played after 1946, leaving the field to Hogan.

Except for failures in clutch situations, Hogan might have won the Open, the Masters, and the PGA in 1946. Where birdies on the last holes would have won both the Open and the Masters, he took three putts from no great distance on either green. His quest for a national championship finally ended when he beat Porky Oliver, 6 and 4, in the final of the

PGA. The PGA, however, did not carry the prestige of the Open, and Hogan wanted that prestige.

Even though Nelson had retired from the Open after 1946, Ben still had strong competition. Lloyd Mangrum had developed into a better player than his brother Ray, and he was good enough to win the championship in 1946; Snead was still around, although his record of failure was becoming a legend; Jimmy Demaret, Jim Turnesa, Lew Worsham, Jug McSpaden, Vic Ghezzi—all were strong players who could beat anybody when their gears meshed.

Hogan had never figured in the 1947 Open—he shot 75 in the second round and 74 in the fourth—but in 1948 the championship was to be played at the Riviera Country Club in Los Angeles. If ever a man were predestined to win, Hogan was then. Because he had won the 1947 and 1948 Los Angeles Opens, they were calling Riviera Hogan's Alley, and as the Open approached, Hogan was playing some of his best golf ever. In his three previous starts he had finished second at Philadelphia and the Colonial, and had won his second PGA, played in May that year, defeating Johnny Palmer, Gene Sarazen, Chick Harbert, and Jimmy Demaret before thrashing Jim Turnesa in the final by 7 and 6. Now he faced the Open, which was becoming as frustrating to him as it was to Snead.

Driven by that flaming will, Hogan played attacking golf from the start. He birdied three of the first four holes, shot 31 on the first nine and 67 for the round. Not much was expected of Lew Worsham, the defending champion—his victory over Snead a year earlier was considered a fluke—but he shot 67 too, and at the end of the day they were tied for first place.

Neither Hogan nor Worsham played as well the next day, Worsham shooting 74 and gradually sliding from view, and Hogan posting 72 and dropping behind Snead, who was in the thick of it once again. Sam's 69-69—138 start set an Open record, a stroke below the 139 Chick Evans had shot in 1916. Watching from the hillside above the 18th green, Evans saw Sam's final putt fall and said, "I'm glad he made it."

Snead began the third round by dropping a fourteen-foot putt for an eagle on the 1st hole, but then hole by hole he fell out of the race and finished with 73-72.

As Snead cooled off, Demaret got hot. Putting for birdies on sixteen of the eighteen holes, he shot 68, but he still couldn't catch Hogan, who had a 68 of his own. With eighteen holes to play, Ben had 207, a record score, and led Demaret by two strokes.

Beginning the last round an hour ahead of Hogan, Demaret went out in a mediocre 36, one stroke over par, but then he began to rally. An eight-foot putt fell on the 10th, a six-footer on the 11th, and at the 12th, a twenty-five-footer with a little too much speed slammed into the back of the cup and dropped for a third straight birdie. Two under now. A lovely long iron stopped five feet away on the 13th, a stout 440-yard par 4, but the putt hung on the lip. A stunning burst of scoring, but it won him nothing.

As Demaret's putt missed, Hogan was on the 8th green on his way to a 33 on the first nine, pushing him five strokes ahead of Demaret for the same number of holes, enough of a cushion to protect him against Jimmy's surge. When Ben birdied the 10th, holing from ten feet, he was safe. He covered the next eight holes in one over par, matched Demaret's 69, and shot 276. Demaret finished with 278, and Jim Turnesa with 280. All three had broken Ralph Guldahl's record of 281 that had stood since 1937. Since Riviera's par was 71, Hogan had played the 72 holes in eight under regulation figures.

His putting had been remarkable. He had taken three putts only twice, once from 75 feet.

The 1948 championship was a landmark Open. Not only had Hogan become only the second man to win both the Open and PGA in the same year—Gene Sarazen had done it first in 1922—but he set two scoring records that would last a generation. His 276 stood until 1967, and his 207 until 1968.

Ben finally had his Open, but he didn't let up. Two weeks later he teamed with Demaret and won the Inverness Four-Ball, and the next week the Motor City Open in Detroit. He won five more tournaments that season, finished 1948 with ten victories, and for the fifth time in his last six full seasons became leading money winner with $32,112. He had been third in 1947, behind Demaret and Bobby Locke.

Since he had rejoined the Tour, Hogan had won thirty-five tournaments. When he began 1949 by winning both the Crosby Pro-Am and the Long Beach Open, then tying for first place in the Phoenix Open, he was off to another great year. It is useless to speculate on what might have been, but Hogan never again led in money winnings, never again won the Vardon Trophy, and never again won more than five tournaments in one year. Instead, he became the standard by whom all others are measured.

THIRTEEN
Top of the World

After winning the 1950 Open, Hogan rejoined the Tour, but his legs couldn't stand the strain, and he gave up the week-by-week grind. Because he could play so seldom, he chose those events he either considered important or that he liked. He usually began with the Seminole Pro-Amateur, at that wonderful course in Florida where he was a member, the Masters, the Colonial Invitational, played in Fort Worth, where he lived, and above all, the Open. Occasionally he entered some others, but that was unusual. A man of strong convictions, he usually refused to play in the "world championship of golf" even though it offered $50,000 in prize money, by far the most money in golf, because he didn't like the circus atmosphere. Nevertheless, he entered in 1951, but he did not play in the PGA again while it remained at match play; to win, he would have to face too many thirty-six-hole days, and he didn't enter anything he didn't expect to win.

Hogan had a strong record in the Masters. He hadn't finished out of the first ten since 1938, and twice he had finished second, losing to Nelson in 1942 and then three-putting the last green in 1946 and missing another playoff by one stroke. In 1950, the year of his comeback, he placed fourth, five strokes behind Demaret, but he had tired badly and shot 76 in the fourth round. Hogan was stronger in 1951 and played Augusta in 70, 72, 70, and 68. His 280 beat Skee Riegel, a former National Amateur champion, by two strokes. By then the Masters had risen in prestige past the

North and South and the Western Opens, and the North and South had been pushed back to the fall. Hereafter, like the dawn sun striking the primitive altar at Stonehenge, the Masters signaled the start of spring.

By 1951, it had become obvious that length alone was no deterrent to the modern player. Oakland Hills had measured 7,037 yards in 1937 and Riviera 7,020 in 1948. Ralph Guldahl had set the record at 281 at Oakland Hills, and Hogan had broken it with 276 at Riviera. Now, with the 1951 Open coming back to Oakland Hills, the course had to be strengthened. It had been designed for the hickory-shafted clubs and unreliable ball, but since the club's opening in 1918, the steel shaft had replaced hickory and had led to a drastic change in techniques: Players *hit* the ball rather than swung at it, and the ball manufacturers had developed techniques that increased distance and consistency. In earlier days, if a man found a ball that was tightly wound and flew predictably, he might use it for more than one round. During the 1930s the ball had become so good, so consistent, and flew so far, the USGA had imposed its initial velocity limit, not only to prevent the old courses from becoming obsolete, but also to assure that the character of the game did not change.

Still, golf wasn't the same as it had been in the 1920s. According to a series of surveys done by Robert Trent Jones, the golf course designer, the modern player carried his shots over old hazards that had baffled and intimidated players of the 1920s, leaving himself little more than a pitch to the green where those who had gone before might have been left with very long irons.

Oakland Hills hired Jones to revise the course. He turned it into a terror, perhaps the most difficult of all Open courses, the one others are compared to. While the finished course measured 6,927 yards, shorter than it had been in 1937, it was still long. Recognizing the work of a genius, Jones retained the green contours that Donald Ross had done so well, but he tightened the approaches by adding more bunkers.

To create the effect he wanted on the fairways, Jones filled in the old bunkers that had been set 200 to 220 yards from the tees and dug new ones 230 to 260 yards out, placing them on both sides, pinching the fairways in the drive zone, and shaping them to resemble the narrow waist of a wasp. On the 8th hole, for example, which had been altered in 1937, Jones relocated the tee and changed it from a three-shot to a two-shot hole, added a bunker on the right that thrust into the fairway and another on the left a few yards farther out, and drew the greenside bunkers in more tightly. The alteration changed a mild par 5 of 491 yards into a brutish 458-yard par 4, more or less restoring Ross's original concept.

The finishing hole, too, was shortened from 537 to 459 yards, and turned into a demanding two-shotter. The fairway was squeezed tight, and two clusters of bunkers created a narrow alleyway no more than twenty yards wide from 230 to 260 yards out.

While no one denied that Oakland Hills was difficult, they questioned if it was good. Hogan didn't think it was. All his life, he said, the golfer strives for length and control so that he can place his shots. When the hole is cut on the left side of the green, with bunkers guarding the direct approach, the smart golfer will try to drive to the right side and set up a better shot at the pin—not at the green but at the pin. He gambles that by playing close to the right border of the fairway he'll have a clear shot at the hole. Ben claimed he couldn't do this at Oakland Hills; the fairways were so narrow a man could do nothing but aim for center-fairway. He believed he had to hit a smaller target with his driver than with his approaches.

Oakland Hills demanded defensive golf, because even the long hitters could not carry the new bunkers; they either tried to hit a perfectly straight ball, hoping to thread through the openings, or they played short of the bunkers, creating longer approaches. Most played short. Watching them, Walter Hagen became annoyed and grumbled, "The course is playing the players instead of the players playing the course."

No one attacked; they used fairway woods from the tees, sometimes even irons. Stay out of trouble, they told each other; play safe. Even with those tactics, no one could handle Oakland Hills. Only Dave Douglas and Johnny Bulla shot a par round over the first thirty-six holes, although Sam Snead had a great chance the first day. Standing three under par with four holes to play, he took six strokes on the 15th, bogeyed both the 16th and 17th, and shot 71. He led, but he shot 78 the next day.

Not even Hogan, the greatest attacking golfer of his time, challenged Oakland Hills. He looked for the safe shots and, as a consequence, shot 76 in the first round and 73 in the second. By then he was five strokes off the lead and behind fifteen players. Bobby Locke led with 144, and Douglas had 145. Since scores of 152 made the thirty-six-hole cut, the fifty-five survivors were all bunched within eight strokes of one another. Literally any one of them could win.

Ben hadn't been optimistic leaving Oakland Hills that afternoon.

"I'd have to be Houdini to win now," he told some reporters. "I'd need one forty, and how can anybody shoot one forty on this course?"

Soaking his legs in his tub that night, Hogan diagnosed the golf course once again. Obviously caution wouldn't work; he would have to attack. Most others agreed. They pulled out their drivers the next morning and fired their approaches at the pins, but that didn't seem to work either. Only Jimmy Demaret matched par, and when the round ended, he was tied with Locke at 218, eight strokes over par. Paul Runyan and Julius

Boros were next, with 219, followed by Hogan, who had passed ten others by shooting 71. He and Clayton Heafner, the gruff, ill-tempered North Carolinian, were tied at 220.

Even though his 71 had been beaten by only three others in fifty-four holes, Hogan was disappointed. Through thirteen holes that morning he had looked as if he had mastered the golf course. He had birdied the 1st, 2nd, and 5th, played the first nine in 32, and with five holes to go seemed on his way to 67. Then his round had collapsed. He overshot the 14th, whose green tilts slightly away from the approach, losing one stroke there, and then dropped two more at the 15th, where Snead had made his 6 in the first round. Trying to avoid the bunker Jones had placed in the middle of the fairway where the hole swings to the left, Hogan drove into the right rough, pulled his second across the fairway into the left rough, dumped his third in a bunker, and made 6.

Surveying the carnage, Hogan stood on the 16th tee with his hands on his hips, his lips drawn tight and curled upward at the corners, and his cold gray eyes wide and staring. It was a cruel stare that had inspired Cary Middlecoff to name him The Hawk. A great round was falling apart, and now he faced one of the most challenging holes in American golf, a dogleg right whose main feature was a pond that crowded against the green's edge and created some pin positions that called for daring approaches. The hole that day was cut in one of the most dangerous locations—on the right side where the green nosed into the pond.

Angry at the way he had butchered the 14th and 15th, Hogan reacted as he had so often when he looked beaten: He struck back. He drilled a screaming drive down the right side of the fairway, as close as he dared to the rough that ran to the water's edge, then rifled an iron that just cleared the pond, bit into the green, and skidded five feet from the cup. It was an aggressive, daring shot, and even though he missed the putt, it was obvious he still had confidence in his swing and in his ability to play the shots he needed to play.

But the round wasn't over yet. Ben lost one more stroke by missing a four-foot putt on the 17th and finished one over par.

Hogan was grim as he strode into the clubhouse for lunch. He had had the course beaten, but he had let a great round slip away. He was still grim when he reached the 1st tee to begin the afternoon round, but now he knew he could handle Oakland Hills, and he simmered with the resolution to beat it.

"I'm going to burn it up," he told Ike Grainger, the referee. But he didn't burn up the first nine. After two routine pars, he overshot the 200-yard 3rd with a 2-iron and bogeyed from a bunker. He took that stroke back on the 381-yard 7th, hitting a 7-iron two feet from the cup. As the ball gripped into the turf and pulled up close to the hole, the crowd cheered. Hogan smiled briefly. "Wait till I make it," he said. He did, and then he showed the patience and intelligence that set him apart from so many others. When he drove into the thick and tangled rough that lined the 8th fairway, he played an 8-iron back to safety, then another 8-iron to five feet and holed the putt for the par 4. Another par at the 9th, and he was out in even par 35.

If the 8th hole was not the toughest on the course, then the 10th was. It measured 448 yards, a bunker probed into the fairway from the right at about 230 yards, and two more pinched in at about 270 yards, creating a walkway barely wide enough to squeeze through. The entrance to the green was narrower still. It was tough enough before Trent Jones had made it so tight. Bobby Jones never could play it; three times in 1924 he had taken 6. Through the first three rounds of the 1951 Open, it had yielded only three birdies. Henry Picard played it four times without making one par, and Bobby Locke made 6 there in the morning, costing him the lead. Locke was playing about an hour and a half behind Hogan now, just beginning his round as Ben stood on the 10th tee.

Hogan had made his pars there in the first three rounds, and now he ripped a drive 260 yards, then drilled a 2-iron that covered the flag from the moment it left the clubface and stopped within four feet of the hole. He said later it was his best shot of the tournament: "It went exactly as I played it, every inch of the way." The putt fell. One under par.

Routine pars on the 11th and 12th, then a 6-iron and a fourteen-foot putt on the 13th put him two under par. Once again he went over the 14th green, and once again he bogeyed. One under again and facing the 15th, which had cost him two strokes in the morning. It would not in the afternoon. He played a safe 3-wood left of the central bunker, then a lovely 6-iron to four feet. The putt fell. Two under again. Now for the 16th.

The gallery was huge; nearly 18,000 people galloped over the course, racing for vantage points. Hogan had three holes to play, and the Open was within his grasp, for Locke had bogeyed three consecutive holes and was unraveling. Hogan must not waver. He rifled his drive 290 yards. Now a 9-iron over the lake to the pin, set dangerously close to the water. The ball floated down gently, bit into the hard ground, and stopped four feet from the cup. The crowd roared, then groaned as the putt slipped past. On to the 17th, where he had bogeyed in the morning. There would be no bogey now. A 2-iron and two putts for the par. One hole to go.

By now only Clayton Heafner was a legitimate threat. Locke was out in 37 and needed a miracle to catch Hogan, Demaret shot 41 on the first nine, and Boros had 38. Ben felt a par 4 would win by a stroke.

The 18th was almost completely ringed by the gallery, with only the front entrance clear, and fans stood twenty and thirty deep, craning to see the finish. Rarely had anyone played the old game as Hogan was playing it now, and they wanted to be a part of it.

With supreme confidence in his swing, Hogan lashed into his drive. The ball rocketed toward the bunkers at the bend of the dogleg, and just when it seemed it must begin to descend, it climbed a little higher, cleared the bunkers and dropped into the fairway. He had only a 6-iron left. The approach floated down softly fifteen feet above the hole, and his putt trickled slowly downhill and fell into the hole for the birdie 3. It could do nothing else.

Hogan had come back in 32. His 67 was the lowest score of the week— Heafner finished with 69, the only other subpar round—and the second lowest ever by the champion, a stroke over Gene Sarazen's 66 at Fresh Meadow in 1932.

It was probably the best round of golf he ever played and certainly the most satisfying, because he had played one glorious shot after another in cold anger inspired by the challenge of the golf course. Even in the glow of victory, the course was on his mind. As he accepted the bright silver trophy and the gold medal that was his permanently, he said, "I'm glad I brought this course, this monster, to its knees."

There have been other great finishes since then—Arnold Palmer's slashing 65 at Cherry Hills in 1960, the 65 by Jack Nicklaus at Baltusrol in 1967, Johnny Miller's 63 at Oakmont in 1973, and the two 68s Cary Middlecoff put together at Inverness in 1957—but none compared to this one, not even Sarazen's. Sarazen, Palmer, and Nicklaus played their great finishing rounds over easier courses, Middlecoff's two 68s earned only a tie (he lost a playoff to Dick Mayer), and Miller made most of his birdies before he realized he was in position to win. Hogan shot his magnificent round over a brutal golf course knowing he needed just such a score to win.

If anyone had clung to the belief that Hogan was anything less than the best of his time, they were convinced now. This was his third Open championship. Only Willie Anderson and Bobby Jones had won four.

After he won the Masters and the Open, Ben relented, played in the World Championship, and won that, too. He appeared in only four seventy-two-hole tournaments and won three of them. After winning the Open, he raised his fee for exhibition matches to $1,000 and played fifteen through the remainder of the year. In November he teamed with Demaret in the Ryder Cup Match and beat Fred Daly and Ken Bousfield, 5 and 4, in foursomes, then beat Charles Ward, 3 and 2, in singles. Nineteen fifty-one had been a great year. A better one lay ahead.

Ben confined himself mainly to exhibitions in 1952 and entered only the Masters, where he finished seventh, the Colonial, which he won, and the Open.

Naturally he was the central figure in the Open, at the Northwood Country Club, in Dallas, particularly when he shot 69-69 in the first two rounds and tied the thirty-six-hole Open record. With only Saturday's double round to go, Hogan stood two strokes clear of George Fazio, who had 71-69—140, and three ahead of Johnny Bulla, with 73-68—141. The world was ready for another Hogan runaway.

Saturday was a hot, humid, uncomfortable day better spent in the swimming pool than on the golf course. Players and spectators dripped perspiration. Perhaps affected by the conditions, Hogan's game, so sharp and precise through the first two days, seemed uninspired. He played two indifferent rounds of 74, ten strokes worse than his first two, and finished with 286.

The Open was won by Julius Boros, a husky, quiet, dark-haired ex-accountant, originally from Bridgeport, Connecticut, but now living in Southern Pines, North Carolina. He had married Buttons Cosgrove, whose family owned the Mid Pines Hotel and golf course. She had died in childbirth earlier in the year. Their son lived.

Thirty-two years old in June, Boros had been a professional for only two and a half years. He had a languid, rhythmic swing, took no time at all to putt, and he had a placid, even phlegmatic temperament. In his first Open at Merion in 1950, Boros' drive on the 18th hole had left him with a fairway wood to the green. A par would have given him a first-round score of 67, three strokes behind Lee Mackey's record 64. He topped the shot. As the ball rolled along the ground, Boros slung the club across his shoulder and strolled along after the ball whistling a snappy little tune. He shot 68.

He was out early that Saturday in 1952. His two opening 71s had left him in good position, only four strokes behind Hogan, and when he shot 68 in the morning, he put a score on the board that no one else could match—210 for fifty-four holes. When he shot 71 in the afternoon, he won cleanly with 281. Fazio finished with two 75s, Bulla two 73s, and Porky Oliver slipped into second place, with 70-72 and 285. Hogan might have tied for second, but Oliver holed a fifty-foot putt on the last green to nose him out by a stroke.

As Bobby Jones had 1930, Ben Hogan had 1953. It was the greatest year of his competitive life, and it was every bit as good as Jones's great year. Hogan played in six seventy-two-hole tournaments and won five. In addition to the Colonial and the Pan American, played in Mexico City, he won the Open, the Masters, and the British Open. This was as close as any professional could come to approximating what Jones had done twenty-three years earlier. While the PGA Championship later became linked with the Open, Masters, and British Open as the professional Grand Slam, its prestige lagged well behind the others in the early 1950s, and Hogan didn't try for all four. He had good reason—first, because the PGA was still at match play, with several days when he would have had to play two matches, and second, because no one could have won both the PGA and British Open that year, since their schedules conflicted. The final match of the PGA was played on Tuesday, July 7, the same day as the second day of qualifying for the British Open, and everyone had to qualify.

Hogan had represented the Hershey, Pennsylvania, Country Club for many years, but in 1952 he had switched to the Tamarisk Country Club in Palm Springs, California. Disappointed in what he considered a poor year in 1952, Hogan spent the winter in Palm Springs, working on his game every day. When he arrived in Augusta for the Masters, he felt he was hitting the ball better than ever. What he did confirmed it. He shot 70-69-66-69—274, broke the seventy-two-hole record by five strokes and won by five over Porky Oliver. Ben considered this the best four rounds he'd ever played. It stopped the growing speculation that he might be through.

Dramatic though it was, the Masters was only the beginning. On April 30 he shot 72 at the Golf Club of Mexico, followed with another 72 the next day, then shot 68 and 74 and won the Pan American Open by three strokes over Dave Douglas. The following week he went to the Greenbrier for a pro-amateur tournament. Snead shot 268, Hogan 272. A week and a half later, Ben was at the Colonial.

Despite his earlier successes—he had won the Colonial three times, including 1952—some said he couldn't repeat under the conditions because he wasn't a very good wind player. Proving them wrong, he shot 282 and won by five strokes over Cary Middlecoff and Doug Ford. Now for the Open.

Once again the championship went to Oakmont, that harsh course above the Allegheny River a few miles north of Pittsburgh. Its greens were still the fastest and most treacherous in championship golf, and its nearly 200 bunkers were still deeply furrowed. By now nearly everyone recognized they were too severe, and after a struggle, the USGA persuaded Oakmont to ease them. New rakes created more shallow furrows—they were still there, but they weren't so deep.

The rest of the course remained the same; the fairways were narrow, the rough deep and dense, and the greens frightening. Par had little meaning at most courses where the professionals played, but it represented excellence here.

Nevertheless, even Oakmont yielded to the steady, forceful, and often inspired play of Hogan. He put pressure on the field from the start. The first hole then was a downhill 493-yard par 5. After a satisfactory drive, Hogan hit his second into the rough short of the green, pitched forty feet past the hole, then holed the putt for a birdie 4. He made routine, though well-played par 4s on the 2nd and 3rd, then reached the green of the 544-yard 4th with two crushing shots and made another birdie. He bunkered his drive at the 5th, a 384-yard par 4, but he reached the collar of the green with his second, and his chip hit the flagstick for another easy par. He played his iron to four feet and made a birdie 2 on the 6th, then rolled in an eighteen-footer for a birdie 3 on the 7th. With pars on the 8th and 9th, Hogan was out in 33; par was 37.

Ben came back in 34, another stroke under par, and shot 67, five under par and three strokes ahead of the field. Three men tied at 70—reliable George Fazio, Walter Burkemo, who had lost to Snead in the final of the 1951 PGA, also at Oakmont, and Frank Souchak, an amateur and an Oakmont member. (Souchak eventually tied for ninth with 296. His was the highest finish by an amateur since Bud Ward had placed fifth in 1947.)

As the second round began, Hogan seemed to be running away from the field. He was on the 1st green in two and birdied, holed a good putt for another birdie at the 2nd, and was close enough to the 4th green with his second to chip and putt for another. He was eight under par for the first twenty-two holes, better than one birdie in every three holes.

Then he cooled off and finished with 72. Snead, meantime, was on a hot streak and closing in. His opening 72 had left him five strokes behind, but with 69 in the second round, he pulled to within two strokes of Ben, and once again his loyal fans raised their hopes. Hope soared into ecstasy as the third round began, because Hogan looked shaky, and Snead picked up four strokes over the first five holes. Sam was actually two strokes ahead by then, and he was still ahead by one after each man had played through the 9th, but once again he broke his fans' hearts by doing his usual swoon. He dropped one stroke at the 10th and another at the 12th. At the end of fifty-four holes he trailed Hogan by one stroke, with 213 against 212, but he was no match for Ben at the finish. Still within one shot of Hogan after eleven holes, Snead lost five strokes to par over the last seven holes and shot 76.

Hogan, meanwhile, had struggled through the early holes, going out in 38, one over par, and he was still one over through fifteen holes. But this was the most dangerous fourth-round player in the game, and he staggered Oakmont with a blistering finish. The 16th is a 234-yard par 3. Hogan's tee shot was in the center of the green, and his first putt stopped so close to the lip of the hole the gallery gasped. A par 3. The 17th then was a short uphill par 4 of 292 yards with a deep bunker guarding the front and right side of the green, set at an angle to the fairway. For the first time that week, Hogan went for the green. He made it; two putts and a birdie 3. Now for the treacherous 18th—462 yards, a narrow fairway lined with deep rough, a cross bunker knifing into the fairway, and a large, two-level green. By then Hogan was certain to win, and nearly every fan on the grounds crowded around the home green, not only to see what they could, but to pay tribute to this great golfer. They created a giant ring from tee to green, and every one of them seemed more tense than Hogan, who remained in total control.

In the stillness, Hogan rifled a drive that Trent Jones measured at 300 yards, right in the center of the fairway. He had only a 5-iron left. With the gallery crowding so close he barely had room to swing, Hogan played a lovely shot that came down toward the front of the green, rolled a few feet, and stopped barely seven feet to the right of the flag. He holed the putt for another birdie 3. He had played the last three holes in 3-3-3 against a par of 3-4-4. His was as strong a finish as any man had ever made in winning the Open. He had played the second nine in 33, the final eighteen in 71, and had finished six strokes ahead of Snead, the runner-up for the fourth time. Hogan's 283 was the lowest score Oakmont had ever yielded for seventy-two holes, and it was sixteen strokes under Sam Parks's winning 299, shot eighteen years earlier.

As the final putt fell, the crowd erupted with a thundering cheer, acclaiming a great champion. Hogan had won his fourth Open; no one had won more. Ben wanted to, but he was not finished with 1953 just yet.

Americans had not begun to return to the British Open in great numbers, but Walter Hagen, Tommy Armour, Bobby Cruickshank, and some other friends had encouraged Ben to try. He filed his entry before he won the U.S. Open.

The British Open was scheduled for Carnoustie, a public course in Scotland, reasonably close to St. Andrews. Hogan had never played in Britain before. He went over early, learned to pick the small ball from the firm ground and tight lies taking very little divot, shot progressively lower scores in each round (73-71-70-68), shot 282 for the four rounds, and won by four strokes over Frank Stranahan, an American amateur, Tony Cerda from Argentina, Dai Rees of England, and Peter Thomson, a young Australian master of the small ball and fast-running courses who eventually would win the British Open five times and would be his successor in 1954.

Hogan was by now as much legend as man. As he limped up Carnoustie's 18th fairway, glowing under the warmth of the Scottish galleries, other players paused to watch him pass, and some sat on the sheer banks of the Barry Burn, which twines through the 17th and 18th holes, with their feet dangling above the stream, watching him hole out on the home green.

If Hogan's career had a peak, this was it. He returned home to a ticker-tape parade up Broadway, the first for a golfer since Bobby Jones in 1930, and then went back to Texas. He'd try for his fifth Open in 1954.

The 1954 Open would be a landmark occasion, but not because of Hogan. Innovations were taking place in other areas. When Snead had holed that curling putt on the 18th hole at St. Louis to tie Lew Worsham seven years earlier, a television camera mounted in the bed of a pickup truck had sent the image through telephone wires to a local station. This was the first known telecast of a golf tournament, certainly the first of the Open. In 1954 the championship was carried nationwide for the first time by the NBC network. The financial effects would be enormous, because television paid tournament sponsors to cover their events, and they paid handsomely. By the 1980s, the ABC network was paying the USGA several million dollars a year for broadcast rights.

The first Open program had been produced in 1928 by Herb and Joe Graffis, two young Chicago entrepreneurs. In 1954, Ed Carter, a Baltusrol member who owned a string of suburban newspapers, took over the program for the club and sold over $50,000 worth of advertising, a huge amount. (When the championship returned in 1980, program advertising sales reached $1 million for the first time; five years later they hit $1.6 million.) In 1954, golf was about to enter an era of escalating prize money, and the players were about to become known on a scale not imagined five years earlier.

One other significant change had taken place. Spectators no longer roamed freely over the fairways. Every hole at Baltusrol was roped from tee to green, and the fans were forced to follow along in the rough. This was unfortunate in a way, because to savor them properly, golf shots should be watched from behind the line of flight, to see if the ball is drawn into the green or faded around a tree. The game is not meant to be watched from the side. But it couldn't be helped. Golf was attracting larger and larger galleries, and if they were allowed on the fairways, they would create bedlam.

Hogan was never really a factor at Baltusrol. Played over the Lower Course (Tony Manero had won over the Upper), the 1954 Open was won by Ed Furgol, a Tour player with an undistinguished record, a permanently bent left arm, the result of falling from a playground swing as a child, and a lively imagination. Needing a par 5 on the seventy-second hole to shoot 72 and 284, Furgol hooked his drive into dense woods that border the left side. He was in so deeply he couldn't play back to the 18th fairway of the Lower Course and be within range of the green, but he had an opening to the 18th fairway of the Upper, which runs parallel. If he could play in that direction, he could reach the green with his third shot. First he checked to see if the Upper Course was in bounds. Assured that it was, Furgol punched his ball through the trees, pitched on, and saved his par. He won by a stroke over Gene Littler, who had become a professional shortly after winning the National Amateur the preceding September. Hogan lay only a stroke behind Furgol after thirty-six holes, but he shot a loose 76 in the morning round Saturday, and he couldn't work his way back into contention. His final score of 289 left him in a tie for sixth place, five strokes out of first.

The Open was Hogan's second disappointment of 1954. In April he had seemed to have the Masters won with eighteen holes to play. He was leading Snead by three strokes, but he shot 75 in the last round and Snead shot 72 and tied. They were even after twelve holes of the playoff, but Snead birdied the 13th, and Hogan, showing the strain, took three putts from eighteen feet on the 16th. Even though Snead bogeyed the 18th, he won, 70-71.

This was Sam's third victory at Augusta, which by then had become almost a two-man show. Snead won in 1949, and after Jimmy Demaret interrupted by winning in 1950, Hogan won in 1951, Snead in 1952, Hogan in 1953, and Snead again in 1954. This was one of the great rivalries in the history of the old game, and even though they were both forty-two that year, they were the game's central figures.

FOURTEEN
Hail and Farewell

Although he was approaching forty-three in June of 1955, Hogan was still the most dangerous player of the age. He was the best striker of the ball who ever lived, as fierce a competitor as Bob Jones, and he still prepared for a tournament with more intelligence and insight than anyone ever. Not since the end of the war had he gone two years without a national title, and he had not won in 1954.

The 1955 Open was scheduled for the Lakeside Course of the Olympic Club, in San Francisco, a few hundred yards from the Pacific Ocean. It hadn't been played on the West Coast since Hogan had set the record in 1948, and remembering how Riviera had been battered, Olympic's members looked around them, saw a 6,430-yard course that had been perfectly adequate when it had opened in 1921, but now could stand to be strengthened. After visiting Baltusrol in 1954, a committee of Olympic members called in Trent Jones. When he finished his revisions, members spent seven months struggling through higher rough, narrower fairways, and more bunkers, for Jones turned Olympic into a test of golf only slightly less severe than Oakland Hills had been four years earlier.

The land originally had been barren sand dunes lying between the ocean and Lake Merced, but years earlier the club had planted 43,000 eucalyptus, pine, and cypress trees, 30,000 of them on the Lakeside Course, the rest on the less ambitious Ocean Course. By 1955 they had grown to impressive heights, from sixty to 100 feet tall, and they bordered every fairway, creating avenues seventy-five to eighty yards wide. The treelines determined the shape of the holes and the lines of play. They were a good starting point for Jones's revisions.

He began by increasing the length to 6,700 yards. Rough lines were drawn in and the fairways narrowed to twenty-five to forty yards, and the rough grass was allowed to grow eight inches tall. Although the rough was higher than it should have been, the other adjustments were commonly done at most Open courses, but Jones went further and altered the 7th and 14th holes dramatically. The 14th originally was a drive-and-pitch par 4 that bent left and had a broad fairway with a wide bulge to the right. Jones pulled the rough in from the right, eliminating the bulge, filled in the left greenside bunker, and in its place swung another bunker diagonally across the right front, moving the opening to the left. The drive now should be played down the left side, closer to the tree line with the constant risk of a hooked shot soaring into the trees or possibly rolling down the slope and into an ugly gully.

Jones affected his most dramatic change on the 7th, a 266-yard par 4 with a green so open and vulnerable it could be driven. He drew a small bunker across the front of the green and practically eliminated the fairway, leaving only what he called a dewdrop landing zone, twenty-seven yards long and twenty-five yards wide, beginning 210 yards out and running to the cross-bunker. It was a radical but effective solution, and while the 7th still wasn't the strongest hole at Olympic, it no longer gave up easy birdies.

With those alterations, Olympic became brutally hard. Players claimed it was unplayable and that the rough around the greens prevented recovery shots for balls that rolled just a little off. The greens themselves seemed unusually small, and the players were asked to hit them from too great a distance.

There was only one way to play Olympic: Hit the fairways and hit the greens. No one did this better than Hogan. Throughout the warmup rounds he laid his plans, and even though his swing looked a bit choppy and flat, he gave the distinct impression that he knew how the Open would develop and how to adjust to it. His plans finished, Ben didn't play the course at all the two days leading up to the championship; instead, he and Claude Harmon went over to the Ocean Course and practiced the shots they knew they'd need.

Nobody had ever heard of Jack Fleck, but he was making his plans, too. He arrived at Olympic a week early and began a strenuous practice schedule, pacing off the yardage of every hole and working on a finesse shot from the rough around the greens. Because the 8th hole ended at the clubhouse, Fleck played forty-four holes every day—two complete rounds and an additional eight holes. He devoted all his time to his preparations; his wife and young son were home in Davenport, Iowa, and he was staying at a small motel and taking his meals at a cafeteria nearby.

Fleck's career as a tournament golfer had not been a wild success. Beginning with the St. Paul Open of 1952, he had played in forty-one tournaments and had won a little under $7,500. Tournament golf, however, was secondary; he relied on the two public courses he ran in Davenport for his primary income.

Like Hogan, Fleck had started as a caddie, and again like Hogan, he had very little luck at the start of his playing career. The similarities ended there, but Fleck did use Hogan clubs. Hogan had left MacGregor by then and had formed his own equipment company. Fleck sent his specifications to the factory in Fort Worth, and asked if Hogan would make up a set for him. By the time Jack arrived in San Francisco, he had his woods and irons, and Hogan himself delivered two wedges.

Although he was an unknown quantity to nearly everyone who followed golf, Fleck was confident in himself. In a letter to a friend written shortly before the Open began, he included himself among the ten men most likely to win. He was alone; hardly anyone else knew he was in the field. Aside from Hogan, those favored to win were Cary Middlecoff, Sam Snead, Ed Furgol, Julius Boros, and among the younger players, Gene Littler, Bob Rosburg, and Peter Thomson, who was now playing the American Tour.

Harvie Ward also drew support, which was unusual since he was an amateur and had yet to win the first of his two consecutive Amateur championships (1955 and 1956).

The morning of the first round brought the promise of a lovely day. The sun was warm and bright, the cool mist had blown away, and the air was light with just a touch of a breeze. It was ideal weather for scoring. What actually happened only emphasized the difficulty of the golf course. Of the 162 starters, eighty-two—more than half the field—failed to break 80. Only Al Besselink birdied the 17th, an uphill, 461-yard par 4. (In seven rounds—six in practice—Hogan hadn't yet hit that green.)

Only Tommy Bolt broke par. An eccentric man with a vile temper, Bolt nevertheless was a fine ball striker. He cruised around Olympic in 67, but that was mainly because of superb chipping and putting. He had eleven one-putt greens and only twenty-five putts in all. When the day of carnage ended, Bolt led by three strokes over Walker Inman, a young Air Force veteran making his second start in the Open. Inman was the only man in the field to match par 70. Hogan, meanwhile, claimed par was misrepresented after he shot 72. ("Par *is* seventy-two, isn't it?" he asked through clenched teeth grinding against his cigarette holder.) Fleck shot 76.

On another sparkling day, Bolt slipped to 77 in the second round but still held a share of the lead, tied at 144 with Harvie Ward, who had 74 and 70. Hogan was next at 145, tied with Fleck, who responded to his disappointing start by shooting 69.

Playing the 16th hole, a 603-yard par 5 that is a continuous right-to-left curve from tee to green, Hogan showed why he was so dangerous. His drive shot off too far left, hit a tree branch about 175 yards out, and dropped straight down. Next he played a magnificent fairway wood and a glorious 2-iron that bored through the light air and braked to a stop twenty-five feet from the cup. He holed the putt for a birdie 4.

On a typically foggy morning the next day, Hogan shot another 72 and moved into the fifty-four-hole lead at 217. Snead was second at 218, after shooting 70, and Bolt came to the 18th hole in position to share the lead, but his drive struck a woman spectator and dropped into an unplayable lie; he made 6, finishing at 219. Fleck, meanwhile, shot 75 and fell three strokes behind Hogan at 220.

Off early in the afternoon, Hogan was out in 35 and heading for his fifth Open. No one else could keep up, and when he came in with 70 for 287, he seemed safe. Gene Sarazen was doing the television commentary and as Hogan strode from the final green, smiling at the thundering roar rising from the 6,000 fans gathered on the amphitheater-like hillside, Gene rushed up, and on a nationwide hookup congratulated Ben on winning his fifth Open. Hogan demurred, reminding Sarazen that some players were within range of him, but Sarazen brushed Ben's caution aside, and Hogan himself went to Joe Dey, handed him his ball, and said, "This is for Golf House," the USGA's headquarters and museum.

Meantime, something wonderful had happened to Jack Fleck. Always reliable from tee to green, he often said he couldn't putt into a tub, but as he had stood over his ball early in the second round, his putter suddenly felt good in his hands, and from that point on he hadn't three-putted a hole. He was on the 10th tee when the roar went up signaling that Hogan had finished, and soon he saw a throng of spectators streaming through the trees, rushing out to watch him. He had been playing wonderful golf through the first nine, shooting 33 and picking up two of the three strokes he needed to catch Hogan, but he would have to cover the second nine in 34, one under par. He played the 10th through the 13th in even par, but then he made a mistake on the 14th. He hit so big a drive he couldn't believe he had only a 7-iron to the green, and so he hit an easy 6-iron into the bunker and missed a saving putt from eight or ten feet. A bogey 5; two behind now with four holes to play.

The gallery was hushed as Fleck moved toward the 15th tee, and some quietly turned away and began the long climb back up the hill toward the clubhouse. Fleck saw them leaving and thought, "They think I'm through."

Most of the deserters hadn't crossed one fairway when Fleck played his iron to the 15th, a little par 3 of 144 yards with a small island green protected by deep bunkers and bordered by eucalyptus trees. Playing now like a man in a trance, Fleck hit a nerveless 6-iron that split the flag and skidded eight feet from the cup. He holed it. As the cheers from his gallery rose through the woods, those who had left turned back, crashing through the trees in a wild rush to see the finish. Fleck was only one stroke behind now, but he had three hard holes to play.

He ripped into his drive on the 16th, but it started off too far left.

"Oh, no," he cried. "I'm in the rough."

He wasn't; he had hit the ball with so much force it carried over the corner of the rough where it swings left and reached the fairway. Safe. Another wood, then a wedge. He pulled it; the ball sailed left of the pin, but it stopped on the collar of the green twenty-five feet from the cup. Taking his putter, he gave the ball a firm rap and almost holed it. A par 5. Now for the 17th, the toughest hole on the course.

Everybody had been playing two woods, and very few had been able to reach the green. Fleck tore into his driver once again and drilled the ball up the left side. He was still a long way from the green, but he was getting great distance with his shots now, and he covered the flagstick with a 3-wood. His ball stopped twenty feet past the hole and left him a putt with a big right-to-left break. He caught a piece of the rim, but the putt wouldn't fall. Still a stroke behind, but now he had only one hole left, a short par 4 of 337 yards through a chute of trees to a narrow fairway below the level of the tee and a small, narrow, heavily bunkered green above fairway level. Fleck had to make a 3 here.

Hogan, meanwhile, had showered, dressed, and packed his gear. He sat in the locker room in an uneasy semisilence, answering occasional nervous questions from reporters, and casting periodic glances out the window at the scene below.

After a momentary pause on the tee, Fleck drove with a 3-wood. As the ball sailed off line to the left, the mighty crowd groaned. He had a slightly uphill lie with his ball sitting up nicely in short rough about 130 yards from the pin. Fleck debated whether to hit an 8-iron or a 7-iron. He chose the 7-iron and hit the ball high. It rose from the grass, arched high against the lead-gray sky, dropped onto the green, and stopped seven or eight feet right of the hole—a perfectly played shot.

Now for the putt, one of the most critical putts a man ever had to play. Some had taken four putts on this green, and a few had putted entirely off. Fleck surveyed the line and figured the ball would break about an inch from right to left. He took one practice stroke, set the putter in front of the ball, then behind it, and tapped it. The ball began creeping down the incline, took the break just right, then tumbled into the hole. The putt had been perfectly read and perfectly struck.

As the ball disappeared into the cup, another cheer ripped the air, and the gallery leaped to its feet and acclaimed the unknown man who had tied the great Ben Hogan by shooting a 67. Hearing the cheers upstairs in the clubhouse, Hogan dropped his head, then called to the attendant:

"Put these sticks back in the locker. Looks like I'll be playing tomorrow."

The playoff was set for two o'clock. To most, that meant Hogan would have to wait one more day for his fifth Open, for Fleck would have no chance. He had played four rounds over his head; certainly he wouldn't play another.

Hogan and Fleck were a contrasting pair as they started out that Sunday afternoon, Hogan the shorter of the two, his bulging forearms covered by a dark sweater. Ben walked with a slight limp, the legacy of his automobile accident six years earlier. Fleck, taller and more slender, had a loose-jointed walk, his arms and legs flapping about as if with no plan, his longer stride eating up the yards more easily than Hogan's shorter choppier steps. Their swings resembled their strides, Hogan's faster, more compact, Fleck's longer, more slowly paced. That most of the gallery expected a runaway didn't seem to bother Fleck; he was inside a special serene world.

Hogan tried to put the pressure on Fleck at the start. When Fleck semi-skied his drive on the 1st hole, a 530-yard par 5, Hogan outdrove him by fifteen yards, then went for the green with a 3-wood. His ball fell into a bunker about thirty yards short of the green, and his third stopped fifteen feet from the hole. Fleck, meanwhile, pitched from the rough to twelve feet, but his putt stopped four inches short of the hole. Pars for both men there and again on the 2nd. Fleck wasn't cracking.

When the break came, it was Hogan who faltered. As Ben prepared to play his tee shot to the 3rd, a 220-yard par 3 from an elevated tee, a frightened rabbit skittered through the crowd and raced across the tee. It looked like a good omen for Ben when he played his 2-iron four feet from the hole. Fleck's shot, also played with a 2-iron, hit the top of a bunker, bounced onto the green, and he made his par. Now, with a chance to begin the expected rout, Hogan lipped out his putt. The rabbit, it seemed, was an omen for Fleck, not for Hogan.

Both men made their pars on the 4th, but then Hogan pushed his drive into the line of tall eucalyptus and pines that border the 5th fairway. He had no chance to reach the green with his second, played a safe shot back to the fairway, hit his third shot on, and his putt, from twenty-five feet, grazed the edge of the cup and missed. Fleck, meanwhile, got down in two from thirty feet and went ahead.

Hogan looked as if he might catch up on each of the next three holes, but Fleck holed an eighteen-foot putt to save par on the 6th, Ben's thirty-five-footer hung on the lip on the 7th, and after Hogan holed a forty-foot putt for a birdie 2 on the 8th, Fleck rolled one in from four feet. Fleck then effectively settled the outcome on the 9th by holing for a birdie from twenty feet while Hogan parred. Fleck was out in 33, Hogan in 35, and with Fleck playing as he was, the pressure had suddenly shifted to Ben. He would have to make some birdies.

Instead, it was Fleck who made them. A putt dropped on the 10th, and now Hogan had fallen three strokes behind with eight holes left.

Caught up in the drama, the fans grew unruly. They broke through the ropes and raced about, generally disturbing the players and disrupting play. It became so bad that Fleck and Hogan were told to wait while the 11th fairway was cleared.

Hogan picked up one stroke there, but lost it on the 12th, where he missed a putt from three feet. He was obviously off his game, and his normally efficient swing was not functioning as it should. He was physically tired from the long program of preparation and emotionally shattered watching the fifth Open he wanted so badly slipping away. He was three strokes behind again with only six holes left, but even then it looked as if he might make it as hole by agonizing hole he fought back. A par 4 on the 14th cut his deficit to two strokes as Fleck made 5, his putt for a birdie on the 16th rolled four inches past the hole, and his fourteen-footer on the 17th grazed the cup. Had it fallen, Ben would have been even, for Fleck made another bogey 5. Now the strain seemed to be working on Fleck. He had bogeyed two of the last four holes, and his lead was down to one bare stroke.

Still, he was ahead, and Hogan had only one chance left. Needing a birdie on the 18th, he set himself as firmly as he could, squirming his feet into the freshly top-dressed tee, then lashed into the ball with that quick, compact swing. But his right foot slipped on the loose soil, and the ball veered sharply left into the knee-high rough. There was no hope. Hogan slashed at it once and moved the ball a foot. He hit it again and moved it three feet. His fourth shot reached the fairway, his fifth flew to the back of the green, thirty feet above the hole, and he holed it for a 6. Fleck, meanwhile, was on with his second and played a safe first putt. His par 4 gave him 69; Hogan shot 72.

While Fleck's victory was a bigger surprise than Sam Parks's winning in 1935, it wasn't a fluke. He played his last thirty-six holes in 67-69—136, as low a score as Sarazen's finish in 1932. Because one round was in a playoff, though, Fleck couldn't share the record. But then he had a different reward. He was invited to the Mark Hopkins Hotel the next morning to visit President Eisenhower, a devoted golf fan, who was in San Francisco for a meeting of the United Nations. Life seemed full.

Fleck never reached those heights again, but he had changed history.

Tired and dejected, Hogan announced he would no longer play tournament golf; the preparation took too much out of him. But he did play, and he had three more opportunities to win—at the Oak Hill Country Club in Rochester, New York, in 1956, at Winged Foot in 1959, and at Cherry Hills in 1960. But he didn't. Nevertheless, his was always a commanding presence. When the Open returned to Oakland Hills in 1961, Jay Hebert, the 1960 PGA champion, said before it began, "Hogan will hit more good shots here than anybody else, but he won't win." Hogan indeed hit wonderful shots, but his 289 placed him fourteenth, eight strokes behind Gene Littler. It was the first time since 1940 he'd been out of the first ten.

This was Hogan's last Open for five years. He entered in 1962 but withdrew with an attack of bursitis. Under the policy of exemption in effect in 1963 he would have had to qualify, and he wouldn't do it. With the 1966 Open coming back to Olympic, the USGA gave him a special exemption to observe his nearly winning there in 1955 (strangely, no invitation was extended to Fleck, the man who beat him). Hogan played well, shot 291, and placed fourteenth, high enough to be exempt from qualifying for the 1967 championship.

He was fifty-four then, and still drove the ball with uncanny precision at Baltusrol, hitting forty-four of the fifty-six fairways on driving holes (only Al Geiberger, with forty-five, did better), but the days were gone when he could play those stinging irons that rattled the flagstick. He hit fifty-one of the seventy-two greens and putted poorly. By contrast, Jack Nicklaus hit sixty-one, an average of a little better than fifteen a round. No one hit more.

After Ben drove from the 18th tee during the first round, play was interrupted by a thunderstorm, but he stayed on the course waiting for the storm to pass. Seeing his idol alone in the rain, a spectator ducked under the gallery ropes and covered Hogan with his umbrella. When play resumed, the fan moved away while Hogan hit his shot, but then he walked back to Hogan's side, and up the hill to the 18th green they walked.

Hogan's 292 was too high to qualify for 1968, and so his Open career ended. He had been in twenty, beginning in 1934, had missed three through injury and illness, and from 1940 on, had been a threat to win until the very end. He won four, but he might have won four more: in

1946, when he three-putted the seventy-second green at Canterbury; in 1955, when Fleck birdied two of the last four holes at Olympic to tie, then beat him in a playoff; in 1956, when he missed a short putt on the seventy-first hole at Oak Hill; and in 1960, when his tee-to-green golf at Cherry Hills was so superb and his putting so bad.

Hogan averaged 72.38 strokes for eighty Open rounds. He shot eighteen rounds under par, beaten only by Jack Nicklaus, who had twenty-nine, and he had fourteen rounds under 70, third best, behind Nicklaus and Palmer. From 1940 through 1956 he was never lower than sixth, and in the eighteen Opens when he made the cut, he was out of the first fifteen only in his first (sixty-second in 1939) and his last (thirty-fourth in 1967). He was second twice, third twice, and fourth and fifth once each. He meant so much to the Open, this gallant figure who fought so hard and worked so hard, it hurt to realize he was gone.

In 1970 Hogan entered the Houston Open at the Champions Golf Club, owned by Jimmy Demaret and Jack Burke, Jr., his close friends. He hadn't played in a professional tournament since the 1967 Open, but he shot 287 and tied for ninth place while other professionals walked in his gallery. A year later, he entered again. He treated the tournament as he had the Open. He came to Houston a week early, and he played superbly in practice. One day he had seventeen pars and a birdie, and in two other rounds he shot 65 and 67.

Once the tournament began, though, he was in trouble from the start. He was two over par when he reached the 4th hole, a big par 3 of 228 yards with a deep ravine bordering the left, and he tried to cut a 3-iron close to the hole. It missed to the left and fell into the ravine. Climbing down the steep hill to see if he could play the ball, Hogan strained his left knee, the one that had been so severely hurt in his accident. The ball was not playable, and so he limped back to the tee. With a hushed gallery silently pleading for him to play well, he hit two more shots into the ditch, finished the hole with a 9, then murmured to Dick Lotz and Charley Coody, his partners, "I'm sorry, fellows."

Ben lasted through the 11th hole. Then, embarrassed and in pain, he called for a cart to take him to the clubhouse. He could go no farther. As he was driven away, he said to a friend, "Don't ever get old."

He never played again.

FIFTEEN
A Legend Is Born

Preeminence fades quickly. After 1953, when he established himself as one of the two or three greatest players the game had known, Ben Hogan won only one more tournament—the 1959 Colonial. At the same time, after beating Hogan in the playoff for the 1954 Masters, Snead won nothing of merit (he did win the Greensboro Open in 1965, two months before his fifty-third birthday). A new group of golfers was taking over, and the brightest of these was Cary Middlecoff, a tall, lean Southerner from Memphis who had won the 1949 Open.

Middlecoff had been a professional for only two years then. The son of a dentist, he had been graduated from the University of Mississippi and the University of Tennessee Dental College, but he played golf too well to practice dentistry. He won the Tennessee Amateur four years running, from 1940 through 1943, and in 1945, while he was still an amateur, he won the North and South Open convincingly, shooting 280 and beating Denny Shute by five strokes and Ben Hogan by six. He reached the quarterfinal round of the 1946 National Amateur, the first postwar championship, and was named to the 1947 Walker Cup team. Because he had decided to turn pro, he declined.

When he made his decision, Cary gave himself two years to prove himself; if he couldn't make it, he'd go back to dentistry. He never drilled another tooth.

Few men over six feet tall had been great players. At six-foot-one, Byron Nelson was the best of them all. At six-foot-two, Middlecoff ranked right behind him. Like Nelson, he was an extraordinary driver. By the middle 1950s, with Snead losing the zip of his youth, Middlecoff was the longest straight driver in the game, hit wonderfully crisp irons, and had incredible streaks of putting; if he holed one thirty-footer, he might hole three or four. He was given to wild bursts of scoring—the 67-69 he shot in the 1949 Open, a 65 at Augusta when he won the 1955 Masters, and two magnificent 68s on the last day of the 1957 Open. At the same time, he was erratic. He began the 1956 Masters with 67 and ended with 77.

Middlecoff was a mass of nerves. He was at once the fastest walker and slowest player on the Tour. He moved along with quick, impatient strides, but once he reached the ball, he studied the shot for long and aggravating periods. He'd pick one club, then go back and pick another. He'd address the ball, then step away. Once over the ball, he'd set the club, then peek down the fairway, set the club, peek again. Endlessly. He chain-smoked. He fidgeted restlessly. He drove the gallery and the other players mad. He had trouble making up his mind and debated with himself over the proper club. During the 1946 Amateur, he tied himself in knots inside and had trouble drawing the club back. He was frustrated easily. During one stretch he pulled out of four tournaments in a row for real or imagined slights. He was so annoyed at his starting time (and at some awful shots) in the 1953 Open at Oakmont, he deliberately hit his ball into the Pennsylvania Turnpike and stormed off the course.

But when he could make those nerves work for him, when he drew the club back in that high arc, paused so deliberately at the top—for an instant he was frozen in place—then thrust himself into the shot, hitting the ball with a loud grunt, and it sailed on and on, and when it seemed it should start down, kept on climbing—then he was a wonderful player to watch.

Middlecoff did indeed have his nerves under control at Oak Hill in 1956—at least until after he finished. Despite two 7s, he shot consistent rounds of 71 and 70 and trailed Peter Thomson by two strokes and Hogan by one with thirty-six holes to play. Gradually, hole by hole through the final day, Middlecoff pulled ahead. Thomson lost four strokes over the last three holes of the morning round and shot 75, Hogan shot 72, and Middlecoff passed them both with 70. With 35 out in the afternoon, he held firm, but he won by scoring three 3s over the next six holes. Now he had a cushion against a wavering finish.

The last three holes at Oak Hill are severe par 4s measuring in order 441, 463, and 449 yards. Middlecoff bogeyed the 16th and drove into the rough on the 17th. After agonizing over the shot, walking about to scout the location of the hole, which hadn't changed since the morning, and switching clubs, he missed the green with his second and dropped another stroke. Clearly in trouble, he drove into the rough again at the 18th, chopped his approach onto the fairway forty yards short of the green, played a wonderful pitch two feet from the cup, and holed the putt to save his par. As the ball dropped, Cary slumped over his putter in relief. He had another 70, 281 for the seventy-two holes, and now he could only wait.

Waiting was agony; three men could catch him without doing anything spectacular. First Hogan. Needing three pars to tie, he got by the 16th safely with a 4, but his approach to the 17th skipped across the green into heavy rough, and his chip rolled perhaps three feet past the cup, leaving him a testy little putt. It was nasty, but it was the kind of putt a man must hole if he is to be Open champion. Hogan's putting, however, had become increasingly shaky the last two years. Facing an eighteen-footer on the 16th at Augusta in his playoff with Snead two years earlier, he had drawn the club back only four or five inches, jabbed at the ball, and three-putted. He had also missed a number of putts that could have saved him at Olympic in 1955. Now, needing this three-footer, Hogan set himself firmly, tapped the toe of his right foot several times, then straightened and stepped away.

At times a man knows in his soul that he can't make even the shortest putts. Hogan knew it then, and it showed. He stepped up to the ball again and missed. Now he needed a birdie 3 to tie. His drive settled in the right rough, just off the 18th fairway. Reaching the ball, he stood for a moment in a characteristic pose—hands on hips, cigarette held firmly in his lips, the lips curled upward at the corners in that curious expression that could never be mistaken for a smile—then pulled a wood from his bag. Cutting the ball out of the grass and giving it a little left-to-right fade, he put the ball onto the left front corner of the green. But he had given himself too long a putt. From thirty feet, his ball turned under the hole, and he made 4. His 282 left him in second place for the second time.

As he limped from the green, the 13,000 fans watching him finish applauded and cheered. So many of them had wanted so badly for him to win a fifth Open, and they knew his time was running out.

Julius Boros next. Needing one birdie on the last four holes to tie, he had one putt die on the lip of the cup on the 15th, another graze the edge on the 16th, and after holing a five-footer to save par on the 17th, he drilled a 3-iron to seventeen feet on the 18th. His putt rolled true to the hole, caught the right edge, disappeared for an instant, then spun out. Serene as ever, Boros smiled: 282.

That left Ted Kroll, a blocky, terse upstate New Yorker, who was a consistent money winner but never much of a threat in major tournaments. Kroll had played wonderfully through the first sixty-three holes.

He was only one stroke behind Middlecoff as he moved to the final nine, but after Cary's wobbly finish, Kroll needed only to par the last four holes to win. The 15th was an innocent par 3 of only 133 yards with a blind tee shot to a green set well above the level of the tee. Although it was only a little pitch, Kroll's shot missed the green, and he bogeyed. Now three pars would tie. Kroll's dream ended on the 16th tee. He hooked into a spruce tree, tried to hack it out, took five strokes to reach the green and two putts to hole out. A 7. He bogeyed the 17th, shot 73, and dropped into a tie for fourth place with Thomson and Ed Furgol at 285.

With his victory at Oak Hill, Middlecoff was at the top of the game, but his hold was shaky. At the height of his career he had become a part-time player, under his doctor's advice not to overexert himself. His right leg was a little shorter than his left, which put a strain on his left hip, leading to tendinitis. He was in such a state after the Open that he skipped the PGA a month later and played very little the rest of the year.

If we can say of any golfer that he reached the peak of his game on one specific day, for Middlecoff it was June 15, 1957, at Inverness.

The 1957 Open began as the 1920 Open had ended—with a storm off Lake Erie. High winds whipped in from the lake in midday of the first round, bending trees and tumbling the small tents set up for tournament officials through fairway and rough. Bolts of lightning ripped through the sky, and rain, driven by the gale winds, struck like bullets. Players caught on the course huddled in bunkers until they were forced out by the rising water. Spectators crowded together among groves of trees, and reporters clung to ropes and poles, trying to hold the press tent in place.

Play was suspended. Hogan had withdrawn earlier in the day with an attack of pleurisy. During the break, the USGA, in a move without precedent, offered to reinstate him if he felt he could play. He couldn't.

With Hogan out of the field, Middlecoff was the clear favorite, but he didn't play like it, shooting 71 and 75 the first two days. With half the championship over, he was eight strokes behind Dick Mayer and Billy Joe Patton, a lively, quick-witted amateur from North Carolina whose swing was a blur but who could escape from any jail it put him in. Both Patton and Mayer shot 70-68, matching the thirty-six-hole record, but Patton had nothing left the next day and closed with a pair of 76s.

Jimmy Demaret was forty-seven. A man everybody liked, he hit his shots in a strange sort of way; the ball streaked off on a dead straight line, but as it lost momentum, it veered sharply right. While it was unorthodox, it was effective, for Demaret controlled it well enough to have won the Masters three times by now. Not the Open, though, and when he finished early on Saturday afternoon with 283, everyone knew this would be his last chance.

Demaret stood in the clubhouse watching through the window as, under a blazing sun, Dick Mayer came to the 18th green. A delicately handsome blond with a rumbling basso voice, Mayer had shot 74 in the morning, and now he needed a par 4 to tie Demaret, a birdie 3 to beat him. The 18th hadn't changed much since Donald Ross designed it: It was a drive and a pitch of only 330 yards with a small green built up like a prayer hassock and guarded by bunkers on the front and left. Mayer's drive split the fairway, his wedge carried over the flagstick, bit into the firm green, and drew back about eight feet beyond the cup. If the putt fell, he would have 282. With Demaret watching through the window, he tapped the ball into the hole for the birdie. Demaret sipped his drink, and with his eyes misting said, "The boy made a wonderful, wonderful putt."

Middlecoff, meanwhile, was approaching the last few holes when he heard the roar of the gallery at the 18th. He had posted one 68 in the morning and needed another to tie, but with four holes to go, he was even par. He would have to birdie two of the last four. He stepped to the 15th, 448 yards, par 4—no birdie there, but a safe par. Two birdies in three holes now. The 16th, 412 yards—terrific drive, pitch within twenty feet, and the putt fell. One more birdie to go. The 17th, 451 yards with a green severely tilted from back to front; no birdie there but another par. One chance left.

Middlecoff sent a drive screaming down the 18th fairway, and his approach was gauged just right for distance and off line only about nine feet to the right. Spectators ringed the green, sitting on the hillside and murmuring quietly as Cary studied the line for agonizing minutes. When he finally struck the putt, it looked as if he had borrowed too much; the ball headed well right of the hole, perhaps by a foot, perhaps by more, but then it swerved left, slowed down, and dropped into the hole. A second 68; the lowest closing rounds since Sarazen's in 1932. He had caught Mayer.

As the putt fell, a great roar burst from the crowd. Fans leaped about, yelled, clapped each other on the back, and said they'd never seen such a finish. Indeed, most hadn't. There had been other great finishes, but this rivaled them all.

The strain of that glorious finish took something out of Middlecoff. He was spent; it was as if all those nerve ends that had held up so well under the grueling tension of the final thirty-six holes broke loose, and he shot some ragged stuff in the playoff. On a hot and humid day, with the temperature close to 100, he missed holable putts, played poorly from bunkers, shot 79, and lost by seven strokes. Mayer shot 72.

Middlecoff was never the same after that Saturday in Toledo, although he came close to winning the 1959 Masters (Art Wall closed with 66 and nipped him by a stroke). Plagued by back problems, he retired in the early 1960s.

Handsome, articulate, and stylish though he was, Mayer never caught on with the public. He wasn't dashing enough, he wasn't consistent enough, and he had problems with alcohol. He finished twenty-third the next year and missed the cut in 1959.

Tommy Bolt succeeded Mayer as champion. A man who could play glorious golf shots, Bolt lacked the strength of will to control his gross tantrums. He threw clubs, swore, insulted anyone he felt like insulting, and he was known to have fistfights.

Still, Bolt had a sense of humor. During the 1958 Open, at the Southern Hills Country Club in Tulsa, Oklahoma, a newspaper published his age as forty-nine instead of the thirty-nine he claimed to be (he was actually forty). Bolt confronted the reporter.

"It was a typographical error, Tommy," the reporter explained.

"Typographical error, hell," Bolt roared. "It was a perfect four and a perfect nine."

Somehow, for one week, Bolt found a reserve of inner peace and direction. Relaxed, he quipped with the gallery, called good-natured insults to the press corps that walked with him, and played one wonderful shot after another. He tamed a difficult and demanding course by shooting 71-71-69-72—283, and won convincingly, finishing four strokes clear of the second man, the twenty-two-year-old South African Gary Player, who was in his first U.S. Open.

Like Middlecoff before him, Bolt was never the same after winning. Barely two weeks later, after declaring himself a new man, he stepped off a plane in New York and abused Frank Shields, the former Davis Cup tennis player, who had arranged to have Tommy and nine other players flown in for the Pepsi Tournament on Long Island. Then he quit after nine holes of a pro-amateur tournament, and two days later walked off the course after nine holes of the Pepsi. The other players complained of his conduct at the airport, and he was fined $500 by the PGA. He had already been on probation after twice being fined in 1957 for conduct the PGA considered detrimental to the game. His vile behavior turned fans against him, and he never threatened to win anything of consequence again (while he finished third in the 1961 Masters, he had to shoot 68 in the last round to creep within five strokes of Player). Defending his Open championship at Winged Foot, a year after winning at Southern Hills, he shot only one round under 75 and finished in thirty-eighth place.

Billy Casper won the 1959 Open with the most remarkable putting ever done in the championship. A good-natured twenty-seven-year-old

Californian who weighed 212 pounds and enjoyed food, Casper was the best putter in the game at that time, and he held onto that delicate stroke throughout his career. It was never better than it was at Winged Foot. It had to be for him to win because others played much better tee-to-green golf.

The championship opened as if time had turned back a decade, and Hogan was still the cold, deadly, efficient scoring machine he had been so many times in the past. He began by blistering Winged Foot's treacherous first nine with a 32, but he wobbled on the home nine, came back in 37, and tied Gene Littler, Gary Player, and Dick Knight at 69. Casper, meantime, one-putted eight greens and shot 71.

Billy's putter continued to behave like Merlin's wand in the second round. He began by missing the 1st green and holing a four-footer to save par, drove into a bunker on the 2nd and holed an eight-footer for another par, missed the 3rd green with his tee shot and holed from nine feet, bunkered his approach to the 4th and holed from seven feet, then ran in an eighteen-footer for a birdie on the par-5 5th. Since he had finished the first round with four consecutive one-putt greens, he had had nine in a row. Facing a twelve-foot birdie chance on the 6th, Casper somehow missed and made a par.

Billy finished with 68 and took over the lead with 139, a stroke ahead of Hogan, who continued to play first-class golf by shooting 71, good for 140. By scoring 69 in the third round, Casper had 208 and opened his lead to three strokes over Hogan, who clung to second at 211 with another 71. A series of thunderstorms struck on Saturday, flooding parts of the course and causing such long delays the fourth round had to be held over until Sunday, the first time the Open was played over four days. On a chilly, gusty afternoon, Casper shot a nervous 74, and Hogan threw away a chance to catch him by scoring 76. He placed tenth. With Hogan gone, only Mike Souchak and Bob Rosburg were within reach of Casper, but they both had to birdie the home hole to tie. Needing to hole a chip shot for his 3, Souchak was short, and Rosburg's thirty-footer was never close. Casper won with 282.

Billy's putting had been sensational. He had used only twenty-eight putts in the first round, thirty-one in the second, twenty-seven in the third, and twenty-eight in the fourth, a total of 114 and an average of about twenty-nine in a round. Three-putt greens are common on Open courses, but Casper had only one. He one-putted thirty-one greens and needed two putts on only forty of the seventy-two. Throughout the week Billy had used a new mallet-headed putter he had never used before, nor would again. As a member of the Wilson advisory staff, he was obligated to use

Wilson clubs. The miracle-working putter was a Golfcraft Glasshaft. He had to give it up. It hangs now in the USGA's museum.

Hogan and Snead were growing old by then, Middlecoff was practically retired, and the last three champions—Mayer, Bolt, and Casper—didn't have mass appeal.

The world was waiting for a new hero.

The world was waiting for Arnold Palmer.

The 13th at the Augusta National Golf Club is the best hole in American golf. A short par 5 of less than 500 yards, it tempts you with the chance for an easy birdie if you can play two well-executed shots, but it makes you pay a heavy price if you try and fail. Its fairway bends left around a forest of tall Georgia pines just short of the drive zone, and a narrow brook purls along the left until just before the green, where it slants across and then curls around the right. The creek makes the hole; it forces the player to choose whether to go for the green with his second, more or less assuring a birdie if the shot works, or to lay up short and hope to pitch close. A long drive that hugs the tree line and turns the corner will put the golfer in position to go for the green. Should he fail to carry the creek, he'll be in serious trouble, because while the shallow water barely covers the rocky rubble lining the bottom, the banks are steep and the stream bed lies well below the surrounding ground. Like the Sirens of mythology, the 13th lured Billy Joe Patton to doom in the 1954 Masters. With a chance to tie Hogan and Snead, if not to win outright, he hit his ball into the creek and made 7.

In the final round of the 1958 Masters, Arnold Palmer faced the decision of whether to go for the green or lay up. It was a difficult decision because his drive had left him barely within range of the green. Further complicating his decision, he didn't know if either he or Ken Venturi was leading, even though they were paired together. Arnold had led by a stroke after eleven holes, but his tee shot to the 12th, a par 3, had embedded in soft ground above a bunker, and because of some uncertainty over whether the embedded ball rule was in effect, he had played an alternate ball, making 5 with the original and 3 with the alternate. If the original ball counted, he was behind; if the alternate was in play, he led. The world waited while the matter was referred to the rules committee. Meanwhile, Arnold had to figure he was behind by one stroke. He might make that up with a birdie here.

With a hitch of his pants, Palmer decided to go for the green. He hit a screaming wood that seemed to be halfway to the green as soon as it left the clubface. The ball cleared the creek easily, hit the green, and rolled fifteen feet from the hole. With that one shot he *became* Arnold Palmer. He made the putt for an eagle 3, learned minutes later that his 3 on the 12th would stand, and won the first of his four Masters Tournaments. He was to grow into the greatest golf hero since Bobby Jones.

If ever a man and a medium were made for each other, it was Palmer and television. Televised golf had been given an enormous boost when Lew Worsham holed a full-blown wedge for an eagle 2 on the seventy-second hole of the World Championship in 1953. The Open went on NBC the next year, and CBS began televising the Masters in 1956.

The Worsham shot was a fleeting image; in Palmer, television had a lasting and highly photogenic hero. Built as an athlete should be built, he stood five-foot-ten and weighed 170 pounds, with broad shoulders, slim hips, and forearms like Schwartzenegger. He was as strong as he looked. He had sandy, wavy hair, a pleasant though not handsome face, blue eyes that crinkled when he laughed, and a tight-lipped smile aimed directly *at* you, a warm, intense, intimate smile that implied you and he shared profound affection. He had a nervous habit of hitching his pants, and he dressed conservatively but impeccably.

All his emotions showed. When he hit a bad shot, he screwed up his face as if he were in pain; when he hit a good shot, he glowed. Like Hogan, Palmer attacked a course; he aimed not at the green but at the pin. He threw himself into every shot, and although he wasn't the longest driver in the game, he looked it, and he was indeed the most accurate. He was an exceptional iron player, and he chipped like a magician. But, like all heroes, he had flaws. He was uncertain with the wedge, and while he seemed to hole his share of long putts, he was not an outstanding putter.

Above all, he was possibly the most confident player who ever lived. He turned pro shortly after winning the 1954 National Amateur, when Ben Hogan was still playing such wonderful golf. Like most young players of the day, Palmer was in awe of the way Hogan played. "But," he said years later, "not for one second did I ever admit, even to myself privately, that I couldn't beat him any time." His confidence stayed with him into his fifties. In 1983, when he was fifty-four and struggling to make thirty-six-hole cuts on the regular Tour, he decided he would retire if he won two tournaments that year. Not just any tournaments—he would quit if he won the Open and the Masters. He didn't.

He played the game for the joy of it, and the television cameras caught it. By winning golf tournaments he became a public figure, and he loved it. By the end of the 1950s, he was the biggest attraction in golf. When a tournament was coming to town, the public wanted to know if Palmer had entered. If he had, they'd watch; if he hadn't, they wouldn't.

Palmer had grown up in Latrobe, Pennsylvania, about forty miles to the east of Pittsburgh. He was born on September 10, 1929, to Doris and Milfred (Deacon) Palmer. A native of the coal and steel valleys of western Pennsylvania, Deacon Palmer became greenkeeper at the new nine-hole Latrobe Country Club in 1921, and when the Great Depression struck and the staff was cut back, he inherited the job of professional. His double role was to last only until times improved. It became permanent.

Arnold was the oldest of five children. He began playing golf when he was three, using a set of junior clubs, and by five he was playing full eighteen-hole rounds accompanied by his father and using his mother's clubs. By seven, he was breaking 100 on the rare occasions he was allowed to play Latrobe. Deacon Palmer was a stern man who held certain conservative beliefs, among them that the club and the golf course were for the members, not for the professional-greenkeeper and his family. Deacon had his meals in his shop or in his house by the 3rd green; he never entered the locker room, the dining room, or the bar unless he was invited by a member.

Arnold grew up under a long list of restrictions: He could not go into the swimming pool, he could not play golf with the members' children, he could not play golf by himself except very early in the morning or late in the evening when no one else was around. He was not allowed to play in a club tournament, but he could play in the annual caddie tournament. He won it four times, but he did not accept the prize; Deacon told him he wasn't eligible for that either.

During the summer, when school was out of session, Arnold worked around the golf course. He caddied, helped out in Deacon's shop or on the course itself. Mostly he practiced, hitting balls for endless hours, occasionally with help from Deacon. While Arnold had no formal instruction, Deacon was always there when Arnold needed him. They had the same kind of relationship as Bobby Jones and Stewart Maiden.

Deacon taught his son to hit the ball as hard as he could, and Arnold did. He swung so hard he'd lose his balance, and sometimes both his feet would fly off the ground, but Deacon believed Arnold's balance would improve as he grew older and that he'd hit the ball hard, as well. He was right.

What Deacon told Arnold stuck. When Arnold was very young, Deacon placed his hands on a club and said, "That's the way you hold it." Arnold held it that way ever after.

"I wouldn't have dared change for fear he'd catch me," Arnold said. "What he said do, I did." At the peak of his career, Palmer had the best grip in the game.

Arnold compiled an impressive amateur record around Latrobe. He won three Western Pennsylvania junior championships and later five

PART THREE

Western Pennsylvania Amateurs. He decided early in his life that he wanted to become a professional and had no plans for college, but he had become close friends with Bubby Worsham, the younger brother of Lew Worsham, and when Bubby was offered a scholarship to Wake Forest, he persuaded the golf coach to take Arnold, too.

Palmer became the school's leading player, won the Atlantic Coast Conference title three times, and in 1950 won the Southern Intercollegiate. But he didn't always win; twice he was beaten badly in the North and South Amateur, but by two of the finest amateurs who ever played the game. Harvie Ward thrashed him, 5 and 4, in a semifinal match in 1948, and a year later Frank Stranahan shocked him, 12 and 11, again in the semifinals. Palmer never won the North and South, then one of the two or three most important amateur tournaments in the country.

Then, in his senior year, Bubby Worsham was killed in an automobile accident. Palmer was so shaken he dropped out of school and enlisted in the Coast Guard. He came out in 1954, found a job representing a paint manufacturer, took up golf again, and in August won the National Amateur, beating Bob Sweeny, a member of high society, 1 up, in the final match. He also beat Stranahan, 3 and 2, in the quarterfinals.

A few weeks later, over the Labor Day weekend, Palmer met Winifred Walzer at a tournament in Shawnee-on-Delaware. They were married in December, and Arnold and Winnie embarked on the professional Tour in a second-hand trailer.

Not exactly a wild success his first year, he did, however, win the Canadian Open and finished the 1955 season thirty-second on the money-winning list with $7,958, about $55,000 less than Julius Boros, the leader. In 1956 he won the Insurance City Open in Hartford, Connecticut, and the Eastern Open in Baltimore, won $16,145 for the year, and finished nineteenth in money winnings. He kept improving, winning four tournaments in 1957 and three in 1958, including the Masters. He was then the leading money winner and the best player in the game, but like all the great players before him, he felt unfulfilled without an Open championship.

Palmer had played in his first Open in 1953 at Oakmont. Still an amateur, he shot 84-78—162 and missed the cut. He missed the cut again in 1954, but he played seventy-two holes for the first time in 1955, shot 303, and tied for twenty-first place. He began to be a threat in 1956, when he shot 287 at Oak Hill and placed seventh, six strokes behind Middlecoff. After two years out of contention, he was in position to win at Winged Foot in 1959, but needing to finish with a sub-70 score, he shot 74 and placed fifth.

Palmer already had a reputation for strong finishes as 1960 began, and he reinforced it when he birdied the last two holes at Augusta and once again beat Ken Venturi. When he arrived at Cherry Hills for the Open, he was on a hot streak. In addition to the Masters, he had won four other tournaments, lost one in a playoff, and had placed among the first five in eleven of his eighteen starts.

Cherry Hills had been stretched to 7,004 yards, but when practice began, hardly anyone believed Hogan's twelve-year-old record of 276 would survive, because at Denver's altitude of 5,280 feet, the ball travels an estimated 8 percent farther than it does at sea level. A shot that normally flies 250 yards in Florida, for example, might go 270 yards in Denver.

On the other hand, the altitude could cause physical problems. Forty-seven at the time, Hogan developed headaches. Believing they were caused by the thin air, he carried a small oxygen canister with a breathing apparatus. He was not alone; thirty-eight players took twelve to fourteen liters of oxygen daily at special facilities in the locker room, and portable tanks were set up around the course. The club hired a physical therapist to supervise the service.

Once the championship began, Palmer was in trouble from the opening shot. The first hole, a downhill par 4, measured a scant 346 yards (reduced by 8 percent, it would measure 318 yards at sea level), and when Palmer tried to drive the green, he pushed his shot into a ditch running parallel to the fairway. After taking a penalty stroke for dropping out of the hazard, he hit a tree with his third, made 6, shot an indifferent 72, and trailed Mike Souchak by four strokes. Souchak, a big, husky man who had played defensive end for Duke when Palmer played golf for Wake Forest in a neighboring North Carolina town, shot 68 (Mike was the younger brother of Frank Souchak, the amateur who finished ninth at Oakmont in 1953). Arnold shot 71 the next day, but Souchak tore around in 67, set a record of 135, and led by three strokes over Doug Sanders.

Saturday, the day of the double round, was sunny and warm, with the snowy peaks of the Rockies glowing in the morning light. Even par after seventeen holes, Souchak showed the first signs that he might crack, taking 6 on the 18th when a movie camera whirred at the top of his backswing and shooting 73. He went to lunch with 208 for fifty-four holes, holding a two-stroke lead over Julius Boros, Dow Finsterwald, and Jerry Barber.

Meanwhile, Palmer was in fifteenth place with 215. To win, he would not only have to make up seven strokes, he'd also have to pass fourteen men. He sat at lunch eating a cheeseburger, drinking iced tea, and talking with Ken Venturi, Bob Rosburg, and Bob Drum, a reporter for the *Pittsburgh Press*. The talk was quick and forced.

"I wonder if Souchak can hold on," Venturi speculated.

"I don't see why he can't," Rosburg answered, "but it's a funny game." Then Palmer brought the conversation to life.

"I may shoot sixty-five," he said, "What would that do?"

"Nothing," Drum scowled. "You're too far back."

Palmer's eyes blazed.

"The hell I am," he snapped. "A sixty-five would give me two-eighty, and two-eighty wins Opens." Angered, he pushed back his chair and stalked from the room.

Three times Palmer had tried to drive the 1st green, and three times he'd failed, but when you're seven strokes behind, you can't be conservative. Arnold went for it again. His ball flew straight at the target, bounded through a belt of rough crossing in front, and rolled onto the green twenty feet from the cup. His putt for the eagle 2 barely slipped past the hole, and he made his birdie.

His confidence buoyed, Arnold raced to the next tee, eager to attack the course. His approach missed the 2nd green, but he chipped in for another birdie. A wedge to a foot set up another birdie at the 3rd, and then he holed from eighteen feet on the 4th. He was finally in the chase now, two under par for the tournament and only three strokes back of Souchak, and the big crowd that had been waiting to follow Mike began breaking up and racing ahead to join the growing Palmer gallery.

With every putt that fell, the cheers grew louder, and spectators poured in from every direction, caught up in the frenzy of one of the wildest days the Open had ever seen. Before it was over, ten men would have their chances to win, and when it finally ended, they had seen the coronation of Arnold Palmer, the emergence of Jack Nicklaus, and the last gasp of Ben Hogan, three men who were the best of their times.

That still lay ahead, though. Now, on the 5th, a par 5 of 538 yards, Palmer drove into the right rough, hit a 3-wood into a greenside bunker, came out twenty feet from the hole, and took two putts. It was his first par of the round. After that pause he went back to work, hitting a 7-iron to the heart of the 6th green and holing a curling twenty-five-footer, then pulling his drive into the left rough at the 7th, pitching to six feet and scoring his sixth birdie in seven holes.

He had most of the frenzied gallery with him now, but those who came late missed the best of the round. He bogeyed the 8th, a long, uphill par 3 of 233 yards, missing from three feet after his 2-iron hooked into a bunker, and then made a par 4 on the 9th. Out in 30, Palmer had turned the Open around.

While Palmer was playing astonishing golf, others were falling all around him. Souchak was among the first to falter. He had always used a

4-wood from the 1st tee, resisting the urge to go for the green, but hearing the thundering roars from Palmer's gallery, he gambled with his driver. His timing off, he pushed the shot into the ditch and made 6, had an unplayable lie on the 9th, and made the turn in 36. In nine holes, Palmer had made up six of the seven strokes he needed to catch Souchak, but by then Arnold had other problems.

As Palmer stood in the bunker at the 8th, Jack Nicklaus was walking off the 9th green. Out in 32, he was five under par for sixty-three holes. Palmer was four under then, but so were Souchak, Ben Hogan, Julius Boros, Jack Fleck, Dow Finsterwald, Jerry Barber, and Don Cherry, the singer, who often arranged nightclub appearances where golf tournaments were played. Palmer then bogeyed the 8th and fell two strokes behind Nicklaus.

For the next half hour it was impossible to know who was leading. Dutch Harrison was out early, and if he could par the last few holes, he would have 283 (he did). Meanwhile, Ted Kroll and Fleck, playing behind Palmer, were tearing up the first nine too. Kroll had begun the last round at 216, one stroke behind Palmer, and birdied five of the first seven holes, and Fleck, who began with 212, birdied five of the first six.

Palmer was ripping the course apart, but not only couldn't he shake free, he couldn't even catch up. It became a matter of whose nerves were steady enough, of who had the stamina to play thirty-six holes in one day under the intense pressure of Open conditions—the fast, hard greens, the narrow fairways, the punishing rough, the lure of fame—of who could play the shots he must play and of who could not.

As Palmer, Kroll, Fleck, Hogan, and Nicklaus played relentlessly on, Souchak cracked. When he bogeyed the 9th, he fell from the lead for the first time, kept piling up bogeys, and shot 75. One man gone.

Up ahead, Nicklaus showed his inexperience. Leading by one stroke after twelve holes, Jack played two perfectly executed shots on the 13th—a 3-wood to level ground short of the creek that intersects the fairway, then a soft 9-iron that stopped twelve feet short of the hole, leaving him an uphill putt, exactly what he wanted. Jack stroked the ball too firmly; it rolled past the hole by about eighteen inches, leaving him with a nasty downhill putt. Nicklaus was only twenty years old, and he was paired with Hogan, in awe of the man and somewhat intimidated by him. Although Ben had been pleasant, even inspiring to play with, Jack knew his reputation for gruff, impatient replies to what he considered stupid questions, and now Jack had a problem. As he looked over his putt, he saw a poorly repaired ball pit directly in his line. Excited, anxious, and under as much pressure as he had ever known, Jack wasn't sure if he could repair the mark (he could), and he was embarrassed to ask either Hogan or an official. When he tapped the putt, the ball hit the depression, lurched off line, caught just the edge of the cup, and spun out. His lead was gone. Shaken, Nicklaus three-putted the 14th too.

It was about 4:45 then, and now Palmer held a share of the lead with Hogan and Fleck at four under par. Boros had dropped behind; he was bunkered on the 14th and missed a three-footer on the 15th.

Now Fleck began to slip, missing the short putts that had fallen for him earlier, and Kroll, playing much later than Palmer, could make up no more ground (eventually he shot 67 and finished at 283).

Palmer, meanwhile, had cooled off, but he continued to play steady, reliable golf. Five under after nine and three under for sixty-three holes, Arnold birdied the 11th, a long par 5 of 563 yards, and parred the next five. When he arrived at the 17th tee, he was four under par for seventy holes and two holes away from the 65 he wanted. Only one man was left between him and the championship. It was Hogan.

After starting with 75-67—142, which had left him seven strokes behind Souchak, Hogan had played the most consistently precise golf he'd ever played in the Open. He had hit thirty-four consecutive greens on Saturday, and if he had putted as he had six or seven years earlier, there's no telling how much he would have won by. The eighteen greens he hit in the morning round earned him only a 69, two strokes under par. After lunch, he hit the first nine greens without making one birdie. Then, playing a 3-wood from the 12th, a par 3 of 212 yards, he hit a lovely soft draw ten feet from the cup. The putt fell, and Ben was three under par for sixty-six holes, in the thick of the fight. His pitch to the 13th dropped just short of the hole, but it hit the pin and bounded nine feet away. Hogan swore, then missed the putt. A twenty-footer dropped on the 15th, and now he had a real chance.

He was four under par; three more pars and he would shoot 280. But 280 might not be good enough. He knew he was level with Palmer and Fleck, a stroke ahead of Nicklaus, but he had to figure one of them would birdie the 17th. He'd better make another birdie. He had a great chance at the 16th, where his pitch braked twelve feet away, but again he missed the putt.

Now he approached the 17th, a long straightaway par 5 of 548 yards with an island green sitting in a lake. Only a twelve-foot-wide band of water separated the green from the fairway, but this was the key feature. It forced the hole to be played with a drive, a layup, then a careful pitch to the green.

After a solid drive and a 3-iron just short of the pond, Hogan decided this was his chance. He had a good lie, with the ball sitting up nicely about an eighth of an inch off the ground, but the pin was very close to the front edge of the green, and with his putting so unreliable, Ben felt he had to play a shot that barely cleared the moat. It was risky, but it was his best chance for the birdie.

The scene was a strange tableau. Palmer and Paul Harney stood on the tee waiting to drive, Boros and Gary Player stood in the fairway waiting to play their second shots, and Hogan and Nicklaus were preparing to play their pitches.

As soon as Hogan hit the ball, Phil Strubing, the referee, shouted, "Oh, no!" It was short. No man could put more backspin on a shot than Hogan, and when his ball hit near the top of the bank rising from the pond, the spin drew it back down the slope and into the water. Had it carried another six inches, just enough to clear the bank, Ben would have had an easy putt for the birdie.

He walked over the causeway linking the fairway with the green, looked down at the ball sitting in shallow water, and took off his shoes and socks. The crowd cheered. He popped the ball onto the green but missed the putt. A stroke gone. Now he needed a birdie on the 18th for 280. The drive had to carry the same lake, but going for the ideal spot that would give him an open approach to the elevated green, Hogan tried to carry the ball too far. It dropped into the water again, about a foot short of land. He made 7 and finished the seventy-two holes in 284, even par. Instead of winning, he placed ninth.

Palmer saw it all, and with the final threat gone, played the last two holes safely. When his final putt fell, he flung his white visor toward the heavens, and the whole world seemed to rejoice.

Meanwhile, back in the locker room, a disappointed Hogan spoke a prophetic sentence.

"I played thirty-six holes today with a kid who should have won this thing by ten strokes."

Having finally won an Open to go with his two Masters victories, Palmer turned his attention to the British Open and the PGA Championship, creating the modern Grand Slam, a four-tournament sweep that resembled but didn't duplicate the Grand Slam Bobby Jones had completed in 1930. While it was impossible for Hogan to have won all four in 1953, it was possible now because the PGA and the British Open dates no longer conflicted, and in 1958 the PGA had changed the format of its championship from match to stroke play. Not only did Palmer's linking it with the Open and Masters raise the prestige of the PGA, his decision to play in the British Open gave that ancient rite a new life. While it wasn't exactly moribund, it had lagged well behind the U.S. Open and the Masters in America's interest, and it hadn't attracted broad attention since Hogan had won in 1953. Since then, Peter Thomson had made it a private affair, winning four of the next five; Bobby Locke won another, and Gary Player the most recent, in 1959. Not one of those three men had what Hollywood called star quality, though. For it to revive, the British Open had to attract the best American golfers.

By coincidence, Palmer's quest for his Grand Slam coincided with the 100th anniversary of the first British Open. With Palmer in the field after already having won the Masters and U.S. Open, combined with its being played at St. Andrews, the 1960 championship was the most popular since Hogan had come over seven years earlier. Palmer made it just as exciting.

With thirty-six holes to go, he was seven strokes behind Kel Nagle, but he made a fight of it to the end. He made up five strokes in the third round, but he couldn't quite pull it off. Nagle beat him by one stroke.

Back in the United States, Arnold finished seven strokes behind Jay Hebert in the PGA.

Arnold Palmer's emergence as the swashbuckling hero of his time—the Harrison Ford of the 1950s and 1960s—meshed with another of those periodic expansions of golf. Unlike those that went before, this spurt was prolonged and sustained. In 1946, at the end of the Second World War, we had 4,817 golf courses in the United States—private, municipal, and daily fee, privately owned but open to the public, a classification that includes resorts. By 1955, when Palmer joined the Tour, the total had grown to 5,218, an increase of 401. Over the next five years it grew by another 1,167, to 6,385. The next ten years saw an increase of 3,805, an incredible expansion, and by 1970 we had more than 10,000 courses. By comparison, growth over the next decade was puny; only 1,817 new courses were added, bringing the total to 12,005 by 1980.

The increase brought about another fundamental change. At the end of the war, 62 percent had been private clubs; the others were either municipal or daily fee. As the number of courses increased, the percentage of private clubs declined—to 50 percent in 1960 and 45 percent in 1970. By 1980, private clubs made up only 40 percent.

How much Palmer stimulated this growth is difficult to say, but his popularity certainly contributed something. Other factors spurred expansion at the same time. Hogan's comeback in 1950 attracted the attention of the non-golf fan; then Dwight Eisenhower was elected president, and golf entered into politics.

America's prosperity contributed. With more leisure time, blue-collar workers spent more of it on golf courses, most often municipal and daily fee. As existing courses became overcrowded, pressure grew on municipalities to build more with tax money, and entrepreneurs saw a future in daily fee and resort operations. By the end of 1974, we had more daily fee operations than private clubs, and more than three times as many as municipally owned courses.

Golf publications revived, too. In 1947, Bob Harlow, the man who once handled the business affairs of Walter Hagen and for a time ran the Tour, began publishing *Golf World*, a weekly magazine devoted mostly to tournament results; Bill Davis, a hustling young Chicagoan who sold commercial radio time, originated *Golf Digest* in 1950, and the brothers Bob and Arnold Abramson launched *Golf Magazine* in 1958. Soon regional publications sprang up throughout the land.

Palmer's magnetism had other effects, particularly on prize money. Every city wanted a golf tournament, and the Tour drove up the prices. The 1950 Tour was worth $419,950, but prize money climbed over $1 million in 1958, and by 1960 it was up to $1.3 million.

Individual money winnings spurted. When Hogan led in 1946, he earned $42,556. Twelve years later, in 1958, it hadn't grown by much; Palmer led with $42,607, only $51 more. Two years later Arnold led again, but he had jumped the leading total to $75,000.

Open prize money grew, too. The 1946 Open offered $8,000; it rose to $10,000 in 1947, and when Hogan made his comeback in 1950, it climbed to $15,000. The Open was never a prize money pacesetter. In 1953, when it reached $20,000 for the first time, seven other tournaments offered more, including the immortal Ardmore (Oklahoma) Open, which was worth $26,000. The World Championship was far ahead of all the others with a purse of $75,000. By 1958, Open prize money was up to $35,000, and then it began to escalate quickly, to $50,000 the next year and to $60,000 in 1960.

The number of entrants grew along with the prize money, and playing in the championship proper became increasingly difficult. The first post-war Open drew 1,175 entrants; by 1952 it was up to 1,688. Concerned that some players who should be in the field might not survive one thirty-six-hole qualifying round—indeed, some didn't—the USGA experimented with the British system for 1953. The original thirty-six holes, played at various locations around the country, qualified 300, who then played thirty-six more at the site—eighteen at Oakmont and eighteen at the Pittsburgh Field Club nearby.

The system was dropped after one trial, but over the next five years more good players failed to qualify, and a new system of two thirty-six-hole qualifying tests went into effect for 1959. All but 500 players were eliminated in the first trials at roughly sixty sites. Those 500, along with some players who had been exempt from the first round, played in the second series, at thirteen locations, to determine the championship field. Some players, however, had been exempt from both stages because of their recent accomplishments—the last five Open champions, low fifteen in the previous year's championship, leading Tour money winners, and the Amateur champion (the list changed over the years).

While this system improved the chances of the better golfers, the odds against one player's getting into the field was growing more prohibitive. In 1959, the Open drew 2,385 entrants. With twenty-one players totally exempt, 129 places were available to the remaining 2,364 entrants, odds of 18-1 against their survival.

Although the size of the entry grew, the size of the starting field shrank. In 1926, when the championship was extended permanently to more than two days, 147 players started. In 1936 the field was boosted to 165 and then to 170 in the first few postwar years. Golfers were taking more time to play though, and by 1949 the starting field was cut back to 162. It fluctuated between the high 150s and low 160s until 1959, when it was reduced to 150, because even at the time of year when the days are longest, a field of 160 modern golfers—mostly professionals—had trouble completing eighteen holes before dark. It took five hours for three men to play eighteen holes at Oakland Hills in 1961.

As more and more people were drawn into the game during the prosperous 1950s, and as golf became a popular spectator sport, the galleries changed, particularly Palmer's. The old decorum was passing; Arnold's gallery didn't come to applaud his spectacular shots with a polite clapping of hands, they came to cheer, just as they cheered for Mickey Mantle or Jim Brown or Bob Cousey. Instead of faintly heard calls of "well played," we heard "Go get 'em, Arnie." His fans acquired a name. Awed by the way his followers stampeded around Augusta National, straining to catch a glimpse of him rifling a long and soaring drive or holing an unlikely chip, or even hitching his pants, Johnny Hendrix, a sports reporter for an Augusta newspaper, added a new term to golf. Reminded of Alexander, Wellington, and Robert E. Lee, Hendrix named Palmer's gallery Arnie's Army.

The army bivouacked at Oakland Hills in June of 1961 expecting a charge up San Juan Hill; instead Palmer behaved more like General Pope at Bull Run. He wasn't really beaten; he was never in the battle. The thirty-six-hole cut fell at 150. Palmer shot 149. His golf was so loose that Bob Drum, the man who said he had no chance at Cherry Hills, warned him that he might be invited to Myrtle Beach, South Carolina, a reference to the annual championship of the Golf Writers' Association of America, a competition in which one man once shot 22 on a par 5 hole and was happy to finish and another swore he would have played one hole more respectably had he not four-chipped. Palmer wasn't amused.

Anticipation rose as the battle between Palmer and Oakland Hills drew close. Only Ben Hogan and Clayton Heafner had broken par 70 there ten years earlier, but if Palmer was on his game, surely he'd tame the monster. Par was indeed broken in the first round, but not by Palmer (he shot 74). Instead, Bobby Brue, an obscure young man not widely known outside Menomonee Falls, Wisconsin, shot 69. The effect was deflating; it was as if the dragon were slain not by St. George but by his page.

While Brue's round failed to inspire the galleries, it had a different effect on the players. They had picked their way cautiously around Oakland Hills in the first round, as if walking barefoot through broken glass, but now they saw the tough old course could be beaten, and they attacked with increased confidence. Four men shot 67 in the second round, one had 68, and five others 69. Brue played progressively worse each day and finished well out of contention.

It was clear by then that the past decade had mellowed Oakland Hills. Somehow the greens were more accessible, the fairways more easily reached, the bunkers shallower, and the rough not so fierce. While the course might have been playing longer with the installation of a watering system, a ball could be controlled on the softer, lusher fairways, and that is more important than length. Ten years earlier it had been common to see a ball hit a fairway and bound into the high and tangled rough. With softer ground, the ball might not roll as far, but it stayed in play.

Gene Littler won, shooting 73, 68, 72, and 68 and finishing with 281, one stroke better than Bob Goalby and Doug Sanders, and six strokes below Hogan's 1951 score of 287. The fifty-four-hole leader, Sanders needed a birdie on the 18th to tie Littler, who had made a nervous par 4 from a bunker by the 18th not long before. Sanders tried gamely to carry the clustered bunkers in the right rough, hoping to shorten his approach, but his ball hung up in the tall grass, his second stopped just off the front edge of the green, and his putt barely slipped past the cup.

The 1961 Open was the only tournament of significance Littler won as a professional. Why he didn't win more is another of the game's mysteries. His swing was every bit as poetic and free-flowing as Snead's, and watching him practice was as thrilling as watching others shoot sub-par scores. He could do anything with a golf ball that anyone else could do. His one failing, at least in terms of golf at the stratospheric level, was emotional. Unlike the great champions, Littler was not a driven man. He was warm and pleasant, a quiet man with an often impish sense of humor. Even now, holding the most important championship in the game, Littler remained what he had always been—something less than a god.

PART THREE

The last decade had been a remarkable period in the development of the game: Hogan had risen to heights only a few had ever climbed, but had grown old; Palmer had reached his peak, and no one knew how many more championships he would win; Nicklaus had given us a glimpse of the future; television had brought the game new popularity; prize money climbed; courses were being built everywhere; and every city wanted its own tournament. Golf was healthy, and as one era ended, another was about to begin.

SIXTEEN
Heavy Hangs the Head

With a chance to win his third Masters in 1961, Palmer bunkered his approach to the last hole and bladed his recovery all the way across and off the green. He made 6, and Gary Player won. Then, in early spring of 1962, it looked as if he had thrown another one away. Leading by two strokes with eighteen holes to go, Arnold shot 75, giving both Player and Dow Finsterwald the opening to catch him, but he was back on his game the next day, shot 68 in a playoff, and beat Player by three strokes and Finsterwald by seven. Since he had won the British Open the previous summer, thoughts of his winning all four of the principal tournaments in one year surfaced once again. With the Masters won, the Open was next, and it looked like a natural, since it was coming back to Oakmont, a course he had played so many times as an amateur. He was the biggest man in golf, and he would be playing in front of people who knew him, who rooted openly for him, and who worshipped him.

Their enthusiasm, along with their disregard for the old decorum, created an atmosphere at Oakmont unlike the feeling at any Open of the past. They came not so much to see a golf tournament as they came to see Arnold beat the pants off everybody else, and they wanted to revel in it.

Meantime, something of significance had happened over the winter. After a remarkable amateur career in which he had won the National Amateur twice and had come close to winning two Opens, Jack Nicklaus joined the pro Tour.

PART THREE

Palmer and Nicklaus were the most appealing attractions in golf, and when they were paired together in the first two rounds at Oakmont, they drew huge galleries. When they finished their warmups and stepped onto the 1st tee for the opening round, they found most of the 12,000 raucous fans who had poured onto the grounds waiting for them. After three holes, the majority had precious little to cheer about, because Jack started with three consecutive 3s, all for birdies, while Palmer had one 4 and two 5s and trailed Jack by five strokes. Matters righted themselves by the end of the day, though. At one point Arnold strung together five consecutive 3s, three of them for birdies, and finished with 71, a stroke better than Nicklaus.

Both of them trailed Littler, who shot 69, a round that included an eagle 3 on the ninth, a mild par 5 whose 485 yards run uphill all the way. Gene holed a pitch of about forty yards. He might have made 68, but his putt on the 18th stopped an inch short of the cup. This by a man who had shot 82 in a practice round on Tuesday.

Littler had trouble with the glassy Oakmont greens the next day, and Palmer and Bob Rosburg surged to the front, Palmer with 68 and Rosburg with 69. They were paired together the third day, and after sixteen holes of the morning round, Rosburg had the lead to himself, but then Palmer drove the 17th green and holed a fifteen-foot putt for an eagle 2, Rosburg made 5, and he was never a threat again. Palmer wasn't clear, though; he was tied with Bobby Nichols, a tall, pleasant Kentuckian who had survived an automobile accident ten years earlier that had left him unconscious for thirteen days and temporarily paralyzed from the waist down. Nichols had shot 70 and stood at 212 for fifty-four holes. Needing only a par 4 to move in front now, Palmer lashed an iron twelve feet from the cup on the 18th, but going boldly for the birdie, he overran the hole and three-putted, shooting 73 and matching Nichols' 212, one stroke under par.

The crowd had been growing all day. By two o'clock, more than 21,000 fans were on the grounds, shattering the attendance record set only a year earlier. Most of them cared for no one but Palmer. Whenever he hit a shot, they raced ahead, calling to one another, not caring that the man with Arnold still might have a shot to play. When Palmer holed a putt, they darted to the next hole, ignoring everyone else. Playing with distractions like that, Nicklaus had been fortunate to get around in 72 and 70 the first two days. He had been three strokes behind Palmer and Rosburg after thirty-six holes, and now, after another 72, he still had to make up two strokes over the last eighteen holes. He might do it if he could keep up his exceptional putting. In fifty-four holes over the most treacherous greens in championship golf, Jack had not had one three-putt green. Palmer had had three in the first round alone.

Then Jack three-putted the 1st green on Saturday afternoon.

Palmer, meanwhile, had gone to lunch feeling a bit let down after missing the birdie opportunity on the 18th, had a ham and cheese sandwich and drank a weird mixture of chocolate milk and Coke. Refreshed, he attacked the course once again while the gallery urged him on.

"Go get 'em. Arnie," they yelled.

"Get tough, Arnie," others whooped.

And Arnie got tough. After a routine par on the 1st, he dropped a six-footer on the 2nd, and following another routine par on the 3rd, he played a wonderful pitch from the rough alongside the 4th hole and birdied again. Now he was two under for the round and three under for fifty-eight holes. A thirty-five-footer hit the hole on the 6th and spun out, a fifteen-footer grazed the cup on the 8th, and then he drilled a long straight drive right up the middle of the 9th fairway. If he could make another birdie here—or better yet an eagle—he might put the Open out of reach. The green was certainly within range of a good solid wood shot, but the pin was set in the front right corner, a tough spot to reach. Arnold pondered his situation. He'd go for the eagle and try to cut a 3-wood in close to the hole. Putting all his power into the shot, he hit the ball solidly enough, but it drifted too much and settled a few yards into the right rough, just about level with the hole and lying on grass that had been flattened by the gallery. No eagle here, but with a simple little flip and a good putt, Arnold should have his birdie, and that might do it.

Then, in a tomblike silence, Palmer stubbed the shot; the ball popped up and dropped quickly back into the grass, still short of the green. Palmer was stunned. He stood for a moment and glared at the ball, then stepped up and played a weak chip that left him eight feet short of the cup. After having a relatively easy shot at a birdie, Arnold would need some luck now to make his par. He didn't have it; his ball slipped past the right edge of the cup, and he made 6. It was like a double bogey. Worse than that, he had given Nicklaus an opening.

Palmer had led Nicklaus by four strokes after his birdie on the fourth, but he lost every one of them over the next nine holes. With five holes to play, Jack and Arnold were tied, and since Rosburg was playing badly and Nichols was struggling, they had the championship to themselves.

The outcome seemed to have turned in Palmer's favor when Nicklaus ran into trouble at the 17th. Trying to reach the green with his tee shot, Jack drove into one of the greenside bunkers, barely cleared the bank with his recovery, and had to chip and putt for his par. It was like losing a stroke, because he had to figure Arnold would make 3. But Jack wasn't ready to give up. Stepping over to the 18th tee, he pounded his drive 300 yards, then spanked a 6-iron twelve feet from the cup. With another chance at the birdie he felt he needed so badly, he missed the putt: 69 and 283.

Playing behind Nicklaus, Palmer always knew exactly what he needed, and when he dropped his approach eight feet from the cup on the 17th, he looked like the winner. He missed the birdie. One more chance, now, but the 18th was no birdie hole. It measured 462 bunker-studded yards, and its green was as slick as a frozen pond. Arnold smashed his drive as hard as he could and dropped a gorgeous approach ten feet from the cup. Another chance to end it. Another missed putt. It was a shame in a way because Palmer had played superbly the last day, missing only four greens in thirty-six holes and twice reaching par 5 holes with his second, but he had shot 73 in the morning and 71 in the afternoon, and fallen into a tie with Nicklaus.

The spark was gone from Palmer's game the next day, and he dropped behind early in the playoff. After Nicklaus birdied the 6th, Arnold lagged four strokes behind. But he wasn't through just yet. With his undisciplined army cheering him on, Arnold birdied the 9th to take one stroke back, then closed to within one stroke with birdies on the 11th and 12th. With six holes to play, Palmer was in high gear, looking as if he might catch up, but all his hope ended on the 13th. He three-putted, fell two strokes behind, and could make no more headway. He shot 74 and Nicklaus shot 71.

This was an Open Palmer should have won because he was the better golfer then. He lost (and Nicklaus won) on Oakmont's greens. In the ninety holes, Jack had only that one three-putt green while Palmer had ten. If one shot cost him the championship, it was that gambling 3-wood on the 9th hole. Had he tried to do no more than put his ball somewhere on the green, the odds are that he'd have made his birdie; by playing a fancy shot, he lost the gamble. But that was his game, that was his appeal. If he hadn't gone for the eagle, he wouldn't have been Arnold Palmer.

Eventually he became another Sam Snead, the man everybody hoped would win the Open, but who never would again. Unlike Snead, though, Arnold won once before learning how vulnerable he could be.

Nevertheless, he was the dominant force in the Open for the next four years, and he remained a strong contender for the next decade. Nicklaus may have been the champion, but Palmer was still the king. As if to emphasize that while we had seen a glimpse of the future at Oakmont, it wasn't here yet, Palmer again very nearly won in 1963, while Nicklaus missed the cut.

The 1963 Open was brought to The Country Club to observe the fiftieth anniversary of Francis Ouimet's having won there in 1913, and as it had on that misty day half a century earlier, the championship was settled by another playoff.

That he was one of the participants in the playoff surprised even Palmer. Late on Saturday afternoon he had needed a drive and a 3-iron to reach the 18th green, which at 385 yards, was hardly worthy of that much artillery, and had had to get down in two from thirty-five feet to tie Julius Boros, who even then was clearing out his locker, getting ready to leave town. Julius had shot 293, nine strokes over par, and had no idea it would be the low 72-hole score. Both he and Palmer expected to finish behind Jacky Cupit, a young Tour player from Texas, who was two strokes ahead playing the 17th hole.

Palmer's first putt glided five feet past the hole, and now he would have to work hard to tie Boros for second place. As Arnold coiled over his ball in that peculiar stance that looked like a panther ready to strike, he heard a groan from the direction of the 17th green. Then a marshal raced along the fairway ropes, and word spread that Cupit had made 6 and both his strokes were gone. Suddenly Palmer's putt became more significant; if he made it, chances are he'd be in a playoff with Boros, who just as suddenly was in the driver's seat. He had his 293; let the others struggle for theirs.

Palmer rammed the ball into the back of the hole. Minutes later, Cupit played a 6-iron to twelve feet and had a chance to win outright, but his ball ran by the low side of the cup.

The 293 was the highest score to lead after seventy-two holes since 1935, when Sam Parks won with 299. It had a number of causes. The course was not in the best condition, principally because of bad luck. In a frigid New England winter, sheets of ice had covered the greens for weeks, causing severe damage, warm spring weather that would have helped them had arrived late, and vandals had sneaked onto the course and carved up one green only days before the Open began.

Condition aside, the main cause of the high scores was a high and unpredictable wind. It swirled around Brookline and tossed flying balls from one side of the fairway to the other. The last day was memorable. Of the fifty-one players who made the cut, only three men shot 72, one stroke over par. Boros was one of them, making his in the fourth round, but it had followed a 76 in the morning that he believed had knocked him out of contention. It hadn't; only nine men had done better. Fourteen shot 80 or higher, and Tommy Aaron shot 91 (as the strokes piled up, Aaron waved his handkerchief aloft and begged, "Where do I surrender?"). Twelve more failed to break 80 in the afternoon, when the wind slackened.

The tournament was begging to be won, but player after player tossed away his opportunity in the blustery afternoon. Tony Lema could have won, but he bogeyed both the 17th and 18th and missed the playoff by two strokes; Paul Harney bogeyed the 18th and missed by one; Bruce Crampton and Billy Maxwell needed only a couple of birdies over the final holes, but they dropped strokes instead. In the end, only Boros, Palmer, and Cupit had held fast, if respective fourth round scores of 72, 74, and 75 could be called that, and in a reprise of 1913, forced a three-man playoff the next day.

Boros was in command from the start. He raced ahead by playing the first five holes in one under par, opening a three-stroke lead, shot 33 on the first nine, and was never in trouble. Whatever remote chance Palmer might have had ended on the 11th hole, a 445-yard par 4 whose green sits on the far side of a pond. Four strokes behind by then after bogeying the 10th, Arnold strained for a little extra distance and hooked his drive into a rotted tree stump standing in the thick woods lining the left side. He had three choices: taking penalties amounting to two strokes, he could either drop the ball out of the stump or he could hit another drive; or else he could play the ball as it lay. Adventurous by nature and not in position to squander strokes, he tried to play the shot. He chopped at it three times to knock it free, made 7, and even though he birdied three of the last four holes, he shot 76 and finished six strokes behind Boros and three behind Cupit. Boros shot 70, Cupit 73, and Palmer 76.

Boros turned out to be a golfer of remarkable longevity. He was forty-three years old when he won at Brookline, the second oldest man ever to have won the Open (Ted Ray had been a few months older in 1920), and in 1968, when he was forty-eight, he won the PGA Championship. No one that old ever won a tournament that important. In the years since he had won his first Open in 1952, he had changed very little. He was thicker in the girth, but he still ambled slowly along, swung with a languid, rhythmic tempo, and played the loveliest soft lob from high grass you ever saw. It popped up in a lazy arc, hit the green gently, and crawled straight toward the cup. It was the kind of shot that fit nicely into Open course tactics.

His record was amazing. From 1950, when he played in his first Open, through 1960, he had placed fifth or better six times. He had not been a factor the next two years, missing the cut in 1961 and filing his entry so late in 1962 it arrived six days after the deadline, but now he was back atop the game. His victory in the Open was his third in recent weeks—he had won the Colonial National Invitation and the Buick Open near Detroit, shooting 66-71-68-69—274 in what some players called the finest four rounds of golf ever played. Boros continued to play reasonably well in the Open for years, but he finished among the low ten only twice again. He was fourth in 1965, and eight years later, in 1973 when he was fifty-three, had a chance to win at Oakmont as he went into the fourth round, but he shot 73 and finished seventh, four strokes behind Johnny Miller.

In 1964, though, one year after winning, he missed the cut, but in the drama of that gripping week, his failure was hardly noticed.

SEVENTEEN
One Brief Shining Moment

As 1963 gave way to 1964, Nicklaus was chipping away at Palmer's pre-eminence, but Arnold was still the game's leading player. While Nicklaus had won the Open in 1962 and the Masters and the PGA in 1963, Palmer's seventy-two-hole score had been beaten only once in the last four Opens, and beginning in 1958 he had won the Masters three times and the British Open twice. As 1964 began, he won the Masters again, becoming the first man to win it four times. Now the Open was coming to Washington for the first time in forty-three years, and once again Palmer was the clear choice.

The championship was scheduled for the Congressional Country Club, which had been stretched out to 7,053 yards, making it the longest Open course ever. It was not particularly strong though. The East had been locked in a drought as well as a heat wave, and because of the dry conditions, Congressional in mid-June was not as punishing as it was expected to be. Its irrigation system had kept the fairways lush and green, but the water didn't reach the rough. Once healthy, thick, and impossible, it had withered and died, and it seemed obvious after thirty-six holes that despite its length, Congressional would yield low, possibly record scores. It was not obvious, however, that the Open would turn into melodrama.

Starting with 68, Palmer was the only man in the field to break par 70 in the first round, but even though he followed with 69, he lost his lead. Tommy Jacobs, a young, curly-haired Californian, exposed Congressional's weakness by shooting 64, matching the eighteen-hole record set by Lee Mackey in 1950. As the day of the double round began, Jacobs was in first place with 136, Palmer was one stroke behind with 137, and then there was a four-stroke gap to Billy Collins at 141. Next, with a solid, steady 72-70—142, stood Ken Venturi.

Finding Venturi so close to the lead shocked everyone in golf; he had played so poorly for the last few years he had trouble getting into Tour tournaments, and he nearly didn't make it into the Open. He had gone through qualifying rounds in Detroit, and because of some withdrawals had played the last round with Larry Mowry, who hadn't yet joined the Tour, Billy Collins, one of the longer hitters, and Mike Souchak. Mowry had gone around the first nine in three under par while Venturi was two over. Clearly discouraged, Venturi said to the others, "I'm sorry, guys, but I've had enough. I'm packing it in."

Both Collins and Souchak pleaded with him to change his mind, and Mowry said, "Kenny, don't let my score discourage you. I'm playing better than I have all year." Then Souchak put his hand on Venturi's shoulder, made a funny remark, and Venturi laughed, changed his mind about quitting, and qualified. Now, as the third round began, he was among the leaders.

Congressional began with a moderate par 4 of 405 yards. Venturi played a precise iron to fifteen feet and rolled his putt to the lip of the hole. The ball hung on the edge for about twenty seconds, then dropped for the birdie. He was off on one of the Open's historic days.

After making his figures on the 2nd and 3rd holes, Venturi's game suddenly turned hot. He ran in putts of fifteen feet on the 4th and 5th, six feet on the 8th, and on the 9th, a misbegotten par 5 of 600 yards whose green is set behind a deep chasm beyond a chute of trees, dropped a wedge ten feet behind the hole, and on a slick and tilted green coaxed it in for his fifth birdie of the round. He had played the first nine in 3-3-4-3-3-4-3-3-4—30, matching the Open's nine-hole record and charging into the thick of the fight. He had hit every fairway and every green, and he had holed every possible putt. When Jacobs completed the first in 36, Venturi had caught him. He hadn't played like that in years.

Thirty-three years old then, Venturi had been a prominent golfer for more than a decade. At seventeen in 1948, he had been runner-up to Dean Lind in the first United States Junior Amateur Championship only five years after taking up the game. He had been encouraged by his father, who had become coprofessional and manager of the golf shop at Harding Park municipal course in San Francisco after thirty years as a ship's chandler. Kenny had played his first round of golf when he was twelve, and at first had no great liking for the game—he shot 172 in his first eighteen-hole round—but he took to it eventually and won the San Francisco Interscholastic championship before losing to Lind in the National Junior. A year later he won the San Francisco City Championship and the California Amateur at Pebble Beach. Since winning either of those is a major achievement in amateur golf, he was chosen for both the 1952 Americas Cup Match (a short-lived series between amateurs from the United States, Canada, and Mexico), and the 1953 Walker Cup. He played devastating golf in the Americas Cup, winning one singles match 10 and 9 and another 12 and 11, and he was a sensation in the Walker Cup, teaming with Sam Urzetta, the 1950 Amateur champion, in beating Joe Carr and Ronald White by 6 and 4 in their alternate shot match, and then destroying Jim Wilson, a good Scottish golfer, by 9 and 8 in singles.

As his reputation grew, he was hired as an automobile salesman by Ed Lowery, Francis Ouimet's caddie in the 1913 Open, who had grown up to be a force in golf as a member of the USGA's executive committee. Realizing he had a prodigy on his hands, Lowery persuaded Byron Nelson to become Ken's tutor. When he shot 66 in their first round together, Venturi assumed Nelson would have very little to criticize. He was wrong. For the next four days Nelson took Venturi's swing apart, then carefully put it together again, basing it on a new set of fundamentals, chiefly position and timing. Under Nelson's guidance, Venturi did nothing but improve.

As a member of the 1953 Walker Cup team, Ken had been invited to the 1954 Masters, shot 297, and tied for sixteenth place, assuring an invitation the next year. Since he was in the Army in 1955 and not available, previous Masters winners, who annually select one player not otherwise eligible, invited him to play in 1956 after his release from the service. Because he was paired in the first round with Billy Joe Patton, who ranked then as the greatest Southern hero since Robert E. Lee (Bobby Jones was a god), he was playing before a huge gallery. The fans began the day whooping it up for Billy Joe, but they left that evening awed by Venturi.

He began with an incredible rush. He birdied the 1st. He birdied the 2nd. He birdied the 3rd. When he birdied the 4th, the gallery was wondering if he could make anything but birdies. He finished the first nine in 32 and came back in 34. His 66 carried the day. When he followed with 69 and 75, he took a four-stroke lead into the last round, and he seemed certain to become the first amateur to win the Masters.

Then he suffered the first of a series of disappointments that would dog him throughout his career. On a chilly, windy day, with a near gale whistling through the Georgia pines, Venturi shot 80 and lost the Masters by one stroke to Jack Burke, Jr., who had begun the round eight strokes behind but made up nine by shooting 71. A disappointment to be sure, but hardly a soul who watched him that week saw anything less than a marvelous future.

Venturi was twenty-four years old that April (he became twenty-five in May). He was tall and slender, standing six feet and weighing 170 pounds, had dark, wavy hair and bright blue eyes, and he wore a happy, open expression. Feet splayed, he swaggered along the fairway with a brisk, confident gait and a soupçon of arrogance, dressed in tones of gray, white, and black, wearing a white linen cap à la Hogan.

He spoke with a stammer, but ah, when he swung he was a joy to watch. He had an elegant, compact, rhythmic motion, and when his hands entered the hitting zone, they whipped through with power and control. He was an exceptionally fine iron player, particularly adroit with the long irons. No doubt about it, he would be a winner.

Venturi joined the Tour in June 1957, won money in all but one of his nineteen starts that year, and had an incredible streak of twelve consecutive rounds under 69. Jay Hebert called him the best player in the game. The following spring he had his second Masters disappointment. Trailing Palmer by one stroke after eleven holes, he lost ground to Arnold's strong finish that included his eagle 3 on the 13th, and placed fourth, two strokes out of first place. Two years later he was in position to win once more, but Palmer birdied the last two holes and beat him again. Nevertheless, through 1960 he had won ten tournaments.

His Open record was not nearly so good. He had placed eighth as an amateur in 1956, and sixth in 1957, four strokes behind Dick Mayer and Cary Middlecoff. Over the next three years, though, he placed no higher than twenty-third, and he missed the cut in both 1961 and 1962.

Although his game had gradually lost its assurance—Harvie Ward had a theory that his swing began to deteriorate as he reached for more length, trying to keep up with Palmer—it really came apart in a pro-amateur tournament in Palm Springs in 1961. Bending over to pick his ball from the hole, Venturi felt a sharp pain in his back. When it wouldn't go away, he withdrew and took several weeks off. To keep his back limber, he took massages and daily heat treatments. It still hurt. To avoid the pain, he restricted his swing. It became flatter and flatter as his game sank lower and lower. Second in winnings in 1960, with $41,230 (Palmer led with $75,262), Venturi won only $3,848 in 1963. Through 1962 and 1963 he played in fifty-four tournaments and only once finished among the first five.

His once lovely and fluid swing gone forever, replaced by a crude, quick, jerky motion you could see any Saturday morning at the local club, Venturi was thirty-two, and he was washed up.

PART THREE

While he played a few tournaments in 1963, he spent most of the year at home in Hillsborough, California, south of San Francisco, laboring over his game, because he believed deep within himself that he could come back. Occasionally he played with the Reverend Francis Murray, a parish priest in Burlingame, a neighboring town. While Ken toiled over the mechanics of his game, Father Murray attacked his spirit. Over time he built a more relaxed and philosophical attitude, one Venturi would need even more after his moment of glory.

The year 1964 did not begin well for Kenny; he was crushed when he wasn't invited to the Masters, and since he was no longer exempt from qualifying for Tour events, he had to plead for sponsors' exemptions. When he played, he grew increasingly encouraged, because he had several good finishes, including a third place in the Thunderbird Classic two weeks before the Open. With his game responding and his spirits reviving, a letter from Father Murray arrived shortly before the Open:

> *Dear Ken,*
>
> *For you to become the 1964 U.S. Open Champion would be one of the greatest things that can possibly happen to our country this year. Should you win, the effect would be both a blessing and a tonic to so many people who desperately need encouragement and a reason for hope.*
>
> *Most people are in the midst of unremitting struggle, involving their jobs, their family problems, their health, frustrations of various sorts, even the insecurity of life itself. For many there is a pressing temptation to give up, to quit trying. Life at times simply seems to be too much, its demands overpowering.*
>
> *If you should win, Ken, you would prove, I believe, to millions everywhere that they, too, can be victorious over doubt, misfortune, and despair. I'll be here with your mother and father and the children watching you on TV.*
>
> > *Your friend,*
> > *Father Murray*

The letter was just what Venturi needed; it gave him the patience to cope with the torments of championship golf. His changed outlook had carried him through the first two rounds of the Open, and now it was helping him control his excitement as he made his surprising move. As Kenny walked past, a scoreboard near the 9th green showed him clearly in the lead. Joe Dey, the referee, suggested he might want to look.

"Not interested," he said. "I can't change what's up there, and I can't control what the other guys are doing. One shot at a time; that's all that interests me."

210

One of the game's great innovators, Byron Nelson won the Open in 1939.

Ben Hogan at the peak of his career, when he combined power with finesse and dominated the game as so few have ever done.

With his lazy, rhythmic swing, Julius Boros compiled an amazing record in the Open. Apart from winning in 1952 and 1963, he was a force in the championship from 1950 through 1973.

Although his left arm was permanently bent at the elbow because of a childhood accident, Ed Furgol was good enough to win the 1954 Open.

Jack Fleck's defeat of Ben Hogan in the 1955 playoff ranks with the greats of Open upsets.

Although at times a mass of nerves, Cary Middlecoff was a glorious striker of the ball. He won the Open in 1949 and 1956.

No one attracted galleries better than Palmer.

Arnold Palmer holing his final putt in the 1960 Open for his only victory.

A putt falls for Ken Venturi in the 1964 championship, which he won in melodramatic circumstances.

Although no one realized it at the time, Gary Player was leading an assault by foreign golfers that would continue to grow when he won the 1965 Open.

The greatest player of his age, Jack Nicklaus, at Baltusrol in 1967, on his way to his second championship.

The Golden Bear winning his third Open, at Pebble Beach in 1972.

Back at Baltusrol in 1980,
and Nicklaus wins a record-tying
fourth Open.

Lee Trevino, the Open champion
of 1968 and 1971, whom Hogan
liked to watch because, he said, "he
uses his hands so beautifully."

No shot has ever been more dramatic than Tom Watson's pitch from the rough into the cup for a birdie on the seventy-first green at Pebble Beach, which won the 1982 championship.

Andy North. He had won three tournaments through 1986, and two of them were Opens.

The United States Open Championship trophy.

Turning for home, Venturi played the 10th and 11th in pars, and then birdied the 12th, a solid par 3 of 188 yards with a kidney-shaped green wrapped around a deep bunker. Six under now. Jacobs, meanwhile, had fought back into the lead, but when Ken played the next four holes in par, once again he slipped a stroke ahead of Tommy, who lost a stroke at the 14th, a difficult though not very good hole of 434 yards with a shallow green cut into the shoulder of a hill.

Heat seemed to collect in the hollows of Congressional, set in the shallow valley of the Potomac River. Even when the temperature was mild, the air hung heavy and still; whatever breeze was about seldom penetrated the thick clusters of maple and oak. The temperature was oppressive, and under a flaming sun it had been climbing throughout the day. It had reached 75 degrees by eight o'clock in the morning, and now it was past 90 and still rising. Venturi had had so little to drink through the morning that by the time he reached the 17th green he was dehydrated, lightheaded, and shaking so badly he could hardly hold his putter. He three-putted from twenty-five feet, making his first bogey of the day and then drove into the woods that line the long sloping fairway of the 18th hole. His feet were like lead weights as he labored down the grade toward his ball. He punched a shot into the fairway, pitched on, then missed a four-foot putt that would have saved his par. Another bogey and a 66. He had 208 for fifty-four holes, but Jacobs finished minutes later with 70 and 206.

Even though he had lost two strokes on the last two holes, Venturi had played a long and difficult course in four under par, a remarkable achievement, but his ordeal was not over. He still had eighteen holes to play, and he was exhausted. Reaching the clubhouse, he slumped on a locker room bench, too drained to stand and unable to speak. His face had no color, and his eyes were vacant and staring. He couldn't eat. He ordered tea and lemon, the first liquid he had taken since early morning, and salt tablets. The other players were concerned for him. Raymond Floyd, who was paired with him, found Ken's wife, Conni, and told her, "He's sick." Dr. John Everett, a Congressional member, took him to one of the bedrooms in the huge clubhouse to lie down and rest. No one was sure if he could play in the afternoon.

After a fifty-minute break, he was back on the 1st tee, apparently recovered. Dr. Everett was with him, carrying a plastic bag of ice cubes wrapped in a white cotton towel. He fed him salt tablets and periodically laid the ice against the back of his neck to cool him throughout the long and difficult afternoon.

Ken began well enough with five sound pars, but he three-putted the 6th, losing a stroke. He was tied for the lead by now, for Jacobs had lost two strokes on the 2nd hole, a sturdy, uphill par 3, and another on the 4th.

PART THREE

The Open was between the two of them now, for Palmer was baffled by his putter and had shot 75 in the morning, dropping six strokes behind Jacobs and four behind Venturi. No one else was in the neighborhood.

When he holed a downhill twelve-footer on the 9th, Venturi was out in 35, and for the first time he looked like a winner. He was two under par for the sixty-three holes, had passed Jacobs, who was two strokes behind him, and no one else was within four strokes of him. But even though he had played superbly in the morning, there were those lingering doubts that his game would hold up.

The temperature continued to climb—95 degrees, 100 degrees; it was becoming unbearable. Still the shots sprang strong and true from Venturi's clubs: a 1-iron missed the long and dangerous 10th, where the water closes in from the right, but a fifteen-footer saved the par. Another par on the 11th, and one more on the 12th. Now for the 13th, a strong par 4 of 448 yards where the ground runs level for the first 200 yards, then falls gently away before rising once again to a green above fairway level. Ken's drive streaked down the middle and rolled to the base of the valley. Hesitating only an instant, he hit a lovely, soft 6-iron that sat down gently on the hard green less than twenty feet from the cup. He took a long time over the putt, and when it fell, he closed his eyes, turned, lifted his face to the sun, and stood silent for a moment. He led now by four strokes, and even though he had five hard holes to play, he was safe, for Jacobs was falling apart.

Venturi's pace had slowed to little more than a crawl, but as soon as he set himself over the ball, he found his strength and played one firm stroke after another. Now, after a fine drive, he began the long walk down the 18th, his head high, his face glowing. Wave upon wave of cheers and applause followed him as step by painful step he marched through the fans who stood five and six deep along both sides of the fairway.

The green of the 18th is a peninsula that juts into a pond. Venturi steered his approach away from the water and caught a bunker. He recovered to about ten feet; when the ball fell into the hole, he dropped his putter, turned away, and beaming as much in relief as in joy, raised his arms and said aloud: "My God, I've won the Open."

As the crowd screamed and yelled, Raymond Floyd picked Venturi's ball from the cup and gave it to him, his eyes wet and tears streaming down his face. He had seen Venturi come as far back as anyone ever had to win the championship. Other players rejoiced with him. Jim Ferrier, the 1947 PGA champion, said, "I think it's just wonderful how he has come back." Gardner Dickinson added, "Other people have come back, but to come back as far as he has . . . I played with him in Florida, and in one round he hit eleven balls out of bounds."

Venturi had played the last round in par 70 and finished the seventy-two holes in 278, only two strokes behind the record of 276 Hogan had set in 1948. His last three rounds of 70-66-70—206 set a record, and his 136 for the last two rounds tied Sarazen's mark at Fresh Meadow. Venturi had played simply marvelous golf. But a question still lingered: Had he come back permanently, or was this only one brief flash of brilliance?

His confidence restored, Venturi continued to play first-class golf the rest of the year, winning the American Golf Classic. It looked as if he had come back to stay. Then it was all over. A problem developed with blood circulation through his wrists. His hands lost some of their feeling, and once again he sank to the bottom. At the Bellerive Country Club in 1965, he missed the cut. As he sat alone in the locker room straddling a bench with his head bowed, a man approached and said how very sorry he was that Venturi had played so badly in the first two rounds, "especially after last year."

Ken sat for a moment, then said quietly, "At least there was a last year."

Few people knew how much the Open meant to him, but he expressed his feelings five years later at a dinner just before the 1969 Open began. He was eloquent. In a wavering voice he said:

"This is my last year of exemption for the Open. How I won it I still don't know. At the end of 1964 I suffered a disease of the hands. I don't know why, but it happened, and I can't question it." His voice faltered and he paused. "Unless a miracle happens, my golf days are limited; I may be forced to leave the game I love. There's Gary," he said, nodding toward Player, "a man with fortitude and determination. There's Jack. He had a lot of early success, but it didn't spoil him. Gene Littler, one of the greatest talents I've ever seen. He won it with a great swing. And Arnold. Articles have been written that may have drawn us apart, but I'll always feel privileged to call Arnold a friend, a champion among champions." Venturi turned to his left and looked down at Lee Trevino, the 1968 champion. "Lee has capitalized financially on his championship, but, Lee, the U.S. Open Championship is more than money. It is something you will cherish forever."

Now he looked out over the audience, hushed by his emotion.

"There's not much I fear, but I do fear leaving the game I love. I just thank God for the moment of glory He gave me. Whoever wins the Open next Sunday, whether it is an unknown or an established player, whoever wins it, treat it well, because the U.S. Open is the greatest championship in golf."

He never played in another.

EIGHTEEN
So Near, So Far

Palmer had won eight tournaments in 1960 and at least five in each of the next three years, but he had won only twice in 1964—one of them the Masters—and in 1965 he won only the Tournament of Champions, an affair in Las Vegas limited to winners of the previous season's Tour events. By the standards he had come to expect, it was a dull year. He had a bad Open, too, shooting two 76s and missing the thirty-six-hole cut for the first time in eight years.

Gary Player won the 1965 Open, beating Kel Nagle in a playoff and becoming the first foreign champion since the Englishman Ted Ray in 1920.

A small man, standing barely five-foot-seven and weighing no more than 150 pounds, Player hit his shots like his countryman Bobby Locke, starting them two holes over and somehow hooking them back to center-fairway. Like Locke, too, he was an exceptional putter. The likenesses ended there. While Locke was given to a slight portliness, Player was lean and hard-muscled. He exercised constantly, twisted towels to build his arm and hand strength, did fingertip pushups, and had the most positive attitude of anybody in the game. Every course was the finest he'd ever seen and every round the greatest he'd ever played. He followed an endless series of fads. He claimed he ate raisins for mysterious health-giving reasons, then switched to bananas. He won the Open using clubs with black shafts, presumably fiberglass, since he endorsed clubs that featured fiberglass shafts. Some said he had merely painted his steel shafts. He even dressed strangely. When he first came to the United States, he dressed in white—shirt, pants, cap, and shoes. When he won the 1959 British Open, he wore pants with one black leg and one white leg. Later he dressed in all-black outfits. He wore the same shirt for four straight days at the Bellerive Country Club in St. Louis, washing it in his room each night. He claimed publicly that he wore black because it absorbs the heat of the sun, but he really wore it as a trademark, something to make him easily identifiable. He didn't have to; he was a first-rate golfer.

Bellerive was a new course, designed by Robert Trent Jones, that was only six years old in 1965 and wasn't ready for anything so important as the Open. Some areas were still raw, and at least one fairway rippled like a washboard with grass that had not yet knitted closely. As it was set up for the Open, it measured an uncommonly long 7,191 yards, with six par 4 holes in excess of 450 yards. Its greens were huge and easy to hit, and under those conditions, the Open turned into a putting contest. Player should have won easily without the playoff. His 70-70—140 put him in front after thirty-six holes, and with 71 in the third round, he was still in front after fifty-four. He was leading by three strokes with three holes to play, then nearly threw it away. He took 5 on the 16th, a long par 3, just as Nagle was making a birdie on the 17th, and suddenly they were tied at 282. Nagle had picked up two strokes over the last eighteen with 69 to Player's 71.

The playoff was anticlimactic. Nagle's shots ran wild—twice he drove into the crowd and hit spectators—and Player rushed to a five-stroke lead after eight holes. Nagle shot 74, and Player won by three strokes with a third straight 71. As if his weird outfits and strange-looking shots didn't attract enough attention, Player made another unorthodox move at the prize ceremony. First prize was $25,000. Gary gave $5,000 to cancer work (his mother died of cancer) and turned $20,000 back to the USGA to promote junior golf.

Player notwithstanding, this was a dull Open, made even more dull by a fundamental change. Since 1926 the championship had been played over three days, one round on Thursday, another on Friday, then winding up with a double round on Saturday.

Open Saturday was like no other day in sport, a day that brought on wonderful comebacks, like Ken Venturi's of 1964, and horrible collapses, like Mike Souchak's of 1960. It drained the emotions, and it demanded the players show who had the stamina, the will, and the control of emotion, as well as the golf shots. Open Saturday was often a wild and wonderful day: a day when Cary Middlecoff could shoot two 68s and come from deep in the pack into a tie; a day when Arnold Palmer could play himself out of contention in the morning, then roar back with an incredible 65 in the afternoon; a day when Ben Hogan could begin the morning leading the

215

field by two strokes, play one flawless shot after another while others were falling all around him, and win by six strokes.

Open Saturday had its human drama too: 1934 and Olin Dutra suffering from dysentery but struggling around Merion and making up eight strokes; 1950 and Ben Hogan, his legs locking but still fighting through those last agonizing holes; 1955 and Jack Fleck blowing himself away in the morning but birdieing two of the last four holes, shooting 67, and catching the mighty Hogan; 1964 and Ken Venturi fighting fatigue and dehydration, but still finding the will to play his best while others around him could not.

These were the qualities that set the champion above the crowd.

But by the middle 1960s, the world was living in a commercial age. Open prize money was climbing, and the cost of running the diversified functions of the USGA was rising as well. Television offered a source of further revenue, but it needed two days over a weekend, not one.

Overriding the financial attractions of a four-day Open, however, the day of the double round had become an administrative horror. Play had become so slow, there was simply no room to maneuver should rain cause a long delay on Friday. The fields of the last three Opens had finished, on the average, at ten minutes after 8. Suppose, the USGA reasoned, that a storm had caused an interruption of an hour or more on Friday. Part of the field wouldn't have finished, and the players would have had to complete their second rounds early Saturday morning. Then a new set of pairings would have had to be made, causing further delays, and the double round itself might not be completed.

These were not hypothetical concerns. Morning fog had caused a twenty-two-minute delay at Oakmont in 1962, and the thunderstorm that struck Inverness in 1957 caused a delay of an hour and ten minutes on Thursday. Players were scattered over the last four holes when the day ended, and they had to finish Friday morning before playing the second round later in the same day. Had the storm struck on Friday, who can tell what might have happened?

Consequently, at a meeting of the executive committee in January of 1965, the USGA announced that hereafter the Open would be played over four days, eighteen holes each day. Open Saturday ceased to exist.

The 1965 Open was the first under the new format, and while the change took away some of the spirit, the wild last day in 1966 put it back.

Palmer hadn't won a major championship since the 1964 Masters, and by now he was wondering if he would ever win another. He felt he might have lost his putting touch, but as the Open approached, the doubts seemed to have flown, and he was playing with élan once again, attacking the golf course as he had when he was younger and bolder. Arnold was thirty-seven years old in 1966, a little beyond prime years for a golfer, and this year he had developed a new style. Always a superb driver, he had played a right-to-left draw ever since he could remember, but in 1966 he began playing the drive dead straight, and he was hitting more fairways than ever. Olympic, however, is essentially a left-to-right course, and as the championship drew near, Arnold made a further slight adjustment that caused his shots to drift a little right. The shot seemed perfect for the golf course.

Arnold began with a typical Palmer tactic: He tried to beat the course to death. The first hole is a mild downhill par 5 of 536 yards. After a good drive, Arnold went for the green with his second. He put all of his slashing power into a 3-wood, but his hands were late, and he pushed the shot into the rough, hole-high to the right. He wedged over the green with his third and made 6. He lost two more strokes going out, turned for home in 38, came back in 33, and completed the round in 71. When the day ended, he was four strokes behind Al Mengert, a club professional from Tacoma, Washington, the type of obscure player who often leads the first round.

Palmer shot 66 the next day, and if he hadn't missed putts of less than four feet on each of the last two holes, he would have matched the Open record of 64. (Rives McBee, an assistant pro from Midland, Texas, had shot 64 earlier in the day.) With this round Arnold climbed into a tie at 137 with Billy Casper, who with 68 was the only other name player to better par. (An early starter, Palmer was with friends that afternoon when he was told that with one exception the scores were high. With a strange look on his face, Arnold said, "I'll bet that exception is Casper.")

This was a new Billy Casper, no longer the roundish 200-pounder. By 1966 he had cut his weight down to 185 pounds through an exotic diet that included buffalo and bear meat. One morning his breakfast consisted of swordfish and tomatoes. He was lean, and he was more somber. And he could still putt.

When he added 73 the next day and Palmer shot 70, Arnold led by three strokes. As coleaders they had played together in the third round, and since they were still the low two, they were paired together again in the fourth.

Arnold felt Olympic's first nine was more difficult than the second, and he would have to play it well to post a low score. After his 38 in the first round, he had followed with 32 in the second and 34 in the third. When he shot 32 again to begin the fourth round, he stood seven strokes ahead of Casper and nine ahead of Jack Nicklaus, whom he considered the more dangerous threat.

If at Cherry Hills General Palmer was Xerxes at Thermopylae, breaching an impregnable defense, at Olympic he was Napoleon at Borodino, blundering into slaughter. Believing he had the Open won, he began playing against the Ben Hogan of 1948 instead of the Billy Casper of 1966, and Casper was the more dangerous opponent. Arnold wanted to break Hogan's record of 276; he had played 239 strokes already, and if he could turn the last nine holes in 36, a stroke above par, he'd have 275. The first blunder.

Arnold bogeyed the 10th as Casper parred, but he took that stroke back with a birdie at the 12th, where Casper also birdied. Six strokes ahead of Casper now with six holes to play, and hot on the trail of Hogan's record. He still had one stroke in hand, but he lost it when he missed the green of the 13th, a solid par 3 of 191 yards. Now Arnold would have to play the last five holes in even par to beat Hogan. Casper, meanwhile, made his 3; Palmer led by five strokes with five holes to play.

Both men made their pars on the 14th. The 15th, a nice par 3 of 150 yards, is not particularly intimidating if the hole is set center or left, but now it was cut in the right corner, close to a bunker, and because Olympic's greens are so small, it was difficult to reach. Arnold was never one to turn down a dare, and in blind pursuit of Hogan, he went for the hole, mis-hit the shot, and watched the ball drop into the bunker. He made 4. Now he needed a birdie to beat Hogan. Casper hit the green, made his putt for a birdie 2, and cut his deficit to three strokes with three to play.

Suddenly Palmer awoke to the simple fact that he had better forget about Hogan and remember Casper. Billy had played the first six holes of the second nine in two under par while Palmer had played them in two over. Four strokes of a seven-stroke lead had gone; it was time to concentrate on winning.

The 16th at Olympic is a long par 5 of 604 yards that follows a sweeping right-to-left curve. Palmer had been playing his faded tee shot all along, but with matters becoming tense, the time was right to switch to his most reliable shot, the right-to-left draw he had grown up with. Another blunder. When he lashed into the ball, it hooked quickly and dived into the rough. Next, Arnold tried a 3-iron. It was too ambitious a shot; the ball squirted across the fairway into even deeper rough on the far side. Now he was in real trouble, probably 300 yards from the green in heavy grass with no chance to reach the green with his third. He chopped back to the fairway with his wedge, drilled a 3-wood into a greenside bunker, and was fortunate to make 6. He did, however, lose two strokes to Casper, who birdied once again. One stroke down with two to play.

Although the 17th hole had been shortened by twenty-six yards since 1955, it remained the hardest hole at Olympic—435 yards uphill to a green set on the shoulder of a hill, the fairway sweeping downward from left to right, and the green cut off by bunkers guarding both the left and right front. Palmer hooked into the left rough once again, flew his second into the right rough, then played a wonderful pitch over the cluster of bunkers banked against the hillside to within ten feet of the hole. His putt grazed the cup, and when Casper holed his putt for the 4, he had pulled even. In a startling turnaround, Billy had made up seven strokes in eight holes, five strokes in the last three, and now they had one more hole to go.

Playing first, Casper split the 18th fairway with his drive, but Palmer, as desperate as he had ever been, switched to an iron and hooked once again. His ball veered into the left rough and settled in heavy grass, leaving him an impossible shot. With his world collapsing, Palmer drew himself together and played the kind of shot that showed how great a player he was. Using all his strength, he tore through the grass with his wedge; the ball shot out, soared in a high arc, dropped onto the right rear, and somehow stayed on that tiny green. It was as fine a pressure shot as any man had ever played.

Arnold was thirty feet above the hole, well outside Casper's ball, the green was slick, and the putt would run downhill. Misreading his line, Arnold rolled his first putt about six feet right of the cup, and because a new rule was in effect for 1966, he had to hole out before Casper would putt at all. If Arnold missed that six-footer, Billy could take two putts and win. Once again Palmer showed he could stand up to the pressure. He holed the putt for the par, Casper made his 4, and both men finished with 278, two strokes under par and two strokes over Hogan's 276. Billy had shot 68 and Arnold 71.

In the frenzy of Palmer's collapse, Casper's steady, impeccable golf was almost forgotten. Over the last nine holes he had hit every fairway, missed only the 17th green, which almost everyone did anyhow, and shot 32. Palmer, on the other hand, lost only four strokes to par, which should have been good enough to win, but he was caught. The tie was as much a result of great golf by Casper as it was of ragged golf by Palmer.

The playoff resembled the fourth round. Hitting his shots solidly while Casper seemed to be hitting his a trifle thin, Palmer rushed to the turn in 33 against Casper's 35. Almost as if it were a replay of the fourth round, Casper picked up two strokes on the 11th, where he birdied as Palmer bogeyed, then went ahead for the first time on the 13th, where a fifty-footer fell for a 2 as Arnold was making a routine 3. When Billy played the next three holes in 4-3-6 against Arnold's 5-5-7, it was all over. Casper shot 69, Palmer 73.

As he had done seven years earlier, Casper had won the Open on the greens. He had used 114 putts at Winged Foot in 1959, thirty under par

PART FOUR

Nicklaus and Beyond

NINETEEN
Baltusrol and the Record

In the five years Jack Nicklaus had been a professional, his rivalry with Palmer had become the hottest matchup since the days of Hogan and Nelson and later Hogan and Snead. They dominated the Tour; week after week, if one of them didn't win, one of them threatened to. After Nicklaus beat him in the 1962 Open, Palmer won the American Golf Classic, and Nicklaus placed third. Nicklaus won at Seattle, and Palmer placed sixth.

It heated up in 1963 when Palmer won seven tournaments and Nicklaus won five. Palmer won at Los Angeles, Nicklaus at Palm Springs, then Palmer again at Phoenix, Nicklaus took the Masters and Tournament of Champions, Palmer the Thunderbird, lost a playoff for the Open, and then won the Cleveland Open. While Nicklaus took the PGA, Palmer came right back to win the Western and the Whitemarsh, and Nicklaus won at Las Vegas. Fan interest grew, prize money grew, and the promise of another duel between Nicklaus and Palmer assured big galleries.

They were back at it again in 1964, but at lower heat. Palmer won the Masters for the fourth time, Nicklaus took such lesser events as the Phoenix, Whitemarsh, Tournament of Champions, and Portland. Palmer won only the Oklahoma City Open in addition to the Masters.

Gradually Palmer began to yield. In 1965, Nicklaus won five tournaments, including his second Masters, Palmer won only one, but a year later they were fairly even again, Palmer with three victories, Nicklaus with two, although one was his third Masters. At the end of the year they paired together to win the PGA Team Championship. Their rivalry was heated but not bitter.

By the beginning of 1967, Jack had established his superiority with his record in the four major events. By then Palmer had won four Masters Tournaments, two British Opens, and one U.S. Open (he had not won the PGA), but since 1962, Nicklaus' first year as a professional, Arnold had won only two Masters and one British Open while Jack had won one U.S. Open, one British Open, one PGA, and three Masters. Throughout this period, however, Palmer maintained a better record in the Open. When Jack missed the cut in 1963, Arnold was in a playoff; when Arnold was in position to win with thirty-six holes to go in 1964, Nicklaus placed thirty-second; when Palmer once again lost a playoff in 1966, Nicklaus was third, but seven strokes behind.

The year 1967 began as so many had in the past. Palmer won at Los Angeles, Nicklaus took the Crosby, and Palmer won at Tucson. As May gave way to June, Palmer had finished second three times and third twice while Nicklaus had been second in one tournament and fourth in four others. The promise that these by now old adversaries once again would be thrust against one another enlivened interest in the 1967 Open, scheduled once again for Baltusrol's Lower Course.

Deane Beman had been one of the world's finest amateurs for nearly a decade, but even though he was twenty-nine, unusually late for such a step, he had decided to play the Tour, and the Open was his second tournament as a professional. He left the 1st tee at 9:08 on Thursday morning, cracked a very good drive that split the fairway between two nests of bunkers, then followed with a 230-yard 4-wood that bored into the overcast sky, easily cleared one set of bunkers fifty to seventy-five yards short of the green, swept through a collar of light rough blocking the entrance, and rolled onto the green and into the hole. Normally a par 5 for the members, the 1st hole was playing that day as a 465-yard par 4. Beman had an eagle 2. He was absolute master of that hole. He scored birdies the next two rounds and finally succumbed and made 4 on the last day.

Beman shot 69 on Thursday. At the end of the day he was tied with six others, two strokes behind Marty Fleckman, a darkly handsome twenty-three-year-old amateur, the son of a lumber dealer in Port Arthur, Texas, across Sabine Lake from Louisiana. Fleckman shot 67. An amateur hadn't attracted this much attention since Billy Joe Patton had led the first round at Baltusrol thirteen years earlier and Harvie Ward had shared the thirty-six-hole lead in 1955.

Fleckman had substantial credentials. An extremely long hitter (he was one of those who could comfortably reach the green of the par 5 18th in two), Marty was the NCAA champion in 1965 and a member of the Walker Cup team that had defeated the British and Irish at Sandwich, England, only a few weeks earlier. While his round excited the galleries, it didn't faze the players. They knew what the galleries would learn later in the week: in this age, unless a player is exposed day after day to the grinding competitiveness of professional golf at its highest levels, he can't win; the nerves will surely fail. No, those who figured to contend for the title were more concerned with Palmer and Nicklaus.

While Arnold had been playing perhaps the best golf of his career as the Open approached, he was having a problem with a sore right hip. It had bothered him so much in a practice round with Nicklaus on Wednesday that his swing was tentative, lacking its usual zest. It had hurt so badly he considered withdrawing, but he bathed it with witch hazel that night, and Winnie Palmer rubbed it with Ben Gay. Still swinging tentatively, Palmer was off slowly on Thursday, and at the end of twelve holes, he was two over par and going nowhere. Then, on the 13th, a short drive-and-pitch par 4, a forty-five-footer dropped, another fell on the 14th, and he finished with a birdie on the 18th. A 69, one under the unbalanced par of 34-36—70.

He had just about finished when Nicklaus teed off. Using a white-painted bull's-eye putter he had borrowed from a friend of Beman's and named White Fang, Jack shot 71. Following his 69 with 68, Palmer stood in first place with 137 after two rounds, a stroke ahead of Nicklaus, who stormed around Baltusrol in 67 the second day. At the same time, Billy Casper was making a strong defense of his championship. Shooting 69 and 70, he was alone in third place.

Palmer and Nicklaus had been especially sharp over the first two rounds, both men hitting thirty-one of the thirty-six greens (Palmer hit seventeen in the second round), but Arnold had putted a little better.

As the two leaders, Jack and Arnold were sent out together in the third round, the last two off the tee. While a pairing of Nicklaus and Palmer seemed like a dream, guaranteeing not only ticket sales but a huge television audience as well, it did not guarantee good golf; too often they forgot the job at hand and played against each other. Predictably, throughout the third round, they played tense, straining golf. While the galleries stormed through the rough, cheering their men on (it was still largely a pro-Palmer group), neither man could do anything right. They missed fairways, missed greens, and even when they hit them, they were yards from the hole. Their putting was so bad it became comic. Facing a putt

225

of about fifteen feet for a birdie on the 16th hole, Palmer stroked the ball terribly. Never for an instant did it look as if it might fall, and he barely scraped out his par. Nicklaus had played a better shot to the green, at least two feet closer to the hole than Arnold. Lining up his putt carefully, he hit an even worse putt than Palmer's. The ball started two feet off line, then broke away from the cup.

Seeing the shocked look on Jack's face, Palmer turned away, bent over from the waist, and began laughing. Still grinning, he turned to Jack and called, "Nice stroke." Nicklaus laughed.

Both men were then four over par for the day. Nicklaus closed with birdies on the 17th and 18th, both par 5s, and shot 72, while Palmer birdied the 18th and shot 73.

Meanwhile, Fleckman, the amateur who everyone said couldn't win, birdied two of the last three holes, shot 69, and led the field with 209. Lurking one stroke behind at 210, Palmer and Nicklaus weren't nearly so concerned with Fleckman as they were with Casper. Out in 33, one under par, Casper led by three strokes at one time, but in a wobbly finish he threw strokes away with bogeys on each of the last three holes, shot 71, and finished the day tied with Nicklaus and Palmer.

Sunday was dull and overcast, carrying with it the threat of rain. The last pair to start, Casper and Fleckman teed off at three o'clock in the afternoon to accommodate television, which was trying for a near prime-time audience.

While Palmer and Nicklaus, who were paired together once again, took most of the gallery with them, a sizable group stayed behind to see if Fleckman could hold together and if Casper could drone around with another subpar score and beat the more glamorous pair ahead. Neither could. Fleckman's first drive screamed off line, clattered through the trees on the right, and he bogeyed. He bogeyed the 2nd, he bogeyed the 3rd, and he bogeyed the 6th. Out in 38, he finished the day with 80. Casper was never really in contention. He didn't make a birdie until the 12th, and by then he was two over par. The crowd left them; the Open was being settled up ahead.

Both Palmer and Nicklaus made routine par 4s on the 1st, but two solid shots put Arnold on the 2nd green within holeable distance, about twelve feet from the cup, while Jack's drive lay in thick and tangled rough close to a chain link fence. His approach dropped into the left greenside bunker, and his recovery rolled ten feet past the hole. Now Arnold had the opportunity to move two strokes ahead should he hole and Jack miss, but his putt slipped past the right edge, and while Nicklaus missed too, Arnold had picked up only one stroke where he might have gained two.

This was a key hole, for Palmer was an emotional player; if that putt had fallen, he might have holed three or four more. As it was, the miss not only took away some of Arnold's fire, it gave Jack a reprieve he didn't expect. He turned the Open around over the next six holes. His pitch to the 3rd covered the flag and braked itself just three feet from the cup for one birdie. Level with Palmer now. A big shot to four feet for another birdie on the 4th. One stroke ahead. A good pitch and a fourteen-footer fell on the 5th. Three straight birdies, and now Palmer was two strokes behind and struggling to keep up.

Nicklaus lost a stroke on the 6th, a long and difficult par 4, and as they stood on the 7th tee, Arnold was only one stroke behind again with plenty of holes left. A few birdies, and he could turn Nicklaus back. The next was one of the key holes of the game's history. Had it gone differently, the Open might have ended differently, and Nicklaus might have become a lesser figure.

Like the 1st hole, the 7th was a par 5 for members, but for the Open the tee had been moved far enough forward to bring the green within range of the second shot, and it was played as a 470-yard par 4. The fairway bends to the right, and the drive has to carry a clutch of bunkers. Another group is set in mounds twenty to thirty yards short of the green, not only blocking the approach, but confusing the judgment of distance as well.

Both men played good drives, Palmer's to the left side of the fairway and Nicklaus' ball more to the center. Palmer was away and played a 1-iron for his second. He never played a better shot. The ball streaked dead on line with the pin, never seemed to rise more than fifteen or twenty feet above the ground, came down on the front of the green, and rolled about ten feet past the hole. The gallery cheered, and Arnold's face broke into a tight-lipped self-satisfied grin.

Jack's turn now. Closer to the green, he hit a 2-iron, but Jack's shots lacked the élan of Arnold's. Palmer's ball seemed a living thing; Nicklaus' ball was simply a projectile. It sailed high and true and came down thirty feet away.

In the minds of the gallery there was never any doubt that Arnold would catch up right there. Nicklaus could not hole that thirty-footer, and Arnold was sure to drop his. He'd missed one like it on the 2nd; surely he couldn't miss another.

But he did. Nicklaus stunned the crowd by ramming his thirty-footer into the center of the hole for the birdie, and Palmer didn't give his putt a chance; hit tentatively, it broke off to the right before it reached the hole. Now Nicklaus was two strokes ahead.

Palmer had nothing left. From the 8th tee he hit his only bad drive of the day and bogeyed while Nicklaus, buoyed by his birdie on the 7th, smashed a long drive, then dropped a soft wedge four feet from the hole for his fifth birdie in six holes.

Four strokes ahead now, Jack was playing one fine shot after another—a wedge to four feet on the 13th, another to five feet on the 14th, his seventh birdie in twelve holes. He was five strokes ahead of Palmer now and four under par. Another birdie, and he could beat Hogan's record.

The skies had turned black by now, threatening rain, and Jack was racing after his ball, not only sensing the victory but trying to beat the storm.

Nicklaus made pars on the 15th and 16th, and then Palmer holed his first putt of the dreary afternoon on the unending 17th. It was too late.

Now they were on the tee of the 18th, another par 5, down a long grade to a creek that runs across the fairway, and then up an incline to a green turned into an island by bunkers right and left and an apron of rough blocking the narrow gap between them. It was here in 1954 that Furgol had hooked into the woods and had to escape to the Upper Course to save his par, and where Dick Mayer had driven into the woods to the right and made 8 where a par 5 would have won.

Nicklaus wasn't about to make those mistakes; he would avoid the risk of a wild drive by playing his 1-iron. But just as Mayer had done thirteen years earlier, he hit his ball into the woods on the right, onto bare dirt next to a television cable drum that was too heavy to move. Allowed to drop the ball clear of the drum, he tried to play an 8-iron just short of the creek, which would then leave him with a comfortable shot to the green with a medium-to-short iron. With the crowd milling about, Nicklaus played a miserable shot; he nipped the ground at least an inch behind the ball, barely moved it to the fairway, and now, instead of an easy shot, he had to cover 230 yards. He didn't need the par, to be sure—he had four strokes in hand, and he could have played short, made an easy 6, and still won—but he took out his 1-iron again and lashed into the ball "harder than I know how." It shot toward the green, rising into the sullen sky, cleared the front bunker by only a foot or so, and rolled twenty feet from the hole. His putt never wavered; it rolled straight at the cup and dived in. A 65 and 275. Hogan's record 276 that had lasted nineteen years was broken, and we were clearly into a new era.

Palmer also birdied the 18th, shot 69, and finished second, with 279.

Pro-Palmer though it was, the crowd burst into applause, hailing its new hero. While the fans had looked on Nicklaus as a villain through most of the week, Jack had turned them around, and he would never be an anti-hero again. His golf had been almost of another world. He had hit sixty-one of the seventy-two greens (no one did better, and only Gardner Dickinson did as well) and thirty-seven of the fifty-six fairways on driving holes. Palmer had played extremely well too, hitting fifty-eight greens and forty-two fairways.

Nicklaus had his second Open. Only eleven others had won as many, but Jack had higher goals. Willie Anderson, Bobby Jones, and Ben Hogan had won four. Nicklaus was only twenty-seven then; he would have time to catch them.

TWENTY
Another Rival

Toward the end of the last round at Baltusrol, a few tournament officials and reporters agreed they should have a look at this fellow Lee Trevino, who had been hovering around the leaders all week, shooting scores that were either even par or not very far from it and who even then was passing well-known golfers. They dashed out to the 5th hole, relatively close to the clubhouse, and found a short (five-foot-seven), pudgy (180 pounds), man of Mexican heritage, with thick, coal black hair, nut brown skin, white even teeth, wearing a faded green shirt, baggy black trousers, black shoes, and a black baseball-type cap.

He stood up to the ball with an open stance, his left foot drawn back from the line of flight, and took the club back on a flat, awkward plane. But when he moved through the ball, his clubhead followed the line of flight for what seemed an exaggerated distance. He had the longest extension through the ball since Hogan.

His drive on the 5th flew out low and flat, drifted slightly right, and dropped gently into the fairway. An iron to the green followed the same flight pattern, then a solid putt, and Trevino had a birdie. It was his second birdie of the day, and it dropped him to one under par.

The officials and reporters had seen enough; with a swing like that, Trevino was obviously playing over his head. Convinced he would never be heard from again, they drifted away, most of them to watch Nicklaus and Palmer.

Trevino shot his second 70 of the week that day, turned in a seventy-two-hole score of 283, and finished fifth behind Nicklaus, Palmer, Don January, and Billy Casper. He collected $6,000, more money than he had ever seen, and walked away wondering how long this had been going on. A week earlier he had been a handyman at the Horizon Hills Country Club in El Paso, cleaning clubs, polishing shoes, and picking up range balls.

Back home again, he invested his $6,000 in the club and became a part-owner, with Don Whittington and Jess Whittenton (the two were cousins, but they spelled their names differently). Sensing that Lee might do well on the Tour, they put up some money and sent him out again, launching one of the great careers in golf.

Over the rest of the year Trevino won more than $27,000 and was voted rookie of the year. He was twenty-seven.

As 1968 unfolded, Trevino became a consistent money winner but an erratic player. He finished eighth in the Los Angeles Open and sixth in the Bob Hope Desert Classic, but he missed the cut at San Diego and placed fifty-ninth in Miami. He was also inexperienced. Only two strokes off the lead going into the last round of the Masters, he shot 80. Leading the Houston Open with two holes to play, he hit two terrible iron shots and lost to Roberto De Vicenzo. "Roberto," he said, "the clubs got heavy."

With a record like this, Trevino was not foremost in the minds of those gathered at the Oak Hill Country Club in Rochester, New York, for the 1968 Open, but when he opened with 69-68—137, he began to attract their attention. Good as it was, though, it left him in second place, because Bert Yancey had matched the Open record by shooting 67-68—135.

When Trevino shot 69 in the third round and Yancey 70, they were one stroke apart, Bert with 205 and Lee with 206, and they had the Open to themselves. Jack Nicklaus and Charlie Coody were tied for third, at 212, but no one else was remotely in contention. Nearly everyone had thrown in at least one bad round on a course that wasn't that difficult. Tom Weiskopf and Billy Casper had shot 75 the first day, Gary Player had opened with 76, and Arnold Palmer had done even worse. A 79 in the third round had left him at 226, the highest score of any professional in the field. Player added some Three Stooges comedy in the last round by swinging at a ball embedded in the bank of a creek and falling over backward into the water. Despite their reputations, they were merely supporting players. The drama was played out between Trevino and Yancey.

Paired together in the last round, they were a study in opposites, Trevino short and dark, slightly pot-bellied, with a flat, unorthodox swing, joking with the gallery, wearing black pants, a red shirt, and a black baseball-type cap, and Yancey tall and blond, quiet and reserved, hiding inside a white visor, and hitting the ball with a regal swing. Once a West Point cadet, Yancey had withdrawn from the academy because of a nervous breakdown, and now, at twenty-nine, he was one of the better players on the Tour, even though he had won nothing of lasting significance.

Both men seemed nervous as the last round began. Yancey drove into the right rough, laid up short of a creek that crosses the fairway, pitched on and took two putts, while Trevino hit his second into a bunker and matched Yancey's 5. It was Lee's last bogey of the day. He saved his par from a bunker at the 2nd to keep level, and then Yancey made a mistake. After missing the 3rd green, he played a nice chip inside four feet but missed the putt. He was stunned. One of the great putters on the Tour—he had once used only 102 strokes for seventy-two holes—he expected to hole putts that short. He looked at his putter as if it had a life of its own and had somehow let him down, and he wondered why.

Now they were tied. Two holes later Yancey missed another holable putt, and Trevino went ahead. One hole later it was tied once more, but then Yancey collapsed. Unable to shake the dogged Trevino, he began to tighten his swing, drove into a bunker on the 7th, caught another bunker on the 8th, and was bunkered again on the 9th. He played the first nine in 38 while Trevino turned in 36.

Trevino put the Open away over the next three holes. Sizing up a thirty-five-footer on the 11th, he rubbed his hands together, stepped up to the ball and rammed it home. He split the 12th fairway with his drive, left his approach twenty-five feet short of the cup, charged the putt, and it dived into the hole for another birdie. He was five under par then, and he had left Yancey far behind. But he wanted more than the championship. If he could birdie the 18th, he'd break the record Nicklaus had set only a year ago. He never had a chance; he drove into the left rough, left his second still in the rough, and had to struggle to make his 4 and 275. He hadn't broken the record, but he had tied it.

Nicklaus had made a brief flurry and shot 67, taking second place with his 279, and after a spirit-crushing 76, Yancey fell to third place with 281.

With scores of 69, 68, 69, and 69, Trevino had become the first man to play all four scheduled rounds in the 60s. His method might not have been classic, but it worked. He had hit forty-five of the fifty-six fairways on driving holes (only one man did better) and fifty-five of the seventy-two greens. Nicklaus hit sixty-one. An effective if not brilliant putter, Trevino had only one three-putt green.

While Trevino left the impression he played a gambling game, he really didn't; his strategy was conservative. His faded tee shots were meant to keep the ball in the fairways, and he usually hit to the widest part of the greens. He played like a gambler who knew the odds and how to take advantage of them. He had learned by hustling golf matches in Texas.

Trevino grew up in a four-room shack with dirt floors in a hayfield near the 7th fairway of the Glen Lakes Country Club in the rural outskirts of Dallas, raised by his mother, Juanita, and his maternal grandfather, Joe Trevino, an immigrant gravedigger. Coming from such a poor environment, he learned the value of money early. A fence separated the Trevino house from the golf course, and at six, Lee was turning a nice profit by picking up balls that had sailed over the fence and selling them back to members. Finding a discarded wooden-shafted 5-iron, he cut it down and used it to hit apples. When the hay was cut in the summer, he laid out a two-hole course.

Trevino quit school after the seventh grade and worked on the grounds crew at Glen Lakes, caddied, played a few holes at dusk, and found he had a natural aptitude for the game. He took no serious interest in golf as a business until, as a marine in Japan, he saw a notice announcing tryouts for the Third Division golf team. Trevino shot 66 and spent the next two years playing in tournaments in the Far East.

Back home in 1961, he played money matches at the Tenison Park golf course in Dallas, a place notorious for gambling action. He had a standard challenge—he'd use one club and give his opponent his full handicap. Trevino claimed he never lost a match. An average week brought in $200. He also worked at a pitch-and-putt course where he'd take on all comers, using a quart-size Dr. Pepper soft drink bottle wrapped with adhesive tape. He rarely shot over 30.

Looking for bigger game, Lee quit the pitch-and-putt course in 1965 and with a financial backer headed for the Panama Open. Obviously the backer hadn't broken the bank at Monte Carlo, because he couldn't afford the air fare; instead, he and Lee drove. They spent seven and a half days threading their way through Central America, bouncing down horse trails and rocky river beds, and sleeping in the car. Trevino finished fifth, won $716.16, said good-by to his backer, and flew home. He spent the rest of the year teaching and playing in local tournaments.

Word of his talents reached Martin Lettunich, a wealthy cotton farmer in El Paso. A golf fanatic, Lettunich had been losing money steadily to one particular man at Horizon City. He offered Trevino a deal. He'd pay his expenses and part of the winnings if Lee would come to El Paso and play as his partner. Lee accepted. He shot 66 and 67, beat Lettunich's tormentor, earned $300, and was offered the job as the club's teaching pro and general handyman.

He still played money matches, once against Raymond Floyd, even then a well-known Tour player. As Floyd drove up to the clubhouse, Trevino approached and asked politely if Raymond wanted his clubs taken to the golf shop.

"Who'm I playing?" he asked.

"Me," Trevino answered.

"You!" Floyd exclaimed. "You mean they bet on you?"

The match was to be over fifty-four holes. Floyd shot 66 the first day and Trevino shot 65. Floyd shot 66 again the next day and Trevino shot 64. The next day Floyd eagled the last hole and beat Trevino by a stroke.

Lee entered his first Open in 1966 at Olympic. Playing with an unmatched set of clubs that included seven different brands, he shot 74 and 73 in the first two rounds, which left him ten strokes behind Casper and Palmer, but he finished with two 78s, shot 303, and won $600. He went home discouraged. While he had played a lot of golf in his lifetime, he had never seen rough like that, and he had never seen bunkers like those. The experience so unnerved him he planned to skip the 1967 Open, but Claudia, his wife, whom he had met when she was a seventeen-year-old ticket-taker at a movie theater, mailed his entry for him. He shot 69-67—136 in the local qualifying rounds, the lowest in the nation, then 141 in the sectionals, and went to Baltusrol. He arrived with a scanty wardrobe, lived in a low-cost motel, and each night walked a quarter of a mile along a dangerous road to a Polynesian restaurant for his dinner. When he wasn't playing, he sat on the clubhouse porch with a Baltusrol member who bought beer as long as Trevino told stories. He told a lot of them, drank a lot of beer, and when the week ended, he was on his way.

Even after he won at Oak Hill, Trevino wasn't accepted as a first-class golfer. The experts scoffed at his swing, which Leonard Crawley, an English writer and a former Walker Cup player, called his "agricultural method," more suited to scything hay than striking golf balls. They looked at his low, flat drives that started left and inevitably worked their way into center fairway and said he'd never be able to play a course that called for long carries over hilly ground. They said his winning at Oak Hill was one of those occasional accidents. When he shot 74 in the first round at the Champions Golf Club in Houston, the next year, then slipped and tumbled into a ravine while he was playing a shot and missed the cut, they smirked.

It took Trevino several more years to establish himself as one of the great players of the age. In the meantime, there were two interesting interludes, the first involving Orville Moody, an ex-Army sergeant, the second involving Tony Jacklin, a young Englishman who for a brief period was a sensational golfer. Orville Moody came first; his winning the 1969 Open was a bigger shock than Sam Parks's winning in 1935.

Trevino had met Moody in the Far East and had been impressed with his golf. Moody eventually left the Army, joined the Tour, and qualified for the 1969 Open at the Champions Golf Club in Houston. Asked early in the week who he thought might win—provided, of course, he did not repeat—Trevino replied, "Orville Moody."

"Why him?" he was asked.

"Because he's one helluva player."

He was indeed. Moody was a wonderful striker of the ball. He hit every shot flush, whether wood, long iron, or short iron; he could make the ball go right or left, or even straight, which is harder to do, and he knew when and under what circumstances to play the shots. He had one fatal flaw: He was the worst putter who ever won the U.S. Open. His stroke was so bad that as a last resort he putted cross-handed, with his left hand below his right on the putter grip. For one week in June, it was effective.

He had a round, moon face, thinning dark curly hair, wore a puzzled expression, and a roll of fat draped over the top of his belt. He had spent fourteen years in the Army, he was thirty-five years old, and he had barely qualified. With nine holes to play he needed two birdies to make it. He had given up.

"I don't mind not qualifying," he had said to Bobby Cole, his playing partner, "because I wouldn't have a chance in the Open."

"Don't be stupid," Cole snapped. "Keep trying."

Moody got the last birdie he needed by holing a bunker shot on the thirty-fifth hole.

Part Choctaw Indian, Moody had won the Oklahoma high school championship and had gone to the University of Oklahoma on a golf scholarship in 1953. Deciding quickly that college was not for him, he dropped out before playing a stroke and enlisted in the Army. He spent a year as a rifle instructor at Fort Chaffee, Oklahoma, and the rest of his tour at golf courses in Japan, Korea, Germany, and the United States. He won the Korean Open and the Korean PGA three times each, and once finished second in the Japan Open.

He left the Army in 1962, hoping to find financial backing to play the Tour, entered the Open, but failed to make the thirty-six-hole cut at Oakmont. He also failed to find anyone with the proper combination of faith and money, so he reenlisted. Five years later he found the backers he needed—a lawyer, a retail clothier, and a mysterious retired Army sergeant. ("Nobody knows what he does for a living," Moody said. "He's a mystery man, always going off somewhere. Maybe he works for the CIA.")

He qualified for the Tour in 1967, and for the next two years he showed a pattern of weak finishes. Leading by a stroke after three rounds at Sutton, Massachusetts, Moody shot 75 and finished fourth. Earlier he had been a factor in the first three rounds at Westchester, New York, but he finished with 76. In Greensboro in early 1969, he did close with a strong 67, but he lost to Gene Littler on the 5th hole of a playoff.

With a record like that he was not considered a serious threat when the championship began under a stifling yellow haze early on Thursday morning. The humidity was fierce, the temperature in the 90s, and rain threatened, but Bob Murphy, a chubby, red-haired former National Amateur champion, sped around in 66 and went into the second round leading Miller Barber by a stroke. While Murphy's game slacked off the next two days, Barber continued to play superb golf, followed his opening 67 with 71 and 68, and went into the last round with 206, protecting a three-stroke lead. Moody, meanwhile, had played progressively better each day, opening with 71, then shooting 70 and 68. He held second place with 209, a stroke ahead of Deane Beman, the thirty-six-hole leader, and Bunky Henry. Bob Rosburg, the 1959 PGA champion, was next at 211, and Arnold Palmer had 212.

Barber had played superbly in the third round. He was hitting his driver flush, and on the 5th hole, a 451-yard par 4, he crushed a drive 285 yards. If he continued playing like this, only a miracle score could beat him. But he didn't. Last off the tee in the final round, he lost four strokes over the first six holes, went out in 39, and allowed Moody to slip into the lead with 35.

Orville was far from clear, though. At that stage Rosburg, Barber, Bruce Crampton, Al Geiberger, Murphy, Beman, and Palmer—seven players— were within two strokes of him. The Open was ripe for taking, and yet, over that last stretch of holes, not one man improved his position with par, and only three held on to what they had.

Barber was the first to fall. He played the 12th and 13th in 5 and 6 against pars of 3 and 5, finished the round in 78, and dropped to sixth place at 284. Sprinting from the 18th green, he tore into the locker room, almost knocked over a policeman, and instead of apologizing snarled, "Get out of my way, I just lost the National Open." When a friend asked if he wanted a drink, he said, "Hell, yes. I might as well get drunk. I can't play golf."

Palmer was next. He had been playing erratically throughout the week, with 70 and 73 in the first two rounds, then a 69 in the third that had driven his fans crazy. His scorecard showed nine 3s, but he had squandered six birdies by making five bogeys. He could still pull out a victory, but he was in trouble on the 15th hole, with his ball in a sandy lie in the woods to the left. From there he hit a stunning shot, a low hook that knifed through an opening in the trees, hit short of the green, skimmed the edge of a bunker, and stopped forty feet from the cup. A birdie would put him in the thick of it.

236

Arnold wasn't up to it. He three-putted, bogeyed the 16th, shot 72, and tied Barber and Crampton at 284.

Geiberger followed Palmer. He three-putted the 16th, struggled to save his par on the 17th, then, needing a birdie on the 18th, missed from twenty feet. He finished with 282. Now Beman. He was two strokes behind Moody by then, but he birdied the 18th to come in with 282, matching Geiberger. Now if Rosburg and Moody slipped, Beman and Geiberger would have a chance. They could only wait.

Rosburg had climbed even with Moody by saving his par from a bunker on the 17th, but he hooked his drive on the 18th, put his next shot into a greenside bunker, played a lovely explosion shot only three feet from the hole, and then, taking very little time, jabbed the putt and missed.

Moody was approaching the 17th green when Rosburg bogeyed the 18th. Seeing his wife in the gallery, he walked over to her and said, "Honey, I just can't line up a putt. I'm stroking it all right, but I can't line it up." She didn't say a word.

Orville made his par on the 17th, and now he needed one more for the championship. He hit his drive with all the power he could find, then played a high, lofted 8-iron fifteen feet left of the hole. When he reached the green, he walked all the way across to the scorer's tent, where Frank Hannigan, the USGA's assistant director, sat watching.

"What's the low score in?" Moody asked.

"You have two putts for the championship," Hannigan answered.

Moody used them both, shot 72, and finished with 281.

Champion or not, Moody remained a humble man. Some weeks later, Frank Chirkinian, who arranged teams for a series of televised matches, recruited him and asked who he'd like for a partner. Chirkinian suggested Gene Littler.

"Oh, no, Frank," Moody answered. "Gene would never want to play with me. None of those good golfers would."

"But you're the U.S. Open champion," Chirkinian argued. "Believe me, they'll play with you."

"No, Frank," Orville insisted. "Why there's a sergeant down on the base who can beat me five days out of seven."

Maybe he could. Except for the World Series of Golf, a thirty-six-hole four-man affair played later that year, Moody never won another tournament.

Tony Jacklin was a different matter; while his winning the 1970 championship was unexpected, it wasn't shocking. He was the British Open champion at the time, and even though he was only twenty-five years old, he had been around for a few years. The son of a golf-playing truck driver from Scunthorpe, England, about 150 miles north of London, Jacklin had begun playing golf at the age of seven, had become a professional in his teens, and had played so well in British tournaments that in 1966 he had been chosen to team with Peter Alliss and represent England in the Canada Cup, later the World Cup.

Jacklin reached a turning point of his career in 1967. As one of the leaders in the British Order of Merit, a statistical ranking based primarily on money winnings, he was invited to the Masters, led briefly in the third round, and learned that if he wanted to play this game properly, he would have to join the PGA Tour. He qualified late in 1967 but accomplished very little that year. Improving remarkably in 1968, he set Britain astir by winning the Jacksonville Open and playing well through the remainder of the season, winning $58,495 and placing twenty-ninth on the money list.

He fell into a slump in 1969. He played in the Open for the first time in June, had a weak 73-75 finish after a strong 71-70 start, and shot 289, eight strokes behind Moody, and tied for twenty-fifth place with Nicklaus and some others. A month later he won the British Open. His victory enthralled the British sports fan. One of their own hadn't won since Max Faulkner in 1951. After years of teeth-grinding agony watching their cherished trophy taken away by Americans, Australians, South Africans, and South Americans (Roberto De Vicenzo won in 1967), the British could glow a little now.

As British Open champion, Jacklin was among those given an outside chance when the 1970 Open went to the Hazeltine National Golf Club, on the outskirts of Minneapolis, once again a relatively new course, short on tradition and long on dogleg holes and blind shots.

Doglegs have been around as long as golf has been played, and there's nothing wrong with them. The 13th at Augusta National and the 17th at St. Andrews, the two best holes in all of golf, are doglegs. Blind shots are something else. Again, there's nothing wrong with playing a hole from memory—knowing at which church steeple to aim on the 13th at St. Andrews—but too often there was no target at all at Hazeltine. On the 1st tee, for example, the players could see neither the green nor the fairway. As targets, they picked a passing cloud or a red Mustang parked in a field off in the distance.

They didn't like the course at all. Nicklaus said it "lacked definition" and claimed that on one hole he had to aim at a chimney on someone's house. Dave Hill, a moderately good player, was fined $150 by the PGA Tour for a bizarre exchange in the press tent. Hill said if he had to play Hazeltine every day, he'd find another game.

"What does it lack?" someone asked.

238

"Eighty acres of corn and a few cows," he quipped. "They ruined a good farm when they built this course."

"What do you recommend they do with it?"

"Plow it up and start over."

This session took place after the second round, when Hill had established himself as the closest challenger to Jacklin, who had surprised everyone by shooting 71 under miserable conditions on Thursday. No one could remember wind of such velocity during an Open. It swept out of the northwest at thirty-five miles an hour at its weakest and gusted over forty, nearly uprooted a huge scoreboard anchored in place by six-by-six pilings driven four feet into the ground, ripped tents covering television towers and left their tattered shreds snapping in the gale like whips, and churned the waters of Lake Hazeltine to froth, littering the 10th green with foam. A glob landed on Gene Littler's line, and he had to wait for it to blow away.

Drives covered ridiculous distances. Playing downwind, Jay Dolan, a club pro, reached the 3rd green with his second shot. The hole measured 585 yards; his drive was measured at 318 yards. He was not among the leaders. Jim Dent sent one screaming 346 yards, and he barely edged Jim Mooney (343), Jim Wright (342), and Andy Borkovich (341).

The scores were as wind-tossed as everything else. Bob Murphy, who had shot 66 in the first round a year earlier, had 42 on the first nine, Dave Marr matched him, and Moody and Palmer had 40. The most shocking score of all belonged to Nicklaus. He hit only four greens on the first nine, had a triple-bogey 7 on the 6th, the best hole on the course, and shot 43. A hard-won 38 on the second nine brought him in with 81, the highest score he'd ever shot in an Open, higher even than at Inverness thirteen years earlier, when he was seventeen.

The scene in the locker room was part comedy, part tragedy. Bill Hyndman, the great amateur, reeled in with a wild look in his eye. "My God," he gasped, "I feel like I lost a fistfight."

Hugh Royer burst in, his eyes glazed, and rushed to a beer cooler. With a blank stare he said, "You get the ball going downwind, and there ain't no place for it to land."

Then came Tommy Bolt. He stormed through the door, his face crimson, his eyes glaring, and his teeth bared and clenched. He wiped a hand over his rubbery face and stalked toward his locker. Everybody drew a breath and waited. Bolt looked straight ahead. He flung open the door to his locker, read a message inside, and slammed it closed. Then, his face still burning red, his nostrils flaring, Tommy Bolt erupted.

"All right, dammit," he barked, "I shot eighty. Now haven't you newspaper sons-of-bitches got something to do on the golf course? If it's too cold for you, I'll lend you my jacket."

It was a moment to treasure.

Bolt's 80 was not that bad. Of the 150 who started, sixty-nine shot 80 or higher, and only eighty-one shot lower. Gary Player had 80, Bert Yancey 81, and Deane Beman and Marr had 82. Moody and Palmer were among the chosen with 79.

Amid the gloom, Tony Jacklin was all smiles and giggles. On a day when birdies were scarce, he made six, four of them on the first seven holes, five of them on the first nine. While others overran the greens, only he had the necessary control to stop his ball. While other balls rolled over the 1st green, driven by a following wind, Jacklin's soft wedge stopped within twelve feet of the cup, and he birdied. His shotmaking was remarkable. He hit a 5-iron eighteen inches from the hole on the 4th, and after hooking his drive on the 5th into rough five inches deep, he choked down on a 7-iron and swung as hard as he could. The ball rolled within three feet of the pin. He was out in 33 and back in 38, shooting 71 and opening a three-stroke lead.

The weather and the scores returned to normal the next day. Dan Sikes went from 81 to 69, Randy Wolff from 78 to a course record 67, Bunky Henry from 80 to 68, Marr from 82 to 69, Nicklaus from 81 to 72, Player from 80 to 73, and Palmer from 79 to 74. Moody had no such luck; he shot 77 and missed the cut.

With the sun shining and the wind stilled, Jacklin shot 70 and Hill 69. Jacklin led, 141 to Hill's 143.

Except for a brief time in the third round when Gay Brewer reeled off four birdies in six holes and climbed within three strokes of the lead, Hill was Jacklin's only threat throughout the championship.

Tony had a few shaky spots that day, but whenever it looked as if he might lose a stroke or two, he saved himself. Par on the 18th gave him his second 70 and increased his lead to four strokes.

While the final round was anticlimactic, it could have been close had some of Hill's early putts fallen; twice he had birdie putts hit the hole and stay out. Only a collapse by Jacklin could help him now, and for a time it looked as if Tony might oblige, taking nervous bogeys on the 7th and 8th.

The 9th hole settled the championship. With strokes slipping away, Jacklin drove into the rough, left his approach twenty-five feet short of the hole, then rapped his putt far too hard. The ball streaked across the green with enough momentum to carry it far past the hole, but it smacked squarely against the back of the cup, shot at least six inches off the ground, then dropped straight down and hovered on the lip. As the gallery sucked in its breath, the ball tumbled in for a birdie. Jacklin threw back his head, spread his arms, and the gallery screamed. He was out in 36, and the second nine, which he played in 34, was a walk in the sun.

Jacklin had been overpowering. He shot 71-70-70-70—281 and beat Hill by seven strokes. Since Hazeltine was a par-72 course, he was seven under par. The Open record of 275, held jointly by Nicklaus and Trevino, was only five under par (Hogan, however, had been eight under par in 1948). Even though he was the first Englishman in fifty years to win the U.S. Open—Ted Ray, in 1920, was the last—Jacklin's victory seemed to have little significance at first. That he was the second foreign champion in five years was of no matter because, the argument went, both he and Gary Player, the 1965 champion, were products of the American Tour. Developments in the 1970s and 1980s, however, were to change that perception.

By the end of 1968, Lee Trevino had begun to give the impression of a golfer with limitless potential. Some critics might point to his clumsy-looking swing and say he couldn't last, but more saw how he kept the ball in the fairways, how he hit it onto the greens, and how well he putted. Some of the more perceptive saw more; they saw how well Trevino maneuvered the ball, how he really could hook it if he wanted, and how he could hit it high or low if those shots were needed, and how wonderfully he played the wedge, a club that makes up for a lot of sins. Ben Hogan rarely spoke about anyone, but he talked about how well Trevino used his hands. Jack Nicklaus admired Trevino's game, and he acknowledged that Lee was not only a fine striker of the ball, but a smart thinker who knew where to hit the ball, what to hit it with, and why.

Lee had followed his Open victory by winning the Hawaiian Open and had finished 1968 with $132,127 in prize money. In 1969 he won the Tucson Open, finished as low individual in the World Cup, and once again won more than $100,000. He was even better in 1970, with $157,037, and he won the Vardon Trophy with a strokes-per-round average of 70.64. By the end of the year he had won more than $400,000 in a career barely two and a half years old, and he was accepted as second only to Nicklaus.

Still, Trevino wasn't sure of himself. Business problems had plagued him throughout 1970 and led to a breakup with Don Whittington and Jess Whittenton, and also with Bucky Woy, an ex-deputy sheriff and pro golfer who had dogged Lee for a year pleading for the chance to manage his affairs. His mother was dying of cancer (she passed away in the fall of 1971), and his marriage was falling apart.

Lee began acting badly. He drank, kept late hours, pulled out of tournaments, missed starting times, and after a late session with friends, he failed to show up at all one morning during the Westchester Classic. He was burning himself out. When the Tour moved to Florida in early

March of 1971, Lee hadn't won a tournament since the National Airlines Open of March 1970. Nicklaus approached him in the locker room at Doral.

"I hope you go right on clowning," Jack said, half jokingly, "and never learn how good you are, because if you do, the rest of us might just have to pack up and go home."

Sobered by Jack's concern for him, Trevino changed his attitude. He went to bed earlier and took better care of himself. In April he won the Tallahassee Open, and in May he won at Memphis. Suddenly he was hot. In the six weeks leading up to the Open, he had a chance to win at Dallas but placed fifth, missed a playoff at Houston by one stroke, finished four strokes out of first at the Colonial Invitation, won at Memphis, missed a playoff at Atlanta by one stroke, and lost a playoff at Charlotte. He was learning that Nicklaus was right.

Including the Open, Trevino had won seven tournaments since June of 1968. Over that same period Nicklaus had won nine, one of them the 1970 British Open, and Billy Casper had also won nine. By then, of course, Nicklaus was in place as the best golfer of the age. He had won three Masters, two Opens, two PGA Championships, and two British Opens, nine of the world's most important competitions. He'd also won the National Amateur twice.

Even though Trevino was on a hot streak, if there was a favorite for the 1971 Open, it was Nicklaus. Already that season he had won the PGA Championship, which had been played in Florida in February, and had finished second in the Masters. Furthermore the Open was going back to Merion, that wonderful old course on Philadelphia's Main Line, where so much of the game's history has been written and where Jack had had one of his finer moments. Eleven years earlier, in 1960, he had played four superb rounds there, shooting 269 in the World Amateur Team championship ten years after Ben Hogan, Lloyd Mangrum, and George Fazio had tied at 287. While it is true that Merion in 1950 was set up as a much more severe test than it was in 1960—the World Amateur field included relatively unskilled golfers from such countries as Norway, Peru, and Ceylon—Jack's rounds of 66, 67, 68, and 68 were a milestone.

This was a new Jack Nicklaus. When he played those four remarkable rounds, Jack had been a big, chunky twenty-year-old, weighing well over 200 pounds. He had a round, chubby face, a substantial girth, and a broad beam. He combed his short blond hair straight back, and his clothes would have caused John Molloy to weep. Throughout the 1960s, in the early years of his professional career, he was still mocked as Ohio Fats and Fat Jack. As the 1970s began, though, he had shed thirty pounds and was down to 180, had his hair refashioned into a modern, less Teutonic style, and dressed in a more tasteful and coordinated fashion. The changes made him into a more attractive (and marketable) personality. If his now svelte figure had cut down on his power, it wasn't evident. He was still the longest straight driver in the game and a deadly ten-foot putter.

Meanwhile, a generation had grown up since the last Open at Merion. Only Julius Boros and Dutch Harrison of the 1971 field had played there in 1950 and knew what it could be like. Consequently, after one practice round, the players were less than awed.

"It's a nice little course," Trevino said, "but it's strictly driving. If you keep the ball down the middle, you've got to burn it up." Two days later he had changed his mind.

"This is the hardest course I've ever seen. I don't see how anybody can break par."

Others agreed.

George Archer: "Ninety-seven percent of the field, myself included, are not equipped to play this course. We just don't have the shots. I heard Byron Nelson say on television that two-seventy-two could win here. I couldn't shoot two-seventy-two if I got a mulligan on every hole."

Tom Weiskopf: "Merion is probably the hardest par seventy for the yardage [6,544 yards] I've ever seen."

Billy Casper: "Modern architects could take a great lesson by looking at this course."

Bobby Nichols: "You can use every club in your bag here. The last five holes are the toughest finishing holes you'll find in this country."

Miller Barber: "You've got to use your head. Fewer players will have a chance here than in most Opens."

Barber's was the most perceptive observation of them all.

Arriving a week early, Nicklaus studied the course and made his plans. He would use his driver on only three holes—the 2nd and 4th, both par 5s, and the 18th, a monstrous par 4 of 458 yards where the drive must carry 210 yards to reach the fairway. He would use his 1-iron on the 7th and 8th, short par 4s that look as if they play through the neighbors' back yards, and the 11th and 15th, which are only slightly longer. He would use his 3-wood on all the rest, and they included some long holes, like the 430-yard 16th.

As he explained his plans, someone remarked that a course that eliminates the driver can't be a good one.

"Why does a driver make a course good?" Nicklaus asked.

"The driver is part of the game, isn't it?"

"Yes," Nicklaus responded, "and so is the three-wood and so is the putter, and so is the one-iron. When you can lean back and belt one three-hundred yards off the tee, it doesn't require thinking. This is a thinking

243

man's golf course, and I like it. I could hit the driver on ten holes, but the thing here is to position the ball in the fairway."

It is not true that Merion took the driver out of the bag. The players could hit the driver on any par-4 or par-5 hole they liked, provided they had the skill to keep the ball in play. Merion tests the skills that count most: accuracy from the tee, judgment, ability to maneuver the ball, and a delicate putting touch, for its greens are nearly as slick as Oakmont's. It has a further tendency to yield strokes on the early holes but take them back later on. Ralph Johnston, a young pro from Florida, was the first man off the tee on Thursday morning. He shot 70, level par, but it was push-and-tug between him and Merion all through the day. Seven times he birdied, but old Merion took away every stroke through five bogeys and a double-bogey 6.

Others had the same experience. Archer was two under after three holes and finished with 71; Ben Crenshaw, then a nineteen-year-old amateur, was two under after three holes, two over after nine, and shot 74; Bob Goalby was four under par with two holes to play, made 5 on the 17th, a long par 3, and shot 68; defending his championship, Tony Jacklin was even par after eleven, then lost five strokes over the last seven and shot 75. Most frustrating of all, Larry Hinson, a young pro with great potential that was never realized, was five under par with five holes to play, then lost six strokes and shot 71.

Some managed to hold on, though. Labron Harris shot 67 and led the first round, Nicklaus shot 69, and Trevino a very quiet 70.

The second day was very trying for both Nicklaus and Trevino; both had more than average difficulty with one hole. Trevino made 7 on the 6th, a 420-yard par 4, without ever going out of bounds or into a bunker, and Nicklaus double-bogeyed the 11th, holing a four-foot putt for his 6. Both shot 72, and neither man seemed likely to make headway unless his game improved significantly. With 141, Nicklaus was three strokes off the lead, and at 142, Trevino was four behind. First place was shared, at 138, by Bob Erickson, an ex-watchmaker struggling to make his way as a tournament golfer, and Jim Colbert, who used the weird putting method of holding his hands steady and moving his body. (Seeing Colbert on the practice green, Dutch Harrison said, "Son, you'll never putt any good that way." Colbert smiled and kept rolling them in.)

The championship took form in the third round. Trevino shot 69 and climbed into a tie for fourth at 211, and Nicklaus shot 68, to take second at 209. The leader at 207 was Jim Simons, a twenty-one-year-old Walker Cupper who had been runner-up to Steve Melnyk in the British Amateur a week earlier. The son of a manufacturer of deodorants in the Pittsburgh suburb of Butler, Simons was about six feet tall, weighed 175 pounds, had a mop of straight, light-blond hair that fell over his forehead, a round pink face with a pug nose, and he wore an expression of perpetual worry.

In a beautifully played round of 65, made up of seven birdies and only two bogeys, Simons was out in 32 and back in 33. His iron play was magnificent; he was inside fifteen feet on every hole he birdied.

He had been paired with Trevino (Lee seemed to lag behind as they approached each green, allowing the young amateur to arrive first and take the applause). Just before Simons holed a fifteen-foot birdie putt on the 16th, Lee holed from an even longer distance and dipped two under par for the day, and when the putt fell, he suddenly realized he was in contention.

Because he was an amateur, Simons was expected to collapse in the last round, but after nine holes he was still leading Nicklaus by one stroke and Trevino by two, despite shooting 38. Paired with him, Nicklaus had thrown away a chance to move ahead by taking 6 on the 5th, a par 4, pulling his drive into a creek. Then, just as it began to look as if an amateur might win an Open after all, Simons faltered, and within the next five holes, Trevino and Nicklaus moved ahead.

Now they had reached Merion's superb finish, and the birdie holes had run out. Those last few holes nearly wrecked both Trevino and Nicklaus, and they did ruin Simons. Lee had to hole a ten-footer to avoid three-putting the 15th and had to chip and putt for his par on the 17th. Now he had the Open in his hand, one stroke up on Jack going to the 18th. A par 4 there would give him 279. His drive, though, was only adequate, leaving him a 3-wood to the green. Feeling the pressure now, Lee pushed the shot into the crowd gathered around the green, dug the ball out, but left it eight feet short of the hole. He missed the putt and shot 69—280.

Nicklaus, meanwhile, was playing the same kind of scrambling golf. He holed from six feet to avoid three-putting the 15th, holed from six feet again after missing the 16th green, and made another six-footer on the 17th, where his tee shot had found a bunker. Now it came down to the last hole, with Jack needing a par 4 to match Lee's 280 and Simons, still in the hunt, needing a birdie 3. When Simons drove into the left rough, his only hope was to dig a 3-wood out of the grass and get the ball close enough for a reasonable chance to hole a putt. He gave it all he had, but the grass was too thick. He made 6, shot 76, and finished with 283.

Nicklaus had his chance, too. He lashed a 280-yard drive to the center of the fairway, leaving himself a difficult shot from the downslope. From a hanging lie, Jack played a glorious 4-iron that flew on line all the way and sat down soft as a feather fourteen feet short of the cup. Hole it, and he had his third Open. After lining it up, he crouched over the putt, and in the stillness you could hear the putter blade tap against the ball. It ran true to the hole, but just as it looked as if it might drop, it skimmed past the right edge. Jack shot 71 and 280. A playoff was set for the next day.

It was settled on the first three holes. Trevino dropped a stroke behind with a bogey on the 1st, but Nicklaus allowed him to move ahead by playing two atrocious bunker shots on the next two holes. On the 2nd, a par 5 of 535 yards, Jack reached a greenside bunker with his second while Trevino took three strokes to reach the green, twelve feet from the hole. Nicklaus squirmed his feet down into the sand and swung. The ball popped up, hit the bank of the bunker, and rolled back in. He made 6. Trevino missed his birdie chance, and now they were tied.

The 3rd hole was almost a replay. In another greenside bunker, Nicklaus again left the ball in the sand, but instead of a bogey, he lost two strokes, and when Trevino made his par 3, he took a two-stroke lead. From then on it was one great shot after another. Nicklaus birdied the 5th, Trevino almost holed his approach to the 8th, and Nicklaus hit it two feet from the cup on the 9th. Trevino out in 36, Nicklaus in 37.

Now another lapse by Nicklaus. The 10th hole is a short par 4 of 312 yards that doglegs sharply left, but it can't be driven, because the green is slanted sideways to the tee and guarded by trees and a deep chasm of a bunker. Nicklaus drove into perfect position, dead center of the fairway where it makes its turn and about forty yards from the green. With a good shot here, he could catch Trevino, who had played an indifferent pitch thirty feet from the hole. Jack hit a terrible shot. The ball popped up weakly and came down yards short of the green. He bogeyed, Lee parred, and now Trevino was ahead by two.

Nicklaus didn't give up. With the holes slipping away he kept the pressure on, but Trevino wouldn't crack. When Nicklaus birdied the 11th, Trevino birdied the 12th; when Lee overshot the 14th, he chipped on and holed an eight-footer to save par. Through it all, Lee seemed to keep smiling while Jack's expression grew more drawn. With all the wonderful shots he'd played, he'd made too many mistakes through these five days, and he could make no headway against Trevino, who was playing such nerveless golf.

All the great shot making reached its climax on the 15th. Trevino was on the green, but he was twenty-five feet from the hole while Nicklaus was well inside him, only eight feet from a birdie. If Jack could hole that putt and climb to within one stroke with the 16th, 17th, and 18th coming up, there was no telling what might happen.

Trevino didn't give him a chance to find out. He rolled in his curling twenty-five-footer, Nicklaus made his, and they were still two strokes apart.

That was as far as Nicklaus could go; he was through as soon as he hit his tee shot on the 17th. The ball drifted to the right and buried itself in a bunker. He made 4, Trevino made 3, and won the playoff, 68 to 71.

Nicklaus was drained. He sat in the scorer's tent and stared at his scorecard in disgust. He looked crushed. He had worked hard to win this tournament, harder than anybody in the field, and yet he had finished second. In the three big tournaments thus far in 1971, he had finished first, second, and second. He had come so close to winning them all.

It is unlikely, however, that anybody could have beaten Trevino that week, because seldom in the history of the game has anyone played such winning golf over so long a period. He had been in position to win every one of the six tournaments leading up to the Open, and when it was over, he went on to win the Canadian Open three weeks later, and in mid-July he won the British Open—three national championships within one month. He was at the very peak of his game, and his confrontation with Nicklaus that June had been one of golf's classic showdowns.

TWENTY-ONE
One More to Go

With the explosion of new golf courses in the ten years since Jack Nicklaus had won his first Open, the game had become increasingly popular. The number of new golfers seemed limited only by the number of courses for them to play. As soon as a new course opened, it had plenty of customers, for Americans were taking to the game in a flood, lured by the exploits of the Palmers and Nicklauses. Where Americans played 87 million rounds of golf in 1962, they played 210 million in 1972, more than two and a half times as many. Manufacturers turned out clubs and balls in staggering amounts: 8.7 million clubs in 1962, 12.7 million in 1972; 5.2 million dozen balls in 1962, 10.5 million dozen in 1972. Americans spent $96 million on clubs and balls in 1962 and $168.6 million in 1972. By 1972 the value of golf course property was estimated at $3.273 billion. Golf was big business.

Sometime in the 1940s colleges realized they could attract publicity with a good golf team more cheaply than with a football team. Coaches scoured the country offering athletic scholarships to promising young players. For good or for bad, many of them did little more than play golf for four years, and when some of them left school, they were equipped to do nothing else. But, my, how they could play. They rushed to the pro Tour, pushing aside some of the veterans and swelling the fields for the weekly tournaments. Where ten years earlier a local club professional could expect to play in a tournament in his home town, by the 1970s he had no chance; there was no room for either him or the good amateurs.

So many of the new pros were so good, survival became increasingly difficult, and they had to be exceptionally skilled just to earn a living. But the living could be good. In 1962, the pros played for $1,790,320. In 1971, prize money soared to $7,116,000. Fortunes could be made.

In this era of rocketing prize money, the Open had to keep up. The purse had been $81,000 in 1962, but it had reached $200,000 by 1971. Nicklaus' first prize had been $17,500 in 1962; Trevino won $30,000 in 1971.

The number of Open entries was climbing as fast as the number of golfers. It reached 2,475 in 1962, and kept rising, setting a record of 4,279 in 1971. It fell off slightly for 1972, but still it reached 4,196, the second-highest total ever, as the Open moved to the West Coast once again. The golf course was part of the attraction.

The championship was scheduled for Pebble Beach, the best golf course on the North American continent and probably the best in the world. Set on craggy headlands above Carmel Bay and the Pacific Ocean and carved from forests of pine, cypress, eucalyptus, and live oaks, it is unmatched among American courses both in strategic concepts and in exquisite natural beauty. While it measures 6,815 yards, it is a par-72 course and, therefore, relatively short. Only one of its ten par 4 holes is as long as 450 yards, and four others are under 400 yards. Its four par 3s range from 120 yards to 218, two of its four par 5s measure 507 and 515 yards, and the other two 555 and 540. Eight holes run along the shoreline, exposed to the winds, seldom offering level lies, but all the while demanding precise, intelligent golf.

It was a familiar sight in the age of television, for two rounds of the Bing Crosby pro-amateur were played there annually. It had also been the setting for the National Amateur Championships of 1929, 1947, and 1961. But this was its first Open. It was overdue.

Pebble Beach was designed by Jack Neville, a good golfer who had been the California Amateur champion five times and had learned the fine points of the game under Macdonald Smith, Mac's brother George, and Jim Barnes, at the Claremont Country Club, near Oakland, where his father held a membership.

In 1915 Neville became a real estate salesman for the Pacific Improvement Company, a subsidiary of the Southern Pacific Railroad, headed by Samuel F. B. Morse, a nephew of the inventor of the telegraph and Morse code. Morse was told to dispose of the railroad's holdings on the Monterey Peninsula, but with an eye for the rugged beauty of the country as well as for a sound investment, he formed Del Monte Properties and bought the land himself, paying $1.3 million for 7,000 acres, including seven miles along the ocean.

249

PART FOUR

One of the earliest to recognize the attraction of golf to sales of building lots, Morse delegated Neville to lay out a course, setting aside some of the best land in the forest, much of it along the oceanfront.

For three weeks Neville walked the property, working out the best routing of the holes. They began simply enough. A log cabin, the original Del Monte Lodge, had been built as a refreshment stand for riders on 17-Mile Drive, a road that winds through the forest, sometimes ranging along the wild rocky shore of the Pacific. With Morse in tow, Neville walked along a path leading from the cabin and drove stakes into the ground for the first two holes. Though they ran parallel to the sea, they were a couple of hundred yards inland. Having reached that point, Neville turned toward the ocean with a shortish par 4 that doglegs slightly left and creates the first loop of the figure 8 routing.

At the 4th, Pebble Beach begins its run along the sea with the shortest par-4 hole on the course, only 327 yards from tee to green but yielding birdies only to the perfectly played shots. Because of a grouping of bunkers on the left of the drive zone, the tee shot must be shaded to the right, close to the cliff's edge, and the approach must settle on a small green crowded by bunkers, with the cliff close at hand, dropping sheer to the white sand beach behind and off to the right. Since this green is tilted from back to front rather more than usual, the approach—hardly ever more than a pitching wedge—must be kept below the hole. While it is short, the 4th is no pushover.

A par 3 moves away from the water, but then Pebble Beach begins a classic stretch of holes, starting with the 6th, a shortish par 5 of 515 yards that rises to a high escarpment above Stillwater Cove, an inlet from Carmel Bay where yachts roll in gentle ocean swells. The course then plunges down to a rocky shelf at the edge of the bay with the 120-yard 7th, a frightening little par 3 played from a high tee to a tiny green ringed with bunkers and bordered on three sides by frothy surf battering rocky outcrops reaching from the sea floor. In troubled weather the green is clouded by lacy spray, and when the wind bears in from the sea in near-gale strength, the tee shot demands a very long club.

Beginning with the 7th, you are playing golf of the most demanding order, each shot flirting with the cliffs along the edge of the bay. No hole could be more intimidating than the 8th, a 425-yard par 4 that begins next to the 7th green. The blind drive must reach a plateau and stop short of a savage chasm that plunges eighty feet to a turbid cove where wild waves churn against the gray cliffs. While the fairway swings left from there and serpentines around the head of the cove, the green is off to the right. The second shot must be played across the gorge to a small green set among deep and punishing bunkers. It is a forbidding sight, but this is nothing less than one of the three finest second shots in golf; only those to the 17th at St. Andrews and the 13th at Augusta rank with it, and this is by far the most spectacular.

The 9th and 10th, par 4s of 450 and 436 yards, are similar to one another, running along the edge of the craggy bluffs over ground that leans toward the sea. Bunkers pinch the landing zones to about twenty yards, and the land from the 6th through the 10th lies open to the sea winds; no trees protect it.

From the 10th, Pebble Beach turns inland, weaving through the forest before returning to the sea once more at the 17th, a par 3 that can play from 175 to more than 200 yards. Its hourglass-shaped green is set at an angle to the line of flight and perches on the brink of the bay. The round ends at one of the great finishing holes, a glorious par 5 of 540 yards that skirts the edge of the rocky shore that gives Pebble Beach its name.

Had the 18th remained as it was created by Neville, it would not have been so great a hole, for in the original design it was a 379-yard par 4. The credit for the change belongs to H. Chandler Egan, the 1904 and 1905 National Amateur champion. A marvelous player, Egan moved from Chicago to Oregon after losing the final of the 1909 Amateur and became a fruit grower. Since he lived 300 miles from a course, he gave up golf, but he moved again in the middle 1920s, settled in California, and took up golf course design.

Hoping to attract the National Amateur, Morse hired Egan to strengthen Neville's original design. He did more than that. His changes were monumental, and while he followed the routing Neville had laid down, he altered the character of Pebble Beach dramatically. He moved the 1st tee and green, creating a nice dogleg, moved the tee of the 2nd and made it into a par 5, rebunkered and reshaped the 7th green, transforming it into the best little par 3 in golf, added 70 yards to the 9th and took fifty yards off the 10th, creating two wonderful par 4s out of a mediocre par 4 and a short, easy par 5. Next he added 100 yards to the 14th, a par 5 that doglegs sharply right and plays up rising ground away from the bay, and he moved the 16th green behind a natural depression and into a grove of trees, adding 105 yards to its length.

He maintained the 18th tee on the rocky promontory where Neville had placed it, keeping the carry across part of the rockstrewn beach, but he moved the green farther back, setting it close to the shoreline and creating one of the finest par 5s in all of golf, a true three-shot hole that hardly anyone tries to reach in two. The penalty for failure is too great.

Egan also re-bunkered almost every green.

When Pebble Beach was announced as the 1972 Open site, television was ecstatic. On the air for five and a half hours over Saturday and Sunday,

PART FOUR

ABC's cameras showed thirteen of the eighteen holes. It was the most extensive coverage ever given to a golf tournament. The network used twenty-three color and two black-and-white cameras, shot aerial scenes from a blimp, and wallowed in the splendor of the setting.

Pebble Beach was a particular favorite of Nicklaus'. He had won the Crosby twice, in 1967 and again in January of 1972, and he'd also beaten Dudley Wysong, 8 and 6, in the final of the 1961 Amateur shortly before he turned pro. Having the Open there was a good omen. There were others.

Jack had played in twelve events by June, had won the Masters, and placed among the ten leaders in seven other tournaments. He skipped the two immediately before the championship and went to California to practice. As usual, he was the heavy choice.

Jack might have expected his stiffest opposition to come from Trevino, particularly after their battle of a year ago, but Lee had had an attack of bronchial pneumonia and spent four days in a hospital in El Paso. He had been released on Tuesday and had flown into Pebble Beach on Wednesday barely in time for one practice round.

Unlike most Open courses that the players see perhaps once in a decade, Pebble Beach was familiar ground. They knew that to score well they would have to make their birdies on the early holes and then hang on through the finish. Few succeeded. Jerry McGee played the first nine in par 36, the second in 43; Bob Murphy and Bob Rosburg were out in 37, back in 42; Jim Simons, still an amateur, shot 35-40, Tom Weiskopf 34-39, Homero Blancas 33-41, and Mason Rudolph 33-38.

Rudolph was among six men who shot 71, the most ever to tie for the first-round lead. Nicklaus was among them. Putting poorly, Jack missed five times from inside twelve feet, four for birdies, one for an eagle. It didn't look good. Nor did he improve in the second round. He had seemed to be coming alive when he played the first thirteen holes in two under par, but on the 14th he let a 4-iron slide off the face of his club and sail out of bounds into a Bloody Mary party on a neighbor's lawn. He saved a bogey by holing a twenty-foot putt, then bogeyed the next two holes, ruining what had been a fine round. He finished with an erratic 73, but when the day ended, he was still in first place, tied with five others at 144. Pebble Beach was not giving away low scores.

Jack had come in early after a nine o'clock start, but Trevino had played late, feeling better after a long rest. He had gone to bed at four o'clock Thursday afternoon and got up at noon Friday. Then he shot 72 and found himself trailing the leaders by only two strokes, with 146.

Palmer had also made a move. He seemed on his way out of the championship after shooting 77 in the first round, but his timing had improved on Friday, and he brought home a 68 that included six birdies. His shot-making was his best in a long time, probably since the 1964 Masters, and he was consistently near the hole with his irons. Like most rounds of this kind, it could have been even lower, but his putting luck had deserted him long ago. He had one sickening stretch where he missed holable birdie putts on the 5th, 6th, and 7th, and then jerked a two-footer past the hole on the 8th, costing him a par. Altogether he missed nine putts of twenty feet or less.

Scores had been running nearly as high as they had been at The Country Club in 1963, and they continued high in the third round. Nicklaus shot 72, and even though he had 216 for three rounds, which was even par, he had the fifty-four-hole lead to himself. Seeming to grow stronger each day, Trevino was only a stroke behind at 217, tied with Bruce Crampton and Kermit Zarley, while Palmer had 218. The only man in the field to improve his score each day, Trevino shot 71 with five birdies, four of them on the second nine. He was keeping himself alive with his putter.

Palmer too had become a serious threat. Playing immediately ahead of Nicklaus, he dropped his tee shot ten feet above the hole on the par-3 5th, and if he could hole the putt, he would be back to even par for forty-one holes and would have caught Jack. The putt was treacherous. Shaved down to three-thirty-seconds of an inch, the greens were slick as oil, and the superintendent was in a perpetual state of panic, wondering if the grass would survive. The greens had never been cut this low, and they were becoming crusty.

Palmer barely touched his ball. It crept slowly down the slope and somehow stopped on the lip of the cup. He made 3, and moments later, when Jack three-putted from thirty feet, Nicklaus and Palmer were even. The deadlock didn't last long; Palmer made 4 on the little 7th just before Nicklaus birdied, and Jack was not caught the rest of the round.

Sunday dawned sunny, but strong westerly winds whipped across the Monterey Peninsula, drying out the greens and churning Carmel Bay to froth. Small craft warnings flew all along the coast, and the sloops that had raced off the 7th hole on Saturday were kept safely moored in Stillwater Cove. It was not a day for low scoring, nor was it a day for taking chances; the wind could turn a moving club off line, upset a man's balance, and hurl a ball into coarse and matted rough.

Nicklaus and Trevino were the last starters, but Lee was not the player he had been earlier in the week, and he couldn't create the duel everyone hoped to see. It was as if his physical condition had overcome his spirit, and he couldn't cope. He was out of it when he made 6 on the 2nd while Nicklaus was making 4. One stroke behind at the start, Lee now trailed by three.

Just when he looked like an easy winner, though, Nicklaus played some indifferent golf, making a shaky bogey on the 4th, another shaky bogey on the 5th, a shaky par on the 6th, and even a shaky birdie on the 7th, where a twenty-five-foot putt bounced and skipped across the crusty green and jumped into the hole on the proper hop.

Although he was ripe to be taken, no one made a substantial move to catch him. Even par by the end of nine holes, he led by four strokes over Trevino, Crampton, playing one hole ahead, and Palmer, then on the 12th tee. The 10th and 12th holes changed the championship from a runaway into a tense battle.

Because the hole was cut in the left rear corner of the 10th green, the best approach was from the right, close to the precipice high above the broad sandy beach. As Nicklaus reached the top of his backswing, a gust of wind tossed the head of his driver out of position, causing him to hit the ball off line, over the cliff's edge, and out onto the beach, sixty feet below. He made 6; two strokes of his lead were gone.

After a par 4 on the 11th, he moved onto the 12th, a 205-yard par 3 calling for a long iron, a difficult shot for the day because the wind had dried out the greens, making them almost impossible to hold with low-trajectory shots. The ground behind the green drops off into heavy grass, and bunkers guard the narrow entrance. At this point Jack had only a one-stroke edge over Palmer, who had made 5 on the 10th where Nicklaus had taken his 6. With the hole slightly sheltered from the winds, Jack needed a high, floating shot that comes down soft as a feather, but he hit a low, burning 3-iron that came in far too hot. Although it hit right on target, the ball took a big bounce and rolled over the back, deep into the shaggy rough. Jack whacked at it with his wedge, but he moved it only a few feet. Once more he chopped at the ball. It jumped on but rolled eight feet past the hole. Now he had a tough putt to save a bogey.

As Nicklaus stood over his eight-footer on the 12th, Palmer stared at an eight-footer on the 14th. Arnold's was for a birdie. The Open hinged on what happened with those two putts. If Arnold's dropped and Jack's didn't, Palmer would take the lead. If they both holed, they'd be tied.

Palmer crouched over his ball in that familiar stance—knees together, shoulders hunched—just as Nicklaus bent over his ball, moving deliberately, setting the clubhead down behind the ball and giving the hole that one last glance before the stroke.

Each man tapped his putt at the same instant. As Jack's ball neared the hole, Trevino urged, "Get in there." The ball dived into the cup. Just then

Arnold's ball eased past. He screwed up his face and turned away, and his shoulders sagged. It was over for Arnold; instead of a stroke ahead, he was a stroke behind, and something went out of him. He drove poorly on the next two holes, dropping strokes on both, and when Nicklaus survived a poor drive on the 13th and holed a twelve-foot birdie putt on the 15th, Palmer fell four strokes behind. That's how he finished.

The struggle was over for Nicklaus. Bruce Crampton was closest to him now, but he was three strokes behind, and Jack had only to avoid throwing strokes away on the last three holes to win easily. After a routine par 4 on the 16th, he hit a nerveless 1-iron to the 17th, playing at 218 yards that day. His ball came down about a foot short of the hole, bounced once, hit the flagstick, and stopped less than a foot from the cup. A birdie; four strokes ahead now with only the challenging 18th left. He played it cautiously, taking three safe shots to reach the green, then three putts for a bogey 6.

He finished the day with 74, and while he had not brought Pebble Beach to its knees, his 290 had to be weighed against the conditions of weather and emotion. He was only two over par on a classic golf course.

This was as much a victory of character as it was of golfing skills, for Nicklaus had assumed the challenge of winning the world's four most important tournaments in one year, and had actually won the first two. He was to go no further, although it took a miracle finish to beat him in the British Open. Six strokes behind Trevino going into the last round at Muirfield, he shot 66, but Trevino chipped in for a par on the 17th and nipped him by a stroke. Jack didn't figure in the PGA, finishing six strokes behind Player.

By winning at Pebble Beach, Nicklaus now had won three Open championships, but Hogan, Jones, and Anderson each had four. Jack had one more to go.

TWENTY-TWO
The Best Round Ever?

Nicklaus had now won thirteen of the major tournaments, the same number but not the same events as Bobby Jones had won. It is difficult for men with the driving ambition and enormous egos necessary to reach apogee in any field to have heroes, but if Nicklaus had one, it was Jones. Jack had grown up in Columbus, Ohio. His father, Charles Nicklaus, was the owner of several pharmacies and held a membership in the Scioto Country Club, where Jones had won the 1926 Open. When Jack was a young boy, his father had told him stories of Jones. Indeed, Jones was a hero to the entire club, and so it was only natural for young Jack to set him up as an idol.

When he retired after winning the original Grand Slam, Jones had won thirteen national championships—five U.S. Amateurs, one British Amateur, three British Opens, and four U.S. Opens. By the beginning of 1973, Nicklaus had won two U.S. Amateurs, four Masters Tournaments, two British Opens, two PGA Championships, and three U.S. Opens. He had not won the British Amateur.

At what point an idol becomes a rival is difficult to say. Indeed, it is not altogether certain that Nicklaus ever looked on Jones as anything other than a hero, but nevertheless Jack was driven to surpass Bobby's record, and by June of 1973 hardly anyone doubted he would.

The key goal was that fourth Open. Twenty years had passed since Hogan had won his fourth in 1953, and eleven years had gone by since Jack had won his first in 1962. Hogan had won his last and Nicklaus his first at Oakmont, and now the Open was back to that homely old course in the rolling hills of western Pennsylvania.

Oakmont was seventy years old by then, but it was expected to be just as tough as ever. It was twenty-seven yards longer than it had been in 1962, its fairways were still narrow, it was well bunkered—perhaps even excessively bunkered (thirty-three new ones had been added, bringing the total to 187)—and its greens were still the fastest in American golf, cut at three thirty-seconds of an inch for everyday play and even shorter for the Open. To emphasize driving accuracy, the USGA set fairway widths to an average of thirty-five yards—some short holes were narrower, some long holes were wider—but Oakmont members must have a masochistic streak in them, because the USGA ordained that two fairways had to be widened; they were too narrow for the Open field.

Oakmont made one other change, revising the 17th, which had always been its weakest hole. Hogan had driven the green in the last round in 1953 and birdied, and Palmer had driven it in the third round in 1962 and eagled. A new tee was built back in a wooded hollow behind and to the left of the old tee, the fairway was shifted to the right, and instead of 292 yards, it played now at 322 yards, with a big, sweeping right-to-left curve that brought into play the bunkers that framed the elevated green. The approach now had to carry those bunkers and hit and hold a shallow green. The 17th was much more satisfactory than it had been; no one could drive it now. But someone did.

Anticipation was at an unusually high pitch as the championship approached, the feeling more feverish than it had been in years. The reasons were varied. In addition to the game's having become a more popular spectator sport to begin with, Nicklaus was going for his fourth Open, his fourteenth major championship, and Palmer was still able to generate excitement, especially so close to home. This had been the scene of the confrontation of 1962, when Nicklaus had beaten Palmer, and Pennsylvania golf fans wanted revenge.

The weather for the first round was ideal for golf. The air was warm and light, and a little breeze blew from the west, helping the tee shots on the 17th. When he had finished sixteen holes, Nicklaus was two over par and unhappy, and seeing a chance to make up the strokes he had lost, he went for the 17th green. Drawing back his driver in his usual high arc, Jack swung with a combination of sheer power and perfect timing. The ball soared off in a high parabola, came down twenty yards short of the green, took one big bounce over the bunkers, and rolled ten feet from the cup. He holed the putt for an eagle 2 and finished the day at 71, four strokes behind Gary Player, who shocked the gallery by shaving four strokes from a sturdy par of 71 and shooting 67.

For Player to be at the front of the field was somewhat surprising, because he had been hospitalized for twelve days in February for surgery on his bladder, and had played in only three tournaments in five months. His 67 was a remarkable score, for Oakmont had been its usual difficult self, yielding birdies grudgingly. Player was enjoying a three-stroke lead over Lee Trevino, Jim Colbert, and Raymond Floyd, the only other men under par. Only six others matched par, and some of the scores were startling. Billy Casper shot 79, Bruce Devlin 76, Dow Finsterwald, Doug Ford and Bob Murphy, 77, Tony Jacklin 75, and Orville Moody 78. It looked as if this would be another trying week.

Then something happened overnight, and Oakmont was a different course on Friday. The greens had become soft, and the players were firing at the flagsticks without fear. The golf course was defenseless; it had never seen a day like this. Early in the day Gene Borek, a club professional from Long Island who was in the field as an alternate, shot 65 and broke the course record. Altogether nineteen men broke par. Brian Allin shot 67, Colbert 68, and nine others had 69, including Vinny Giles, the National Amateur champion, who had a great finish. Against a par of 4-3-4-4 he shot 2-3-3-3, holing a full 6-iron on the 15th, barely missing a birdie on the 16th, and holing short birdie putts on the 17th and 18th.

The sprinkling system was blamed. Unlike those at Pebble Beach and Merion, Oakmont's greens are large, and to be at their best, they must be firm and fast. Simply hitting them shouldn't be enough; you should be forced to hit the right spot. Reaching those spots is difficult if the greens are firm, but Pittsburgh had had a rainy spring, and on the Tuesday night before the championship began, Oakmont was hit by a thunderstorm. The weather had been clear and dry since then, and the course was becoming fast, just as it should be. When he shot his 67, Player said that by Sunday everybody would know just how good a round that was. Both P. J. Boatwright, the man most responsible for running the Open, and Harry Easterly, then the chairman of the championship committee, were satisfied the greens had the proper pace, and after a conversation with Lou Scalzo, the club's greenkeeper, they agreed to sprinkle for only five minutes overnight. Exactly what happened was never clear, but most likely someone made a mistake and allowed the sprinklers to run longer than they should have. Oakmont was never right again.

In the easier conditions, Player went around in 70, and while he clung to his lead, he was only a stroke ahead of Colbert, with 137 to 138. It was evident by now that Player's game was not as steady as his scores implied. With only twenty-nine putts for the round, he should have done better than 70, but five times he had to one-putt to save pars. Because he had been away from the game for so long, he did not have his usual competitive edge.

Nicklaus was hardly playing any better, but he was sharper competitively, and he could score. He birdied three of the last six holes, shot 69, and climbed to within three strokes of Player with 140. Palmer stood two strokes farther back after a second 71, but he was erratic. Every time he birdied, he threw the stroke away with a bogey. In thirty-six holes, he had had eight birdies, eight bogeys, and twenty pars.

Already saturated, Oakmont was hit by another storm early Saturday morning. Rain began falling heavily at about 5:30, stopped briefly three hours later, but began in earnest once again at about 9:30. It stopped in time for the first starting time at 10:20, but then fell heavily off and on throughout the day, occasionally interrupting play. While the greens had been soft on Friday, they were like mush on Saturday. Where the ball hit, it stopped. The course was playing easier than it ever had, but Player's game collapsed, and he shot 77. Six men broke 70, and when the round ended, four shared the lead at 210, another had 211, and three others had 212. Eight men were bunched within two strokes.

Jerry Heard was one of those at 210, after shooting 66, the low round of the day. A strapping six-footer who had dropped out of college to join the pro Tour in 1969, Heard said hitting irons to the greens was like throwing darts. He was tied with John Schlee, a lean, sandy-haired veteran with a flat, unattractive swing, fifty-three-year-old Julius Boros, and Palmer.

With so many bunched so close, and with Palmer among the leaders, a dramatic climax was shaping up for Sunday's final round, but some spectators who flooded through the gates came only to see Arnold. They had only a vague acquaintance with golf. To wit:

One man ran up to another and asked, "Where's the next par?"

Another wondered, "Do they change the pins for every group coming through?"

Still another looked at Arnold with green envy. Watching how the female spectators reacted as Palmer strode by, he turned to his companion and said, "Can you imagine being Arnold Palmer and single?"

Sunday was an uncomfortable day. Clouds hung low and the humidity pressed down, and because the overcast blocked the sun, the greens remained soft and receptive, raising the probability of low scoring. Nevertheless, no one was prepared for what happened.

Johnny Miller, a lanky, blond Californian who hit wonderfully straight and crisp irons and who had won two tournaments since dropping out of Brigham Young University to join the Tour in 1969, left the 1st tee

an hour before the leaders. When he had left his motel that morning, he
had told his wife to pack and be ready for a quick exit from Pittsburgh;
after shooting an untidy 76 on Saturday, Miller had 216 for fifty-four
holes and stood six strokes behind the leaders. To reach the top, he would
have to pass twelve men; clearly, he was going nowhere.

Miller began the last round by playing a straight drive down the middle
and then drilling one of his pretty, precise irons—a 5-iron here—five
feet from the cup and holing the putt for a birdie.

"That's not too bad," he told himself. On to the 2nd.

After another straight drive, Miller almost holed his 9-iron; the ball sat
down six inches from the cup for another birdie. On the 3rd he looked
out at the Church Pew bunkers and smacked another long, straight drive
and a 5-iron twenty-five feet past the hole. The putt fell; three under.

The fairway of the 4th, a 549-yard par 5, swings in a long crescent
through a narrow opening past the Church Pews on the left and a grouping of five other bunkers on the right, through coarse and heavy rough to
another slick and undulating green set at an angle to the approach. After
another fine drive, Miller tried to reach the green with his second, but his
3-wood drifted into a greenside bunker on the right. He almost holed
his recovery and had his fourth straight birdie. He had begun the day
three over par and now he was one under for fifty-eight holes. For the
first time it occurred to him that he could win.

No one was paying attention to Miller yet though, because at about
this time the leaders were going off the 1st tee. Schlee was paired with
Palmer, playing ahead of Boros and Heard, who were the last two men
off. After Saturday's round, Schlee had tried to explain why he was playing so well. A disciple of astrology, he said, "My horoscope is just outstanding. Mars is in conjunction with my natal moon." Something must
have tilted overnight, because he pushed his drive out of bounds and made
6 on the 1st hole. He would be back, though.

With so many players grouped so tightly, and almost all of them playing
so well, it was impossible to tell what was happening through the first nine
holes. Nicklaus set off a roar when he birdied the 2nd, but then so did
Colbert, Trevino, Bob Charles, and Tom Weiskopf. From then on
through the end of the first nine, the situation changed quickly and
repeatedly. Caught up in the frenzy, spectators dashed back and forth
as one man after another went ahead, then fell back. Three men held the
lead at one time or another—Heard after he birdied the 2nd, Palmer
after a birdie on the 4th, then Boros after birdies on the 4th and 6th. As
soon as they grabbed the lead, they lost it. After nine holes, Boros, Palmer,
and Weiskopf shared the lead at four under par, and Trevino, Schlee,
and Heard were three under.

Miller, meantime, had cooled off. After reeling off routine pars on the 5th, 6th, and 7th, he three-putted the 8th from thirty feet. Three under for the day now, he was four strokes behind the leaders, but he could pick up one with a birdie on the 9th, a short, uphill par 5. A drive, then a 2-iron, and he was on the green, but forty feet from the cup. A good lag putt put him close, and he holed the short second putt for the birdie. Out in 32 and four under par for the round, one under for sixty-three holes. Now he was closer, but a quick glance at the scoreboard showed him how tight the race had become. No one was folding; he needed more birdies.

A drive and 5-iron to twenty feet on the 10th. No birdie there. Then a break on the 11th. His wedge from the crest of the hill stopped fourteen feet away, and the putt fell. Five under for the day, two under for the distance. Closing in. Now for the 12th, 603 yards winding through wiry rough and deep bunkers. A drive into the rough, his first off-line drive of the day. No chance to do anything with this shot; just play it out to safety. A 7-iron to the fairway, then a marvelous 4-iron to fifteen feet. The putt dropped. Six under for the day, three under for the distance. Almost there.

Most of the gallery was still across the Pennsylvania Turnpike following Palmer, Boros, Nicklaus, and the others, but as word of Miller's hot streak spread, they raced for the footbridge that spans the Turnpike, clogging the approaches and cramming their way through. Risking serious injury, some fans climbed onto the foot-wide railing and crawled across on hands and knees while cars and trucks whizzed past below at mile-a-minute speeds. Others slipped off the course and fought their way through heavy traffic inching along a road that borders the club, then cut back onto the Oakmont grounds.

Miller kept up the pace. A 4-iron to five feet on the 13th and another putt dropped. Seven under for the day, four under for the distance. He'd caught up, and now only Palmer was tied with him. Another birdie chance on the 14th from twelve feet, but the ball stopped an inch from falling. Now for the 15th, one of the strongest holes in American golf, a 453-yard par 4 with a narrow fairway only thirty-four yards wide, bordered on the left by a smaller version of the Church Pews and on the right by a mammoth bunker that begins twenty yards ahead of the green and runs almost to the back edge. Putting something extra into the shot, Miller drove his ball 280 yards. Now a 4-iron. The ball hit the green, hopped once, and skidded ten feet away. Miller rolled the ball into the center of the hole. Eight under par for the round and finally into the lead at five under par for sixty-nine holes. Only three holes left.

Palmer, meanwhile, was coming up the 11th not aware of Miller's surge. He was four under par then, and after a good tee shot he played a lovely pitch just four feet to the right of the hole. It seemed just like old times. If he kept playing as he was, he would surely win and have that second Open he had tried so hard for all those years. He was forty-three years old then, and he would probably have no more opportunities; he had to take advantage of this one. When he made this putt, he would be five under par, and that should be good enough.

Arnold was about to suffer three shocks that upset him so badly he never recovered.

First, he missed the putt and remained four under par. It hurt, but he believed he was still leading by a stroke over Schlee, Weiskopf, and Boros. Still confident, he strode over to the 12th tee and played what he thought was a perfect drive, shading the left side where the ground slants to the right and will kick the ball to center-fairway. He was so confident he had played the shot perfectly, he hitched his pants, and with an assured, tight-lipped smile, he turned away and didn't watch the ball land.

Then, as he and Shlee left the tee, Arnold glanced at a scoreboard. Squinting through the branches of a tree, Palmer made out a red 5 down on the bottom of the board indicating that someone was five under par and a stroke ahead of him. He couldn't quite make out the name.

Palmer was stunned. His confident grin faded and, bewildered, he asked Schlee, "Who's five under?"

"Miller," Schlee answered. "Didn't you know?" Shock number two.

Then, as he and Schlee approached the landing area, they saw only one ball in the fairway. Assuming it was his, Arnold strode up to it, but when he looked down, he saw it was Schlee's. Instead of bouncing right, Palmer's ball had jumped left into heavy rough. Shock number three. He bogeyed the 12th, then followed with two more bogeys on the 13th and 14th. There would be no second Open.

Now it was only a matter of Miller's holding on. A 3-wood to forty feet on the 16th and two putts for a par 3; a 1-iron and a wedge to ten feet on the 17th and another par; then a huge drive on the 18th, a 7-iron to twenty feet, and two more putts for his final par. Out in 32, back in 31. A 63, the lowest round ever shot in the Open.

Miller finished with 279, four strokes better than Hogan had shot in 1953 and than Nicklaus and Palmer had shot in 1962, and twenty strokes under Sam Parks's 299 of 1935.

But it wasn't over yet; two men could still catch him.

Schlee had rallied after his 6 on the 1st hole, and now he could tie Miller with a birdie on the 18th. His second shot rolled over the green into clumpy rough about fifty feet from the hole. He would have to chip. The crowd hushed and Miller stood and watched as Schlee set himself. He played a courageous shot, gauging the distance just right, but he pulled the ball a trifle left of the hole and made 4.

Miller relaxed. Only Weiskopf was left, and he would have to hole his second shot on the 18th to tie. He didn't, and Miller was the champion. Schlee finished second, one stroke behind at 280, and Weiskopf was third at 281. Palmer, Trevino, and Nicklaus all shot 282, and Boros and Heard finished with 283, tied with Lanny Wadkins.

Miller had played a phenomenal round. He had hit every green and had missed only one fairway on the driving holes. His irons were inspiring. He had hit five shots inside six feet (two of them inside one foot), two more to ten feet, and three others to fifteen feet or less. He had birdied nine holes and had bogeyed only the 8th, where he had three-putted. His 63 had broken the record set first by Lee Mackey at Merion in 1950, then matched by Tommy Jacobs at Congressional in 1964, and by Rives McBee at Olympic in 1966.

As soon as Miller posted his score, a natural question arose: Was it the greatest round ever played in the Open? Did it rank with the 65 Arnold Palmer shot at Cherry Hills in 1960, the round that carried him to the championship from seven strokes behind, or with Ben Hogan's closing 67 at Oakland Hills in 1951?

No, it didn't. While it was an extraordinary score, it was done over a course softened by rain. Miller's shots required nowhere near the control of Palmer's and Hogan's, because they played their rounds over fast and firm courses. For them to hold those hard greens, Palmer and Hogan had to play to certain spots on the greens and apply fierce backspin to stop the ball. Miller didn't have to do that: Oakmont's greens were so soft and mushy, any kind of shot would hold.

Nevertheless, Miller had played the course as he found it, and he had played it better than anyone else. As for controlling his emotions, while it is true he had no thoughts of winning when he had begun in the morning, he had realized he had a chance after he birdied the first four holes, and he had birdied five more after that. Furthermore, a 63 on no matter what kind of course is something special, and even though Oakmont was playing easier in 1973 than it had ever played, it was still among the more challenging tests in American golf.

Miller's 63 wasn't the best ever, but it was close.

TWENTY-THREE
The Journeymen

Except for certain special events like the Open, the Masters, and the PGA, the game had become little more than a driving and putting contest in the early 1970s. As golf courses were set up for the weekly Tour tournaments, they seldom asked for finesse; the players had only to swing hard, scrape the ball onto the green, and rely on a delicate putting touch.

Under conditions like these, scores in the 60s were not only common, they had become necessary for survival, and par had become an insignificant figure. On the American tour in 1973, only the World Open, played at Pinehurst, had been won with a score over par. In the week before the 1974 Open, Hubert Green, a slender Alabaman with a quick, flat, wristy swing, had won at Philadelphia with 271, seventeen under par. In Charlotte, North Carolina, earlier, all but one man had finished the seventy-two holes under par.

Some of the better players complained.

"Finesse has been replaced by muscle," Lee Trevino said, "and it's due to the way our courses are set up. On the whole, the rough has been eliminated; it doesn't make any difference if you keep the ball in the same county, let alone the same fairway. Sometimes you'll have better lies in the so-called rough than in the fairway."

Tom Weiskopf agreed.

"Our officials are setting up the courses so they play too easy. Instead of making the game a test of the players' abilities, they turn it into a putting contest."

There was truth in the complaints. In 1970 the Dow Jones Open was played at the Upper Montclair Country Club in Clifton, New Jersey, within sight of the towers of Manhattan. The Metropolitan Golf Association had played its amateur championship over the same course a week earlier, but before the professionals arrived, the greenkeeper was ordered to cut the rough back and widen the fairways.

Players accustomed to these easy layouts had more trouble than they should at demanding courses.

Weiskopf expressed his opinion while Hubert Green was ripping apart the Whitemarsh Valley Country Club. The next week the players arrived at Winged Foot for the Open and found a course with punishing rough, hard and quick greens, and trees pressing in on narrow fairways, requiring a lot of long iron shots. Nobody could play it.

Although it had changed very little since the days of Bobby Jones, Winged Foot was the most severe test since Olympic in 1955. It was much too hard. It was long, measuring 6,961 yards, and the fairway lines were drawn in too tight for a course of its length. The landing zone was wider than thirty-four yards only on the 8th hole, a brutish par 4 of 442 yards. Some were much tighter. The short little 6th, a par 4 of 324 yards, allowed only twenty-eight yards between rough lines. The 5th, an uphill par 5 of 515 yards, demanded the drive hit a narrow alley of twenty-nine yards. Adding to its difficulty, Winged Foot was heavily wooded; its holes wove among an assortment of trees that could stock an arboretum: five varieties of oak, four of maple, as well as linden, ash, birch, beech, pine, fir, spruce, golden raintree, along with flowering trees such as white and pink dogwood, purplish Japanese lilac, and the scarlet-blossomed Eastern redbud.

Its greens required high shots that come down softly, but too often they had to be played with long irons, and the greens were both framed and guarded by steep-faced bunkers. Heavily contoured with humps and hollows, at best they're difficult to putt; as they were shaved down for the Open, they were terrifying. Faced with a downhill twenty-five-footer on the first hole, Jack Nicklaus tapped his ball gently, then watched horrified as it glided past the cup and scooted off the green. He was still twenty-five feet away. Not only were they fast, they broke wildly. Johnny Miller said that on one green he felt silly standing with his back to the hole and looking over his left shoulder to see the cup. They were also hard. Vandals drove a car across the 1st green the evening after the opening round, but nobody noticed except the men who set the cups early Friday morning.

The rough was as difficult as the greens. Largely bluegrass, a more coarse, wide-bladed strain than the bentgrass used on tees, greens, and fairways, it stood five inches high just six feet off the fairway. Playing more than a 4-iron from this stuff was chancy.

PART FOUR

All of these factors, of course, affected scoring. Gary Player had been playing wonderful golf through the early months of 1974. He had won the Masters in April for the second time, won again at Memphis a month later, and had been out of the top twenty only once in nine tournaments. Winged Foot had him baffled. While he shot 70, matching its demanding par, he had to scramble, scraping the ball around, hitting only twelve greens, but somehow willing the ball into the cup. No one could match him. When the day ended, he had a one-stroke lead over Lou Graham, Jim Colbert, and Mike Reasor, a new Tour player who had caddied for Palmer at Olympic in 1966.

Winged Foot took a heavy toll. Early in the day the scoreboards had dripped red numbers, indicating holes played under par, but the players were under unrelenting pressure from this punishing course, and as the hours passed, the red numbers disappeared. Only twenty-three men shot under 75. Billy Casper and Gene Littler shot 80 and Lee Trevino 78. Miller had won five tournaments already that year, but with 76, he had no answer to Winged Foot's problems. Nor did others:

John Schlee, after shooting 78: "I don't know whether to practice or cut my wrists."

Bob Goalby with 81: "I tried on every damn shot."

Ralph Johnston with 87: "If I hadn't been putting well, I wouldn't have broken ninety."

Asked, "Is the USGA trying to embarrass the best players in the world?" Sandy Tatum, the newly appointed chairman of the championship committee, riposted, "No, we're trying to identify them."

Winged Foot was more forgiving the next day, but Player's game collapsed on the first nine. With a 7 on the 4th hole, he played the first six holes in six over par, fought back with 33 on the second nine, shot 73, and at the end of the day shared the lead with Raymond Floyd, Arnold Palmer, and Hale Irwin.

Showing the first signs of his potential, Tom Watson slipped ahead in the third round. Only twenty-four, Watson had come close to winning some Tour events, but now he was in position to win the most important title of all. After shooting 69, he was ahead by a stroke, with 213 for fifty-four holes. Irwin had 214 and Palmer 215.

As Watson left the 18th green on Saturday, he spied Tatum, a fellow Stanford alumnus. Tatum was as pleased and excited as Tom. Grim-faced, Watson approached him and asked, "Do you think I can do it?"

"Do *you* think you can do it?" Tatum replied.

"Yes, I do," Watson said.

No, he couldn't. Paired with Irwin the last day, he was out in 38 with a couple of three-putt greens and stumbled back in 41. A 79 and 292.

Palmer failed, too. He three-putted from twelve feet on the 2nd hole, then, desperate for birdies, tried to play too good a shot on the little 6th, hit his pitch about a yard short of the green and into a bunker, made 5, and shot a dispirited 76.

The championship developed into a battle between Irwin and Forrest Fezler, a relatively obscure player. Six strokes behind Watson when the round began, Fezler made up ground steadily, birdied the 12th, holed a gritty twenty-footer for a par 4 on the 16th, and made another gritty par from a bunker on the 17th. He was eight over par then, but he was playing shaky golf.

Irwin, meanwhile, had been wavering, too. He had coaxed in a thirty-five-footer on the 9th that climbed a hump, then ghosted into the cup for a birdie 3, and had finished the first nine in 36, dropping him to five over par for sixty-three holes, but then he played some strange golf that almost cost him the championship. Over the next seven holes he had one par, two birdies, and four bogeys. He was then seven over par and wobbly, and his situation didn't improve when he drove into the left rough on the 17th, a fierce par 4 of 444 yards. From where his ball lay, he had no chance to reach the green.

Just then Fezler came to his rescue, driving into the left rough on the 18th, taking a bogey 5, and finishing with 289, nine over par.

Back at the 17th, Irwin still had problems. He had moved his second shot only about 100 yards into the fairway, and he still had 100 yards to the green. Now he lofted a pitch ten feet from the pin and holed the putt for his par. It was the decisive stroke of the week. Still seven over and leading by two, Irwin relaxed and played the 18th perfectly—a safe drive, then a heroic 2-iron dead on line, and two putts for the par. He had played the last eighteen holes in 73, not a very exciting round, and he had bogeyed two of the last four holes.

His final score was 287, seven over par. Two years earlier Nicklaus had won at Pebble Beach with 290, but he had been only two over par. This was the highest score in relation to par since 1963, when Julius Boros, Jacky Cupit, and Palmer had tied at 293, nine over par, but the scores had been high at The Country Club because of fluky weather. To find the last winning seven-over-par score shot under normal conditions, we had to go back nineteen years, to Olympic in 1955.

Although he projected very little of his personality, Hale Irwin was an attractive golfer. He was twenty-nine years old, a trim six feet and 170 pounds, with dark hair and a long, thin face. He wore gold-rimmed glasses, and he was an articulate speaker. He had won the National Collegiate Athletic Association golf championship in 1967, while he was at the University of Colorado, and had played football in the same defensive backfield as Dick Anderson, who was with the undefeated Miami Dolphins of 1972. Irwin was not that good. While he was not drafted, he did receive a questionnaire from the St. Louis Cardinals, but when he came to the line asking about his speed, he chucked it into the trash can. The Cards did not pursue the matter.

Even though he lacked the fluid graceful swing of a Snead, the dedication of a Player, the majesty of a Nicklaus, or the Hollywood ambiance of a Miller, he was an accomplished golfer, at home on courses that required the long iron. He had won the Heritage Classic twice, over the Harbour Town Golf Links in Hilton Head Island, South Carolina, but he was usually just one of the crowd. The Open, however, has a way of setting one golfer apart from the others.

During the 1974 championship, though, the public had seen a new star rising. Not Irwin, but Tom Watson. He had boyish appeal, a shock of rumpled auburn hair, an open friendly face, and a warm smile that showed a wide gap between his two front teeth. The All-American boy—the real life image of Jack Armstrong.

Watson had been born into an affluent and fairly prominent Kansas City family. His grandfather Isaac Newton Watson, a lawyer, had helped break the Pendergast machine that had ruled Missouri politics, and his father, Raymond E. Watson, was a well-known insurance broker and scratch golfer. Ray Watson had won the Kansas City Country Club championship several times and had gone to the fourth round of the 1950 National Amateur, beating Tom Strange, the father of Curtis Strange, and Bill Hyndman in the early rounds.

Tom began hitting golf balls when he was six, using a cut-down spade-mashie (about a 7-iron). Stan Thirsk, a former Tour player, took over as the club professional when Tom was ten and worked with him to develop an upright swing. Even at that age, Tom could move the ball right or left, and he became one of the few players with much interest in learning to play different kinds of shots.

He was a prodigy. At thirteen he shot 67, and at fourteen he won the Kansas City Match Play championship. At fifteen, in an exhibition match against Arnold Palmer, he ripped his first drive 300 yards. "Who's *this*?" Palmer quipped. Three years later he played another exhibition match with Nicklaus and lost by two strokes.

He attended the Pembroke-Country Day school, won the state high school golf championship twice, played quarterback on the football team and guard on the basketball team. Shortly after graduation from high school, he won the Missouri Amateur, and then won it three more times while he was in college.

Continuing a family tradition, he went to Stanford—his father and both of his brothers were Stanford men—and played four years on the golf team without the spectacular success that would indicate he was a future star. He didn't come close to winning the Pacific Eight Conference championship, finished fifth in the NCAA championship in his junior year and sixth in his senior year, couldn't get past the quarterfinals in the Western Amateur, and from 1967 through 1970, when the National Amateur was at stroke play, he placed, in order, sixteenth, twenty-fifth, fifth, and twenty-sixth.

Watson could hit the ball long distances, and he could chip and putt, but he was wild. He didn't have a sound, reliable swing. Nevertheless, as a senior at Stanford, he decided to try professional golf. He qualified for the Tour in 1971 and won $2,185 the remainder of the year. He began to improve. In 1972 he won $31,000, in 1973 he won $75,000, and in 1974 he went over $100,000 for the first time, winning $135,474. By then he had come under the influence of Byron Nelson, who had seen him play in early 1974 and had liked Watson's aggressiveness and his ability to concentrate.

While Watson was winning money, he hadn't won a tournament through the first half of 1974, and his dismal last round at Winged Foot had raised some question about his nerve, but two weeks later he won the Western Open over the Butler National Golf Club, near Chicago, almost as tough a course as Winged Foot. Six strokes behind Tom Weiskopf after fifty-four holes, Watson shot 69 in the last round, only the fourth sub-70 score of the week, and nipped Weiskopf and J. C. Snead by two strokes, showing he could play first-class golf when it mattered.

Promising though he was, Watson was only one of a growing number of outstanding young golfers coming out of college programs that sometimes pushed them into more competitive situations in one spring than Jack Nicklaus might take on in a year. When Watson joined the Tour in 1972, Lanny Wadkins, John Mahaffey, and Steve Melnyk already had months of experience. Grier Jones and Bob Murphy had joined the Tour in 1968, and Johnny Miller and Jerry Heard in 1969. Tom Kite came on in 1972, the same year as Watson, then Andy North joined them in 1973.

No one, however, had come into professional golf in quite the style of Ben Crenshaw in late 1973. A player with enormous potential, along with a shy, friendly appeal that earned him the nickname Gentle Ben, Crenshaw had won the NCAA championship three times, once sharing first place with Kite, his teammate at the University of Texas. He led the Tour's qualifying competition by twelve strokes, and in his last round shot 30 on the second nine of the Dunes Golf and Beach Club, a testing layout on the shores of the Atlantic Ocean in Myrtle Beach, South Carolina. The very next week, in his first tournament as a professional, Crenshaw won the Texas Open, and a week later shot 64 over Pinehurst Number 2 in the World Open.

Crenshaw was after bigger game than the Texas Open; he thirsted to win one of the major championships, and he very nearly won the 1975 Open, played once again at Medinah, where Cary Middlecoff had won in 1949.

For the second time in three years, weather became a dominant factor in an Open championship. Medinah was soaked by an all-day rain on Sunday, and more fell on Monday, Tuesday, and Wednesday. Great shards of lightning crackled through the skies, the weather bureau issued tornado warnings, and the course was closed a good part of each day. Consequently, the greens were soft enough to hold even a low-trajectory long iron, and they putted much slower than they should have.

Apparently forgetting his bad experience at Winged Foot, Watson was off to a marvelous start, shooting 67-68—135. With par set at 71, he was seven under regulation figures and had matched the thirty-six-hole record. Crenshaw was next with 138, somehow saving pars while hacking trails through the trees following his erratic drives. Playing the 16th hole in the first round, he pushed his drive deep into the woods, found an opening about eight feet wide, hit a 5-iron twelve feet from the hole, and birdied. The next day, when his drive on the 13th shot into the woods and bounced back toward him, he played a 9-iron over the trees, a full 6-iron to twenty feet, and holed the putt. He struggled around Medinah in 76 in the third round and dropped into a tie for fourth place at 214.

Meantime, Watson's world was falling apart as, strangely, his putter turned sour. While he was to become one of the most reliable short putters the game has ever known, he began the third round by taking three putts from twenty feet on the 1st hole, then astonishing the gallery by missing from less than two feet on the 2nd. Stunned as the ball spun around the lip of the hole and sat on the edge, he never recovered. He lost his timing, went out in 40, shot 78 for the day, followed with 77 on Sunday when a par round would have won easily, and tied for ninth place, three strokes behind the leaders. Questions about his nerve revived.

Crenshaw, meanwhile, remained in the hunt, but he became just one more of a group of players who could have won but didn't. Watson could have won, Nicklaus could have won, Frank Beard, the third-round leader, could have won, John Mahaffey could have won, and Lou Graham, who eventually did win, could have won more easily.

Every one of them except Mahaffey threw away the championship over the last few holes of the fourth round. Mahaffey played the 14th through the 18th in one under par, posted his 287, then waited.

Needing one birdie over the last three holes for 286, Nicklaus pulled his drive into the woods on the 16th and bogeyed, then, after overshooting the 220-yard 17th, played a weak chip, leaving his ball still short of the green, and bogeyed again, finishing with 289.

Crenshaw needed two pars to beat Mahaffey, but on the 17th tee he caught his ball toward the toe of his 2-iron, and it splashed into a pond. A 5 and 288.

Lou Graham next. A pleasant man in his late thirties, he had been on the Tour for eleven years and had won two tournaments. He was two over par through sixteen holes and had been standing on the 17th tee watching Beard bogey the 16th hole. Frank had been playing miserably all day, and now he had slipped to six over par for the day and three over par for seventy holes. He would need three more pars for 287. Graham had passed him; two more pars and Lou would have 286, which would beat Mahaffey and probably Beard, unless Frank turned his game around quickly.

One of the game's finest shotmakers, Graham played a screaming 2-iron that covered the flag, hit the green, and taking the roll of the ground, swerved fifteen feet away from the hole. His putt looked like it was in all the way, but it took too much break, skimmed the edge of the cup, and stopped inches away.

Beard then bogeyed the 17th and dropped to four over par. He finished at 288.

When Graham split the 18th fairway with his 2-iron, he seemed to have the Open won, but his 6-iron approach hit too close to a bunker and jumped into the sand. A weak recovery left him twenty feet away, and he left his first putt short. A bogey. He had tied Mahaffey.

The playoff the next day was dull. Graham birdied the 4th, 5th, and 10th, played every hole on the second nine in 4s, shot even par 71, and won by two strokes even though Mahaffey had played better golf. John hit every green after the 6th, and he putted for birdies on half the holes, but he was constantly short.

While Graham was not a demonstrative man, he was thrilled. Sitting with a friend and cradling the silver trophy, his big, very white teeth gleaming through a wide smile, he said, "Now my name will be on that trophy just like Ben Hogan and Bobby Jones."

Watson would have to wait for his name to join theirs, but three weeks later he won the British Open by defeating Jack Newton of Australia in a playoff at Carnoustie. His nerves had been good enough in Scotland.

The next four years were a period of waiting—waiting to see if Nicklaus could win his fourth Open, and if Watson would ever win his first. Meanwhile, three young players won from 1976 through 1978, and then Hale Irwin took the fourth, once again showing he could stay close to par on an extremely difficult course. Before Irwin came through at Inverness, Jerry Pate won at Atlanta, Hubert Green at Southern Hills, and Andy North at Cherry Hills. Each championship was absorbing in its own way.

Until 1976, the Open had never been played in the southeastern quadrant of the country—east of the Mississippi and south of the Potomac—but that year it went into the heart of the Confederacy, to the Atlanta Athletic Club. It was there because Bobby Jones had written to the USGA asking for it to be played at his old club (this was, however, a different golf course; he grew up playing the old East Lake Course). His letter was dated November 16, 1971; he died thirty-one days later. There was never any doubt he would have his wish. Unfortunately, the golf course, which was only a few years old, was nothing special, and if not for a stunning 5-iron shot on the last hole, it would rank among the least memorable of all the Open championships.

It began with Mike Reid, a short-hitting amateur then, just as later he became a short-hitting pro, shooting 67 and not only leading the field, but baffling and contradicting the pros, who complained they couldn't control the ball because the fairway grass, cut to about three-quarters of an inch, was too long. The wheels on some new mowing equipment were too big and raised the cutting blades higher off the ground than they should have been. The players claimed the extra quarter of an inch allowed grass blades to get between the clubface and the ball, preventing them from applying enough spin. Reid had no trouble on Thursday, but once the grass was cut lower, he shot 81 and dropped from sight.

John Mahaffey was back in contention again, leading after three rounds with 207, Pate, the 1974 Amateur champion, was two strokes back at 209, and Al Geiberger and Tom Weiskopf had 210 and 211. They were all there at the end. Geiberger and Weiskopf finished with 279 and stood by the 18th green waiting for Mahaffey and Pate, who were playing behind them.

Pate caught Mahaffey with a birdie on the 15th, a long par 3, and then John committed a series of errors that cost him the Open. One of the shorter hitters, he hooked his drive into a fairway bunker on the 16th and bogeyed, then hit a terrible 3-iron shot miles away from the flagstick on the 17th and took three putts. Now he was two strokes behind Pate coming to the long and difficult 18th, a par 4 of 460 yards with a body of water in front of the green. He would have to do something dramatic here to catch Pate, but he pushed his drive deep into the wiry Bermudagrass rough and had no realistic chance to reach the green. He had to try, though, because, he said later, "You don't win the Open by laying up." He took a hard swing with his 3-wood, but he knew it was short as soon as he hit the ball. He pressed his lips tight, and with a forlorn look, he turned away. The ball splashed into the pond.

It wasn't over just yet, because Pate had a problem, too. He needed a par 4 for 278, a stroke better than Weiskopf and Geiberger, but his ball also lay in the rough. The question now was whether he should try to reach the green and risk going into the pond or play short of the water and hope to pitch close enough to have a 4. Looking at his ball, Pate realized he had a stroke of luck. Instead of lying deep down in the grass, it was propped up almost as if it were on a tee. He'd go for it.

Pate then played one of the great shots of golf lore, a 5-iron that flew straight at the flag and stopped less than three feet from the cup. He holed the putt, finished the round in 68, and shot 277.

A former National Amateur champion, he was twenty-two years old, in his first season on the Tour, and this was his first victory as a professional. The comparison with Nicklaus was inevitable. Pate, however, was no Nicklaus. He played well enough for a while, losing the 1978 PGA in a sudden-death playoff to Mahaffey, but eventually developed a disk condition in his neck and gradually faded.

A year later it was Hubert Green's turn, but this was an Open remembered less for the quality of the golf than for unusual circumstances. With eighteen holes to play under searing heat at Southern Hills Country Club, Green was two strokes under par with 208, and leading Andy Bean by one stroke. They were paired together in the last round, and as they drove from the 10th tee, an extraordinary meeting was taking place inside the clubhouse.

A Tulsa police lieutenant told the USGA's Harry Easterly, Sandy Tatum, and P. J. Boatwright a chilling story. A clerk in the Oklahoma City office of the FBI had answered a telephone call from a frantic woman who claimed three men were on their way to Tulsa to kill Hubert Green.

"I know they're serious," she cried. "They showed me their guns."

The nature of the meeting was kept secret, but several actions were taken. A phalanx of uniformed policemen suddenly sprang up around Green, the clubhouse was closed to everyone, plainclothesmen patrolled the gallery, and a mysterious person materialized within the ABC television control trailer, where no outsider is permitted, and quietly gave orders to Roone Arledge, the president of ABC Sports, and Chuck Howard, who was producing the telecast. He told them to instruct their cameramen to scan the crowd around the 15th hole and not ask questions.

Green obviously had to be told, and he was already playing shaky golf. He had bogeyed the 9th and 10th, and now Lou Graham was closing in. Out in 37 and losing ground, Graham had suddenly turned his game around and run off four birdies in five holes. He had just birdied the 16th as Green was finishing the 13th, and now they were only a stroke apart, with Green ahead.

Graham then hooked his drive into a line of trees that border the 17th fairway. His ball was lying on bare ground deep in the trees, and his line was blocked by some low-hanging branches. To reach the green, he would have to play a shot that would start low to clear the branches, rise, turn left to avoid sailing into the woods on the far side, land short of the green in the cushiony Bermudagrass to take the speed off the ball, then hop up onto the green. Using a 3-iron, Graham played the shot perfectly; the ball stopped seven or eight feet from the cup. It was one of the most imaginative shots ever played under the pressure of an Open championship. Then he missed the putt and remained a stroke behind Green.

As Graham walked toward the 18th tee, Green was leaving the 14th green. Easterly, Tatum, and the police lieutenant called him aside and explained the threat and the reason for the unusual number of policemen. They gave him three options: He could withdraw, he could ask for play to be suspended, or he could continue to play. Green chose to play on, and he even joked that the threat probably came from an old girlfriend.

Nothing happened; the threat probably was a hoax.

Green hung on through some anxious moments, scraped out a par on the 15th, birdied the 16th from the rough, got down in two putts from fifty feet on the 17th, then left his approach to the 18th short and in a bunker. He needed a 5 here, for Graham had played the last nine in 31 and was in with 279.

"Don't chunk it," Green said to himself as he dug his feet into the loose sand.

He chunked it, leaving his ball twenty feet short. Two putts now for 278. He left his first putt three and a half feet short. But he holed the second for the 5, shot par 70, and with 278, won by a stroke.

Two days earlier, Sam Snead had said good-by to the Open. It had been forty years since he had played in his first, back in 1937, and he had been invited to play again as an observance. Sam was sixty-five. He shot 74-78—152 and missed the cut.

While Green's victory was unexpected, he was at least playing winning golf in 1977, and he was at a high point of his career. The next spring he nearly won the Masters, missing a short putt on the seventy-second green that would have tied him with Gary Player. Since he joined the Tour in 1970, Hubert had won eleven tournaments, although none since the Heritage Classic of 1976. Andy North, on the other hand, was in his sixth

274

year as a professional when the championship returned to Cherry Hills in 1978, and he had won only the Westchester Classic of 1977. His winning the Open was almost as big a shock as Orville Moody's.

This was an Open Jack Nicklaus could have won had his mind not wandered at strange moments. With a thirty-six-hole score of 142, he was only two strokes behind North going into the third round. He had just rapped a twenty-footer three and a half feet past the cup on the 5th, but as he approached his ball, he saw Gary Player and J. C. Snead on the 7th. Since they were the pairing immediately ahead, he wondered how they got there so fast, and he was still thinking about it when he stood over his putt. He missed and bogeyed. Then he bogeyed the 6th, a par 3. Worse was coming.

An eagle 3 after two monstrous drivers onto the 10th green brought him back to even par, and he was still even after the 12th, trailing Player by three strokes and North by two. Now they were approaching the 13th, a relatively innocent par 4 of 382 yards whose fairway ends about seventy-five yards short of the green, where the ground begins a gentle drop to a creek, then rises to a green guarded by five bunkers. As an inexperienced amateur in the 1960 Open, Jack had three-putted the 13th, because he wasn't sure he could repair a ball mark. He'd have settled for that 5 now.

Nicklaus played a gorgeous 3-wood into perfect position, short of the creek. On his way to his ball though, he stopped at a portable comfort station, then came back to face a short wedge, a shot he never liked. The interruption probably upset his rhythm, because he played an awful shot; he hit the ground at least an inch behind the ball and took a divot the length of a hall rug. The ball didn't even reach the creek on the fly; it hit short and rolled into the water. He made 7, using six strokes from 103 yards. He finished the day with 74, not quite out of it, but on his way.

North shot 71 and with 211 went into the last round nursing a one-stroke lead over Player. One by one the challengers faded as the last round began. Five strokes behind at 216, Nicklaus made an early run with two birdies on the first three holes, but he dropped two strokes on the 4th and was done. Player three-putted two of the first three holes, and when North birdied the 4th, he moved four strokes ahead.

North managed to make it close with some mediocre golf on the last five holes, but he was so far ahead, he squeezed through even though he shot 74. Anyone close to the lead could have won with a decent round, but Player, who needed 73, shot 77; J. C. Snead and Dave Stockton, who needed 71, shot 72, and Andy Bean, Johnny Miller, and Seve Ballesteros, the young Spaniard who had burst onto the golf scene in the British Open two years earlier, needed 70s, but shot, in order, 74, 74, and 77.

PART FOUR

The Open had been going through a series of loose finishes by the champion ever since Miller's 63 at Oakmont. Irwin had scored 73 in the last round at Winged Foot, Graham had finished with 73 and John Mahaffey with 71 at Medinah, North had shot 74 at Cherry Hills, and in 1979 Irwin closed with 75 at Inverness.

Irwin had the rare knack of playing winning golf over classic and difficult courses—Harbour Town twice, Riviera, Butler National (not a classic course but certainly difficult), and Pinehurst Number 2, where he had shot 62 in one round and 264 for seventy-two holes, twenty strokes under par. Inverness was similar to Winged Foot with its abundant and heavy rough, constricted fairways, and small, well-guarded greens, both humpy and quick to the touch.

Extraordinarily consistent, Irwin once played through eighty-six consecutive tournaments without missing a thirty-six-hole cut, but it was surprising he didn't win more often. Since he joined the Tour in 1968, he had won ten tournaments in ten years—none at all since 1977—and neither he nor anyone else could explain why, for if he had one quality in abundance, it was his competitiveness. When Tom Weiskopf played a great shot ahead of him in the third round of the 1979 championship, he refused to yield and instead played an even better one.

Irwin had gone into the third round at 142, three strokes behind Tom Purtzer, a twenty-seven-year-old graduate of Arizona State University who had won the 1977 Los Angeles Open, and Larry Nelson, who had learned to play golf by reading a book. This was the best scoring day of the tournament. The wind was light, the pin placements were reasonable, and more of the players were on their games. No one had broken 70 in the first round and only Irwin, Nelson, and Purtzer had done it in the second, but nine men shot 69 or better in the third. Amid the sudden spurt of low scoring, Purtzer and Nelson were doing poorly, but Irwin and Weiskopf were playing inspired golf, hitting one superb shot after another and driving each other to new levels.

The round—indeed the championship—reached its climax on the 13th hole, now a par 5 after the course had been revised. Playing immediately ahead of Irwin, Weiskopf smashed a powerful drive that rolled down an incline onto level ground, then rifled a 4-iron onto the green and holed from eight feet for an eagle 3.

Watching Weiskopf, Irwin's aggressive juices began to flow. He pressed his lips together, muttered to his caddie that he'd make an eagle of his own, then drilled a 2-iron to three feet. The shot was classic; it traveled about 225 yards and flew directly at the flagstick all the way. It was the shot that won the Open. Holing the putt, Irwin was five under par for the

276

day and four strokes ahead of Weiskopf, who was then in second place. Weiskopf picked up one stroke on Irwin over the closing holes, and both men finished the round in 67.

Weiskopf had nothing left in the last round. He began with two bogeys, played the first nine in 38, and lost three strokes to Irwin. Pate had begun the last round five strokes behind and was falling back, and Nelson made no move at all. Only Purtzer seemed to have a chance when he began with four straight 3s, but he threw everything away with an unorthodox drive on the eighth.

The 1979 Open will be forever remembered for "Hinkle's tree." In re-modeling Inverness, the architects George and Tom Fazio created a new 8th hole from elements of the old 6th and 7th, making it into a par 5 of 528 yards that turns gently left beyond the drive zone and runs roughly parallel to the 17th. During practice rounds, Lon Hinkle, a hulking pro known for little else but his long drives, noticed that if he turned a little to his left, he could hit down the 17th fairway and cut about sixty yards off the length of the 8th. Instead of 528 yards, it would play to about 470, and he could reach the green with a medium iron, provided, of course, that his second shot carried the copse of evergreens growing close to the green.

He tried it in the first round, and it worked. Word spread, and others used the same trick. Hearing of Hinkle's novel idea, the USGA acted. Early Friday morning a scrawny Black Hills spruce sprang up alongside the tee. It stood twenty-four feet high and measured sixteen feet across at its base, but it looked as if it had been left over from last December's stock of rejected Christmas trees. It was intended to block shots aimed down the 17th, but the tree was so scraggly, players continued to attack the hole this way. It was risky, but sometimes it worked.

It didn't for Purtzer. He hit a wild shot to the bottom of a ravine and made 7. He rallied briefly, but dropped four strokes over the last four holes. He was gone, and now Pate was closest to Irwin, but he was six strokes behind and had no chance. Nor did Player, even though he was on his way to a 68. Gary had started the last nine from eight strokes back.

While a six-stroke lead seemed safe enough, Irwin had lost his rhythm, and he was struggling for every par on the home nine. His driving was erratic—in the right rough here, the left rough there—and he was missing greens. Still, he was scraping out pars, and everyone else was miles behind. Even though he made 6 on the 17th, a par 4, he was still three strokes in front heading to the 18th tee. With a gallery of more than 20,000 sitting tense and quiet, Irwin pushed his drive into the right rough, and from a grassy lie pulled his second into the left greenside bunker.

Then he played as good a shot as he needed; the ball floated up softly and stopped six feet past the hole. He got down in two, shot 40 on the second nine, and 75 for the round, the highest fourth round by a champion since Cary Middlecoff thirty years earlier. Still, his 284 was even par and two strokes ahead of Player and Pate, who finished with 286. Living up to his reputation for playing his best on the toughest courses, Irwin became the fourteenth man to win the Open more than once.

TWENTY-FOUR
Jack Is Back

Twenty-one years had passed since Jack Nicklaus had won the 1959 Amateur, his first national championship. That was a long time to stay at the top of any game—indeed, few men had—but as the 1980 Open approached, Jack was no longer the overpowering force he had been for two decades. He had become forty years old in January, a time when hand-to-eye coordination is on the ebb and the nerve ends jangle from a generation of competition at the highest level.

He had won his third British Open in mid-July of 1978 and the Philadelphia Classic a week later, but he had won nothing in the twenty-three months since. If he never won again, he would have played winning golf for a remarkably long period, but Nicklaus wasn't content to step aside and savor what had passed. He lusted to win, as he had from the first time he had played the game as a ten-year-old in one of Jack Grout's junior classes at Scioto. He had been a gifted golfer from the start. At eleven, one year after taking his first group lesson, he shot 81. At twelve, after eight consecutive rounds of even 80, he shot 74, and at thirteen he shot 69 for the first time, holing a thirty-five-foot putt across a wet green in semi-darkness for an eagle 3.

He was a genuine prodigy, and Grout nurtured and developed his natural talent. Under Grout's guidance, Nicklaus learned to play his tee shots with a slight left-to-right drift, because, as Grout pointed out, the strong golfer has more control over a fade than over a hook. Besides, any finished golfer must occasionally play the fade to reach pins tucked away to the right. At the same time, the polished golfer must play a right-to-left draw when the fairway bends left or when the pin is on the left.

Grout also impressed on Nicklaus that he should hit the ball high in order to hold a hard green with a long iron. Because of the way Jack set himself up, with his head farther behind the ball than most players, high shots came naturally.

He was becoming a first-class golfer, learning not only how to hit the ball, but also how to play shots and when to play them. In competition, he was a consistent winner from the start. At thirteen he won the Ohio Junior, for boys from thirteen to fifteen, and the Columbus, Ohio, Junior, and in his introduction to national golf, he won three matches in the National Junior Championship. At fourteen he played in the Ohio Amateur but didn't go far (Arnold Palmer won). He also shot 64 in a high school tournament.

By the time he was fifteen he dominated junior competition around Columbus, and in September he played in his first National Amateur. With Bobby Jones watching, Nicklaus went to the 11th tee of the Country Club of Virginia leading Bob Gardner, a good player from California, by one hole, but he lost the next three with some sloppy golf and Gardner won, 1 up.

Nicklaus was building a reputation. At sixteen he won the Ohio Open, shooting 64 in the third round and beating a good field that included Frank Stranahan. In the midst of the tournament, he squeezed in an exhibition match with Sam Snead. He hit every fairway, every green, two-putted every hole, and shot 72. Snead shot 68.

He qualified for the Open at seventeen, shot two rounds of 80 at Inverness, and missed the cut. He qualified for the Open again in 1958 and shot 304 at Southern Hills, won the Trans-Mississippi Amateur, shot 66 and 67 in the first two rounds of the Rubber City Open, a Tour event, and finished twelfth, and in the second round of the National Amateur took Harvie Ward to the 18th hole at Olympic, Ward's home course. Ward had a medal score of 70, Nicklaus 71. Ward won, 1 up.

Jack was picked for the 1959 Walker Cup Match, at Muirfield in Scotland. He was part of a remarkable team that included Deane Beman, Tommy Aaron, Bill Hyndman, Charlie Coe, Billy Joe Patton, and Ward. As they began their practice rounds, they were followed by a group of British supporters who wanted to see this new crop of young Americans. They arrived at the 2nd hole, a 349-yard par 4, just in time to see Nicklaus drive. They watched in awe as the ball arched high against a steel-gray sky, dropped onto the hard fairway, and bounded onto the green. Without saying a word they walked slowly back to the clubhouse and straight into the bar. With Jack winning his alternate shots and his singles matches, the United States won, 9–3.

The Walker Cup was played in late May. Returning home, Nicklaus won the North and South Amateur, his second consecutive Trans-Mississippi, and in a close match with Charlie Coe, birdied the last hole at The Broadmoor in Colorado Springs to win the National Amateur, 1 up. Against a par of 71, Nicklaus shot 71-69—140 and Coe 69-73—142. Nicklaus had reached the pinnacle of amateur golf, but he was going higher, and he was getting better.

He had missed the cut in the 1959 Open, but he had nearly won the 1960 championship and then finished fourth in 1961, three strokes behind Gene Littler. He had lost in the fourth round of the 1960 Amateur, but he had won again in 1961 after winning the NCAA and Western Amateur championships. It was time to move on. In the fall he gave up amateur golf and became a professional.

No one had gone into professional golf with so much promise, and no one had been more successful in winning the tournaments that mattered. By the end of 1979 Nicklaus had won sixty-six tournaments in the United States, plus three British Opens and five Australian Opens. Until then he had never gone a year without winning at least two Tour events, nor had he finished lower than fourth in money winnings. In 1979 he was seventy-first, and he hadn't won a tournament since mid-1978. Suspicions were growing that he might be through and that it was time to retire gracefully. He didn't think so.

A winner all his life, Nicklaus was not accustomed to *not* winning, and he was determined to do something about it. He thought he knew the problem. Lee Trevino had said God gave Nicklaus everything but a wedge, and Paul Runyan, one of the great players of the 1930s and 1940s, had said Nicklaus had the short game of a ten-handicapper. Phil Rodgers, on the other hand, was a wizard around the greens. Rodgers had been a Nicklaus rival in their amateur days. A cocky ex-marine, he had bragged that he would beat Jack in their third-round match in the 1960 Amateur, but in an inspired round of golf, Jack shot seven-under-par golf for thirteen holes and wiped him out, 6 and 5. Rodgers by now had dropped off the Tour and had put on quite a bit of weight, but he still knew how to handle the wedge. Jack asked him for help, and he answered the call. Rodgers went to Florida, and for two weeks he lived in the Nicklaus house, spending hours on the practice green in the Nicklaus back yard working on Jack's chipping and pitching every morning and every afternoon. Jack practiced as he had seldom practiced before. Day after day they worked, and gradually he grew better, although the results weren't evident for a time. From January through mid-June, he played in nine tournaments, and aside from a tie for second place in Miami in March, he finished in such unglamorous positions as thirty-third, forty-third, and fifty-third. Poor finishes aside, he had begun hitting the ball with his old authority. When he shot 67 in the Atlanta Classic, the week before the Open, he was encouraged, even though he had scored 78 in the first round and missed the cut. The 67 buoyed his confidence.

He was confident for another reason: The championship was back to Baltusrol, where he had won in 1967 and set the seventy-two-hole record.

The Open began on a sunny, windless day. From a hill above the first tee, the Manhattan skyscrapers glistened in the morning light, and the air was clear and cool, with the heat of the day still to come. Nicklaus was to start in midmorning, but it was evident long before then that this would be an unusual day. Raymond Floyd, by now an old campaigner, ripped the first nine apart, shooting 30, four under par. Arnold Palmer, Calvin Peete, and Bob Zender shot 32, and Tom Weiskopf, playing just a little ahead of Nicklaus, was out in 31. Clearly Baltusrol was not the stern test it was expected to be, again because the greens were soft from twenty-four inches of rain that had fallen through the spring. Floyd was firing his shots right at the flagsticks—fifteen feet on the 1st, five inches on the 4th, eight feet on the 6th, and five feet on the 8th. The road home was tougher; he came back in 37, finishing with 67.

Weiskopf, meanwhile, had birdied five holes on the first nine, added three more from the 13th through the 18th, and shot 63, matching the Open record.

Nicklaus began his round tentatively, one-putting to save par on the 1st, then hitting a poor 1-iron from the 2nd tee and taking a bogey. Not an encouraging beginning, but Jack birdied three of the next five holes and went out in 32. After a par on the 10th, he ran off three more birdies following precise irons, saved par from a bunker on the 14th, then birdied both the 15th and 17th. Seven under par now, he needed a birdie on the last hole to shoot 62. He covered almost all of the 542 yards with a drive and 3-wood, then played a soft little lob that cleared the edge of the green, dropped gently, coasted down an incline, and stopped three feet from the cup. It was a lovely shot, played with touch and finesse, justifying all the work he had done with Rodgers. Now for the putt.

The gallery hushed as he settled over his ball. The putt would break left, and he would have to tap the ball just right for it to fall. He tapped it gently, but the ball rolled past the right edge of the hole and never once looked as if it might fall. It was the only holeable putt he had missed all day. He shot 31 on the second nine and shared first place with Weiskopf.

Never had opening round scores been so low. The 63s tied the record set by Johnny Miller seven years earlier, but seventeen others broke par

70. Three men shot 66, three more 67, and four had 68. Clearly this would be a week of low scoring.

Nicklaus shot a struggling 71 in the second round, moving him into a two-stroke lead over Isao Aoki, a lean, thirty-seven-year-old Japanese who had won the World Match Play tournament two years earlier, Lon Hinkle, Mike Reid, and Keith Fergus, a young Texan who had been runner-up in the 1975 National Amateur.

Jack's 134 was a thirty-six-hole record. When he went out in 32 the next day, he was running away from the field, but then he wobbled, bogeyed both the 14th, where he was in the rough and a bunker, and the 15th, where he left a twenty-footer six feet short and three-putted, shot 38 on the second nine, and 70 for the round. Aoki caught him with his third consecutive 68. They would go into the last round tied at 204, once again a record score. Now even the seventy-two-hole record was at risk; Nicklaus and Aoki would need only par 70 to break it.

Despite their record scores, however, they did not have the Open to themselves. Hinkle was only a stroke behind at 205, while Fergus, Mark Hayes, and Tom Watson lurked at 206.

The day of the final round was warm and sunny, with hardly the suggestion of a breeze, an altogether fine day for golf, and everyone anticipated an exciting climax. Television had progressed so much that toward the end of the 1970s it had become customary to show all eighteen holes of the Open, the only tournament given such treatment. With Nicklaus in position to win the championship, the Open was a gigantic attraction. When it was over, television people estimated it had reached 90 million homes, more than any other tournament in 1980 except the Bob Hope, whose field was laced with movie and television personalities.

Everyone had reason to expect something special. Here was the greatest player of the age battling an unorthodox Japanese whose putting style had caused spectators to snicker and whose results caused them to gasp, with their most obvious challenger expected to be Tom Watson, the best player of the last few years.

A streaky golfer, Watson had spurted into contention by birdieing five holes in a six-hole span in the third round and shooting 67, but he had nothing left on Sunday. He drove poorly on the 1st hole and bogeyed, made up for it with a birdie on the 2nd, but didn't make another until the 16th, when it was far too late. Hayes dropped behind early and shot 74; Fergus hung on and could have been a threat if more putts had fallen, and while Hinkle once came within a stroke of Nicklaus, Jack and Aoki gradually pulled away.

Paired together for the fourth consecutive day, they played what amounted to match-play golf. Jack jumped ahead when Isao bogeyed the

2nd and then opened a two-stroke lead with a birdie from five feet on the 3rd. Except for a loose shot on the 4th, Nicklaus had been playing beautifully, hitting firm, crisp irons and swinging with a solid tempo, but suddenly he lost control of his driver, drove into the left rough on the 6th and the right rough on the 7th and 8th. Luckily, he dropped only one stroke to par over those three holes, and when he finished the first nine in 35, he was still ahead by two strokes.

The tee shot on the 8th was his last error; after that his golf was of another world. He hit every fairway in just the right spot, and he hit every green. Not only was his direction dead on, he gauged the distance of his shots perfectly. When the hole was on the back of the green, he hit the back; when the hole was on the front, he hit the front. On the 10th, with the pin well to the back, he placed his drive on a level area right of center fairway and then played a precisely judged 7-iron hole high and three feet to the right. On the 11th, which doglegs left, he drove to the ideal spot, beyond the turn and safely away from the fairway bunkers, and his pitch barely skimmed the overhanging branches of a tree close against the left side of the green.

One flawless shot followed another. On the 15th he hit the only shot that looked as if it might be off line, twenty-five or thirty feet left of the flag, but there was hardly a doubt that he had aimed for that general area because the hole was cut to the right rear, and no one leading the Open by two strokes would risk going for it.

Still, Nicklaus couldn't shake Aoki, and with two par-5 holes coming up, he couldn't afford a slip. Both men made their 3s on the 16th, and from the 17th tee Nicklaus hit a thunderous drive that arched high, drifted slightly right, and covered 275 yards. Although the 17th measures 630 yards, Jack couldn't go all out with his second because the green is set on a plateau beyond an abrupt rise covered with scraggly rough and scarred with bunkers. To stay short of the rise he played a 2-iron over the cross bunkers beyond the drive zone to level ground on the right side of the fairway, leaving himself about ninety yards short of the hole, set on the left front corner of the green.

Aoki was away and played a soft pitch right at the hole. Now Nicklaus. Thinking his shot through very carefully, he played a sand iron and aimed it to the right of the hole, toward the wide part of the green and away from the trouble along the left. When they climbed up the grade, they saw Aoki's ball sitting five feet from the cup and Jack's about twenty-two feet away.

Aoki had been putting so well Jack assumed he would birdie, and unless he birdied too, he would be going to the 18th with only a one-stroke lead. He wanted this putt desperately.

He examined the line and stood over the putt with his usual deliberation, and then, drawing on that inner resolve and strength of will, Jack holed the putt. The Open was his. Watching him, it was like a great weight had been lifted from his back. His face had been drawn as he stood over the ball, but now it was breaking into the widest grin he had ever shown, and he was taking on a glow he hadn't shown before.

Aoki made his putt, as Jack had expected, but now he would need a miracle eagle on the 18th to have any hope at all. There was no miracle. Nicklaus played a 3-wood from the tee, a 3-iron short of the bunkers before the green, then pitched on to ten feet. He tried to coax his ball close to the hole, and it dropped in for another birdie.

The gallery had broken through the restraining ropes by now and had crowded to the edges of the green, and as Jack's putt fell, the spectators began to charge toward him. Acting quickly, he thrust out his right hand, palm toward the gallery, much as a traffic policeman stops onrushing cars, and the crowd stopped long enough for Aoki to hole his putt. Nicklaus had finished with 68, and Aoki had shot 70. Both men had broken the old record of 275, Nicklaus with 272, Aoki with 274.

As Aoki's final putt dropped, blue-uniformed New Jersey State troopers rushed to form a wall around Nicklaus and led him through the cheering throng, into a corridor between sections of the grandstand toward the big Tudor-style clubhouse. Fans, grinning almost as happily as Nicklaus, reached toward him, hoping for a brief handclasp or simply to touch him.

Off to the side, attendants at the big scoreboard spelled out a message:
JACK IS BACK

Time fled. It hardly seemed he had been away.

TWENTY-FIVE
Waiting for Watson

Nicklaus had now won four Open championships and had pulled even with Willie Anderson, Bobby Jones, and Ben Hogan. But like Hogan, he wanted a fifth. He felt he had a good chance to win at least one more, because the next two were going to courses he knew and liked—Merion in 1981 and Pebble Beach in 1982—and he was playing at his peak. Two months after winning at Baltusrol, he had won the PGA Championship for the fifth time.

He had a further ambition. The Open had been his eighteenth victory in the five major championships (including the Amateur), and the PGA was his nineteenth. But twenty is a nicer number.

As usual, he played a limited schedule through the early months of 1981, finishing two strokes behind Watson in the Masters (a 75 in the third round ruined him), and by June he had won over $100,000 for the eighteenth time in nineteen years. He believed he was hitting the ball better than he had a year earlier, and he was confident he could score at Merion. He was right. Others, however, scored better, and even though he shot 280, the same score that had tied for first ten years earlier, he placed sixth. The 1981 Open belonged not to Nicklaus, but to David Graham.

Graham was a superior craftsman who had scrapped and fought and reached the top even though no one else had faith in him. Two years earlier Nicklaus had advised him to give up the game and devote his career to designing clubs. Graham ignored the advice, then went out and won the 1979 PGA Championship at Oakland Hills.

His background was very different from Nicklaus' and Watson's.

Where they were the sons of fairly well-off families, Graham had had a troubled childhood of constant family bickering. He was born in Melbourne, Australia, and grew up independent, resolute, and determined. Against the objections of his father, he left school on his fourteenth birthday to become a professional golfer, causing a rift that never healed. Until 1970 they hadn't seen each other in years, but his father came to the 1970 Open in Minneapolis and approached David. Graham invited him into the clubhouse to talk. The meeting was a bitter failure. They argued once again, and David stood up and walked away.

Graham began his career as a shop boy in a Melbourne club, but he was dismissed for allegedly calling a member by his first name. At eighteen he became head pro at a club in Tasmania, the island state off the southern coast, but in three years he accumulated debts of $6,000. A man of enormous integrity, he was determined to pay back his creditors. He took a job with Precision Golf Forgings, an Australian golf club manufacturer, and for eighteen months he never went out, lived on baked beans and fish-and-chips, and paid off his debts. He had the streak of self-discipline so necessary to succeed in professional golf.

He did not become a first-class golfer easily; he had to learn everything. In his early life he had played left handed, but he was converted to a right-hander by George Naismith, the man who gave him his first job. After playing through Australia and the Far East, he tried to qualify for the American Tour in 1970 but failed. A week later he teamed with Bruce Devlin and won the World Cup for Australia. A year after that he qualified for the Tour and became one of its more reliable and consistent players. He won the World Match Play Championship in England in 1976, and in 1977 he realized a boyhood dream by becoming the Australian Open champion.

By now he had built a reliable repeating swing that was effective even though it looked awkward. He stood erect to the ball, his back straight as a board, took the club back at a slow, steady pace in an upright plane, then came through with a measured precise stroke. He always seemed to play within himself, never pushing for extra distance, content to place the ball where he wanted.

His game seemed particularly well suited to Merion, which asks for control more than power. David played the first three rounds in 68, 68, and 70 and posted 206, three strokes behind George Burns, a burly man who had once played football at the University of Maryland (he quit with a knee injury after one year). In spite of an unusual method—his right elbow was shoulder high at the top of his backswing instead of pointing downward in the classical manner—Burns had broken the year-old record with 203, built on rounds of 69, 66, and 68.

PART FOUR

Rain fell on Saturday night, softening the greens for the final round, but leaving them still extremely fast. By Sunday morning the skies had cleared, and the air was light and calm.

Nicklaus was still in range with 208, but he couldn't get a good round going and dropped out of the race. Bill Rogers remained close enough to have a shot at the lead, but he couldn't make up enough ground.

The duel was between Burns and Graham, and Graham went after the lead from the start, rolling in a twenty-footer on the 1st and then nearly holing a 9-iron for an eagle 3 on the 2nd; his ball stopped six inches from the cup for an easy birdie. Two under now and only one stroke back. When Burns dumped his approach to the 4th into a brook, Graham had made up three strokes in four holes. Burns fought back, though, and held a one-stroke lead after nine holes, but he broke on the 10th, taking a bogey, and even though Graham played a loose sort of hole himself, leaving a sand iron twenty-five feet short of the hole, he made his par and caught up.

That misjudged approach was Graham's last lapse. He made a routine par 4 on the 11th, missed a birdie chance from ten feet on the 12th, lipped the cup from eight feet on the 13th, and then came to those last five demanding holes. No one could have played them better. He drove to just the right spot on the 14th fairway (he was feeling so confident, he used a driver for the first time that week), and his 7-iron covered the flag, setting up a birdie from six feet. The 15th was a copy of the 14th—a 1-iron from the tee, then an 8-iron to ten feet and another birdie. The 16th, 3-wood and 5-iron to ten feet, then a putt that grazed the edge of the cup. The 17th, 2-iron onto the collar twenty feet away, two putts. The 18th, perfectly placed drive, a 4-iron to eighteen feet, again a putt that grazed the lip. Graham played those last five terrifying holes in two under par and shot 67, three under par. His final score of 273 was the second lowest ever in the Open. Burns had been even with Graham going to the 14th tee, played the last five in one over par, and lost three strokes. He dropped into a tie with Rogers for second place, with 276.

Graham's precision that day was beyond anything since Johnny Miller's 63 at Oakmont in 1973. He missed only one fairway, and while he was not exactly on the putting surface of all eighteen holes in the regulation allotment of strokes, he was on the collars of the three greens he missed, and he was able to putt on each of them. As for flaws, he drove into the left rough on the first hole but still birdied, and he three-putted the severely tilted fifth from eighteen feet. He made four birdies, all from fifteen feet or less, missed three from inside ten feet, and six more from inside twenty feet. Three putts that missed actually touched the hole.

Beyond Miller's 63, Graham's precision must also be compared to

Hogan's last two rounds at Cherry Hills in 1960, when he hit thirty-four consecutive greens. It does not, however, compare with the 67 Hogan shot at Oakland Hills in 1951. That course was infinitely more brutal than Merion in 1981.

Still, Graham's was a marvelous accomplishment, one of the finest rounds ever played in championship golf, done when it was needed, under conditions that strain the steadiest of nerves, over one of the world's most testing courses, for the world's most important championship.

Graham was the latest in a series of journeymen golfers who had won the national championship. While all of them had played exceptional golf to win, they would not be remembered as the great players of their time. Still, Lou Graham, Jerry Pate, Hubert Green, Andy North, Hale Irwin, and now David Graham had won the Open. Tom Watson had not.

Watson was an enigma. Since 1975 he had been the biggest tournament winner and the hottest money winner in golf. He had won over $300,000 in each of the last five years, once he won $462,000, and in 1980 he had won $530,000, more than anyone ever. Since he had joined the Tour in 1972, he had won twenty-five American tournaments and three British Opens. He had won the Masters twice, and he had established himself as the successor to Nicklaus as the game's leading player. But he had not won the Open.

By now he had settled doubts about his nerve, principally through two unforgettable confrontations with Nicklaus in 1977, first in the Masters and then in the British Open. With Nicklaus breathing down his neck, he had gone into the third round at Augusta with a three-stroke edge over Jack, played the last thirty-six holes in 70-67 while Nicklaus shot 70-66, and won by two. The British Open at Turnberry later that season was probably the best exhibition of shotmaking by two players the game has seen. Tied after thirty-six holes, they were paired together in the last two rounds and finished a stroke apart. Watson shot 65-65 and Nicklaus 65-66.

Theirs had grown into a rivalry that compared with some of the great matchups of earlier times—Nicklaus and Palmer, Nicklaus and Trevino, Snead and Hogan, Hogan and Nelson, Sarazen and Hagen, Hagen and Jones.

During 1977, they played 288 holes against each other in the Masters, Open, PGA, and British Open. Watson scored one stroke lower. They didn't play quite so evenly again. When Nicklaus won the Open in 1980, Watson finished four strokes behind; a month later, when Watson won the British Open, Nicklaus trailed by nine; another month after that, when Nicklaus won the PGA, Watson finished fourteen strokes behind.

Then, when Watson won the 1981 Masters, he beat Nicklaus by two. They were to have one more classic confrontation, in 1982, when the championship again went to Pebble Beach.

Although he had not won the Open, Watson had often played well. He had thrown away a chance to win in 1974, probably should have won in 1975, and he had placed no lower than seventh in four of the next six. Now the championship was coming to familiar ground. Not only had Watson played Pebble Beach in the 1972 Open during his first season as a professional, he had often come there during his college days at Stanford, about an hour and three quarters' drive to the north. Three or four times a year a gang would organize for the early morning drive down the Pacific shore. They would play twice around, then begin a third round, play the 1st through the 5th, skip the holes at the outer reaches of the course, cut across to the 14th and hit something like an 8-iron to the green, and play in from there, sneaking in forty-five holes for one green fee.

Knowing Pebble Beach as he did, Watson understood he must make his birdies early, but the first nine defeated him in both the first two rounds. Starting with three 5s in a row on Thursday, he shot 37. He was worse on Friday, posting 38. His homeward nines were much better. Three over par with four holes to play and headed for a 75 on Thursday, he reeled off three straight birdies, shot 35, and finished with 72. The next day he birdied the 14th and 17th, and came back in 34 for another 72.

With 144 for the first thirty-six holes, Watson stood five strokes off the lead, and while he seemed to be on his way to another also-ran finish, a little study showed he was actually in quite a good position. Bruce Devlin was leading with 139, but he couldn't expect to hold on. He was forty-four years old, and he hadn't won a tournament in ten years. Larry Rinker and Scott Simpson were next at 141 and 142, but they didn't figure, and next at 143 sat Calvin Peete, Lyn Lott, Andy North, and Bill Rogers. Of those, only Rogers might be a serious threat, since he had proved himself by winning the 1981 British Open and had slipped into a tie for second at Merion a year earlier. At 6,825 yards, Pebble Beach seemed too long for Peete, at once the most accurate and the shortest hitter in the field as well as an unreliable putter; North hadn't won anything since the 1978 Open, and Lott and Rinker had simply played two good rounds and probably wouldn't play two more.

Watson wasn't alone, however, for there beside him at 144 sat Nicklaus, who had recovered from a dismal 74 start with a rock-steady 70 in the second. Three others also had 144—Bobby Clampett, a young Californian, Tom Kite, and George Burns, who had had one of those strange days. Opening the second round with a par 4, Burns ran off six consecutive birdies, due largely to outstanding iron play. His longest putt was from ten feet, and with a chance for an eagle 3 on the 6th, he two-putted from eight feet. Out in 30, Burns had matched the Open's nine-hole record. Then he lost it all with 42 on the second nine.

Beginning his move in the third round, Watson shot 68 and, from a tie for eighth, shot into a tie for first with Rogers. Devlin had the 75 he was expected to shoot and dropped two strokes behind, level with Burns, Simpson, and David Graham, who had come to life with 69.

Nicklaus, meanwhile, had played some steady but dull stuff, hitting greens reasonably close to the cups, but failing to hole the putts he needed. He had the ball within twenty feet on each of the last four holes, but while ten years earlier he could have expected to hole at least one of them, he missed them all. Like Palmer before him, he wasn't the putter he used to be. He shot 71, a stroke under par, and his 215 left him behind six men—Watson and Rogers at 212, Devlin, Graham, Burns, and Simpson at 214. But if Jack could get something going, he could make up strokes quickly.

Nicklaus was in the fourth-from-last group Sunday, paired with Peete. A fine drive from the 1st tee left him in prime position for his pitch to the green, but for the second straight day he played a loose shot. The ball hit the lower right corner of the green and spun off into shaggy grass at the top of a downslope. From there he played a miserable chip that never once moved in the direction of the hole. It stopped at least twelve feet away, and he missed the putt. When he failed to birdie the 2nd, the weakest hole on the course and the easiest par 5 in championship golf, it seemed that this would not be Jack's Open.

But Jack was never through as long as there were holes to be played. He would fight on.

Suddenly he began playing superb golf. A sand iron to fifteen feet on the 3rd, another pitch to twenty-four feet on the 4th, a 6-iron tee shot to two feet on the 5th—three straight birdies. His drive settled in a close lie in the fairway on the 6th, but this was no time for caution; a 1-iron onto the green, two putts, and another birdie. A sand iron to eleven feet on the 7th and still another putt fell. Five consecutive birdies. Jack was four under par for the round, five under for fifty-nine holes, and at that moment he was tied for the lead with Rogers, playing two holes behind him. Watson was one stroke back, tied with Devlin, who was still hanging on. A hole later, Devlin birdied the 6th and he too was five under par. At least five men stood within a stroke or two of one another.

As soon as Nicklaus grabbed a share of the lead, he lost it. He drove well enough on the 8th, to the top of the hill where he had a good look at the green sitting across the chasm, but his iron drifted into heavy grass and settled in so deeply he had trouble finding it. When he did, he played another mediocre chip and missed the putt. One stroke gone. A par on the 9th, and he was out in 33 and stood four under par for sixty-three holes. Another par on the 10th, then an uncharacteristic bogey on the 11th. For years Nicklaus had been the most dangerous fourth-round player in golf and the most reliable putter, but here he three-putted from twenty feet, giving away a stroke when he needed birdies.

Devlin, meantime, was falling apart, and Watson had edged ahead of Rogers briefly with a birdie on the 2nd, dropping him five under par. Tom had thrown away one glorious opportunity on the 7th by jabbing at a putt of two feet, and after the first nine, he was four under par while up ahead Nicklaus was walking off the 11th green at three under.

Watson's driver had usually been his most unreliable club, but it had been behaving wonderfully so far, and he had not missed a fairway. A man of no more than average size (five-foot-nine and 160 pounds), he was powerful, nonetheless; with forearms like Hogan's, he generated terrific clubhead speed and hit the ball tremendous distances. On the 10th, he crushed his drive and sent it thirty or forty yards past Rogers' ball, leaving him with only a 7-iron to the green. Close though he was, he had to play his approach from a downhill lie, and something went wrong. His ball shot off on a line that would take it to the right of the green, and unless it came down quickly, it would soar over the cliff to the beach below. Luckily it fell short, onto a shelf below the level of the green and burrowed down in the coarse and wiry grass.

A quick player, Watson took hardly any time, popped the ball onto the collar, then holed from twenty feet for his par.

Rogers, meantime, had lost three strokes in four holes, and now only Nicklaus and Watson were left in the chase.

Turning inland now, Watson birdied the 11th. Five under and two ahead of Nicklaus. Not for long. A bogey on the 12th, and back to four under. Ahead by one.

Walking toward his drive on the 13th, Tom heard a roar from the Nicklaus gallery; Jack had birdied the 15th. Tied now.

A routine 4 on the 13th, then a forty-footer dropped on the 14th after an unlucky pitch had rolled to the back fringe. Five under again.

Nicklaus, meanwhile, was finishing his round with three immaculate pars and was in with 69 and 284, waiting for Watson. If Tom wavered, the fifth Open would be his.

Tom wavered. He hadn't missed a fairway through the first fifteen holes, but a drive got away from him on the 16th and bounced into a bunker on

292

the right. With his ball sitting so close to a high front wall he had no chance to reach the green, he played out sideways, pitched on with his third, and bogeyed. Four under once again, and even with Nicklaus.

As Tom missed his twenty-footer on the 16th, the crowd raced for the 17th tee, for this could be the critical hole of the week. A par 3 set up to play at 209 yards, the 17th has a green shaped like an hourglass with a ridge separating the two halves. It sits on a promontory that pokes into Carmel Bay and perches above a rocky beach where rounds have been ruined. This would be no easy par.

Watson frowned as he watched Rogers play a 4-wood with a soft draw that hit the right side of the green and held. Tom next. He would play his 2-iron. After the usual preliminaries, he settled himself, drew the club back with his quick rhythm, and lashed into the ball with terrific force. He had been a little quick with his hands; the ball shot off on a line a trifle right, but then it began to curve left, turned more than he had planned, hit the left edge of the green, then hopped into weedy rough between two bunkers, settling about fifteen or eighteen feet from the hole.

Forget beating Nicklaus; now he'd need luck to tie.

He looked grim as he walked toward his ball. All his hard work might have meant nothing because of one shot that slipped out of control. But as he drew close, he saw that instead of nestling deep in the grass, his ball was sitting up high enough for him to work under it with his sand wedge. No man ever had a better break than Watson had here. He had practiced this shot for hours, and he felt sure he could make his 3. Maybe he could do better.

"Get it close," his caddie said.

Tom said, "I'm not going to get it close, I'm going to make it."

Watson chopped into the grass. The ball popped up, hit the collar of the green, and began rolling toward the cup. As he saw how it was running, Watson cried out, "That's in the hole!"

Then it slammed against the flagstick and dropped from sight. A birdie 2 where a 4 was likely, and now Watson leaped from the ground and raced around the green, smiling and laughing. He was in front by a stroke once more, with only the long and testing 18th to play.

He took no chance there; a 3-wood from the tee, a 7-iron well short, setting up a full 9-iron rather than a delicate little pitch that might test the nerves too much, and then a lag putt he hoped would stop within easy holing distance. Instead, it dropped for another birdie. Watson shot 70. His 282 beat Nicklaus by two strokes. He was the Open champion at last.

Nicklaus had seen it all on a television monitor in the scorer's tent behind the 18th green. As Watson's ball fell into the cup on the 17th, Jack's face collapsed. He knew he had lost. Now, as Watson walked off the green, Nicklaus was waiting. They shook hands, and Jack smiled and said, "You little son-of-a-bitch, you're something else. I'm proud of you."

With his arm across Watson's shoulder, Nicklaus walked him away, his fifth Open still a dream, and Watson's second a strong possibility. Maybe Nicklaus could do it next year, when once again he returned to Oakmont, where he had won his first so long ago.

TWENTY-SIX
From Nelson to North

A month after winning at Pebble Beach, Watson shot 284 at Royal Troon in Scotland and won his fourth British Open. With his two Masters, he had won seven major championships and was acknowledged as the game's leading player. He was thirty-two, and he seemed ready for a long rule. Those ranked closest to him were Seve Ballesteros and Jack Nicklaus. Tall, dark, and handsome, Ballesteros had blossomed into an exceptional golfer and a major box-office attraction. He hit glorious long irons and could putt like Wyatt Earp could shoot—he was deadly. He was the best golfer ever to develop on the European continent. He had won the British Open in 1979 when he was twenty-two and the Masters in 1980 and again in 1983, but those tournaments had been won over courses with thinnish rough, if there was any at all. He had had no success at all in the U.S. Open. It demands patience, and Seve's Latin blood bubbled too easily when he was in tangled grass, which was common for him, because he could be a wild driver. By 1983 he had completed seventy-two holes only twice in five starts, and in 1980 he had been disqualified for arriving at Baltusrol too late to make his starting time for the second round.

Nicklaus, however, was always at his best in the Open. He was forty-three then, past his prime, but he couldn't be measured by normal standards. Only Watson's miracle finish had snatched the championship from him at Pebble Beach, and there was no way of knowing how long he could go on.

The 1983 championship might answer that question.

PART FOUR

This would be the sixth Open played at Oakmont, and it was almost the Oakmont of old. The greens were glassy, the narrow fairways snaked around bunkers that protruded into the landing areas, and the thick ankle-deep rough was so intimidating some players shunned their drivers and drove with irons or fairway woods. A club repair van that followed the Tour did a brisk business sharpening the leading edges of the players' pitching clubs. While an unusual amount of rain had fallen throughout the spring, nourishing that unyielding rough, the weather had moderated in the last few weeks, and the greens were not only fast, they were firm—perhaps hard.

At 1:30 on Friday afternoon, well into the second round, its character changed.

The day had begun with overcast skies and thick, heavy air, and the weather had become more threatening as the day wore on. As Ballesteros strode down the last fairway, dark clouds glowered overhead, and the rumble of thunder drew close. His putt had barely hit the bottom of the hole when lightning ripped through the sky and monsoon rains showered down. The 20,000 spectators dashed for cover. They ducked under trees, raced for their cars, and some lucky ones shouldered into the old clapboard clubhouse. Five young men squeezed into one phone booth and still had room to hoist a beer.

As the first bolts streaked across the lowering sky, sirens wailed, and play was suspended. Players close enough sped back to the clubhouse.

Out on the course it was frightening. Falling much harder now, the rain flooded bunkers, and the gray-black clouds pressed closer to the ground. Lightning bolts flashed in rapid order—one, then another. Hale Irwin, Lanny Wadkins, and David Graham and his wife were trapped at the 2nd green. Too far away to reach the clubhouse, they huddled in a drainage ditch, but the water level was rising, and they wondered how long they could stay.

The storm was savage. For ten minutes the skies crackled as lightning struck all around them. A bolt ripped into a tree. Another cracked into a telephone pole, then leaped to another tree. A bolt streaked to earth. Two men fell to the ground and lay still.

The fury lasted but a short time. The electricity slackened, but the rain poured down for another hour. The two men felled by lightning were rushed to a hospital. Both recovered, although one was temporarily paralyzed overnight. Only when the rage of the storm eased were the players able to reach the clubhouse. For a time they had been less concerned with their swings than with survival.

Oakmont was unplayable. Some greens were ankle deep in water, and low areas had turned into ponds. Play was suspended for two and a half hours and not everyone finished that day; thirty-eight men had to come back at seven o'clock on Saturday morning to complete their rounds.

When play resumed Friday, Oakmont was different. The greens were soft enough that the players could stop their approaches easily—until the storm it had been common to play short of the green on some downhill holes and let the ball roll on. Now they could attack. The change affected Larry Nelson more than anyone else.

Nelson was among the more unusual professionals. A thirty-five-year-old Georgian, he had played his first round of golf when he was twenty-one, learning the basics of the golf swing by reading *The Modern Fundamentals of Golf*, a book by Ben Hogan and the author Herbert Warren Wind. The lessons he learned from that book led to a sound, compact, uncomplicated, repeating swing. When he had first begun playing, he had given himself three months to break 40 for nine holes. He shot 37. Next he went for a par round, shot it, then aimed for a subpar round. Within a year he had shot 68. He quit his job and became an assistant pro at a small club in Kennesaw, Georgia. Two years later he had determined to play tournament golf. He qualified for the Tour in 1973 and six years later won the Inverrary Classic. In 1981 he won the PGA Championship. He had been playing golf for only thirteen years.

So far in 1983 he had been playing poorly, missing the cut in nine of his sixteen tournaments and withdrawing from another, and he had barely survived the cut in the Open. Opening with 75, he added 73 in the second round. The cut fell at 151; Nelson had 148. He was in twenty-fifth place, seven strokes behind John Mahaffey and Joe Rassett, the coleaders at 141. Watson had 142, and Ballesteros 143. Nicklaus was not a contender. He had opened with 147, then finished with 77 and 76. He had answered no questions.

The championship had been unmemorable so far, but it perked up midway through the third round when, after a slow start, Nelson began making birdies. Six over par as the day began, he bogeyed the 3rd, driving into the Church Pews. Seven over par now and heading nowhere. Then, Nelson found his game. He had hit only twenty-one greens through the first thirty-six holes, but now he couldn't miss. A 9-iron to three feet on the 5th, then a 6-iron to ten feet and a 5-iron to twenty-five feet on the 6th and 7th. He holed all three putts, then reached the 9th green with his second for still another birdie. Four birdies in five holes and three over par through forty-five holes.

Still more birdies on the home nine—from twenty-five feet on the 11th, from fifteen feet on the 14th, then a blistering 3-iron to six feet on the long and hard 15th. Seven birdies in eleven holes. He was six under for the day and even par for the distance. Three strokes to get down from a foot off the 16th green and a bogey, but another birdie at the 18th, where his 5-iron skidded to five feet. Out in 33, back in 32. A 65. Now Nelson was at 213 and had climbed within a stroke of Watson and Ballesteros, who were staging a furious head-on duel and had moved in front, each with 212.

Even though Nelson was challenging the leaders, hardly anyone was taking him seriously. Surely Watson and Ballesteros would settle this Open between them and, at the same time, determine who had the right to be called the greatest player in the game. Nelson had only a supporting role; he'd have to prove his great round wasn't a fluke.

Nelson began the last round paired with Calvin Peete, just ahead of Watson and Ballesteros, the last men off the tee, and unbelievably, he was keeping up his pace of the previous day. His irons were flying at the flagsticks, and his putts continued to fall. After seven holes he was three under par, but he took three putts on the 8th, then made up for it by reaching the 9th green with his second, scoring his fourth birdie of the day. He was out in 33. But he had lost ground.

Watson had been playing miracle golf. He was making one birdie after another and gaining confidence with every shot. Six birdies on the first nine and Tom was out in 31. Ballesteros couldn't keep up, and the showdown everyone expected didn't develop. With par 36, Ballesteros had lost five strokes to Watson and had no chance. Even Nelson had lost two strokes in spite of his hot round. Peete had been hitting fairways and greens but missing holeable putts, had gone out in 37, and stood seven strokes behind. Only Nelson was within reach, and he trailed Watson by three strokes. He would have to keep up the pressure and hope Watson would cool down.

Tom did. After his blistering first nine, his shots grew tentative and lost their assurance. He dropped one stroke on the 10th, where he went from rough to rough, and another at the 12th, where a short putt hit the lip and stayed out. Only a stroke behind now, Nelson caught Watson with a soft, floating pitch to the 14th that dropped a foot from the hole. Both men were four under par now, with Watson playing the 14th and Nelson heading down the 15th.

Just then another thunderstorm broke. Rain pelted down and more lightning shredded the leaden sky. Bunkers flooded, and pools of water collected on the greens, already waterlogged from earlier rain. It was 5:30 in the afternoon. Play was suspended, and the finish was postponed. They would begin at ten o'clock Monday morning with Watson facing a thirty-five-foot putt on the 14th (he chose not to complete the hole) and Nelson the frightening tee shot across the valley to the par-3 16th.

Arriving early the next day, Watson worked on longish putts while

Nelson spent his warm-up time hitting 4-wood shots. As play began, Nelson aimed at the left side of the 16th green, planning to fade his ball toward the hole, set in the right corner close to a sharp downslope that fell into matty rough. The fade didn't take, and the ball soared straight, leaving him sixty feet or so from the hole. Just then Watson missed his putt and headed for the 15th tee.

From where Nelson's ball lay, he might need luck to get down in two. His putt would have to coast down two gentle inclines and take a right-to-left break of about four feet. He stroked the ball firmly, and as it rolled toward the hole, it began to look better and better. As it drew close and took the break, Nelson began trotting along behind it, urging it on as it glided down the last dip. When it dived into the cup, Nelson yelped and galloped across and around the green, raising his arms and his putter above his head. He had gone ahead for the first time. Now to hold on.

A missed chance from eight feet on the 17th, but a par 4. Now for the 18th. Two good shots onto the green, but three putts from forty feet. That could cost him. He had finished with 280, and now Watson could win with a birdie on one of the last two holes.

The short 17th offered Tom his best chance, especially after a solid drive left him only a 9-iron, but he hit the ball badly and pushed it into a downhill lie in a bunker. No chance for a birdie, but a par here and another on the 18th would still tie. A weak recovery, though, five feet short, and his putt grazed the hole. Watson was finished. To tie now he'd have to birdie the 18th, but after a drive measured at 310 yards, he overshot the green and had to hole a good putt to save his par 4. Watson had shot 38 on the second nine, had 69 for the day, and finished with 281, one stroke too many.

Nelson had shot 67. Combined with his 65 in the third round, he had played the last thirty-six holes in 132, breaking the old record by four strokes. Set by Gene Sarazen in 1932, it had lasted for fifty-one years. It had been matched several times since then, but never beaten. Of the 156 players who had begun the first round at Oakmont, only Arnold Palmer and Miller Barber had been alive at the time of Sarazen's whirlwind 70-66 finish at Fresh Meadow. The wonder of it all was that it had lasted so long.

The trend of records, however, is inevitably downward, and there seems to be no reason why any of the standing records shouldn't fall. While barriers exist, they are largely psychological. Once they're broken, what seemed improbable to one generation becomes commonplace to the next.

Until Chick Evans' 286 in 1916, no one had been under 290 for seventy-two holes of an Open, but after that, scores under 290 were customary.

PART FOUR

Evans' record stood for twenty years, until Tony Manero shot 282 in 1936. After that:

281—Ralph Guldahl in 1937
276—Ben Hogan in 1948
275—Jack Nicklaus in 1967
272—Jack Nicklaus in 1980

For sixteen years Hogan's 276 stood out as an almost freakish score; 280 remained a barrier. Then Ken Venturi shot 278 at Congressional, three years later Nicklaus shot his 275, and scores under 280 were to be expected. For a time, scores over 280 had indicated a stronger than usual golf course, but by the middle 1980s, a score that high had become rare. The modern golfer had learned that under the proper conditions, he might shoot any score.

Still, the players were wary when they came back to Winged Foot in June of 1984. It had been brutal in 1974 when Hale Irwin had won with 287 and only one other man had been under 290. They remembered, too, how heavy and dense the rough had been at Oakmont, and they wondered how tough Winged Foot would be.

They were relieved once they arrived and tested the course in practice. They found it more manageable than it had been ten years earlier and the rough not nearly so dense as it had been at Oakmont in 1983. The differences were deliberate. Believing it might have been making its courses too punishing over the last few years, the USGA set up Winged Foot to be much more playable. The scoreboard showed it. Where scores of 143 had shared the thirty-six-hole lead in 1974, a score of 136 led in 1984. Where only two men had broken 290 in 1974, ten years later twenty-four men were under 290. And, while Hale Irwin bettered his 1974 total by three strokes, shooting 284, he was nowhere near the lead at the end. But he had his moments.

Returning to the site of his first Open championship, Irwin was among the leaders from the beginning, and for a time he seemed to be a solid bet to win his third. With two rounds of 68, he was in first place at the end of thirty-six holes, one stroke ahead of Fuzzy Zoeller, and two ahead of Greg Norman, a tall, lean Australian with stark white hair and a friendly manner. Somewhat shaky on the first nine, where he hit only four greens, Irwin shot 69 in the third round and remained in front at 205, with eighteen holes to play. He could go no further. He was thirty-nine then, and perhaps his nerves had taken all they could take. The next day, with the gallery almost out of control, he shot 40 on the first nine, 39 on the second, and finished with 79. The battle was between Norman and Zoeller.

Norman had gone into the last round at 207, one stroke behind Zoeller, but while all the other contenders had collapsed, he had climbed into a tie with one hole to play. The championship reached its climax on the 18th.

Playing a hole ahead of Zoeller, Norman could pick up a valuable stroke here if he could birdie, but he had played some loose irons on the last two holes, missing both the 16th and 17th greens and scrambling for his pars, and the strain was telling. A long and straight drive had placed him in excellent position in the center of the 18th fairway, only a 6-iron from the green. From there he hit a terrible shot; the ball squirted so far right it sailed into a grandstand set far away from the green, eliminating any chance at all for a birdie and making a par unlikely, for this would be no easy recovery. He was allowed to drop the ball without a penalty stroke, but then he flew the shot all the way across the green and onto the far collar, about forty feet from the hole. Most likely he'd bogey now.

While it is impossible to be certain, he seemed to have the same line to the hole that Bobby Jones had in 1929 when, after throwing away strokes like confetti at a parade, he had to hole a curling twelve-footer to tie Al Espinosa. His putt had fallen, and he had won in a playoff.

In the fifty-five years since that sultry summer day, Jones's putt had become one of the landmark shots in American golf history. Certainly it had never been forgotten at Winged Foot. The club had invited Jones back in 1954 for a twenty-fifth anniversary celebration featuring an exhibition match involving Tommy Armour, Gene Sarazen, Johnny Farrell, and Craig Wood. After the match a group gathered around the 18th green to re-create Bobby's putt. Walking with canes then, Jones indicated where the hole had been set and a greenkeeper cut a new cup. Then Bobby pointed to where his ball had lain, and all four tried to re-create history. All four missed. They tried again, and they missed again. Some others tried. Findlay Douglas, the 1898 Amateur champion, missed. Everybody missed.

In a gesture toward tradition, the USGA had cut the hole in about the same place for the final round in 1984, and now Norman had to hole his putt or probably lose the Open, and he was thirty feet farther from the cup than Jones had been.

The putt had to be played three or four feet left, and for the last ten feet or so it would be rolling downhill. Holing it would be as much a problem of pace as of line. With his ball on the collar, Norman left the flagstick in place and picked a patch of browned-out grass midway to the cup as his target. He struck the ball perfectly. When it held its line through the brown grass, Greg felt sure he had holed the putt. The ball ran up to the cup, hit the flagstick squarely, then dropped.

PART FOUR

Norman went wild. He leaped and galloped across the green, grinning and waving his putter high above his head.

Back on the fairway, Zoeller saw the ball fall, but he had been playing the 17th when Norman had hit his approach into the bleachers, and he assumed Greg had birdied. Now, he thought, he needed a birdie to tie. He smiled, walked a few strides to his bright orange golf bag, lifted his white towel from the handle of his umbrella, and waved it overhead in a sign of surrender.

Shouts from the gallery alerted Fuzzy that Norman had parred, not birdied, and that he needed only a 4 to tie. He made it. Both men finished at 276, the only scores under Winged Foot's still demanding par.

Norman was no match for Zoeller in the playoff the next day. Fuzzy jumped three strokes ahead on the 2nd by holing a long birdie putt from sixty-five to seventy feet while Norman was taking a double-bogey, and he kept building on his lead. Out in 34, he was five strokes ahead after the 9th, seven ahead after the 14th, eight ahead after the 15th, and nine ahead after the 16th. Norman cut his deficit by one stroke with a birdie on the 17th, but the outcome had been settled long ago. Zoeller played a superb 67, and Norman shot 75. They walked off the last green arm in arm.

By the middle 1980s it seemed clear the game was in a period of transition. The old heroes and some of the new ones were not performing as they had been, particularly on the great occasions. Nicklaus was not playing up to his standard, Watson was not the sensational putter he had been, Ballesteros was still erratic, winning one week, missing the cut the next, and Bernhard Langer, the German sensation who won the Masters in the spring of 1985, was not quite ready for U.S. Open conditions. Once again the world was looking for a new hero. For a time it looked as if it might be T. C. Chen, an ex-sailor in the Chinese navy.

Oakland Hills, where so much had happened over the years, was acting as host to its fifth Open in 1985, but the game had changed. Maintenance techniques had improved so dramatically that by the 1980s the players knew that if they read the green correctly and stroked the ball properly, it could do nothing but go in the hole. Greenkeepers, pushed by members, were overwatering their greens and making them softer, and the clubs and balls were better and more reliable. And the players were hitting the ball farther than anyone had dreamed of in the 1950s and 1960s.

When Gene Littler eagled the 9th hole at Oakmont in 1962, he had been short of the green with a 3-wood second and had pitched in for his 3. When Arnold Palmer made a 6 there later in the week, he too had played his second shot with a wooden club. Littler was thirty-one in 1962 and Palmer thirty-two. Eleven years later, when they were forty-two and forty-three and logically not as strong, they had reached that green with irons. In 1974, when the 9th hole at Winged Foot was set up as a par 4 of 466 yards, it had been almost unreachable with two shots, and the 18th, which measured 448 yards, asked for medium-to-long irons. Ten years later, with the 9th shortened by only ten yards, Tom Watson played a 7-iron for his second and Jay Sigel, an amateur, a 5-iron. Meanwhile, at the 18th, where Hale Irwin had played a stirring 2-iron in 1974, Andy Bean hit an 8-iron, and in the last round both Fuzzy Zoeller and Greg Norman had hit 6-irons.

By remodeling Oakland Hills for 1951, Trent Jones had introduced the modern school of golf course design, with bunkers drawing the fairways tight in the landing areas and the greens not only guarded by bunkers but framed by them as well. When Jones had finished, hardly anyone could drive over those fairway bunkers, and only the daring or the desperate tried to thread their way through the openings. Most played short.

Then, a survey done in 1983 convinced both Jones and Oakland Hills officials that further revisions were needed to keep the field in check for 1985. Some of the bunkers had grown shallower as sand had been added over the years. Jones deepened them. He added a new bunker on the left side of the 8th fairway, probably the most difficult of the par 4s in 1951, and another new bunker on the left of the 18th.

Above all, some holes had to be lengthened. Under the onslaught of the modern player and the modern ball, the fairway bunkers that had been in place for thirty-four years would have as little effect as the original Donald Ross bunkers Jones had relocated so long ago. To bring them back into play, he built new tees and stretched the old course to 6,996 yards, seventy yards longer than it had played in 1951.

But distance didn't intimidate the modern golfer. Once the championship began, holes beyond reach thirty-four years earlier were being hit easily. Ben Hogan had needed a 2-iron to reach the 10th green on his way to his historic 67 in 1951, but in 1985, Andy North was comfortably on with a 3-wood tee shot and a 7-iron second. T. C. Chen reached it with a drive and 4-iron, and Mike Reid, the shortest hitter of all the leading professionals, also needed only a 4-iron. Jones had lengthened the 2nd to 527 yards, but Fred Couples was on the green with only a drive and a 6-iron. It was the same all around the course. Where the fields had played defensively in 1951, they attacked in 1985.

An extremely long hitter, Couples raced around in 66 the first day. He had teed off a few minutes before two o'clock, and par was under siege already. Craig Stadler, Lanny Wadkins, and Bill Glasson, a relatively unknown young man with platinum hair and knees so bad he had to wear braces, were in with 70, and Mike Reid was about to finish with 69. Despite the low scoring, the fans felt none of the excitement they would have had one of the great players of the day been on his game. The championship was, in fact, a little dull. Then one shot changed the tone.

Couples had barely made the nine-hole turn when Chen brought the championship to life back at the 2nd. Playing in the fifth-from-last group, he drove into the narrow gap between bunkers, then drilled a 3-wood toward the green, 240 yards away. He knew he had hit a good shot as soon as he saw his ball begin to climb and streak toward the pin, tucked away in the right rear corner, but he didn't realize how good it would be. The ball hit the front of the green, ran straight toward the cup, about fifty-five feet away, hit the flagstick, and dived into the hole. A double eagle 2—as far as anyone knew, the first ever in the Open and, again as far as anyone knew, only the second in a major championship: Gene Sarazen had made a double eagle on the 15th at Augusta fifty years earlier and had won the Masters. But Sarazen was one of the great players. Who was Chen? Sarazen had also seen his ball drop into the cup, but Chen hadn't. The green sits well above eye level, and by this time of day hardly anyone was watching the early holes. The twenty or so spectators sitting in the bleachers raised so feeble a cry Chen didn't realize he had holed the shot until he climbed the grade, and a scoreboard attendant called out the news.

When he followed with another 2 on the par-3 3rd, he was four under par for the first three holes. Over the next thirteen he played some good and some bad golf, gradually giving back some of the strokes he'd taken, and with two holes to play, he was three under par. Then he put on a strong finish. His 3-iron to the 17th came down within six feet of the cup, and his 4-iron to the 18th was even better, stopping only four feet away. He made both putts, shot 65, and so overshadowed everything else that happened that day that Couples' 66 was hardly noticed.

Chen's round, together with the revelation of his quiet, friendly personality, seemed to be nothing more than a refreshing interlude, for this was the first Open he'd played in, and first-time-starters don't win. Then he shot 69 the next day and equaled the thirty-six-hole record.

While he led, his 134 placed him only one stroke ahead of North, who was having his best tournament in years, and Jay Haas. North had matched par 70 in the first round, and then shot a flawless 65 of his own in the second—five birdies, no bogeys. Haas had 66 to go with his opening 69. Oakland Hills was being torn apart. Denis Watson matched North's 65, and three others shot 67—six men with 67 or better, five more with 68, and thirteen with 69, including two who didn't make the cut, which fell at 146, six strokes lower than in 1951, three strokes under 1961.

Playing the third round through a steady, all-day rain, the first time an Open round had been played under those conditions since 1913, Chen shot another 69. He should have been a stroke lower, but he missed a putt from less than two feet on the 17th, where he was distracted by water dripping from the bill of his cap. When the day ended, he had 203 and stood two strokes ahead of North, who had another 70. It looked as if the U.S. Open was about to have its first Asian champion.

The rain stopped during the night, but the weather remained threatening on Sunday, with heavy clouds hanging low overhead. By the time Chen and North teed off, at 2:30 in the afternoon, 37,000 fans were scattered through the grounds, several thousand of them jammed into large grandstands and seated on the hillsides by the 18th green.

North began badly, driving into the left fairway bunker and losing a stroke. When Chen birdied the 2nd, he had moved four strokes ahead, with North still clinging to second place. Both men made their pars on the next two holes, and at 3:25, an hour after they had begun, Chen stood eight under par and North four under. Dave Barr, playing a hole ahead, was two under through five holes, and Payne Stewart, eight strokes behind at the start, had birdied three of the first eight holes and caught him.

It looked like an easy victory for Chen. He was playing steady, forceful golf, making no mistakes, showing no signs of nervousness, and giving no openings.

The 5th hole is a 457-yard par 4 whose fairway runs level for a couple hundred yards, then falls gently downhill, crosses a narrow brook about 300 yards out, and levels off again as it approaches the green. The pin was set close to a huge white oak whose upper branches could block a shot coming in from the right.

Chen's drive split the fairway, and from where his ball lay he had a clear line at the pin. He should have no trouble here. Within the next few minutes, everything changed.

Chen pushed a wild 4-iron thirty yards wide of the green into thick, tangled rough among a copse of trees. Luckily he had an opening; he could pitch on and save a bogey with little harm to his lead. He saw it differently; he wanted the 4. He tried to drop his pitch on the edge of the green and give it a chance to run close to the hole, but he hit the ball a shade too softly, and it fell short into tall grass. Now he was in deep trouble, facing the loss of two strokes.

Chen chopped down into the grass with his wedge. The ball popped almost straight up and seemed to hang in midair. Meantime, the heavy grass had checked the clubhead for an instant; when it broke free, it hit the ball once again and flipped it high and to the left, onto the collar of the green. By hitting the ball twice on the same stroke, Chen had incurred a penalty stroke. He was stunned. His face became a blank mask. Now he lay 5, still not on the green. After a pause to settle himself, he chipped again but rolled the ball well past the hole and took two putts. He made 8. His lead, which had seemed so safe only a few minutes ago, was gone, and a colossal stroke of bad luck had turned the 1985 Open into a wild scramble and opened the way for five men to win—Chen, North, Barr, Stewart, and Denis Watson.

Now Chen was tied with North. Not for long. Badly shaken, he three-putted the 6th and followed with bogeys on the 7th and 8th. Within four holes he had gone from four strokes ahead of North to three strokes behind him, for through it all, North had held steady. With nine holes to play, he was three under par and led Barr by one stroke, Chen and Stewart by two.

Back and forth it went. First Barr pulled even with North, then went ahead. Then he lost strokes and North passed him again. Next Chen struggled back into a tie with North. It was happening so fast, no one was quite sure how they stood until Barr, in a weak finish, bogeyed the last two holes and tied Denis Watson at 280, even par. Stewart made no further progress and came in with 281.

North was coming to the 17th as Barr was finishing, as confused over the situation as everyone else. He had been playing shaky golf, bogeying four holes, and now he pushed his tee shot into the right greenside bunker that looked as deep as a mineshaft. But with the championship slipping away, he played the kind of stroke he had to play, an explosion shot that cleared the high front wall of the bunker by inches, barely missed the left edge of the cup, and stopped less than a foot away. He made his par, then strode to the 18th tee. But to do what?

No one in North's gallery knew how he stood; they didn't know that Barr had bogeyed the 18th, and they weren't sure if Andy needed his par to win. North didn't know either, but he pounded a solid drive down the right that cleared the bunkers, bounced off the hillside, and ran to the center of the fairway. As he stood over his ball waiting to play his second, rumors flew through the gallery. He needed a 4 to beat Barr. No, Barr had bogeyed; Andy could lose a stroke here and still win. The huge scoreboard by the green was too far off to read.

Taking his 4-iron, Andy drilled his shot directly at the flagstick, but he had hit the ball a bit fat, and it dropped into a band of rough between two bunkers. Now he was in trouble. The ball lay deep in the grass about twenty-five yards short of the hole, and as far as he knew, he needed a 4 to win—maybe to tie.

Just then the referee, who had been in radio contact with the scoring system, told Andy he had two strokes in hand. Relieved, he pitched on and took two putts to hole out.

He had played the last round in 74, the highest fourth round by a winner since Hale Irwin's 75 in 1979, and equal to his own close at Cherry Hills seven years earlier. He finished with 279, one stroke under par.

How he won was a mystery. He had made only nine birdies in seventy-two holes, five of those in shooting 65 in the second round, and he had made only two birdies over the last thirty-six holes, one with a monstrous putt all the way across the 16th green on Saturday and the other from ten feet following a gorgeous 5-iron to the 13th green on Sunday.

His driving in the last round had been atrocious. He had hit only four fairways and driven into fairway bunkers on the first four driving holes, and he had not hit a single fairway until the 6th, where he had played a 1-iron from the tee.

With his awkwardly upright swing, North was not a pretty golfer to watch, especially as he struggled to survive the final round at Oakland Hills. Still, he had survived, and that is all anyone could ask.

He had been bothered by injuries throughout his career, and even though he had won only three tournaments, two of those were Opens, the one that matters.

The Open had always demanded more of a golfer than any other competition, and yet it had some surprising winners, perhaps none more surprising than those who had won ninety years apart. In winning the 1895 Open Championship, Horace Rawlins had outplayed the best golfers in America, men like Willie Dunn, Willie Campbell, Jim Foulis, and Willie Davis. They weren't the best in the world—the greatest were in Britain—but they were the best in North America.

When North won in 1985, he did indeed beat the best in the world, because by now all but a handful of the game's leading players were Americans. North could not claim to be among them, but he had done what so many others had failed to do. By winning at Oakland Hills, he had become one of an elite group of fifteen men who had won the Open twice. He had won the ultimate challenge.

EPILOGUE

Willie Davis had been given a month's leave of absence by the Royal Montreal Golf Club to come to the United States and build a golf course near the Shinnecock Indian Reservation on Eastern Long Island. Using the Indians as his labor force, Davis laid out twelve holes through the sandy scrub, occasionally scraping away the face of one of the ancient burial mounds scattered here and there to create a bunker. (The bunkers were ideal hiding places for the Indians' whisky bottles. For a long time afterward an explosion shot might bring up not only the ball, but perhaps a bone or a bottle as well.)

Willie Dunn, who came later, had expanded Shinnecock to eighteen holes by 1896, when Jim Foulis won the Open championship, but it measured only 4,423 yards, and it became obsolete when the rubber-cored ball came into wide use. It was altered over the years; some holes were kept and lengthened and some new ones were built, but in the late 1920s, Suffolk County planned a road through the property that would destroy some holes. Shinnecock realized it was time to build an entirely new course.

The club engaged the organization of Toomey and Flynn, and with Bill Flynn as the designer, the firm created a course that belongs in the upper echelon of the world's finest. Where Davis had begun his routing on the ocean side of the clubhouse, facing the broad sweep of land that runs to the Atlantic, Flynn turned away from the sea and built the new course over rolling, sandy ground, covered with thick growths of blackberry bushes on the other side of the clubhouse. From the lofty hill, the waters of Peconic Bay sparkle over the pines, and the windmill that is the symbol of the National Golf Links of America stands clear only a few hundred yards away.

Shinnecock Hills is closer to the game's roots than any other course in the United States. When golf came to North America in the late nineteenth century, it moved inland, away from its seaside origins, and when it did, it lost its original flavor. The land was more level—not flat, for indeed there are some terribly hilly American courses—but not as undulating and rippling as the linksland. Furthermore, the effects of the wind were lost as well, for wind is not nearly so much a part of the game on America's parkland courses as it is along the seacoasts of Britain and Ireland.

Golf on a typical American course has a different feel from golf on the links.

Shinnecock Hills is as near as an Open caliber American course can be to the game's Scottish origins. The ground resembles the appearance of the British dunes, where the sea receded in eons past and left the land barren of all but scrub growth. Shinnecock has trees, but they seldom affect play. Furthermore, the eastern end of Long Island is exposed to high winds blustering in from the Atlantic Ocean to the south and Long Island Sound to the north. The wind can be a formidable force on a normal day, as in the old tradition.

When Flynn finished, he had created a masterpiece that was both a challenge and a joy to play. The holes serpentine through the prickly scrub, seldom running arrow-straight from tee to green, and the fronts of most of the greens are open, not shut off by bunkers. Although bunkers border every green, it is not necessary to carry over them to reach the putting surface. In designing Shinnecock, Flynn had the wisdom to take the wind into account and allow for the runup shot.

It is a par 70 course with two par 5s, one of 544 yards and the other of 535, four par 3s, the longest at 226 yards and the shortest at 158, and twelve par 4s. While the par 3s and par 5s offer a good variety, the strength of Shinnecock, as it is with any great course, is its par 4s. Four are under 400 yards, and four others measure 450 yards or more. Almost all the shorter holes play into the fresh sea wind that can bend flagsticks nearly horizontal, while the longer holes usually play downwind. Most of the fairways are islands; to reach them the drive must carry a formidable stretch of wilderness. The faces of the bunkers may seem unkempt, but this is a highly natural course; it is not heavily groomed.

Here, then, was a superb golf course set where the seeds of American golf had been planted, adjacent to the National Links, which remains as Charles B. Macdonald designed it in the early years of the century. And yet no Open had been played there since 1896.

EPILOGUE

Why it had not explains a lot about a modern sports spectacle. As the Open grew from its rather primitive beginnings, the USGA had relied on the clubs to supply volunteer labor for marshals, scorers, for selling tickets and for arranging housing for players, officials, and the press, providing for parking, producing a program, arranging with police for traffic control, and also for seeing that the golf course was in the best possible condition. Clubs normally begin serious work two years in advance.

Shinnecock Hills, though, is not a normal club. It has a small seasonal membership, and its old wooden clubhouse, which was designed by the architect Stanford White and built in the early 1890s, is neither heated nor air-conditioned. The flagsticks are taken from the holes on election day and not replaced until early May. The club is simply closed during the winter. Two hours by car from Manhattan, Southampton is largely a summer colony for the well-to-do. Since Shinnecock Hills could supply no volunteer labor force, conducting an Open championship there seemed beyond all logic.

Still, there sat that magnificent golf course—strong, unusual for the general run of American courses, of a type the modern professional never sees. The prospect of testing the Open field over this course was so tantalizing that in the early 1980s the USGA decided to take the Open to Shinnecock by assuming responsibility for the entire organization of the championship. And so, in 1986, exactly ninety years after its first, Shinnecock had its second Open.

It was a triumph. The players raved about the golf course, some of them saying it was the best Open course they'd ever played, that they liked its traditional design, that it gave them the opportunity to play runup shots to the greens, and that it reminded them of the great seaside courses of the British Isles.

As the first round began they had reason to wonder if the similarities with British golf weren't too strong. High winds are often a factor at Shinnecock, but as the first round began, a fresh, chilling breeze whipped in from the northeast at a force of between twenty and thirty miles an hour, with sudden gusts of even greater velocity; at the same time the temperature dropped into the high 40s, and rain began to fall. No one could remember an Open day quite like this (indeed, not many could recall a British Open played under worse conditions).

Coming from an unusual direction, the wind turned Shinnecock into a terror. Of the 156 players who made up the starting field, only forty-seven shot 75 or better, with forty-five scoring 80 or more. Twenty-four men stood at 75; twelve others shot 74, three had 73, six shot 72, one had 71, and Bob Tway led the field with 70. Of the four par 4s that measure over 450 yards, only the 6th was helped by the high winds. It played at about

460 yards, and those who found the fairway with their drives usually had less than a 6-iron to the green. On the other hand, the 9th and 18th, which played directly into the wind, were practically unreachable in two strokes, and the 12th, played through a right-to-left crossing wind, was very difficult.

Under conditions like these, Tway's 70 was an exceptional score indeed. A tall (six-foot-four), lean (180-pound), twenty-seven-year-old with bushy, sandy hair, Tway finished the day holding a one-stroke lead over Greg Norman, with six others two strokes behind.

This round demonstrated so well that players of Open caliber can scrape out their figures even on days when they don't hit many greens. With the wind tossing the ball about, Tway hit only eight greens, but through thirteen holes he had saved pars from off the greens of four holes, birdied four of the seven holes where he hit the greens, and bogeyed only twice. He was two under par with only five holes to play, but he dropped one stroke by driving into the deep tangled rough on the 14th, a par 4 of 444 yards that plays as a slight dogleg to the right, and the other by under-clubbing on the 15th, landing his approach in a bunker.

Others were having similar problems. Norman hit only seven greens, and Denis and Tom Watson, among those tied at 72, hit nine greens each. Jack Nicklaus had perhaps the most remarkable round of the day. He hit only four greens and yet brought in a 77. His little chips and pitches, never one of his strengths, often left him with little work to do on the greens.

Tway had been something of a sensation during the first half of the season. After five years on the Tour without a victory, he had won at San Diego in February and only the week before the Open had won the Westchester Classic. He was, therefore, no idle threat. It was surprising then to see him shoot 73 the next day when the weather eased, and everyone else seemed to play better.

The wind had swung around to the southwest overnight and lost most of its force, but it was still chilly in the morning. The clouds became thin and wispy through the day, and finally they drifted away. The sun was warm, the sky a bright blue, and the ball became controllable. Whereas no one had broken par in the first round, nine men were in the 60s in the second. Joey Sindelar, a twenty-eight-year-old professional who had come out of nowhere to win two tournaments in 1985, was the first to solve Shinnecock's mysteries. Beginning shortly after noon, as the sun was growing stronger, Sindelar matched par going out, but then, firing his irons directly at the flagsticks, he birdied four straight holes coming in, none from outside fifteen feet, and sped home in 31. His 66 was a competitive course record, and while it had no effect on the championship, it indicated what was coming.

EPILOGUE

Playing two groups behind Sindelar, Danny Edwards shot 30 on the second nine, matching the Open's nine-hole record; and of more significance, Greg Norman, in the group behind Edwards, raced around the first nine in 31. Never in command of his game on the home nine, he shot 37, but nevertheless, with 139 he had clawed his way into first place, three strokes ahead of Lee Trevino, still dangerous at forty-six, and Denis Watson. Trevino had gone around in 68 and Watson in 70. Behind them at 143 lurked Tway, Tom Watson, and also Raymond Floyd, who had come to life with a 68 after opening with a shaky 75. He had hit only six greens in the first round, but he made up for it by chipping and putting beautifully.

Norman had been playing sensational golf throughout the year, and he seemed ready to win a significant event. When he played the first nine of the third round in 33, dropping to three under par, it looked as if this would be the one. Although he lost a stroke to par by overshooting the 10th green, he still held a three-stroke lead as he climbed the gentle grade to the 13th tee. Trevino, who was paired with him, was his closest challenger, at one over par, while up ahead Hal Sutton, Bob Tway, Mark McCumber, and Denis Watson were two over. Lots of holes were left to play, but Norman was looking good.

Although it measures only 377 yards and begins from an elevated tee, the 13th at Shinnecock is a marvelously conceived par 4. The drive approaches the fairway at an angle, which has the effect of making it play narrower than its measured width of thirty-two yards, and adding to the problem, it bends left in the drive zone. Although the second shot is only a medium iron—or in some winds a pitch—the green is guarded by deep bunkers.

Unlike most good players, who tend to hook under tension, Norman is inclined to lose shots to the right. Now, holding a comfortable lead, he pushed his drive into deep rough, and then, after Trevino nearly holed his approach, carried his second over the green into tangled grass and underbrush bordering a parking lot. With not enough room to take a full backswing and drop the ball softly onto the green, Norman tried to punch it against the bank and let it hop on, but his sharp downward blow carried the ball over the bank, across the green, and into the rough on the other side. From there he chipped on and missed from four feet. A 6. When Trevino holed for his birdie 3 from less than two feet, he and Norman stood at even par, and both Sutton, who had finished seventeen holes by then, and Tway, who had played through the 15th, were one stroke behind. Within fifteen minutes, the Open had been thrown into a tangle that led into another wild last day.

Norman held on well through the remaining holes, but Trevino dropped a stroke behind when he drove into the right rough on the 18th and could not reach the green with a wooden-club second. As the round ended, Norman stood at 210, Trevino and Sutton at 211, Tway at 212, and Floyd, who had shot 70, was tied with four others at 213. With eighteen holes to play, fourteen men were within four strokes of one another, another lurked five strokes behind, and six more lay six strokes off the lead. No one could remember a more tightly bunched field, and soon the chase would become even tighter.

Sunday was another clear day. Early in the day a soft wind came out of the south, barely strong enough to ripple the coves and inlets of the Atlantic, which lay calm and glassy at dawn, but by early afternoon, when the leaders began teeing off, it had backed to the southwest and picked up strength. By the time Norman and Sutton left the 1st tee together, the wind was blowing at more than twenty miles an hour, and as it gathered force, Trevino's chances began looking better, since he was perhaps the game's best wind player. He showed how well he could control the ball in those conditions by dropping a nice little pitch onto the 1st green, hole high to the right of the cup, and holing the putt for a birdie 3. Even par now and tied with Norman, who had just driven. Moments later Norman parred, but Sutton matched Trevino's birdie, and now Norman, Trevino, and Sutton were all even par and tied for the lead.

It went on like this for most of the day, with first one man and then another taking the lead and just as quickly losing it. Ben Crenshaw, one of the five men who had begun the day at 214, ripped off four consecutive birdies beginning at the 3rd hole, and suddenly had the lead to himself, since Norman, Trevino, and Sutton had stumbled and lost strokes. Then Mark McCumber, who had begun at 213 and was playing three groups behind Crenshaw, birdied three of the first five, dropped to even par, and assumed the lead, for by then Crenshaw had bogeyed the difficult redan 7th. Moments later, McCumber, too, bogeyed the 7th.

As player after player gained, then lost strokes, it was impossible to tell how anyone stood. Tway moved ahead, then fell back, and at one time the scoreboard showed nine men tied for the lead at one over par, for up ahead, playing an hour and a half ahead of the leaders, Lanny Wadkins and Chip Beck had thrust themselves into the chase. Both men had begun the day six strokes off the lead, but after going out in 34, Wadkins had run off three straight birdies beginning at the 14th, and after sixteen holes had climbed to one over par, while Beck, after a 35 out, had birdied five of the next six holes, and with three holes to play had matched Wadkins.

Meanwhile, Payne Stewart suddenly shot ahead by dropping to even par, and now he began looking like the man to beat. He had played the first five holes in three under par, and after making the nine-hole turn in

33, had birdied the scary 11th, a short, 158-yard par 3 with a small green that left no room for error, and then played a wonderful iron from the right rough to within five feet of the cup for another birdie on the 12th. One under par now for sixty-six holes, but with strokes being won and then thrown away all over the course, Stewart couldn't be sure if he was one stroke ahead, two strokes ahead, or even if he had the lead at all.

Stewart was playing the last round with Floyd, who had been pretty much ignored. Raymond had gone out in 34, which left him two over par, but then he too had birdied the 11th. Suddenly, as if he had come from nowhere, Floyd was in the thick of the fight. It was as if no one was quite prepared to deal with him, for when Floyd is on his game, when his face wears that set, grim expression, his lips in a straight, thin line, his eyes glaring straight ahead, never looking right or left as he walks with a quick, determined stride, he can frighten anyone. Raymond had been around a long time—he was playing in his twenty-second Open—and although he had placed among the leading ten scorers only twice (the last time in 1971), he had won the Masters once and the PGA twice, and he had won Tour tournaments in three decades. Floyd knew how to win.

Not a pretty swinger, he took the club back on a flat plane with an even, measured pace, his left wrist supinated rather more than most good players, then lashed into the ball with a lot of body motion and good power. He was not particularly accurate, hitting on average two out of three greens in the regulation number of strokes, but he was a remarkably good putter. He stood erect and stiffbacked, placed the putterhead behind the ball with tedious care to assure the clubface was square to the line, set his feet with equal care, then tapped the ball with a smooth rhythmic stroke. He seldom missed when he was within holing range.

Raymond could be erratic, though, and he had just had a bad experience at Westchester. Particularly dangerous when he was in front, he had gone into the last round tied for the lead with Tway, but while Tway was finishing with 67, Floyd had shot 77 and fallen to twelfth place. Now, as he drove from the 12th tee, it looked as if he might have thrown away another opportunity just as he seemed to have seized it, for he pushed his drive into a big bunker with a high front wall that cut off his line to the green. But, with so many years of experience in golf at this level, Floyd had learned patience; he pitched sideways to the fairway, then dropped a sand wedge twenty feet beyond the hole and rolled in the putt for a par 4. Still one over, but two behind Stewart. Up the hill to the 13th tee.

Driving with a 1-iron, Floyd placed his ball in perfect position in the center of the fairway. He had determined earlier that he would play the last round conservatively, for experience had taught him that bogeys are made by trying to force birdies, and that players in contention for the great championships often beat themselves by playing straining, careless shots. It was good strategy, but here he ignored it and stung a 6-iron directly at the pin, set on a shallow tongue of the green about twenty-four feet beyond one of the deep bunkers protecting the front and twenty feet from the right edge. The ball hit, bit into the green, and braked to a dead stop four feet from the cup. It was a daring shot, the kind the great golfers play when it counts the most.

Stewart's ball, meanwhile, played with no less daring, seemed to have little stuff on it; it rolled off the back edge and into some scruffy grass beyond the collar. Using his putter Stewart put too much force into a sharp descending blow. The ball caught a corner of the cup but slid four or five feet past. Stewart missed. Floyd holed, and now Floyd had caught Stewart.

While Floyd was picking up strokes, everyone else seemed to be throwing them away. Norman had fallen apart and was on his way to a 75 and 285; Crenshaw had begun scattering shots and finished with 69 and 282; McCumber lost two strokes on the 16th, a par 5 hole, shot 71 and 284; Sutton slipped on the home nine for 71 and 282; Trevino was two over after the 9th and never recovered, shooting 71 and 282; Tway also took 7 at the 16th, finishing with 72 and 284; and Stewart finished poorly, too, making bogeys on three of the next five holes for a 70 and falling to 283. Wadkins and Beck had finished with 281s by then, each breaking the course record with blistering 65s.

The Open belonged to Floyd—if he could hold on. A 7-iron approach rolled over the 14th green, but he holed a four-footer to save par. At the 15th he played a 3-wood and pitching wedge to six feet, but missed the birdie opportunity. Then he won the championship with an attacking 8-iron into the 16th green, punched low to fight the wind. It skidded dead ten feet from the cup, he holed the putt, and for the first time in those four days he dipped a stroke under par.

It was all he needed.

After another daring shot into the narrow neck at the left rear of the 17th, which won him another par, Floyd drove to the center of the 18th fairway, then played a 4-iron to the front of the green. Two putts and he had turned the last nine in 32 and the final eighteen in 66, a stunning score on so trying a course under the emotional tension of contending for the Open.

After his opening 75, Floyd had played the last fifty-four holes in 204 strokes; no one had ever done better, although Jack Nicklaus had shot 204 over the last fifty-four holes at Baltusrol in 1967, when he won his second Open. Before Floyd, only Ben Hogan in 1951 and Johnny Miller in 1973 had played the last nine holes in 32 to win the championship. (Billy Casper closed with 32 in 1966, but it earned him a tie.) Furthermore, Floyd

315

had made only three bogeys in the last three rounds, with none at all in either the 2nd or the 4th—nor had he bogeyed after the 12th hole of the third round.

Admittedly, Floyd's golf had hardly been a model of precision. He had hit only thirty-eight of the fifty-six fairways on driving holes, and only forty-five of the seventy-two greens (Nicklaus had hit sixty-one in 1967). On the other hand, Raymond had been in only two bunkers, and his putting had been deadly: only twenty-five putts in the first round, twenty-nine in each of the next two, and twenty-eight in the fourth, for a record of 111, three fewer than Casper had used in 1959.

At forty-three years, nine months, and eleven days, he was the oldest man ever to win the Open, and no other man had ever won after trying so many times without success.

It was understandable, then, that when Floyd climbed the steep hill leading from the home green to the sanctuary of the scorer's tent, he slumped into a chair, took a deep breath, and sighed, "I finally won me an Open."

While Floyd was playing the last thirty-six holes in 70-66—136, Jack Nicklaus was shooting 67-68—135. Only Beck, with 68-65—133, played them better. Jack, however, had begun with 149; his strong finish had pushed him into a tie for eighth place. It was his eighteenth finish among the leading ten scorers, more than any other man.

Nicklaus had been going through a revival in 1986, a year after he seemed through as a dominating player or even a regular contender. He had labored through the first thirty-six holes at Oakland Hills, missing fairways, missing greens, and missing the putts he'd normally have gobbled up. After a 39 over the first nine holes, he needed a miracle to make the cut, but the miracles wouldn't come, and he shot 76-73—149, three strokes too many. He hadn't missed the cut in an Open since 1963, when, as a very young man, he had failed at The Country Club in defense of his first Open championship.

In an Open career dating back to 1957, Nicklaus had played through seventy-two holes in twenty-one consecutive championships through 1984. Only three men had done better. Walter Hagen, Gene Sarazen, and Gary Player had made the cut in twenty-two in a row. By 1985 Jack had been in twenty-eight Opens and had played all seventy-two holes in twenty-five.

Nicklaus had been through a lot in those twenty-eight years. Coming out of college when Arnold Palmer ruled golf, he had beaten off Palmer, withstood the challenge of Trevino, and finally locked Watson in inspiring battles. A month after his failure at Oakland Hills, Nicklaus also missed the cut in the British Open, the first time since he had begun participating in that ancient rite in 1962. It looked as if it might be over.

But it was never wise to underestimate this remarkable man. Just when his career seemed at its end, in April of 1986, he stunned the Masters field by playing the last nine holes of the Augusta National Golf Club in 30, shooting 65 the last day, and winning the tournament for the sixth time. Then he had his astonishing finish in the Open; obviously he was not ready to close his career.

Jack was forty-six. He had played tournament golf at the international level for nearly thirty years, and he'd won more tournaments of international significance than any man had ever won. No one could match his record, and perhaps no one ever will.

He had played in thirty Opens through 1986, and had shot twenty-nine rounds under par, twenty-four of them under 70. He set the Open's seventy-two-hole record twice, first in 1967, when he shot 275 at Baltusrol, and again in 1980, with 272, once more at Baltusrol. He also shared the record for the low individual round at 63, the thirty-six-hole record of 134, and the record for the last fifty-four holes at 204. He had played 112 rounds in the Open and averaged 72.24 strokes.

While he had won four championships, it might have been more, but his inexperience and Arnold Palmer's wild surge beat him by two strokes at Cherry Hills, Lee Trevino beat him in a playoff at Merion, and when he had seemed to have the Open won at Pebble Beach, Tom Watson had holed his pitch on the 17th, and Jack was second for the fourth time. He'd also been second to Trevino in 1968, but then atrocious putting had cost him pretty much any chance of winning by the final stages. He'd also placed third once, fourth twice, fifth once, tenth or better on ten other occasions, and he'd either won or been within three strokes of first place in seven of the twelve championships from 1971 through 1982.

For twenty-five years he had been the man to fear in every Open, indeed, in every tournament he entered. He was the best golfer of his time, and no one could ask more of anyone. He was the longest straight driver the game had ever known, hit as many greens as any man, and although he was weak with the wedge, he was the best putter of all the great players. His accomplishments were so vast, his dominance so complete, that he ranks with Harry Vardon, Bobby Jones, and Ben Hogan as the four greatest golfers who ever lived.

Like them Nicklaus raised the game to new levels, and like Jones, Hogan, and Willie Anderson, he won four United States Open Championships.

That is the modern measure of greatness.

On a hazy morning in 1970, when, at fifty-eight, Hogan played the first round of the Houston Open, his gallery included a number of prominent players. After the round, R. H. Sikes, another professional, spent ten minutes studying a shot-by-shot account. As his career drew to its inevitable close, we were drawing nearer to the day when golfers too young to have seen him at his peak will follow in Jack's gallery, staring in wonder as he drills a 1-iron to the heart of some distant green.

Some say we'll never see their likes again, that no one will ever dominate the game as Nicklaus, Hogan, Jones, and Vardon had done.

But someone will. Someone always does.

APPENDICES
U. S. Open Champions

Date	Winner, Runner-Up	Score	Site	Entry
1894 October 11–12	Willie Dunn d. Willie Campbell	2 Up	St. Andrew's GC Yonkers, N.Y.	4
1895 October 4	Horace Rawlins Willie Dunn	173 175	Newport GC Newport, R.I.	11
1896 July 18	James Foulis Horace Rawlins	152 155	Shinnecock Hills GC Southampton, N.Y.	35
1897 September 17	Joe Lloyd Willie Anderson	162 163	Chicago GC Wheaton, Ill.	35
1898 June 17–18	Fred Herd Alex Smith	328 335	Myopia Hunt Club South Hamilton, Mass.	49
1899 September 14–15	Willie Smith Val Fitzjohn George Low W. H. Way	315 326 326 326	Baltimore CC Roland Park Course Baltimore, Md.	81
1900 October 4–5	Harry Vardon J. H. Taylor	313 315	Chicago GC Wheaton, Ill.	60
1901 June 14–16	Willie Anderson Alex Smith	331–85 331–86	Myopia Hunt Club South Hamilton, Mass.	60
1902 October 10–11	Laurie Auchterlonie Stewart Gardner *Walter Travis	307 313 313	Garden City GC Garden City, N.Y.	90

* Denotes amateur.

Date	Winner, Runner-Up	Score	Site	Entry
1903 June 26–29	Willie Anderson David Brown	307–82 307–84	Baltusrol GC Original Course Springfield, N.J.	89
1904 July 8–9	Willie Anderson Gil Nicholls	303 308	Glen View Club Golf, Ill.	71
1905 September 21–22	Willie Anderson Alex Smith	314 316	Myopia Hunt Club South Hamilton, Mass.	83
1906 June 28–29	Alex Smith Willie Smith	295 302	Onwentsia Club Lake Forest, Ill.	68
1907 June 20–21	Alex Ross Gil Nicholls	302 304	Philadelphia Cricket C St. Martins Course Philadelphia, Pa.	82
1908 August 27–29	Fred McLeod Willie Smith	322–77 322–83	Myopia Hunt Club South Hamilton, Mass.	88
1909 June 24–25	George Sargent Tom McNamara	290 294	Englewood GC Englewood, N.J.	84
1910 June 17–18, 20	Alex Smith John McDermott Macdonald Smith	298–71 298–75 298–77	Philadelphia Cricket C St. Martins Course Philadelphia, Pa.	75
1911 June 23–24	John McDermott Mike Brady George Simpson	307–80 307–82 307–85	Chicago GC Wheaton, Ill.	79
1912 August 1–2	John McDermott Tom McNamara	294 296	CC of Buffalo Buffalo, N.Y.	131
1913 September 18–20	*Francis Ouimet Harry Vardon Ted Ray	304–72 304–77 304–78	The Country Club Brookline, Mass.	165
1914 August 20–21	Walter Hagen *Chick Evans	290 291	Midlothian CC Blue Island, Ill.	129
1915 June 17–18	*Jerry Travers Tom McNamara	297 298	Baltusrol GC Revised Course Springfield, N.J.	141
1916 June 29–30	*Chick Evans Jock Hutchison	286 288	Minikahda Club Minneapolis, Minn.	94
†1917 June 20–22	Jock Hutchison Tom McNamara	292 299	Whitemarsh Valley CC Philadelphia, Pa.	
1918	No championship: First World War			
1919 June 9–12	Walter Hagen Mike Brady	301–77 301–78	Brae Burn CC West Newton, Mass.	142

† 1917: Open Patriotic Tournament conducted by the USGA for the benefit of the American Red Cross.

Date	Winner, Runner-Up	Score	Site	Entry
1920 August 12–13	Ted Ray Harry Vardon Jack Burke, Sr. Leo Diegel Jock Hutchison	295 296 296 296 296	Inverness Club Toledo, Ohio	265
1921 July 21–22	Jim Barnes Walter Hagen Fred McLeod	289 298 298	Columbia CC Chevy Chase, Md.	262
1922 July 14–15	Gene Sarazen *Bobby Jones John Black	288 289 289	Skokie CC Glencoe, Ill.	323
1923 July 13–15	*Bobby Jones Bobby Cruickshank	296–76 296–78	Inwood CC Inwood, N.Y.	360
1924 June 5–6	Cyril Walker Bobby Jones	297 300	Oakland Hills CC Birmingham, Mich.	319
1925 June 3–5	Willie Macfarlane *Bobby Jones	291–75 72 295–75 73	Worcester CC Worcester, Mass.	445
1926 July 8–10	*Bobby Jones Joe Turnesa	293 294	Scioto CC Columbus, Ohio	694
1927 June 14–17	Tommy Armour Harry Cooper	301–76 301–79	Oakmont CC Oakmont, Pa.	898
1928 June 21–23	Johnny Farrell *Bobby Jones	294–143 294–144	Olympia Fields CC No. 4 Course Mateson, Ill.	1,064
1929 June 27–30	*Bobby Jones Al Espinosa	294–141 294–164	Winged Foot GC Mamaroneck, N.Y.	1,000
1930 July 10–12	*Bobby Jones Macdonald Smith	287 289	Interlachen CC Minneapolis, Minn.	1,177
1931 July 2–6	Billy Burke George Von Elm	292–149 148 292–149 149	Inverness Club Toledo, Ohio	1,141
1932 June 23–25	Gene Sarazen Bobby Cruickshank Phil Perkins	286 289 289	Fresh Meadow CC Flushing, N.Y.	1,011
1933 June 8–10	*John Goodman Ralph Guldahl	287 288	North Shore CC Glenview, Ill.	915
1934 June 7–9	Olin Dutra Gene Sarazen	293 294	Merion Cricket Club Ardmore, Pa.	1,063

APPENDICES

Date	Winner, Runner-Up	Score	Site	Entry
1935	Sam Parks	299	Oakmont CC	1,125
June 6–8	Jimmy Thomson	301	Oakmont, Pa.	
1936	Tony Manero	282	Baltusrol GC	1,277
June 4–6	Harry Cooper	284	Upper Course	
			Springfield, N.J.	
1937	Ralph Guldahl	281	Oakland Hills CC	1,402
June 10–12	Sam Snead	283	Birmingham, Mich.	
1938	Ralph Guldahl	284	Cherry Hills CC	1,223
June 9–11	Dick Metz	290	Denver, Colo.	
1939	Byron Nelson	284–68	Philadelphia CC	1,193
June 8–12		70	Spring Mill Course	
	Craig Wood	284–68	Philadelphia, Pa.	
		73		
	Denny Shute	284–76		
1940	Lawson Little	287–70	Canterbury GC	1,161
June 6–9	Gene Sarazen	287–73	Cleveland, Ohio	
1941	Craig Wood	284	Colonial CC	1,048
June 5–7	Denny Shute	287	Fort Worth, Texas	
‡1942	Ben Hogan	271	Ridgemoor CC	1,540
June 18–21	Jimmy Demaret	274	Chicago, Ill.	
	Mike Turnesa	274		
1943–1945	No championships: Second World War			
1946	Lloyd Mangrum	284–72	Canterbury GC	1,175
June 13–16		72	Cleveland, Ohio	
	Byron Nelson	284–72		
		73		
	Vic Ghezzi	284–72		
		73		
1947	Lew Worsham	282–69	St. Louis CC	1,356
June 12–15	Sam Snead	282–70	St. Louis, Mo.	
1948	Ben Hogan	276	Riviera CC	1,411
June 10–12	Jimmy Demaret	278	Los Angeles, Calif.	
1949	Cary Middlecoff	286	Medinah CC	1,348
June 9–11	Sam Snead	287	No. 3 Course	
	Clayton Heafner	287	Chicago, Ill.	
1950	Ben Hogan	287–69	Merion GC	1,379
June 8–11	Lloyd Mangrum	287–73	Ardmore, Pa.	
	George Fazio	287–75		

‡ 1942: Hale America National Open conducted by the USGA in cooperation with the Chicago District Golf Association and the PGA for the benefit of the Navy Relief Society and the United Service Organization.

Date	Winner, Runner-Up	Score	Site	Entry
1951 June 14–16	Ben Hogan Clayton Heafner	287 289	Oakland Hills CC Birmingham, Mich.	1,511
1952 June 12–14	Julius Boros Ed (Porky) Oliver	281 285	Northwood Club Dallas, Texas	1,688
1953 June 11–13	Ben Hogan Sam Snead	283 289	Oakmont CC Oakmont, Pa.	1,669
1954 June 17–19	Ed Furgol Gene Littler	284 285	Baltusrol GC Lower Course Springfield, N.J.	1,928
1955 June 16–19	Jack Fleck Ben Hogan	287–69 287–72	Olympic Club San Francisco, Calif.	1,522
1956 June 14–16	Cary Middlecoff Julius Boros Ben Hogan	281 282 282	Oak Hill CC Rochester, N.Y.	1,921
1957 June 13–15	Dick Mayer Cary Middlecoff	282–72 282–79	Inverness Club Toledo, Ohio	1,907
1958 June 12–14	Tommy Bolt Gary Player	283 287	Southern Hills CC Tulsa, Okla.	2,132
1959 June 11–14	Billy Casper Bob Rosburg	282 283	Winged Foot GC Mamaroneck, N.Y.	2,385
1960 June 16–18	Arnold Palmer *Jack Nicklaus	280 282	Cherry Hills CC Denver, Colo.	2,453
1961 June 15–17	Gene Littler Doug Sanders Bob Goalby	281 282 282	Oakland Hills CC Birmingham, Mich.	2,449
1962 June 14–17	Jack Nicklaus Arnold Palmer	283–71 283–74	Oakmont CC Oakmont, Pa.	2,475
1963 June 20–23	Julius Boros Jacky Cupit Arnold Palmer	293–70 293–73 293–76	The Country Club Brookline, Mass.	2,392
1964 June 18–20	Ken Venturi Tommy Jacobs	278 282	Congressional CC Washington, D.C.	2,341
1965 June 17–21	Gary Player Kel Nagle	282–71 282–74	Bellerive CC St. Louis, Mo.	2,271
1966 June 16–20	Billy Casper Arnold Palmer	278–69 278–73	Olympic Club San Francisco, Calif.	2,475
1967 June 15–18	Jack Nicklaus Arnold Palmer	275 279	Baltusrol GC Lower Course Springfield, N.J.	2,651
1968 June 13–16	Lee Trevino Jack Nicklaus	275 279	Oak Hill CC Rochester, N.Y.	3,007

APPENDICES

Date	Winner, Runner-Up	Score	Site	Entry
1969	Orville Moody	281	Champions GC	3,397
June 12–15	Bob Rosburg	282	Cypress Creek Course	
	Al Geiberger	282	Houston, Texas	
	Deane Beman	282		
1970	Tony Jacklin	281	Hazeltine National GC	3,605
June 18–21	Dave Hill	288	Minneapolis, Minn.	
1971	Lee Trevino	280–68	Merion GC	4,279
June 17–21	Jack Nicklaus	280–71	Ardmore, Pa.	
1972	Jack Nicklaus	290	Pebble Beach GL	4,196
June 15–18	Bruce Crampton	293	Pebble Beach, Calif.	
1973	John Miller	279	Oakmont CC	3,580
June 14–17	John Schlee	280	Oakmont, Pa.	
1974	Hale Irwin	287	Winged Foot GC	3,914
June 13–16	Forrest Fezler	289	Mamaroneck, N.Y.	
1975	Lou Graham	287–71	Medinah CC	4,214
June 19–23	John Mahaffey	287–73	No. 3 Course	
			Chicago, Ill.	
1976	Jerry Pate	277	Atlanta Athletic Club	4,436
June 17–20	Tom Weiskopf	279	Atlanta, Ga.	
	Al Geiberger	279		
1977	Hubert Green	278	Southern Hills CC	4,608
June 16–19	Lou Graham	279	Tulsa, Okla.	
1978	Andy North	285	Cherry Hills CC	4,897
June 15–18	J. C. Snead	286	Denver, Colo.	
	Dave Stockton	286		
1979	Hale Irwin	284	Inverness Club	4,853
June 14–17	Gary Player	286	Toledo, Ohio	
	Jerry Pate	286		
1980	Jack Nicklaus	272	Baltusrol GC	4,812
June 12–15	Isao Aoki	274	Lower Course	
			Springfield, N.J.	
1981	David Graham	273	Merion GC	4,946
June 18–21	Bill Rogers	276	Ardmore, Pa.	
	George Burns	276		
1982	Tom Watson	282	Pebble Beach GL	5,255
June 17–20	Jack Nicklaus	284	Pebble Beach, Calif.	
§1983	Larry Nelson	280	Oakmont CC	5,039
June 16–20	Tom Watson	281	Oakmont, Pa.	
1984	Fuzzy Zoeller	276–67	Winged Foot GC	5,195
June 14–18	Greg Norman	276–75	Mamaroneck, N.Y.	

§ Fourth round suspended June 19 because of rain. Completed June 20.

Date	Winner, Runner-Up	Score	Site	Entry
1985 June 13–16	Andy North Tze-Chung Chen Dave Barr Denis Watson	279 280 280 280	Oakland Hills CC Birmingham, Mich.	5,274
1986 June 12–15	Raymond Floyd Chip Beck Lanny Wadkins	279 281 281	Shinnecock Hills GC Southampton, N.Y.	5,410

Progress of Scoring Records

Eighteen holes:

82—Horace Rawlins, Newport Golf Club, 1895.
74—James Foulis, Shinnecock Hills Golf Club, 1896.
73—Gil Nicholls, Garden City Golf Club, 1902.
72—Willie Anderson, Glen View Club, 1904.
68—David Hunter, Englewood Golf Club, 1909.
67—Willie Macfarlane, Worcester Country Club, 1925.
66—Gene Sarazen, Fresh Meadow Country Club, 1932.
65—Jimmy McHale, St. Louis Country Club, 1947.
64—Lee Mackey, Merion Golf Club, 1950.
63—John Miller, Oakmont Country Club, 1973.

Seventy-two holes:

328—Fred Herd, Myopia Hunt Club, 1898.
315—Willie Smith, Baltimore Country Club, 1899.
313—Harry Vardon, Chicago Golf Club, 1900.
307—Laurie Auchterlonie, Garden City Golf Club, 1902.
303—Willie Anderson, Glen View Club, 1904.
295—Alex Smith, Onwentsia Club, 1906.
290—George Sargent, Englewood Golf Club, 1909.
286—Chick Evans, Minikahda Club, 1916.
282—Tony Manero, Baltusrol Golf Club, 1936.
281—Ralph Guldahl, Oakland Hills Country Club, 1937.
276—Ben Hogan, Riviera Country Club, 1948.
275—Jack Nicklaus, Baltusrol Golf Club, 1967.
272—Jack Nicklaus, Baltusrol Golf Club, 1980.

Other Notes of Interest

Champions who led all the way. Only four men have led after every round: Walter Hagen in 1914; Jim Barnes in 1921; Ben Hogan in 1953; and Tony Jacklin, in 1970. Seven other champions have led or were in a tie all the way: Willie Anderson in 1903; Alex Smith in 1906; Chick Evans in 1916; Tommy Bolt in 1958; Jack Nicklaus in 1972 and 1980; and Hubert Green in 1977.

Clubs most often host. Baltusrol Golf Club and Oakmont Country Club six times. Opens were played at Baltusrol in 1903, 1915, 1936, 1954, 1967, and 1980, and at Oakmont in 1927, 1935, 1953, 1962, 1973, and 1983. Five Opens were played at Oakland Hills Country Club, in 1924, 1937, 1951, 1961, and 1985. Four clubs were host four times: Myopia Hunt Club in 1898, 1901, 1905, and 1908; Inverness Club in 1920, 1931, 1957, and 1979; Merion Golf Club in 1934, 1950, 1971, and 1981; and Winged Foot Golf Club in 1929, 1959, 1974, and 1984.

Consecutive winners. Five players: Willie Anderson (1903, 1904, 1905); John J. McDermott (1911, 1912); Robert T. Jones, Jr. (1929, 1930); Ralph Guldahl (1937, 1938); Ben Hogan (1950, 1951).

Finishes in first ten. 18 by Jack Nicklaus. Walter Hagen finished in the first ten sixteen times and Ben Hogan fifteen times.

Highest thirty-six-hole cut. 155 in 1955 (low 50 and ties).

Lowest nine-hole score. 30: by Danny Edwards on the second nine in the second round in 1986; by George Burns on the first nine of the second round in 1982; by Raymond Floyd on the first nine of the first round in

1980; by Tom Shaw in the first round and Bob Charles in the last round in 1971, both on the first nine; by Steve Spray on the second nine of the fourth round in 1968; By Ken Venturi on the first nine of the third round in 1964; by Arnold Palmer on the first nine of the final round in 1960; and by Jimmy McHale, on the first nine in the third round in 1947.

Lowest round. 63: by Jack Nicklaus and Tom Weiskopf in the first round at Baltusrol in 1980; by John Miller in the final round at Oakmont in 1973.

Lowest first thirty-six holes. 134: by Tze-Chung Chen in 1985 and by Jack Nicklaus in 1980.

Lowest last thirty-six holes. 132: by Larry Nelson in 1983.

Lowest thirty-six-hole cut. 146: in 1980 and 1985.

Most consecutive Opens. Gene Sarazen teed off in thirty-one successive Opens, from 1920 through 1954 (no championships in 1942–1945 because of the Second World War). Arnold Palmer teed off in thirty-one consecutively, from 1953 through 1983.

Most consecutive Opens completed seventy-two holes. 22: by Walter Hagen from 1913 through 1936 (no championships 1917–1918 because of the First World War); Gene Sarazen from 1920 through 1941; and Gary Player from 1958 through 1979.

Most Opens completed seventy-two holes. Sam Snead played through twenty-seven Opens between 1937 and 1973. Gene Sarazen played through twenty-six and Jack Nicklaus twenty-five.

Most victories. Four men have won four times: Willie Anderson (1901, 1903, 1904, 1905); Robert T. Jones, Jr. (1923, 1926, 1929, 1930), Ben Hogan (1948, 1950, 1951, 1953), and Jack Nicklaus (1962, 1967, 1972, 1980). Eleven men have won two times: Alex Smith (1906, 1910), John J. McDermott (1911, 1912), Walter Hagen (1914, 1919), Gene Sarazen (1922, 1932), Ralph Guldahl (1937, 1938), Cary Middlecoff (1949, 1956), Julius Boros (1952, 1963), Bill Casper (1959, 1966), Lee Trevino (1968, 1971), Hale Irwin (1974, 1979), and Andy North (1978, 1985).

Most times runner-up. Sam Snead, Robert T. Jones, Jr., Arnold Palmer, and Jack Nicklaus, four times each.

Most subpar rounds in career. Twenty-nine by Jack Nicklaus, eighteen by Ben Hogan, seventeen by Sam Snead.

Pace-setters' fate. The man who led after eighteen holes has won only fourteen of the eighty-six Opens. A player who led or tied for the lead after thirty-six holes has won twenty-four of the eighty-three Opens at seventy-two holes. A man who led or tied for the lead after fifty-four holes has won thirty-six of the eighty-three Opens at seventy-two holes.

Under-70 finishes by champions. The following champions broke 70 in the fourth round: Gene Sarazen, 68 in 1922 and 66 in 1932; Tony Manero,

67 in 1936; Ralph Guldahl, 69 in 1937 and 1938; Byron Nelson, 68 in 1939; Ben Hogan, 69 in 1948 and 67 in 1951; Jack Fleck, 67 in 1955; Arnold Palmer, 65 in 1960; Gene Littler, 68 in 1961; Jack Nicklaus, 69 in 1962, 65 in 1967, and 68 in 1980; Bill Casper, 68 in 1966; Lee Trevino, 69 in 1968 and 1971; John Miller, 63 in 1973; Jerry Pate, 68 in 1976; David Graham, 67 in 1981; Larry Nelson, 67 in 1983; and Raymond Floyd, 66 in 1986.

SELECTED BIBLIOGRAPHY

Alles, Jane P. *The History of the Philadelphia Country Club, 1890–1965*. Wilmington: Kaumagraph Company, 1965.

Barkow, Al. *Golf's Golden Grind*. New York: Harcourt Brace Jovanovich, 1974.

Bisher, Furman. *The Birth of a Legend: Arnold Palmer's Golden Year 1960*. Englewood Cliffs, N.J.: Prentice-Hall, Inc., 1972.

Corcoran, Fred, ed. *The Official Golf Guide 1948*. New York: A. S. Barnes & Company, Inc., 1948.

————. *The Official Golf Guide 1949*. New York: A. S. Barnes & Company, Inc., 1949.

Corcoran, Fred, and Bud Harvey. *Unplayable Lies*. New York: Duell, Sloan and Pearce, 1965.

Cotton, Henry. *This Game of Golf*. London: Country Life Limited, 1948.

Golf at Merion 1896–1976. Privately printed, 1976?

Goodner, Ross. *Golf's Greatest*. Norwalk, Conn.: Golf Digest, Inc., 1978.

Gregston, Gene. *Hogan: The Man Who Played for Glory*. Englewood Cliffs, N.J.: Prentice-Hall, Inc., 1978.

Hagen, Walter, as told to Margaret Seaton Heck. *The Walter Hagen Story*. New York: Simon and Schuster, 1956.

Jones, Robert T., Jr. and O. B. Keeler. *Down the Fairway*. New York: Minton, Balch & Company, 1927.

SELECTED BIBLIOGRAPHY

Jones, Robert T., Jr. *Bobby Jones on Golf*. New York: New Metropolitan Fiction, Inc., 1929–1930.

Leach, Henry. *The Happy Golfer*. London: Macmillan & Co., Ltd., 1914.

McCormack, Mark. *Golf '67*. London: Cassell, 1967.

McCormack, Mark H. *Arnie*. New York: Simon and Schuster, 1967.

McCormack, Mark H., ed. *Dunhill Golf Yearbook 1979*. Garden City, N.Y.: Doubleday & Company, Inc., 1979.

McCormack, Mark H., ed. *Dunhill Golf Yearbook 1980*. Garden City, N.Y.: Doubleday & Company, Inc., 1980.

———. *Dunhill World of Professional Golf 1981*. New York: A. S. Barnes & Company, Inc., 1981.

———. *Dunhill World of Professional Golf 1982*. New York: A. S. Barnes & Company, Inc., 1982.

———. *Dunhill World of Professional Golf 1983*. London: Springwood Books, 1983.

———. *Ebel World of Professional Golf 1984*. Washington, D.C.: Acropolis Books Limited, 1984.

———. *Ebel World of Professional Golf 1985*. Ascot, Berkshire: Springwood Books, 1985.

———. *Ebel World of Professional Golf 1986*. Ascot, Berkshire: Springwood Books, 1986.

———. *The World of Professional Golf 1968 Edition*. New York: The World Publishing Company, 1968.

———. *The World of Professional Golf: Golf Annual 1969*. Great Britain: International Literary Management, Inc., 1969.

———. *The World of Professional Golf: Golf Annual 1970*. London: Hodder and Stoughton, 1970.

———. *The World of Professional Golf: Golf Annual 1971*. London: Hodder and Stoughton, 1971.

———. *The World of Professional Golf: Golf Annual 1972*. New York: Atheneum, 1972.

———. *The World of Professional Golf: Golf Annual 1973*. New York: Atheneum, 1973.

———. *The World of Professional Golf: Golf Annual 1974*. New York: Atheneum, 1974.

———. *The World of Professional Golf: Golf Annual 1975*. New York: Atheneum, 1975.

———. *The World of Professional Golf: Golf Annual 1976*. New York: Atheneum, 1976.

SELECTED BIBLIOGRAPHY

———. *The World of Professional Golf: Golf Annual 1977*. New York: Atheneum, 1977.

———. *The World of Professional Golf: Golf Annual 1978*. Garden City, N.Y.: Doubleday & Company, Inc., 1978.

Macdonald, Charles Blair. *Scotland's Gift—Golf*. New York: Charles Scribner's Sons, 1928.

Martin, H. B. *Fifty Years of American Golf*. New York: Dodd, Mead & Company, 1936.

Miller, Dick. *Triumphant Journey*. New York: Holt, Rinehart and Winston, 1980.

Nicklaus, Jack, and Herbert Warren Wind. *The Greatest Game of All*. New York: Simon and Schuster, 1969.

Ouimet, Francis. *A Game of Golf*. Boston: Houghton Mifflin Company, 1932.

Price, Charles. *Golfer-at-Large*. New York: Atheneum, 1982.

———. *The World of Golf*. New York: Random House, 1962.

Rice, Grantland. *The Bobby Jones Story* from the writings of O. B. Keeler. Atlanta: Tuper & Love, 1953.

Richardson, Bill, ed. *The Official Golf Guide 1947*. New York: A. S. Barnes and Company, 1947.

Sarazen, Gene, and Herbert Warren Wind. *Thirty Years of Championship Golf*. New York: Prentice-Hall, Inc., 1950.

Snead, Sam, and Al Stump. *The Education of a Golfer*. New York: Simon and Schuster, 1962.

Spalding's Athletic Library. *Golf Guide for 1921*. New York: American Sports Publishing Company, 1921.

Spalding's Athletic Library. *Golf Guide—1924, 1925, 1927, 1931, 1932*. New York: American Sports Publishing Company, 1924, 1925, 1927, 1931, and 1932.

Taylor, J. H. *Golf: My Life's Work*. London: Jonathan Cape, 1943.

Travers, Jerome D. *The Winning Shot*. New York: Doubleday, Page & Co., 1916.

Vardon, Harry. *My Golfing Life*. London: Hutchinson & Co., Ltd., 1933.

Wind, Herbert Warren. *The Story of American Golf*. New York: Simon and Schuster, 1956.

The American Golfer, 1909–1936.

Golf Digest, 1950 to date.

Golf Illustrated, 1923–1935.

SELECTED BIBLIOGRAPHY

Golf Journal, 1948 to date.
Golf Magazine, 1960 to date.
Golf World, 1947 to date.
Golf World (British), 1980 to date.
Golfers Magazine, 1914–1915.
Golfing, 1950, 1954.
National Golf Review, 1939–1940.
The New Yorker, 1960 to date.
Newsweek, 1962.
Playfair Golf Annual, 1950.
PGA Magazine, 1930–1940.
Reader's Digest, 1960.
Rx Sports and Travel, 1969.
Sports Illustrated, 1954 to date.

Baltimore Evening Sun
Dallas Morning News. Southwest Scene, Sunday, June 14, 1970.
Miami Herald
New York Herald Tribune
The New York Times
Washington Evening Star

INDEX

Aaron, Tommy, 204, 280
ABC, 167, 252, 273
Abramson, Arnold, 195
Abramson, Bob, 195
Adair, Perry, 64
Agua Caliente Open, 150
Ainsley, Ray, 116
All American Open, 133
Allegheny Country Club, 26
Allin, Brian, 258
Allis, Peter, 238
American Golf Classic, 213, 223
American Golfer, The, 85, 110–111
American Red Cross, 46, 48, 64, 127
Americas Cup Match, 208
Anderson, Arthur, 123
Anderson, John G., 38
Anderson, Tom, Sr., 21
Anderson, Willie, 19–22, 24–26,
    30, 37, 89, 116, 162, 229, 255,
    286, 317
Aoki, Isao, 3–4, 7, 283–285
Apawamis Club, 21

Archer, George, 243, 244
Ardmore Open, 8, 195
Arledge, Roone, 273
Armour, Tommy, 76, 90, 94–95,
    166, 301
Armour Research Foundation of
    Chicago, 124
Asheville Land of the Sky Open,
    151
Associated Press, 82
Atlanta Athletic Club, 272
Atlanta Classic, 282
Atlanta Journal, 62
Atlantic City Country Club, 28
Atlantic Coast Conference, 188
Auchterlonie, Laurie, 17, 18, 19,
    22, 24
Augusta National Golf Club, 80,
    86, 122, 133, 157, 164, 168,
    179, 185, 188, 196, 238,
    251, 304, 317
Australian Open, 281, 287

INDEX

Balfour, Arthur, 111
Ball, John, 24
Ballesteros, Severiano, 7, 295, 297, 298, 302
Baltimore Country Club, 17, 73
Baltusrol Golf Club, 3, 5, 7, 24, 46, 71, 104, 108–109, 110, 116, 118, 124, 133, 150, 162, 167–168, 169, 176, 224–229, 230, 234, 282–285, 286, 295, 315, 317
Banks, Charles, 109
Barber, Jerry, 189, 191
Barber, Miller, 236, 237, 243, 299
Barker, H. K., 28
Barnes, Jim, 35, 46, 47, 53–54, 59, 65–66, 116, 249
Barr, Dave, 305, 306
Barron, Herman, 128
Bean, Andy, 275, 303
Beard, Frank, 270, 271
Beardsley Park, 92
Beck, Chip, 313, 315, 316
Behr, Max, 70, 111
Bell, Dave, 18, 19
Bell, Rex, 116
Bellerive Country Club, 213, 215
Beman, Deane, 224, 236, 237, 240, 280
Bendelow, Tom, 70, 71
Ben Hogan Open, 143
Besselink, Al, 8, 171
Bill, W. H., 74
Bing Crosby Pro-Amateur Tournament, 5, 113, 134, 142, 143, 156, 224, 249, 252
Blancas, Homero, 252
Boatwright, P. J., 6, 147, 258, 273
Bob Hope Desert Classic, 231, 283
Bolt, Tommy, 171, 172, 183, 185, 239–240
Boomer, Aubrey, 76

Borek, Gene, 258
Borkovich, Andy, 239
Boros, Julius, 5, 145, 159–160, 161, 171, 180, 188, 189, 191, 192, 193, 203–205, 220, 243, 259, 260, 261, 262, 263, 267
Boston Interscholastic Championship, 37
Boston Post, 122
Bousfield, Ken, 162
Bradley, Alva, 112
Brady, Mike, 28–29, 30, 46, 48–49
Brae Burn Country Club, 18, 49, 116
Braid, James, 20, 83
Brentwood Country Club, 103
British Amateur Championship, 65, 66, 74, 75, 80, 81, 92, 120, 122, 244, 256
British Open, 4, 12, 13, 15, 17, 18, 20, 24, 30–31, 32, 33, 48, 50, 53, 56, 60, 65, 73, 74, 75, 76, 78, 81–82, 85, 86, 93–94, 95, 102–103, 139, 143, 153, 163, 164, 166–167, 193, 194, 199, 206, 215, 224, 238, 242, 247, 255, 256, 271, 275, 279, 281, 289, 290, 295, 317
The Broadmoor, 271
Brooklawn Country Club, 92
Brown, David, 22, 24
Brown, Joe E., 86
Brue, Bobby, 197
Bucky Woy, 241
Buffalo Country Club, 29
Buick Open, 205
Bulla, Johnny, 118–119, 145, 159, 163
Bunky, Henry, 236, 240
Burke, Billy, 91, 112
Burke, Jack, 150

Burke, Jack, Jr., 177, 208
Burkemo, Walter, 165
Burns, George, 278, 288, 290–291
Bush, Prescott, 85
Butler National Golf Club,
    269, 276
Byers, Eben, 26

Cagney, James, 86
California Amateur, 208
Campbell, Alex, 18, 37
Campbell, Willie, 12, 13, 14,
    15–16, 307
Canada Cup, 143, 238
Canadian Golf Association, 101
Canadian Open, 65, 93, 101,
    188, 247
Cann, George, 18
Canterbury Golf Club, 120, 127–
    129, 134, 177
Capital City Open, 102
Carnoustie, 103, 166–167, 271
Carr, Joe, 208
Carter, Ed, 167
Cascades Course, 118
Cascades Open, 112
Casper, Billy, 183–184, 185, 217–
    220, 225, 226, 231, 234, 242,
    243, 258, 266, 315, 316
CBS, 186
Cerda, Tony, 166
Champions Golf Club, 177, 234,
    235
Charles, Bob, 260
Chen, T. C., 302, 303–306
Cherry, Don, 191
Cherry Hills Country Club, 58,
    71, 116, 117, 118, 162, 176–
    177, 189, 263, 272, 275,
    276, 289, 306–307, 316
Chicago District Golf
    Association, 152

Chicago Golf Club, 13, 14, 16,
    18–19, 72, 124
Chirkinian, Frank, 237
Chisholm, Willie, 116
Christie, Agatha, 111
Clampett, Bobby, 290
Claremont Country Club, 151,
    249
Cleveland Open, 223
Cobb, Ty, 94
Cochrane, Mickey, 78
Coe, Charlie, 280, 281
Colbert, Jim, 244, 258, 260, 266
Cole, Bobby, 235
Collins, Billy, 207
Colonial Country Club, 122, 142
Colonial Invitational, 133, 134,
    143, 155, 157, 163, 164, 178,
    205, 242
Columbia Country Club, 59
Compston, Archie, 81–82
Congressional Country Club, 133,
    206–207, 211–212, 263, 300
Coody, Charley, 177, 231
Cooper, Harry, 76, 83, 84, 90, 103,
    117, 151
Corcoran, Fred, 122, 147
Cotton, Henry, 103
The Country Club, 12, 14, 33,
    34–37, 39–41, 66, 124, 203,
    253, 267, 316
Country Life, 72, 111
Couples, Fred, 303, 304
Cox, Wiffy, 106
Crampton, Bruce, 204, 236, 237,
    253, 254, 255
Crawley, Leonard, 234
Crenshaw, Ben, 244, 269–270, 271,
    313, 315
Crosby, Bing, 127
Cruickshank, Bobby, 60–62, 67–68,

69–70, 93, 96–97, 99,
105–106, 166
Crump, George, 71
Cunningham, Bill, 122
Cupit, Jacky, 203–204, 267
Curtis, Laurence, 14
Cypress Point, 71

Daly, Fred, 162
Darwin, Bernard, 72, 85–86, 111
Davis, Bill, 195
Davis, Willie, 12, 13, 15, 16, 307
Dean, Simpson, 64
Del Monte Properties, 249
Demaret, Jimmy, 111, 126, 140,
142, 143, 152, 153, 155–156,
157, 159, 161, 162, 168,
177, 181–182
Democrat and Chronicle, 43
Dempsey, Jack, 78
Dent, Jim, 239
Denver Open, 133
De Vicenzo, Roberto, 231, 238
Devlin, Bruce, 258, 287, 290,
291, 292
Dey, Joe, 121, 140, 144, 172, 210
Dickinson, Gardner, 212, 229
Diegel, Leo, 54, 55, 56, 82, 90
DiMaggio, Joe, 126
Dolan, Jay, 239
Dorais, Gus, 42
Douglas, Dave, 159, 164
Douglas, Findlay, 301
Dow Jones Open, 264–265
Down the Fairway (Jones), 111
Drum, Bob, 189–190, 196
Dudley, Ed, 103
Dunes Golf and Beach Club, 269
Dunn, Jamie, 12
Dunn, Tom, 16

Dunn, Willie, Jr., 11–16, 17, 18,
307, 308
Dunn, Willie, Sr., 12
Dunwoodie, 73
Dutra, Mortie, 91
Dutra, Olin, 103, 105, 216
Dye, Pete, 109

Easterly, Harry, 258, 273–274
Eastern Open, 188
East Lake Golf Course, 63, 64, 272
Edgar, Doug, 65
Edwards, Danny, 312
Edwards, Kenneth, 64
Egan, H. Chandler, 37, 99, 251
Eisenhower, Dwight, 194
Elm, George Von, 74, 75, 77
Emmet, Devereaux, 70, 109
Englewood Golf Club, 27, 30
Erickson, Bob, 244
Esmeralda Open, 133
Espinosa, Abe, 99
Espinosa, Al, 79–80, 114, 301
Essex County Country Club, 17
Euclid Club, 24
Evans, Chick, 38, 44–45, 47–48,
56, 64, 85, 98, 100, 104, 110,
123, 155, 299–300
Everett, Dr. John, 211

Fairbanks, Douglas, Jr., 86
Farrell, Johnny, 73, 76–78, 90, 301
Faulkner, Max, 238
Fazio, George, 109, 111, 145–146,
148, 163, 165, 242, 277
Fazio, Tom, 109, 277
Fergus, Keith, 283
Ferrier, Jim, 145, 212
Fezler, Forrest, 267
Fields, W. C., 86
Finsterwald, Dow, 189, 191,
199, 258

Fitzgerald, Maury, 121
Fitzsimmons, Bob, 71
Five Farms, 108, 109
Fleck, Jack, 170–176, 177, 191–192, 216
Fleckman, Marty, 224–225, 226
Floyd, Raymond, 211, 212, 233– 234, 258, 266, 282, 312, 313, 314–316
Flynn, Bill, 70, 71, 118, 308, 309
Ford, Doug, 164, 258
Fort Wayne Country Club, 92
Foulis, Jim, 15–17, 18, 307
Foulis, Richard, 18
Fownes, Henry C., 106–107, 108, 109
Fownes, William C., 26, 107–108, 109
Fox Hill Club, 26
Francis, Richard S., 104
Franco, Francisco, 79
Franklin Park, 37
Fresh Meadow Country Club, 86, 94–98, 99, 162, 213, 299
Furgol, Ed, 167–168, 171, 181, 228

Ganton Golf Club, 142
Garden City Golf Club, 38
Gardner, Bob, 58, 64, 280
Gardner, Stewart, 22, 24, 25
Gehrig, Lou, 78
Geiberger, Al, 176, 236, 237, 272, 273
Georgia Amateur Championship, 59
Gershwin, George, 79
Ghezzi, Vic, 111, 127–129, 151, 155
Giles, Vinny, 258
Glasson, Bill, 303
Glen Garden Caddie Championship, 150

Glen Garden Country Club, 149
Glen Lakes Country Club, 233
Glen View Club, 25
Goalby, Bob, 197, 244, 266
Golf, 18, 110
Golf Club of Mexico, 164
Golf Digest, 195
Golfers Magazine, 110, 111
Golf House, 172, 185
Golf Illustrated, 101, 108, 110, 111
Golf Illustrated Gold Vase, 80
Golf Is My Game (Jones), 111
Golf Magazine, 195
Golf World, 195
Golf Writers Association of America, 196
Goodall Round Robin, 151
Goodman, Johnny, 99–100, 101, 112, 113, 115
Graffis, Herb, 167
Graffis, Joe, 167
Graham, David, 286–289, 291, 296
Graham, Lou, 4, 266, 270, 271, 273–274, 276, 289
Grainger, Ike, 137, 149, 160
Grand Slam, 105, 164, 193, 256
Green, Hubert, 264, 265, 272, 273–275, 289
Greenbrier Pro-Am, 143
Greenbrier's Old White, 112
Greensboro Open, 151, 178
Griscom, Rodman E., 104
Grout, Jack, 150, 279–280
Guilford, Jesse, 48
Guldahl, Buddy, 116
Guildahl, Ralph, 100, 103, 111, 114–117, 118, 126–127, 149, 152, 156, 158, 300

Haas, Jay, 304
Hagen, Walter, 4, 33, 34, 43–45, 47, 48–50, 54, 57, 59, 66, 69,

73, 74, 77, 78, 81, 83, 90,
91, 93, 101, 102, 103,
110, 126, 159, 166, 195, 289,
297, 316
Hale America National Open,
152–153
Hamilton, Bob, 142
Hancock, Roland, 77
Hannigan, Frank, 237
Harbert, Chick, 134, 142, 155
Harbour Town Golf Links, 268,
276
Harding Park, 207
Harlow, Bob, 195
Harmon, Claude, 126, 170
Harney, Paul, 193, 204
Harper & Bros., 18
Harris, Labron, 244
Harrison, Dutch, 111, 142, 145,
146, 191, 243, 244
Haskell, Coburn, 23, 89
Havemeyer, Theodore, 14
Hawaiian Open, 241
Hayes, Mark, 283
Hazeltine National Golf Club,
238–241
Heafner, Clayton, 118, 137, 142,
160–161, 197
Heard, Jerry, 259, 260, 263, 269
Hendrix, Johnny, 196
Henry Hurst Invitational, 126
Herbert, Jay, 176, 194, 209
Herd, Fred, 17, 20, 22, 24
Herd, Sandy, 24
Heritage Classic, 268, 274
Herreshoff, Fred, 37
Herron, Davey, 65
Hershey Country Club, 164
Hershey Four-Ball, 151
Hershey Open, 112
Hill, Dave, 238, 239, 240
Hines, Jimmy, 126, 147

Hinkle, Lon, 277, 283
Hinson, Larry, 244
Hitchcock, Tommy, 79
Hitler, Adolf, 79
Hogan, Ben, 4, 5, 6, 8, 88, 111,
121, 125, 126, 127, 128, 134,
138, 140–177, 178, 179–
180, 181, 184, 185, 186, 189,
190, 191–193, 194, 197,
198, 213, 215, 216, 218, 229,
241, 242, 255, 256, 257,
262, 263, 286, 289, 297, 300,
303, 315, 317, 318
Hogan, Valerie, 140, 141, 142, 150
Homans, Gene, 76, 86, 105
Homestead, The, 118
Hope, Bob, 127
Horizon Hills Country Club, 231
Houston Open, 177, 231, 317–318
Howard, Chuck, 273
"How To Play Golf" (film), 86
Hoylake, 30–31, 33
Hoyt, Fred, 38
Hudson River, 73
Hunter, David, 29
Hunter, Ramsey, 92
Hunter, Willie, 66, 92
Hutchison, Jock, 47–48, 53, 54, 55,
56, 60–61, 93
Hutchison, Tom, 18
Hyndman, Bill, 239, 268, 280

Indian Creek Course, 118
Inman, Walker, 171
Insurance City Open, 188
Interlachen Country Club, 83–85
Inverness Club, 53–56, 57, 58,
65, 90–91, 93, 181, 216, 239,
272, 276–277
Inverness Four-Ball, 117, 156
Inverray Classic, 297

Inwood Country Club, 60–62, 66–68
Irwin, Hale, 266–268, 271–272, 276–278, 289, 296, 300, 303, 306

Jacklin, Tony, 234, 237–241, 244, 258
Jacksonville Open, 238
Jacobs, Tommy, 206–207, 211–212, 263
James River Course, 118
January, Don, 231
Japan Open, 235
Johnston, Jimmy, 76
Johnston, Ralph, 244, 266
Jones, Bob, Jr., 109
Jones, Grier, 269
Jones, Rees, 109
Jones, Robert Purmedas, 62
Jones, Robert Trent, 109, 158, 161, 166, 169–170, 215, 303
Jones, Robert Tyre (grandfather), 63
Jones, Robert Tyre, Jr., 4, 45, 46, 58–68, 69–88, 90, 92, 93, 94, 95, 96, 99, 102, 103, 105, 108, 110–111, 116, 122, 123, 125, 126, 153, 161, 162, 163, 167, 169, 186, 187, 193, 229, 255, 256, 265, 272, 280, 286, 289, 301, 317, 318
Jones, Thomas, 62

Kansas City Country Club, 268
Kansas City Match Play, 268
Keeler, O. B., 62, 66–67, 81, 107
Keller, Louis, 108–109
Kempa, Loddie, 146
Kibbee, Guy, 86
Kite, Tom, 269, 290
Kittansett Course, 118

Knight, Dick, 184
Knoxville Open, 126
Korean Open, 235
Korean PGA, 235
Kroll, Ted, 180–181, 191, 192

Lacy, Charlie, 84
LaGorce Open, 76, 101
Landon, Alfred M., 120
Laney, Al, 87
Langer, Bernhard, 302
Latrobe Country Club, 187
Lawrence, W. G., 13
Leach, Bill, 77
Lema, Tony, 204
Lettunich, Martin, 233
Lido Country Club, 71–73
Lind, Dean, 207, 208
Lindbergh, Charles A., 79
Little, Lawson, 99, 112, 120–122, 123, 152, 153
Littler, Gene, 168, 171, 176, 184, 197, 200, 213, 236, 237, 239, 266, 281, 302
Lloyd, H. Gates, 104
Lloyd, Joe, 14, 17, 19, 22
Locke, Bobby, 134–135, 156, 159, 161, 193, 214
Lockhart, Robert, 12
Long Beach Open, 156
Long Island Open, 93
Lorms, Charley, 53
Los Angeles Open, 101, 102, 112, 123, 142, 143, 150, 155, 231, 276
Lott, Lyn, 290
Lotz, Dick, 177
Low, George, 26
Lowery, Eddie, 36, 39, 208

McBee, Rives, 217, 263
McCarthy, Maurice, 76, 100

INDEX

McCumber, Mark, 312, 313, 315
McDermott, John, 27–32, 33, 34,
    39, 108, 116
Macdonald, Charles Blair, 13, 15,
    71–72, 109, 309
McDonald, Robert, 46
McFarlane, Willie, 73, 76
McGee, Jerry, 252
MacGregor Sporting Goods
    Company, 149, 171
MacKenzie, Alister, 70, 71, 72
McKenzie, Fred, 25
Mackey, Lee, 144, 163, 207, 263
Mackie, Isaac, 26
McLeod, Fred, 123
McNamara, Tom, 29–30, 34, 37,
    44, 46, 48
McSpaden, Harold (Jug), 126,
    127, 155
Mahaffey, John, 269, 270–271, 272,
    273, 276, 297
Maiden, Stewart, 63, 187
Manero, Tony, 103, 104, 110, 167,
    300
Mangrum, Lloyd, 111, 121, 128–
    129, 134, 142, 145–146,
    148–149, 155, 242
Mangrum, Ray, 155
Marr, Dave, 239, 240
Martin, Eddie, 128
Martin, Fred, 112
Massachusetts Amateur, 35, 38
Massachusetts Open, 29
Masters Tournament, 7, 86–87,
    113, 116, 117, 118, 126–127,
    134, 139, 143, 151, 152,
    153, 157, 162, 163, 164, 168,
    178, 179, 182, 183, 185,
    186, 188, 189, 193, 199, 206,
    208, 209, 214, 216, 223,
    224, 231, 242, 256, 253, 264,

    266, 286, 289, 290, 295,
    302, 304, 314, 317
Maxwell, Billy, 204
May, George S., 133
Mayer, Dick, 162, 181–182, 183,
    185, 209, 228
Meader, Frank, 63
Medinah Country Club, 5, 137,
    270–271, 276
Mehlhorn, Bill, 59–60, 69–70, 90,
    101
Melnyk, Steve, 244, 269
Mengert, Al, 217
Mercer, Tom, 21
Merchantville Field Club, 28
Merion Golf Club (Merion
    Cricket Club), 5, 32, 46, 47,
    65, 70, 71, 86, 103, 104–105,
    106, 108, 118, 134, 143–
    149, 150, 163, 216, 242, 243,
    244–247, 258, 263, 286,
    288–289, 290, 316
Merrick, Clara, 62–63
Merrill, John, 39
Met PGA, 93
Metropolitan Golf Association,
    101, 265
Metropolitan New York Open,
    20, 93
Metropolitan Open, 29, 101
Metz, Dick, 116, 117, 136
Metzger, Sol, 66
Miami Beach Open, 101
Miami Four-Ball, 76, 117
Miami Open, 76, 93, 101, 123
Middlecoff, Cary, 137, 145, 146,
    160, 162, 164, 171, 178–183,
    209, 215, 220, 278
Midlothian Country Club, 19, 43–
    45, 47
Mid Ocean Club, 72
Mid Pines, 163

Mid-South Open, 102
Miller, Johnny, 7, 162, 205, 259–
    263, 265, 266, 269, 275,
    276, 282, 288, 315
Minikahda Country Club, 47–48,
    76
Misquamicut Golf Club, 21
Missouri Amateur, 268
Modern Fundamentals of Golf,
    The (Hogan and Wind),
    297
Montgomery Invitational, 64
Moody, Orville, 5, 234–237, 238,
    239, 240, 258
Mooney, Jim, 239
Moran, Pat, 43
Moreland, Gus, 149
Morgan, J. Pierpont, 79
Morris, Tom, 12
Morse, Samuel F. B., 249, 251
Motor City Open, 156
Mowry, Larry, 207
Murder on the Links (Christie),
    111
Murphy, Bob, 236, 258, 269
Murray, Francis, 210
Myopia Hunt Club, 17, 21, 22,
    25, 124
Myrtle Beach, 196, 269

Nagle, Kel, 194, 214, 215
Naismith, George, 287
National Airlines Open, 242
National Amateur Championship,
    8, 13, 14, 15, 17, 24, 29, 38,
    58, 62, 64, 65, 66, 71, 76, 78,
    86, 92, 99, 110, 111, 168,
    178, 179, 186, 188, 199, 249,
    251, 252, 256, 268, 269,
    279, 280, 281, 286, 301
National Capital Open, 134

National Collegiate Athletic
    Association, 267
National Golf Links of America,
    71, 309
National Junior, 207, 280
National Open, 113, 122, 140
NBC, 167, 186
Nelson, Byron, 5, 103, 111, 113,
    117, 119–120, 121, 122, 124,
    125–139, 149–150, 151,
    152, 153, 154, 155, 157, 178,
    208, 269, 289
Nelson, Larry, 276, 297–299
Nelson, Louise, 129
Neville, Jack, 70, 249–250, 251
Newport Golf Club, 14–16
Newton, Jack, 271
New York Herald Tribune, 87
Nicholls, Ben, 33
Nicholls, Bernard, 18, 22
Nicholls, Gil, 25, 26, 33
Nichols, Bobby, 200, 243
Nicklaus, Charles, 256
Nicklaus, Jack, 3–4, 5–6, 7, 58, 125,
    150, 162, 176, 177, 190–193,
    198, 199–202, 206, 217,
    223–229, 231, 232, 239, 241,
    242–247, 248, 252–255,
    256–257, 259, 260, 261, 263,
    265, 267, 268, 270–271,
    275, 279–285, 286, 289–
    290, 291–294, 295, 297, 300,
    302, 311, 315, 316–317, 318
Norman, Greg, 7, 300–302, 303,
    310, 311, 313, 315
North, Andy, 269, 272, 274, 275,
    276, 289, 290, 303–307
North and South Amateur, 188,
    281
North and South Open, 29, 60–61,
    119, 127, 151, 152, 158, 178
Northcliffe, Lord, 33

INDEX

North Shore Country Club,
99–100
Northwood Country Club, 163
Norton, Reg, 96
Norton, Willie, 14

Oak Hill Country Club, 176, 177,
179–181, 188, 231–232, 234
Oakland Hills Country Club, 5,
69–70, 71, 76, 113, 118,
158–162, 169, 170, 176, 196–
197, 263, 286, 289, 302–307,
316, 317
Oakland Open, 113
Oakmont Country Club, 5, 6, 7,
65, 76, 77, 93, 104, 106–108,
138, 164–166, 179, 188,
189, 195, 199–202, 205, 216,
235, 244, 257–263, 276,
288, 294, 296–299, 300, 302
Oak Ridge, 73
Ohio Amateur, 280
Ohio Junior, 280
Ohio Open, 280
Oklahoma City Open, 223
Oland, Warner, 86
Oliver, Ed (Porky), 120–121, 129,
154, 163, 164
Olympia Fields, 71, 76–78
Olympic Club, 5, 6, 71, 169–170,
177, 179, 216–220, 234, 263,
265, 267, 280
Onwentsia Club, 25–26
Open Patriotic Tournament, 48
Ormond Beach, 18
Ouimet, Francis, 44, 45, 46, 47, 48,
65, 66, 73, 76, 92, 100, 110,
203
Ouimet, Wilfred, 37

Pacific Eight Conference, 269
Palmer, Arnold, 5, 125, 162, 177,
185–207, 209–212, 213, 215,
216, 217, 220, 223–229,
231, 236, 237, 239, 240, 252–
255, 257, 259, 260, 261–262,
263, 266, 267, 268, 280,
282, 289, 291, 299, 302, 316,
317
Palmer, Doris, 186
Palmer, Johnny, 142, 145, 155
Palmer, Milfred (Deacon), 187
Palmer, Winifred, 188
Panama Open, 233
Pan American Open, 163, 164
Park, Willie, Sr., 14, 71
Parks, Sam, 103–104, 175, 203, 234
Patch, Dan, 21
Pate, Jerry, 272–273, 277, 278, 289
Patton, Billy Joe, 181, 185, 208,
224, 280
Paulsen, Guy, 91
Pebble Beach Golf Links, 5, 7, 71,
99, 106, 208, 249–255, 258,
267, 286, 290–294, 295, 316
Peete, Calvin, 282, 290, 291, 298
Pelham Country Club, 74
Penna, Toney, 111
Pensacola Open, 101
Pepsi Tournament, 183
Perkins Phil, 95–97
PGA Championship, 5, 6, 7, 48,
50, 54, 60, 69, 78, 93, 94,
103, 110, 113, 116, 122, 127,
129, 134, 135, 139, 152, 154–
155, 156, 157, 164, 165, 176,
181, 193, 194, 204, 206,
212, 223, 224, 236, 238, 242,
256, 264, 273, 286, 289,
297, 314
PGA of America, 108
Philadelphia Classic, 279
Philadelphia Country Club, 118
Philadelphia Cricket Club, 26

Philadelphia Inquirer Open, 133
Philadelphia Open, 27
Phoenix Open, 119, 140, 156, 223
Picard, Henry, 112–113, 116, 117,
    121, 126, 127, 152, 161
Pinehurst, 101, 153, 264, 270, 276
Pinehurst No. 2, 71
Pine Valley, 71, 106
Piping Rock Golf Club, 72
Pittsburgh Field Club, 195
Pittsburgh Press, 189
Player, Gary, 183, 184, 193, 199,
    213, 214–215, 231, 240, 241,
    255, 257, 258–259, 266,
    274, 275, 277, 278, 316
Point Comfort, 18
Portland Open, 223
Powers, Francis, 66
Precision Golf Forgings, 287
Prestwick Golf Club, 14
Princes, 95
Purtzer, Tom, 276–277

Quaker Ridge, 73

Radix, Harry, 146
Radix Trophy, 116
Ransom, Henry, 134
Rassett, Joe, 297
Rawlins, Horace, 16–17, 18, 307
Ray, Ted, 31, 33–35, 39–41, 53,
    54, 55, 56, 73, 83, 107, 142,
    204, 214
Raynor, Seth, 109
Reasor, Mike, 266
Rees, Dai, 166
Reid, John, 12–13
Reid, Mike, 272, 283, 303
Reid, Wilfred, 34–35, 47
Reno Open, 133
Revolta, Johnny, 112, 151
Richmond Open, 133

Ridgemoor Country Club, 152–153
Riegel, Skee, 157
Rinker, Larry, 290
Riviera Country Club, 140, 155,
    169, 276
Robertson, Allan, 12
Robertson, Peter, 26
Robinson, Bill, 20
Robinson, Edward G., 86
Robson, Fred, 76, 81
Rochester Country Club, 43
Rockaway Hunting Club, 23
Rockne, Knute, 42, 78
Rodgers, Phil, 281, 282
Rogers, Bill, 288, 290, 291, 292, 293
Roosevelt, Theodore, 42
Rosburg, Bob, 171, 184, 189, 200,
    201, 236, 237, 252
Rosenthal, Elaine, 64
Ross, Alex, 28, 34
Ross, Donald, 28, 53, 70, 71, 109,
    151, 158, 182, 303
Round Hill Club, 91
Royal & Ancient Golf Club of
    St. Andrews, 4, 12, 13, 14,
    56, 76, 81, 89, 90, 106, 123,
    194, 238, 251
Royal Liverpool Golf Club, 81
Royal Lytham, 74
Royal Troon, 295
Royer, Hugh, 239
Rubber City Open, 280
Rudolph, Mason, 252
Runyan, Paul, 117, 159, 281
Ruth, Babe, 78
Ryder Cup Match, 110, 153, 154,
    162
Ryder Cup Team, 142

St. Andrew's Golf Club, 13
St. Annes, 74
St. Louis Country Club, 134

INDEX

St. Louis Open, 102
St. Paul Open, 102, 123, 171
San Antonio Open, 133
Sande, Earl, 78
Sanders, Doug, 189, 197
San Francisco City Championship, 208
San Francisco Golf Club, 108
San Francisco Interscholastic, 207–208
San Francisco Match Play, 102
Saraceni, Eugenio. *See* Sarazen, Gene
Saraceni, Federico, 92
Sarazen, Gene, 4, 20, 59–60, 66, 69, 76, 79, 85, 86, 90, 92–98, 99, 101, 103, 105, 117, 120–122, 150, 152, 155, 156, 162, 172, 176, 182, 213, 289, 299, 301, 304, 316
Sargent, George, 27, 30, 44
Savannah Open, 80
Scalzo, Lou, 258
Schlee, John, 259, 260, 262–263, 266
Scioto Country Club, 74, 256, 279
Scott, J. A., 64
Seaver, Charlie, 99
Seminole Pro-Amateur, 157
Shawnee Invitational, 53
Shawnee Open, 108
Shields, Frank, 183
Shinnecock Hills Golf Club, 17, 71, 118, 124, 308–315
Shinnecock Indian Reservation, 12, 308
Shute, Denny, 103, 113–114, 117, 118, 122, 126, 152, 178
Sigel, Jay, 303
Sikes, Dan, 240
Sikes, R. H., 318
Simons, Jim, 244–245, 252

Simpson, George, 28–29
Simpson, Scott, 290, 291
Sindelar, Joey, 311, 312
Skokie Country Club, 59–60, 92, 93
Slazenger, Frank Legh, 21
Smith, A. W., 16
Smith, Alex, 18, 20, 22, 25–26, 27, 29, 31, 34, 37
Smith, George, 249
Smith, Horton, 80, 81, 82, 83, 90, 103
Smith, Macdonald, 27, 34, 69, 76, 82, 83, 85, 90, 91, 95, 100, 103, 249
Smith, Tom, 26
Smith, Willie, 17, 18, 19, 22, 26, 27
Snead, J. C., 269, 275
Snead, Sam, 5, 103, 111–115, 117–120, 121, 125–126, 134–139, 142–143, 151, 155, 159, 160, 165–166, 167, 171, 172, 178, 179, 185, 197, 202, 274, 280, 289
Somerville, Ross, 100
Souchak, Frank, 165, 189
Souchak, Mike, 184, 189, 190–191, 192, 207
Sound Beach Golf Club, 21
South Central Open, 102
Southeastern Open, 80
Southern Amateur Championship, 59, 64
Southern Hills Country Club, 6, 183, 273–274, 280
Southern Intercollegiate, 188
Southern Open, 59, 65, 75
Spalding (A. G.) Company, 17, 70, 86
Sports Illustrated, 111
Spring Mill Course, 117–118, 122, 124, 125

Stadler, Craig, 303
Standish, Jim, 64
Stewart, Earl, 8
Stewart, Payne, 305, 306, 313–314, 315
Stirling, Alexa, 64
Stockton, Dave, 275
Stoddard, L. B., 13
Stranahan, Frank, 147, 166, 188, 280
Strange, Curtis, 268
Strange, Tom, 268
Strubing, Phil, 193
Sunningdale, 74, 81
Sutton, Hal, 312, 313, 315
Sweeny, Bob, 188
Sweetser, Jess, 66, 74, 86

Tallahassee Open, 242
Tallmadge, Henry O., 14
Tamarisk Country Club, 164
Tam O'Shanter Country Club, 133, 134
Tam O'Shanter Open, 123, 126
Tatum, Sandy, 266, 273, 274
Taylor, J. H., 17–19, 20, 22, 23–24, 31, 85–86, 89
Tellier, Louis, 34, 35, 46, 48
Tennessee Amateur, 178
Tennison Park, 233
Texas Open, 101, 102, 270
Thirsk, Stan, 268
Thomas, Harold A., 124
Thomson, Jimmy, 104, 113
Thomson, Peter, 166, 171, 179, 181
Thorne, Howard, 63
Thorpe, Jim, 42
Thunderbird Classic, 210, 223
Tilden, Bill, 78
Tillinghast, A. W., 70, 79, 108–109, 111
Time, Inc., 111

Times, 111
Times (London), 33, 72
Timms, Cecil, 143
Todd, Harry, 134
Tolley, Cyril, 81, 82–83
Toomey, Howard, 118, 308
Toulmin, Dr. Henry, 104
Tournament of Champions, 8, 214, 223
Trans-Mississippi Amateur, 280, 281
Travers, Jerry, 18, 37, 38, 44, 45, 46–47, 100
Travis, Walter, 24, 37, 66, 110
Trevino, Claudia, 234
Trevino, Joe, 233
Trevino, Juanita, 233
Trevino, Lee, 5, 213, 230–235, 241–242, 243, 244, 245–247, 252, 253–254, 255, 258, 260, 263, 264, 266, 281, 289, 312–313, 315, 316, 317
True Temper Open, 116
Tucker, Samuel, 13
Tucson Open, 241
Turnesa, Jim, 155–156
Turnesa, Joe, 74–75, 83, 84
Turnesa, Mike, 153
Turney, Gene, 78
Tway, Bob, 310–312

United States Junior Amateur Championship, 207
Upper Montclair Country Club, 265–266
Urzetta, Sam, 208
USGA (United States Golf Association), 4–6, 8, 14, 16, 17, 20, 32, 38, 41, 47, 48, 71, 74, 77, 87, 89, 90, 92, 94, 102, 118, 121, 123–124, 135, 137, 138, 140, 144, 152,

INDEX

158, 164, 167, 172, 181, 183,
195, 208, 215, 216, 257,
258, 272, 277, 300, 301, 310
U.S. Open, 4–8
  in 1894, 16
  in 1895, 14–16, 71
  in 1896, 17, 71
  in 1897, 17, 19
  in 1898, 17, 20, 24
  in 1899, 17
  in 1900, 18–19, 23
  in 1901, 20, 21, 22
  in 1902, 20, 24
  in 1903, 20, 24
  in 1904, 20, 25
  in 1905, 20, 25
  in 1906, 25–26
  in 1907, 26
  in 1909, 17, 27, 29
  in 1910, 27
  in 1911, 28–29
  in 1912, 29–30
  in 1913, 32, 33–37, 39–42, 43, 45,
203, 208
  in 1914, 32, 43–45, 46
  in 1915, 46
  in 1916, 46, 47–48
  in 1917, 48
  in 1919, 49, 54
  in 1920, 53–56, 65, 71, 73, 93,
181, 241
  in 1921, 59, 93
  in 1922, 59–60, 66, 93
  in 1923, 60–62, 66–68, 71, 81
  in 1924, 69–70
  in 1925, 71, 72–73, 94
  in 1926, 74–75, 94, 110, 256
  in 1927, 76, 94, 107
  in 1928, 76–78, 94
  in 1929, 79–80, 110, 301
  in 1930, 83–85, 86, 94
  in 1931, 90–91, 150

in 1932, 86, 94–98, 102, 162
in 1933, 100, 113
in 1934, 103, 105–106, 150
in 1935, 103–104, 175, 234
in 1936, 103, 116
in 1937, 113–115, 116, 274
in 1938, 116
in 1939, 118–120, 125, 127,
151, 177
in 1940, 117, 120–122
in 1941, 122, 125
in 1946, 125, 127–129, 195
in 1947, 134–137, 155, 195
in 1948, 155–156
in 1949, 137–138, 178, 179, 270
in 1950, 142–149, 163, 195
in 1951, 159–162, 263, 289
in 1952, 163, 204
in 1953, 138, 164–166, 179, 188,
256, 262
in 1954, 167–168
in 1955, 169–176, 180
in 1956, 179–181
in 1957, 179, 181–182, 216
in 1958, 183, 195
in 1959, 183–184, 281
in 1960, 58, 189–193, 195, 263,
275, 281, 289
in 1961, 176, 196–197, 281
in 1962, 199–202, 206, 216, 223,
235, 302
in 1963, 203–204, 206–207,
210–213, 253
in 1965, 214, 215, 216
in 1966, 176, 216–220, 234, 263
in 1967, 177, 224–229, 234
in 1968, 213, 231–232, 238
in 1969, 213, 234, 236–237
in 1970, 238–241, 287
in 1971, 32, 243–247
in 1972, 249–255
in 1973, 257–263

in 1974, 264, 265–267, 268
in 1975, 270–271
in 1976, 272–273
in 1977, 138, 273–274
in 1978, 275, 290
in 1979, 276–278
in 1980, 8, 279, 282–285, 289
in 1981, 286, 288–289
in 1982, 7, 290–292
in 1983, 7, 295–299
in 1984, 13–14, 300–302
in 1986, 310–315

Valentine, Joe, 104
Valentino, Rudolph, 79
Vanderbilt, W. K., 11
Vardon, Harry, 4, 17–19, 20, 21,
    22, 28, 31, 33–35, 39–41, 53–
    56, 58, 83, 89, 123, 142,
    317, 318
Vardon Trophy, 151, 152, 153, 241
Venturi, Conni, 211
Venturi, Ken, 5, 185, 189, 207–213,
    215, 216, 300
Virginia, Country Club of,
    118, 280
Voigt, George, 81
Von Elm, George, 91, 111

Wadkins, Bobby, 296
Wadkins, Lanny, 263, 269, 303,
    313, 315
Wahconah Country Club, 87
Walker, Cyril, 64, 69–70, 114
Walker, Jimmy, 79
Walker Cup Match, 73, 74, 80–81,
    122, 178, 208, 280, 281
Wall, Art, 182–183
Walsh, Frank, 121
Ward, Bud, 136, 165
Ward, Charles, 154, 162

Ward, Harvie, 171, 172, 188, 209,
    224, 280
Warner Brothers, 86
Warren K. Wood Memorial, 76
Washington Post, 121
Washington Times Herald, 121
Watrous, Al, 74
Watson, Denis, 304, 306, 311, 312
Watson, Raymond E., 268
Watson, Robert, 38
Watson, Tom, 5, 7, 35–42, 44, 266,
    268–269, 270, 271, 283, 286,
    289–294, 298, 299, 300,
    302, 303, 311, 312, 316, 317
Weiskopf, Tom, 231, 243, 252,
    260, 262, 263, 264, 269, 272,
    273, 276–277, 282
Weissmuller, Johnny, 127
Wellesley Country Club, 39
Wentworth Golf Club, 143
Westchester Biltmore, 93
Westchester Classic, 241, 275, 311
Western Amateur, 269, 281
Western Golf Association, 24–25,
    47
Western Open, 20, 24, 25, 60, 77,
    93, 101, 116, 126, 127,
    133, 158, 223
Western Pennsylvania Amateurs,
    187
Western Pennsylvania Junior
    Championship, 187
Wethered, Roger, 81
White, D. K. (Deke), 53
White, George, 79
White, Ronald, 208
White, Stanford, 310
Whiteman, Paul, 79
Whitemarsh Valley Country Club,
    48, 223, 265
Whiting, Sam, 71
Whittenton, Jess, 231, 241

349

INDEX

Whittington, Don, 231, 241
Whittlesey, Merrell, 121
Why Didn't They Ask Evans?
  (Christie), 111
Willard, Ernest, 43
Williams, Harold, 146
Wilson, Hugh, 70, 104, 109, 118
Wilson, Jim, 208
Wilson Sporting Goods, 134
Wind, Herbert Warren, 297
Winged Foot Golf Club, 5, 7, 71,
  79–80, 108, 138, 176,
  183–184, 188, 219, 265–267,
  269, 270, 276, 300–302,
  303
Wodehouse, P. G., 111
Wolff, Randy, 240
Wood, Craig, 112, 118, 119–120,
  122, 124, 126, 152, 153, 301
Wood, Warren K., 64
Woodmont Country Club, 145
Woolsey, Robert, 116
Worcester Country Club, 72

World Amateur Team, 242
World Championship, 186, 195
World Cup, 238, 241, 287
World Match Play, 283, 287
World Open, 264, 270
World Series of Golf, 237
Worsham, Bubby, 188
Worsham, Lew, 135–137, 155, 167,
  186
Wright, Jim, 239
Wright and Ditson, 38, 64
Wykagyl, 133
Wykagyl Open, 29
Wysong, Dudley, 252

Yale Golf Club, 72
Yancey, Bert, 231–232, 240
Young, Loretta, 86

Zarley, Kermit, 253
Zender, Bob, 292
Ziegfeld, Florenz, 79
Zoeller, Fuzzy, 7, 300–302, 303

ROBERT SOMMERS began playing his version of golf at the age of four on a nine-hole course with sand greens. He has played many times since then without significant improvement, and decided long ago that since he couldn't beat anybody playing the game, perhaps he could make a career of writing about it.

In compiling this book, Sommers has called on his observations from over thirty years of watching golf at its highest levels on five continents. He saw his first Open in 1950, the year of Ben Hogan's comeback. Soon after, he began reporting the game for the *Baltimore Evening Sun*, then for the *Washington Star*, and for the last twenty years he has been editor of the magazine *Golf Journal*. Sommers has been a frequent contributor to other magazines, and his articles have appeared in a number of golf anthologies. He grew up in Baltimore and now lives in Bridgewater, New Jersey.